M

Edward S. Her
ton School of t
books are *Co*
Real Terror Ne... ...rrorism in Fact and Propaganda; *Demonstration Elections: U.S.-Staged Elections in the Dominican Republic, Vietnam and El Salvador* (with Frank Brodhead) and *The Rise and Fall of the Bulgarian Connection* (with Frank Brodhead).

Noam Chomsky is Institute Professor, Department of Linguistics and Philosophy, at the Massachusetts Institute of Technology. He is the author of *The Chomsky Reader*; *Towards a New Cold War*; *Deterring Democracy*; *Reflections on Language* and *Language and Responsibility*, among other notable titles.

BY NOAM CHOMSKY
ALSO AVAILABLE IN VINTAGE

Deterring Democracy

Edward S. Herman and
Noam Chomsky

MANUFACTURING CONSENT

The Political Economy of the Mass Media

VINTAGE BOOKS
London

Published by Vintage 1994

3 5 7 9 10 8 6 4 2

First published in the United States of America by Pantheon Books, a division of Random House, Inc., New York and simultaneously in Canada by Random House of Canada Limited, Toronto in 1988

Vintage
Random House, 20 Vauxhall Bridge Road, London SW1V 2SA

www.vintage-books.co.uk

Addresses for companies within The Random House Group Limited can be found at: www.randomhouse.co.uk/offices.htm

The Random House Group Limited Reg. No. 954009

A CIP catalogue record for this book is available from the British Library

ISBN 9781784708146

Penguin Random House is committed to a sustainable future for our business, our readers and our planet. This book is made from Forest Stewardship Council® certified paper.

FSC www.fsc.org MIX Paper from responsible sources FSC® C018179

Printed and bound in Great Britain by Clays Ltd, Elcograf S.p.A.

TO THE MEMORY OF ALEX CAREY

The Iran-contra scandals were blamed on the President's easygoing habits, though the people had every opportunity to know this was his way of doing things or not doing before they put him in the White House, not once but twice.

James Reston

They who have put out the people's eyes, reproach them of their blindness.

John Milton

Contents

TABLES

Preface

IN THIS BOOK, WE SKETCH OUT A "PROPAGANDA MODEL" AND apply it to the performance of the mass media of the United States. This effort reflects our belief, based on many years of study of the workings of the media, that they serve to mobilize support for the special interests that dominate the state and private activity,[1] and that their choices, emphases, and omissions can often be understood best, and sometimes with striking clarity and insight, by analyzing them in such terms.

Perhaps this is an obvious point, but the democratic postulate is that the media are independent and committed to discovering and reporting the truth, and that they do not merely reflect the world as powerful groups wish it to be perceived. Leaders of the media claim that their news choices rest on unbiased professional and objective criteria, and they have support for this contention in the intellectual community.[2] If, however, the powerful are able to fix the premises of discourse, to decide what the general populace is allowed to see, hear, and think about, and to "manage" public opinion by regular propaganda campaigns, the standard view of how the system works is at serious odds with reality.[3]

The special importance of propaganda in what Walter Lippmann referred to as the "manufacture of consent" has long been recognized by writers on public opinion, propaganda, and the political requirements of social order.[4] Lippmann himself, writing in the early 1920s, claimed that propaganda had already become "a regular organ of popular government," and was steadily increasing in sophistication and importance.[5] We do not contend that this is all the mass media do, but we believe the propaganda function to be a very important aspect of their overall service. In the first chapter we spell out a propaganda model, which describes the forces that cause the mass media to play a propaganda role, the processes whereby they mobilize bias, and the patterns of news choices that ensue. In the succeeding chapters we try to demonstrate the applicability of the propaganda model to the actual performance of the media.

Institutional critiques such as we present in this book are commonly dismissed by establishment commentators as "conspiracy theories," but this is merely an evasion. We do not use any kind of "conspiracy" hypothesis to explain mass-media performance. In fact, our treatment is much closer to a "free market" analysis, with the results largely an outcome of the workings of market forces. Most biased choices in the media arise from the preselection of right-thinking people, internalized preconceptions, and the adaptation of personnel to the constraints of ownership, organization, market, and political power. Censorship is largely self-censorship, by reporters and commentators who adjust to the realities of source and media organizational requirements, and by people at higher levels within media organizations who are chosen to implement, and have usually internalized, the constraints imposed by proprietary and other market and governmental centers of power.

There are important actors who do take positive initiatives to define and shape the news and to keep the media in line. It is a "guided market system" that we describe here, with the guidance provided by the government, the leaders of the corporate community, the top media owners and executives, and the assorted individuals and groups who are assigned or allowed to take constructive initiatives.[6] These initiators are sufficiently small in number to be able to act jointly on occasion, as do sellers in markets with few rivals. In most cases, however, media leaders do similar things because they see the world through the same lenses, are subject to similar constraints and incentives, and thus feature stories or maintain silence together in tacit collective action and leader-follower behavior.

The mass media are not a solid monolith on all issues. Where the powerful are in disagreement, there will be a certain diversity of tactical judgments on how to attain generally shared aims, reflected in media debate. But views that challenge fundamental premises or suggest that the observed modes of exercise of state power are based on systemic factors will be excluded from the mass media even when elite controversy over tactics rages fiercely.

We will study a number of such cases as we proceed, but the pattern is, in fact, pervasive. To select an example that happens to be dominating the news as we write, consider the portrayal of Nicaragua, under attack by the United States. In this instance, the division of elite opinion is sufficiently great to allow it to be questioned whether sponsorship of a terrorist army is effective in making Nicaragua "more democratic" and "less of a threat to its neighbors." The mass media, however, rarely if ever entertain opinion, or allow their news columns to present materials suggesting that Nicaragua is more democratic than El Salvador and Guatemala in every non-Orwellian sense of the word;[7] that its government does not murder ordinary citizens on a routine basis, as the governments of El Salvador and Guatemala do;[8] that it has carried out socioeconomic reforms important to the majority that the other two governments somehow cannot attempt;[9] that Nicaragua poses no military threat to its neighbors but has, in fact, been subjected to continuous attacks by the United States and its clients and surrogates; and that the U.S. fear of Nicaragua is based more on its virtues than on its alleged defects.[10] The mass media also steer clear of discussing the background and results of the closely analogous attempt of the United States to bring "democracy" to Guatemala in 1954 by means of a CIA-sponsored invasion, which terminated Guatemalan democracy for an indefinite period. Although the United States supported elite rule and helped to organize state terror in Guatemala (among many other countries) for decades, actually subverted or approved the subversion of democracy in Brazil, Chile, and the Philippines (again, among others), is "constructively engaged" with terror regimes on a global basis, and had no concern about democracy in Nicaragua as long as the brutal Somoza regime was firmly in power, nevertheless the media take government claims of a concern for "democracy" in Nicaragua at face value.[11]

Elite disagreement over tactics in dealing with Nicaragua is reflected in public debate, but the mass media, in conformity with elite priorities, have coalesced in processing news in a way that fails to place U.S. policy into meaningful context, systematically suppresses evidence of U.S. violence and aggression, and puts the Sandinistas in an extremely bad light.[12] In contrast, El Salvador and Guatemala, with far worse records, are presented as struggling toward democracy under "moderate" leaders, thus meriting sympathetic approval. These practices have not only distorted public perceptions of Central American realities, they have also seriously misrepresented U.S. policy objectives, an essential feature of propaganda, as Jacques Ellul stresses:

> The propagandist naturally cannot reveal the true intentions of the principal for whom he acts. . . . That would be to submit the projects to public discussion, to the scrutiny of public opinion, and thus to prevent their success. . . . Propaganda must serve instead as a veil for such projects, masking true intention.[13]

The power of the government to fix frames of reference and agendas, and to exclude inconvenient facts from public inspection, is also impressively displayed in the coverage of elections in Central America, discussed in chapter 3, and throughout the analysis of particular cases in the chapters that follow.

When there is little or no elite dissent from a government policy, there may still be some slippage in the mass media, and facts that tend to undermine the government line, if they are properly understood, can be found, usually on the back pages of the newspapers. This is one of the strengths of the U.S. system. It is possible that the volume of inconvenient facts can expand, as it did during the Vietnam War, in response to the growth of a critical constituency (which included elite elements from 1968). Even in this exceptional case, however, it was very rare for news and commentary to find their way into the mass media if they failed to conform to the framework of established dogma (postulating benevolent U.S. aims, the United States responding to aggression and terror, etc.), as we discuss in chapter 5. During and after the Vietnam War, apologists for state policy commonly pointed to the inconvenient facts, the periodic "pessimism" of media pundits, and the debates over tactics as showing that the media were "adversarial" and even "lost" the war. These allegations are ludicrous, as we show in detail in chapter 5 and appendix 3, but they did have the dual advantage of disguising the actual role of the mass media and, at the same time, pressing the media to keep even more tenaciously to the propaganda assumptions of state policy. We have long argued that the "naturalness" of these processes, with inconvenient facts allowed sparingly and within the proper framework of assumptions, and fundamental dissent virtually excluded from the mass media (but permitted in a marginalized press), makes for a propaganda system that is far more credible and effective in putting over a patriotic agenda than one with official censorship.

In criticizing media priorities and biases we often draw on the media themselves for at least some of the facts. This affords the opportunity for a classic *non sequitur,* in which the citations of facts from the mainstream press by a critic of the press is offered as a triumphant "proof" that the criticism is self-refuting, and that media coverage of disputed issues is indeed adequate. That the media provide some facts about an issue, however, proves absolutely nothing about the adequacy or accuracy of that coverage. The mass media do, in fact, literally suppress a great deal, as we will describe in the chapters that follow. But even more important in this context is the question of the attention given to a fact—its placement, tone, and repetitions, the framework of analysis within which it is presented, and the related facts that accompany it and give it meaning (or preclude understanding). That a careful reader looking for a fact can sometimes find it with diligence and a skeptical eye tells us nothing about whether that fact received the attention and context it deserved, whether it was intelligible to the reader or effectively distorted or suppressed. What level of attention it deserved may be debatable, but there is no merit to the pretense that because certain facts may be found in the media by a diligent and skeptical researcher, the absence of radical bias and de facto suppression is thereby demonstrated.[14]

One of our central themes in this book is that the observable pattern of indignant campaigns and suppressions, of shading and emphasis, and of selection of context, premises, and general agenda, is highly functional for established power and responsive to the needs of the government and major power groups. A constant focus on victims of communism helps convince the public of enemy evil and sets the stage for intervention, subversion, support for terrorist states, an endless arms race, and military conflict—all in a noble cause. At the same time, the devotion of our leaders and media to this narrow set of victims raises public self-esteem and patriotism, as it demonstrates the essential humanity of country and people.

The public does not notice the silence on victims in client states, which is as important in supporting state policy as the concentrated focus on enemy victims. It would have been very difficult for the Guatemalan government to murder tens of thousands over the past decade if the U.S. press had provided the kind of coverage they gave to the difficulties of Andrei Sakharov or the murder of Jerzy Popieluszko in Poland (see chapter 2). It would have been impossible to wage a brutal war against South Vietnam and the rest of Indochina, leaving a legacy of misery and destruction that may never be overcome, if the media had not rallied to the cause, portraying murderous aggression as a defense of freedom, and only opening the doors to tactical disagreement when the costs to the interests they represent became too high.

The same is true in other cases that we discuss, and too many that we do not.

We would like to express our thanks to the following people for their assistance in the preparation of this book: James Aronson, Phillip Berryman, Larry Birns, Frank Brodhead, Holly Burkhalter, Donna Cooper,

Carol Fouke, Eva Gold, Carol Goslant, Roy Head, Mary Herman, Rob Kirsch, Robert Krinsky, Alfred McClung Lee, Kent MacDougall, Nejat Ozyegin, Nancy Peters, Ellen Ray, William Schaap, Karin Wilkins, Warren Witte, and Jamie Young. The authors alone remain responsible for its contents.

MANUFACTURING CONSENT

1

A Propaganda Model

THE MASS MEDIA SERVE AS A SYSTEM FOR COMMUNICATING messages and symbols to the general populace. It is their function to amuse, entertain, and inform, and to inculcate individuals with the values, beliefs, and codes of behavior that will integrate them into the institutional structures of the larger society. In a world of concentrated wealth and major conflicts of class interest, to fulfil this role requires systematic propaganda.[1]

In countries where the levers of power are in the hands of a state bureaucracy, the monopolistic control over the media, often supplemented by official censorship, makes it clear that the media serve the ends of a dominant elite. It is much more difficult to see a propaganda system at work where the media are private and formal censorship is absent. This is especially true where the media actively compete, periodically attack and expose corporate and governmental malfeasance, and aggressively portray themselves as spokesmen for free speech and the general community interest. What is not evident (and remains undiscussed in the media) is the limited nature of such critiques, as well as the huge inequality in command of resources, and its effect both on access to a private media system and on its behavior and performance.

A propaganda model focuses on this inequality of wealth and power and its multilevel effects on mass-media interests and choices. It traces the routes by which money and power are able to filter out the news fit to print, marginalize dissent, and allow the government and dominant private interests to get their messages across to the public. The essential ingredients of our propaganda model, or set of news "filters," fall under the following headings: (1) the size, concentrated ownership, owner wealth, and profit orientation of the dominant mass-media firms; (2) advertising as the primary income source of the mass media; (3) the reliance of the media on information provided by government, business, and "experts" funded and approved by these primary sources and agents of power; (4) "flak" as a means of disciplining the media; and (5) "anticommunism" as a national religion and control mechanism. These elements interact with and reinforce one another. The raw material of news must pass through successive filters, leaving only the cleansed residue fit to print. They fix the premises of discourse and interpretation, and the definition of what is newsworthy in the first place, and they explain the basis and operations of what amount to propaganda campaigns.

The elite domination of the media and marginalization of dissidents that results from the operation of these filters occurs so naturally that media news people, frequently operating with complete integrity and goodwill, are able to convince themselves that they choose and interpret the news "objectively" and on the basis of professional news values. Within the limits of the filter constraints they often are objective; the constraints are so powerful, and are built into the system in such a fundamental way, that alternative bases of news choices are hardly imaginable. In assessing the newsworthiness of the U.S. government's urgent claims of a shipment of MIGs to Nicaragua on November 5, 1984, the media do not stop to ponder the bias that is inherent in the priority assigned to government-supplied raw material, or the possibility that the government might be manipulating the news,[2] imposing its own agenda, and deliberately diverting attention from other material.[3] It requires a macro, alongside a micro- (story-by-story), view of media operations, to see the pattern of manipulation and systematic bias.

Let us turn now to a more detailed examination of the main constituents of the propaganda model, which will be applied and tested in the chapters that follow.

1.1. SIZE, OWNERSHIP, AND PROFIT ORIENTATION OF THE MASS MEDIA: THE FIRST FILTER

In their analysis of the evolution of the media in Great Britain, James Curran and Jean Seaton describe how, in the first half of the nineteenth century, a radical press emerged that reached a national working-class audience. This alternative press was effective in reinforcing class consciousness: it unified the workers because it fostered an alternative value system and framework for looking at the world, and because it "promoted a greater collective confidence by repeatedly emphasizing the potential power of working people to effect social change through the force of 'combination' and organized action."[4] This was deemed a major threat by the ruling elites. One MP asserted that the working-class newspapers "inflame passions and awaken their selfishness, contrasting their current condition with what they contend to be their future condition—a condition incompatible with human nature, and those immutable laws which Providence has established for the regulation of civil society."[5] The result was an attempt to squelch the working-class media by libel laws and prosecutions, by requiring an expensive security bond as a condition for publication, and by imposing various taxes designed to drive out radical media by raising their costs. These coercive efforts were not effective, and by mid-century they had been abandoned in favor of the liberal view that the market would enforce responsibility.

Curran and Seaton show that the market *did* successfully accomplish what state intervention failed to do. Following the repeal of the punitive taxes on newspapers between 1853 and 1869, a new daily local press came into existence, but not one new local working-class daily was established through the rest of the nineteenth century. Curran and Seaton note that

> Indeed, the eclipse of the national radical press was so total that when the Labour Party developed out of the working-class movement in the first decade of the twentieth century, it did not obtain the exclusive backing of a single national daily or Sunday paper.[6]

One important reason for this was the rise in scale of newspaper enterprise and the associated increase in capital costs from the mid-nineteenth century onward, which was based on technological improvements along with the owners' increased stress on reaching large audiences. The expansion of the free market was accompanied by an "industrialization of the press." The total cost of establishing a national weekly on a profitable basis in 1837 was under a thousand pounds, with a break-even circulation of 6,200 copies. By 1867, the estimated start-up cost of a new London daily was 50,000 pounds. The *Sunday Express*, launched in 1918, spent over two million pounds before it broke even with a circulation of over 250,000.[7]

Similar processes were at work in the United States, where the start-up cost of a new paper in New York City in 1851 was $69,000; the public sale of the *St. Louis Democrat* in 1872 yielded $456,000; and city newspapers were selling at from $6 to $18 million in the 1920s.[8] The cost of machinery alone, of even very small newspapers, has for many decades run into the hundreds of thousands of dollars; in 1945 it could be said that "Even small-newspaper publishing is big business . . . [and] is no longer a trade one takes up lightly even if he has substantial cash—or takes up at all if he doesn't."[9]

Thus the first filter—the limitation on ownership of media with any substantial outreach by the requisite large size of investment—was applicable a century or more ago, and it has become increasingly effective over time.[10] In 1986 there were some 1,500 daily newspapers, 11,000 magazines, 9,000 radio and 1,500 TV stations, 2,400 book publishers, and seven movie studios in the United States—over 25,000 media entities in all. But a large proportion of those among this set who were news dispensers were very small and local, dependent on the large national companies and wire services for all but local news. Many more were subject to common ownership, sometimes extending through virtually the entire set of media variants.[11]

Ben Bagdikian stresses the fact that despite the large media numbers, the twenty-nine largest media systems account for over half of the output of newspapers, and most of the sales and audiences in magazines, broadcasting, books, and movies. He contends that these "constitute a new Private Ministry of Information and Culture" that can set the national agenda.[12]

Actually, while suggesting a media autonomy from corporate and government power that we believe to be incompatible with structural facts (as we describe below), Bagdikian also may be understating the degree of effective concentration in news manufacture. It has long been noted that the media are tiered, with the top tier—as measured by prestige, resources, and outreach—comprising somewhere between ten and twenty-four systems.[13] It is this top tier, along with the government and wire services, that defines the news agenda and supplies much of the national and international news to the lower tiers of the media, and thus for the general public.[14] Centralization within the top tier was substantially increased by the post–World War II rise of television and the national networking of this important medium. Pre-television news markets were local, even if heavily dependent on the higher tiers and a narrow set of sources for national and international news; the networks provide national and international news from three national sources, and television is now the principal source of news for the public.[15] The maturing of cable, however, has resulted in a fragmentation of television audiences and a slow erosion of the market share and power of the networks.

Table 1-1 provides some basic financial data for the twenty-four media giants (or their controlling parent companies) that make up the top tier of media companies in the United States.[16] This compilation includes: (1) the three television networks: ABC (through its parent, Capital Cities), CBS, and NBC (through its ultimate parent, General Electric [GE]); (2) the leading newspaper empires: *New York Times, Washington Post, Los Angeles Times* (Times-Mirror), *Wall Street Journal* (Dow Jones), Knight-Ridder, Gannett, Hearst, Scripps-Howard, Newhouse (Advance Publications), and the Tribune Company; (3) the major news and general-interest magazines: *Time, Newsweek* (subsumed under *Washington Post*), *Reader's Digest, TV Guide* (Triangle), and *U.S. News & World Report*; (4) a major book publisher (McGraw-Hill); and (5) other cable-TV systems of large and growing importance: those of Murdoch, Turner, Cox, General Corp., Taft, Storer,[17] and Group W (Westinghouse). Many of these systems are prominent in more than one field and are only arbitrarily placed in a particular category (Time, Inc., is very important in cable as well as magazines; McGraw-Hill is a major publisher of magazines; the Tribune Company has become a large force in television as well as newspapers; Hearst is important in magazines as well as newspapers; and Murdoch has significant newspaper interests as well as television and movie holdings).

These twenty-four companies are large, profit-seeking corporations, owned and controlled by quite wealthy people. It can be seen in table 1-1 that all but one of the top companies for whom data are available have assets in excess of $1 billion, and the median size (middle item by size) is $2.6 billion. It can also be seen in the table that approximately three-quarters of these media giants had after-tax profits in excess of $100 million, with the median at $183 million.

Many of the large media companies are fully integrated into the market, and for the others, too, the pressures of stockholders, directors, and bankers to focus on the bottom line are powerful. These pressures

TABLE 1-1

Financial Data for Twenty-four Large Media Corporations (or Their Parent Firms), December 1986

COMPANY	TOTAL ASSETS ($ MILLIONS)	PROFITS BEFORE TAXES ($ MILLIONS)	PROFITS AFTER TAXES ($ MILLIONS)	TOTAL REVENUE ($ MILLIONS)
Advance Publications (Newhouse)[1]	2,500	NA	NA	2,200
Capital Cities/ABC	5,191	688	448	4,124
CBS	3,370	470	370	4,754
Cox Communications[2]	1,111	170	87	743
Dow Jones & Co.	1,236	331	183	1,135
Gannett	3,365	540	276	2,801
General Electric (NBC)	34,591	3,689	2,492	36,725
Hearst[3]	4,040	NA	215 (1983)	2,100 (1983)
Knight-Ridder	1,947	267	140	1,911
McGraw-Hill	1,463	296	154	1,577
News Corp. (Murdoch)[4]	8,460	377	170	3,822
New York Times	1,405	256	132	1,565
Reader's Digest[5]	NA	75–110 (1985)	NA	1,400 (1985)
Scripps-Howard[6]	NA	NA	NA	1,062
Storer[7]	1,242	68	(−17)	537
Taft	1,257	(−11)	(−53)	500
Time, Inc.	4,230	626	376	3,762
Times-Mirror	2,929	680	408	2,948
Triangle[8]	NA	NA	NA	730
Tribune Co.	2,589	523	293	2,030
Turner Broadcasting	1,904	(−185)	(−187)	570
U.S. News & World Report[9]	200+	NA	NA	140

COMPANY	TOTAL ASSETS ($ MILLIONS)	PROFITS BEFORE TAXES ($ MILLIONS)	PROFITS AFTER TAXES ($ MILLIONS)	TOTAL REVENUE ($ MILLIONS)
Washington Post	1,145	205	100	1,215
Westinghouse	8,482	801	670	10,731

NA = not available

1. The asset total is taken from *Forbes* magazine's wealth total for the Newhouse family for 1985; the total revenue is for media sales only, as reported in *Advertising Age,* June 29, 1987.
2. Cox Communications was publicly owned until 1985, when it was merged into another Cox family company, Cox Enterprises. The data presented here are for year-end 1984, the last year of public ownership and disclosure of substantial financial information.
3. Data compiled in William Barrett, "Citizens Rich," *Forbes,* Dec. 14, 1987.
4. These data are in Australian dollars and are for June 30, 1986; at that date the Australian dollar was worth 68/100 of a U.S. dollar.
5. Data for 1985, as presented in the *New York Times,* Feb. 9, 1986.
6. Total revenue for media sales only, as reported in *Advertising Age,* June 29, 1987.
7. Storer came under the control of the Wall Street firm Kohlberg Kravis Roberts & Co. in 1985; the data here are for December 1984, the last period of Storer autonomy and publicly available information.
8. Total revenue for media sales only; from *Advertising Age,* June 29, 1987.
9. Total assets as of 1984–85, based on "Mort Zuckerman, Media's New Mogul," *Fortune,* Oct. 14, 1985; total revenue from *Advertising Age,* June 29, 1987.

have intensified in recent years as media stocks have become market favorites, and actual or prospective owners of newspapers and television properties have found it possible to capitalize increased audience size and advertising revenues into multiplied values of the media franchises—and great wealth.[18] This has encouraged the entry of speculators and increased the pressure and temptation to focus more intensively on profitability. Family owners have been increasingly divided between those wanting to take advantage of the new opportunities and those desiring a continuation of family control, and their splits have often precipitated crises leading finally to the sale of the family interest.[19]

This trend toward greater integration of the media into the market system has been accelerated by the loosening of rules limiting media concentration, cross-ownership, and control by non-media companies.[20] There has also been an abandonment of restrictions—previously quite feeble anyway—on radio-TV commercials, entertainment-mayhem programming, and "fairness doctrine" threats, opening the door to the unrestrained commercial use of the airwaves.[21]

The greater profitability of the media in a deregulated environment has also led to an increase in takeovers and takeover threats, with even giants like CBS and Time, Inc., directly attacked or threatened. This has forced the managements of the media giants to incur greater debt and to focus ever more aggressively and unequivocally on profitability, in order to placate owners and reduce the attractiveness of their properties to outsiders.[22] They have lost some of their limited autonomy to bankers, institutional investors, and large individual investors whom they have had to solicit as potential "white knights."[23]

While the stock of the great majority of large media firms is traded on the securities markets, approximately two-thirds of these companies are either closely held or still controlled by members of the originating family who retain large blocks of stock. This situation is changing as family ownership becomes diffused among larger numbers of heirs and the market opportunities for selling media properties continue to improve, but the persistence of family control is evident in the data shown in table 1-2. Also evident in the table is the enormous wealth possessed by the controlling families of the top media firms. For seven of the twenty-four, the market value of the media properties owned by the controlling families in the mid-1980s exceeded a billion dollars, and the median value was close to half a billion dollars.[24] These control groups obviously have a special stake in the status quo by virtue of their wealth and their strategic position in one of the great institutions of society. And they exercise the power of this strategic position, if only by establishing the general aims of the company and choosing its top management.[25]

The control groups of the media giants are also brought into close relationships with the mainstream of the corporate community through boards of directors and social links. In the cases of NBC and the Group W television and cable systems, their respective parents, GE and Westinghouse, are themselves mainstream corporate giants, with boards of directors that are dominated by corporate and banking executives. Many of the other large media firms have boards made up predomi-

TABLE 1-2

Wealth of the Control Groups of Twenty-four Large Media Corporations (or Their Parent Companies), February 1986

COMPANY	CONTROLLING FAMILY OR GROUP	PERCENTAGE OF VOTING STOCK HELD BY CONTROL GROUP (%)	VALUE OF CONTROLLING STOCK INTEREST ($ MILLIONS)
Advance Publications	Newhouse family	Closely held	2,200[F]
Capital Cities	Officers and directors (ODs)	20.7 (Warren Buffett, 17.8)	711[P]
CBS	ODs	20.6[1]	551[P]
Cox Communications	Cox family	36	1,900[F]
Dow Jones & Co.	Bancroft-Cox families	54	1,500[P]
Gannett	ODs	1.9	95[P]
General Electric	ODs	Under 1	171[P]
Hearst	Hearst family	33	1,500[F]
Knight-Ridder	Knight and Ridder families	18	447[P]
McGraw-Hill	McGraw family	c.20	450[F]
News Corp.	Murdoch family	49	300[F]
New York Times	Sulzberger family	80	450[F]
Reader's Digest	Wallace estate managed by trustees; no personal beneficiaries	NA	NA
Scripps-Howard	Scripps heirs	NA	1,400[F]
Storer	ODs	8.4	143[P]
Taft	ODs	4.8	37[P]
Time, Inc.	ODs	10.7 (Luce 4.6, Temple 3.2)	406[P]
Times-Mirror	Chandlers	35	1,200[P]
Triangle	Annenbergs	Closely held	1,600[F]
Tribune Co.	McCormick heirs	16.6	273[P]
Turner Broadcasting	Turner	80	222[P]

COMPANY	CONTROLLING FAMILY OR GROUP	PERCENTAGE OF VOTING STOCK HELD BY CONTROL GROUP (%)	VALUE OF CONTROLLING STOCK INTEREST ($ MILLIONS)
U.S. News & World Report	Zuckerman	Closely held	176[2]
Washington Post	Graham family	50+	350[F]
Westinghouse	ODs	Under 1	42[P]

Sources: P means taken from proxy statements and computed from stock values as of February 1986; F means taken from *Forbes* magazine's annual estimate of wealth holdings of the very rich.

1. These holdings include William Paley's 8.1 percent and a 12.2 percent holding of Laurence Tisch through an investment by Loews. Later in the year, Loews increased its investment to 24.9 percent, and Laurence Tisch soon thereafter became acting chief executive officer.

2. This is the price paid by Zuckerman when he bought *U.S. News* in 1984. See Gwen Kinkead, "Mort Zuckerman, Media's New Mogul," *Fortune*, Oct. 14, 1985, p. 196.

nantly of insiders, a general characteristic of relatively small and owner-dominated companies. The larger the firm and the more widely distributed the stock, the larger the number and proportion of outside directors. The composition of the outside directors of the media giants is very similar to that of large non-media corporations. Table 1-3 shows that active corporate executives and bankers together account for a little over half the total of the outside directors of ten media giants; and the lawyers and corporate-banker retirees (who account for nine of the thirteen under "Retired") push the corporate total to about two-thirds of the outside-director aggregate. These 95 outside directors had directorships in an additional 36 banks and 255 other companies (aside from the media company and their own firm of primary affiliation).[26]

In addition to these board linkages, the large media companies all do business with commercial and investment bankers, obtaining lines of credit and loans, and receiving advice and service in selling stock and bond issues and in dealing with acquisition opportunities and takeover threats. Banks and other institutional investors are also large owners of media stock. In the early 1980s, such institutions held 44 percent of the stock of publicly owned newspapers and 35 percent of the stock of

TABLE 1-3

AFFILIATIONS OF THE OUTSIDE DIRECTORS OF TEN LARGE MEDIA COMPANIES (OR THEIR PARENTS) IN 1986*

PRIMARY AFFILIATION	NUMBER	PERCENT
Corporate executive	39	41.1
Lawyer	8	8.4
Retired (former corporate executive or banker)	13 (9)	13.7 (9.5)
Banker	8	8.4
Consultant	4	4.2
Nonprofit organization	15	15.8
Other	8	8.4
Total	95	100.0
OTHER RELATIONSHIPS		
Other directorships (bank directorships)	255 (36)	
Former government officials	15	
Member of Council on Foreign Relations	20	

* Dow Jones & Co.; Washington Post; New York Times; Time, Inc.; CBS; Times-Mirror; Capital Cities; General Electric; Gannett; and Knight-Ridder.

publicly owned broadcasting companies.[27] These investors are also frequently among the largest stockholders of individual companies. For example, in 1980–81, the Capital Group, an investment company system, held 7.1 percent of the stock of ABC, 6.6 percent of Knight-Ridder, 6 percent of Time, Inc., and 2.8 percent of Westinghouse.[28] These holdings, individually and collectively, do not convey control, but these large investors can make themselves heard, and their actions can affect the welfare of the companies and their managers.[29] If the managers fail to pursue actions that favor shareholder returns, institutional investors will be inclined to sell the stock (depressing its price), or to listen sympathetically to outsiders contemplating takeovers. These investors are a force helping press media companies toward strictly market (profitability) objectives.

So is the diversification and geographic spread of the great media companies. Many of them have diversified out of particular media fields into others that seemed like growth areas. Many older newspaper-based media companies, fearful of the power of television and its effects on advertising revenue, moved as rapidly as they could into broadcasting and cable TV. Time, Inc., also, made a major diversification move into cable TV, which now accounts for more than half its profits. Only a small minority of the twenty-four largest media giants remain in a single media sector.[30]

The large media companies have also diversified beyond the media field, and non-media companies have established a strong presence in the mass media. The most important cases of the latter are GE, owning RCA, which owns the NBC network, and Westinghouse, which owns major television-broadcasting stations, a cable network, and a radio-station network. GE and Westinghouse are both huge, diversified multinational companies heavily involved in the controversial areas of weapons production and nuclear power. It may be recalled that from 1965 to 1967, an attempt by International Telephone and Telegraph (ITT) to acquire ABC was frustrated following a huge outcry that focused on the dangers of allowing a great multinational corporation with extensive foreign investments and business activities to control a major media outlet.[31] The fear was that ITT control "could compromise the independence of ABC's news coverage of political events in countries where ITT has interests."[32] The soundness of the decision disallowing the acquisition seemed to have been vindicated by the later revelations of ITT's political bribery and involvement in attempts to overthrow the government of Chile. RCA and Westinghouse, however, had been permitted to control media companies long before the ITT case, although some of the objections applicable to ITT would seem to apply to them as well. GE is a more powerful company than ITT, with an extensive international reach, deeply involved in the nuclear power business, and far more important than ITT in the arms industry. It is a highly centralized and quite secretive organization, but one with a vast stake in "political" decisions.[33] GE has contributed to the funding of the American Enterprise Institute, a right-wing think tank that supports intellectuals who will get the business message across. With the acquisition of ABC, GE should be in a far better position to assure that sound views are given proper attention.[34] The lack of outcry over its takeover of RCA and NBC resulted in part from the fact that RCA control over NBC had already breached the gate of separateness, but it also reflected the more pro-business and *laissez-faire* environment of the Reagan era.

The non-media interests of most of the media giants are not large, and, excluding the GE and Westinghouse systems, they account for only a small fraction of their total revenue. Their multinational outreach, however, is more significant. The television networks, television syndicators, major news magazines, and motion-picture studios all do extensive business abroad, and they derive a substantial fraction of their revenues from foreign sales and the operation of foreign affiliates. *Reader's Digest* is printed in seventeen languages and is available in over 160 countries. The Murdoch empire was originally based in Australia, and the controlling parent company is still an Australian corporation; its expansion in the United States is funded by profits from Australian and British affiliates.[35]

Another structural relationship of importance is the media companies' dependence on and ties with government. The radio-TV companies and networks all require government licenses and franchises and are thus potentially subject to government control or harassment. This technical legal dependency has been used as a club to discipline the media, and media policies that stray too often from an establishment orientation could activate this threat.[36] The media protect themselves from this contingency by lobbying and other political expenditures, the cultivation of political relationships, and care in policy. The political ties of the media have been impressive. Table 1-3 shows that fifteen of ninety-five outside directors of ten of the media giants are former government officials, and Peter Dreier gives a similar proportion in his study of large newspapers.[37] In television, the revolving-door flow of personnel between regulators and the regulated firms was massive during the years when the oligopolistic structure of the media and networks was being established.[38]

The great media also depend on the government for more general policy support. All business firms are interested in business taxes, interest rates, labor policies, and enforcement and nonenforcement of the antitrust laws. GE and Westinghouse depend on the government to subsidize their nuclear power and military research and development, and to create a favorable climate for their overseas sales. The *Reader's Digest*, *Time*, *Newsweek*, and movie- and television-syndication sellers also depend on diplomatic support for their rights to penetrate foreign cultures with U.S. commercial and value messages and interpretations of current affairs. The media giants, advertising agencies, and great multinational corporations have a joint and close interest in a favorable climate of investment in the Third World, and their interconnections and relationships with the government in these policies are symbiotic.[39]

In sum, the dominant media firms are quite large businesses; they are controlled by very wealthy people or by managers who are subject to sharp constraints by owners and other market-profit–oriented forces;[40] and they are closely interlocked, and have important common interests, with other major corporations, banks, and government. This is the first powerful filter that will affect news choices.

1.2. THE ADVERTISING LICENSE TO DO BUSINESS: THE SECOND FILTER

In arguing for the benefits of the free market as a means of controlling dissident opinion in the mid-nineteenth century, the Liberal chancellor of the British exchequer, Sir George Lewis, noted that the market would promote those papers "enjoying the preference of the advertising public."[41] Advertising did, in fact, serve as a powerful mechanism weakening the working-class press. Curran and Seaton give the growth of advertising a status comparable with the increase in capital costs as a factor allowing the market to accomplish what state taxes and harassment failed to do, noting that these "advertisers thus acquired a de facto licensing authority since, without their support, newspapers ceased to be economically viable."[42]

Before advertising became prominent, the price of a newspaper had to cover the costs of doing business. With the growth of advertising, papers that attracted ads could afford a copy price well below production costs. This put papers lacking in advertising at a serious disadvantage: their prices would tend to be higher, curtailing sales, and they would have less surplus to invest in improving the salability of the paper (features, attractive format, promotion, etc.). For this reason, an advertising-based system will tend to drive out of existence or into marginality the media companies and types that depend on revenue from sales alone. With advertising, the free market does not yield a neutral system in which final buyer choice decides. The *advertisers'* choices influence media prosperity and survival.[43] The ad-based media receive an advertising subsidy that gives them a price-marketing-quality edge, which allows them to encroach on and further weaken their ad-free (or ad-disadvantaged) rivals.[44] Even if ad-based media cater to an affluent ("upscale") audience, they easily pick up a large part of the "downscale" audience, and their rivals lose market share and are eventually driven out or marginalized.

In fact, advertising has played a potent role in increasing concentration even among rivals that focus with equal energy on seeking advertising revenue. A market share and advertising edge on the part of one paper or television station will give it additional revenue to compete more effectively—promote more aggressively, buy more salable features and programs—and the disadvantaged rival must add expenses it cannot afford to try to stem the cumulative process of dwindling market (and revenue) share. The crunch is often fatal, and it helps explain the death of many large-circulation papers and magazines and the attrition in the number of newspapers.[45]

From the time of the introduction of press advertising, therefore, working-class and radical papers have been at a serious disadvantage. Their readers have tended to be of modest means, a factor that has always affected advertiser interest. One advertising executive stated in 1856 that some journals are poor vehicles because "their readers are not purchasers, and any money thrown upon them is so much thrown away."[46] The same force took a heavy toll of the post–World War II social-democratic press in Great Britain, with the *Daily Herald, News Chronicle,* and *Sunday Citizen* failing or absorbed into establishment systems between 1960 and 1967, despite a collective average daily readership of 9.3 million. As James Curran points out, with 4.7 million readers in its last year, "the *Daily Herald* actually had almost double the readership of *The Times,* the *Financial Times* and the *Guardian* combined." What is more, surveys showed that its readers "thought more highly of their paper than the regular readers of any other popular newspaper," and "they also read more in their paper than the readers of other popular papers despite being overwhelmingly working class. . . ."[47] The death of the *Herald,* as well as of the *News Chronicle* and *Sunday Citizen,* was in large measure a result of progressive strangulation by lack of advertising support. The *Herald,* with 8.1 percent of national daily circulation, got 3.5 percent of net advertising revenue; the *Sunday Citizen* got one-tenth of the net advertising revenue of the *Sunday Times* and one-seventh that of the *Observer* (on a per-thousand-copies basis). Curran argues persuasively that the loss of these three papers was an important contribution to the declining fortunes of the Labor party, in the case of the *Herald* specifically removing a mass-circulation institution that provided "an alternative framework of analysis and understanding that contested the dominant systems of representation in both broadcasting and the mainstream press."[48] A mass movement without any major media support, and subject to a great deal of active press hostility, suffers a serious disability, and struggles against grave odds.

The successful media today are fully attuned to the crucial importance of audience "quality": CBS proudly tells its shareholders that while it "continuously seeks to maximize audience delivery," it has developed a new "sales tool" with which it approaches advertisers: "Client Audience Profile, or CAP, will help advertisers optimize the effectiveness of their network television schedules by evaluating audience segments in proportion to usage levels of advertisers' products and services."[49] In short, the mass media are interested in attracting audiences with buying power, not audiences per se; it is affluent audiences that spark advertiser interest today, as in the nineteenth century. The idea that the drive for large audiences makes the mass media "democratic" thus suffers from the initial weakness that its political analogue is a voting system weighted by income!

The power of advertisers over television programming stems from the simple fact that they buy and pay for the programs—they are the "patrons" who provide the media subsidy. As such, the media compete for their patronage, developing specialized staff to solicit advertisers and necessarily having to explain how their programs serve advertisers' needs. The choices of these patrons greatly affect the welfare of the media, and the patrons become what William Evan calls "normative reference organizations,"[50] whose requirements and demands the media must accommodate if they are to succeed.[51]

For a television network, an audience gain or loss of one percentage point in the Nielsen ratings translates into a change in advertising revenue of from $80 to $100 million a year, with some variation depending on measures of audience "quality." The stakes in audience size and affluence are thus extremely large, and in a market system there is a strong tendency for such considerations to affect policy profoundly. This is partly a matter of institutional pressures to focus on the bottom line, partly a matter of the continuous interaction of the media organization with patrons who supply the revenue dollars. As Grant Tinker, then head of NBC-TV, observed, television "is an advertising-supported medium, and to the extent that support falls out, programming will change."[52]

Working-class and radical media also suffer from the political discrimination of advertisers. Political discrimination is structured into advertising allocations by the stress on people with money to buy. But many firms will always refuse to patronize ideological enemies and those whom they perceive as damaging their interests, and cases of overt discrimination add to the force of the voting system weighted by income. Public-television station WNET lost its corporate funding from Gulf + Western in 1985 after the station showed the documentary "Hungry for Profit," which contains material critical of multinational corporate activities in the Third World. Even before the program was shown, in anticipation of negative corporate reaction, station officials "did all we could to get the program sanitized" (according to one station source).[53] The chief executive of Gulf + Western complained to the station that the program was "virulently anti-business if not anti-American," and that the station's carrying the program was not the behavior "of a friend" of the corporation. The London *Economist* says that "Most people believe that WNET would not make the same mistake again."[54]

In addition to discrimination against unfriendly media institutions, advertisers also choose selectively among programs on the basis of their own principles. With rare exceptions these are culturally and politically conservative.[55] Large corporate advertisers on television will rarely sponsor programs that engage in serious criticisms of corporate activities, such as the problem of environmental degradation, the workings of the military-industrial complex, or corporate support of and benefits from Third World tyrannies. Erik Barnouw recounts the history of a proposed documentary series on environmental problems by NBC at a time of great interest in these issues. Barnouw notes that although at that time a great many large companies were spending money on commercials and other publicity regarding environmental problems, the documentary series failed for want of sponsors. The problem was one of excessive objectivity in the series, which included suggestions of corporate or systemic failure, whereas the corporate message "was one of reassurance."[56]

Television networks learn over time that such programs will not sell and would have to be carried at a financial sacrifice, and that, in addition, they may offend powerful advertisers.[57] With the rise in the price of advertising spots, the forgone revenue increases; and with increasing market pressure for financial performance and the diminishing constraints from regulation, an advertising-based media system will gradually increase advertising time and marginalize or eliminate altogether programming that has significant public-affairs content.[58]

Advertisers will want, more generally, to avoid programs with serious complexities and disturbing controversies that interfere with the "buying mood." They seek programs that will lightly entertain and thus fit in with the spirit of the primary purpose of program purchases—the dissemination of a selling message. Thus over time, instead of programs like "The Selling of the Pentagon," it is a natural evolution of a market seeking sponsor dollars to offer programs such as "A Bird's-Eye View of Scotland," "Barry Goldwater's Arizona," "An Essay on Hotels," and "Mr. Rooney Goes to Dinner"—a CBS program on "how Americans eat when they dine out, where they go and why."[59] There are exceptional cases of companies willing to sponsor serious programs, sometimes a result of recent embarrassments that call for a public-relations offset.[60] But even in these cases the companies will usually not want to sponsor close examination of sensitive and divisive issues—they prefer programs on Greek antiquities, the ballet, and items of cultural and national history and nostalgia. Barnouw points out an interesting contrast: commercial-television drama "deals almost wholly with the here and now, as processed via advertising budgets," but on public television, culture "has come to mean 'other cultures.' . . . American civilization, here and now, is excluded from consideration."[61]

Television stations and networks are also concerned to maintain audience "flow" levels, i.e., to keep people watching from program to program, in order to sustain advertising ratings and revenue. Airing program interludes of documentary-cultural matter that cause station switching is costly, and over time a "free" (i.e., ad-based) commercial system will tend to excise it. Such documentary-cultural-critical materials will be driven out of secondary media vehicles as well, as these companies strive to qualify for advertiser interest, although there will always be some cultural-political programming trying to come into being or surviving on the periphery of the mainstream media.

1.3. SOURCING MASS-MEDIA NEWS: THE THIRD FILTER

The mass media are drawn into a symbiotic relationship with powerful sources of information by economic necessity and reciprocity of interest. The media need a steady, reliable flow of the raw material of news. They have daily news demands and imperative news schedules that they must meet. They cannot afford to have reporters and cameras at all places where important stories may break. Economics dictates that they concentrate their resources where significant news often occurs, where important rumors and leaks abound, and where regular press conferences are held. The White House, the Pentagon, and the State Department, in Washington, D.C., are central nodes of such news activity. On a local basis, city hall and the police department are the subject of regular news "beats" for reporters. Business corporations and trade groups are also regular and credible purveyors of stories deemed newsworthy. These bureaucracies turn out a large volume of material that meets the demands of news organizations for reliable, scheduled flows. Mark Fishman calls this "the principle of bureaucratic affinity: only other bureaucracies can satisfy the input needs of a news bureaucracy."[62]

Government and corporate sources also have the great merit of being recognizable and credible by their status and prestige. This is important to the mass media. As Fishman notes,

> Newsworkers are predisposed to treat bureaucratic accounts as factual because news personnel participate in upholding a normative order of authorized knowers in the society. Reporters operate with the attitude that officials ought to know what it is their job to know.... In particular, a newsworker will recognize an official's claim to knowledge not merely as a claim, but as a credible, competent piece of knowledge. This amounts to a moral division of labor: officials have and give the facts; reporters merely get them.[63]

Another reason for the heavy weight given to official sources is that the mass media claim to be "objective" dispensers of the news. Partly to maintain the image of objectivity, but also to protect themselves from criticisms of bias and the threat of libel suits, they need material that can be portrayed as presumptively accurate.[64] This is also partly a matter of cost: taking information from sources that may be presumed credible reduces investigative expense, whereas material from sources that are not prima facie credible, or that will elicit criticism and threats, requires careful checking and costly research.

The magnitude of the public-information operations of large government and corporate bureaucracies that constitute the primary news sources is vast and ensures special access to the media. The Pentagon, for example, has a public-information service that involves many thousands of employees, spending hundreds of millions of dollars every year and dwarfing not only the public-information resources of any dissenting individual or group but the *aggregate* of such groups. In 1979 and 1980, during a brief interlude of relative openness (since closed down), the U.S. Air Force revealed that its public-information outreach included the following:

140 newspapers, 690,000 copies per week
Airman magazine, monthly circulation 125,000
34 radio and 17 TV stations, primarily overseas
45,000 headquarters and unit news releases
615,000 hometown news releases
6,600 interviews with news media
3,200 news conferences
500 news media orientation flights
50 meetings with editorial boards
11,000 speeches[65]

This excludes vast areas of the air force's public-information effort. Writing back in 1970, Senator J. W. Fulbright had found that the air force public-relations effort in 1968 involved 1,305 full-time employees, exclusive of additional thousands that "have public functions collateral to other duties."[66] The air force at that time offered a weekly film-clip service for TV and a taped features program for use three times a week, sent to 1,139 radio stations; it also produced 148 motion pictures, of which 24 were released for public consumption.[67] There is no reason to believe that the air force public-relations effort has diminished since the 1960s.[68]

Note that this is just the air force. There are three other branches with massive programs, and there is a separate, overall public-information program under an assistant secretary of defense for public affairs in the Pentagon. In 1971, an *Armed Forces Journal* survey revealed that the Pentagon was publishing a total of 371 magazines at an annual cost of some $57 million, an operation sixteen times larger than the nation's biggest publisher. In an update in 1982, the *Air Force Journal International* indicated that the Pentagon was publishing 1,203 periodicals.[69] To put this into perspective, we may note the scope of public-information operations of the American Friends Service Committee (AFSC) and the National Council of the Churches of Christ (NCC), two of the largest of the nonprofit organizations that offer a consistently challenging voice to the views of the Pentagon. The AFSC's main office information-services budget in 1984–85 was under $500,000, with eleven staff people.[70] Its institution-wide press releases run at about two hundred per year, its press conferences thirty a year, and it produces about one film and two or three slide shows a year. It does not offer film clips, photos, or taped radio programs to the media. The NCC Office of Information has an annual budget of some $350,000, issues about a hundred news releases per year, and holds four press conferences annually.[71] The ratio of air force news releases and press conferences to those of the AFSC and NCC taken together are 150 to 1 (or 2,200 to 1 if we count hometown news releases of the air force), and 94 to 1 respectively. Aggregating the other services would increase the differential by a large factor.

Only the corporate sector has the resources to produce public information and propaganda on the scale of the Pentagon and other government bodies. The AFSC and NCC cannot duplicate the Mobil Oil company's multimillion-dollar purchase of newspaper space and other corporate investments to get its viewpoint across.[72] The number of individual corporations with budgets for public information and lobbying in excess of those of the AFSC and NCC runs into the hundreds, perhaps even the thousands. A corporate *collective* like the U.S. Chamber of Commerce had a 1983 budget for research, communications, and political activities of $65 million.[73] By 1980, the chamber was publishing a business magazine (*Nation's Business*) with a circulation of 1.3 million and a weekly newspaper with 740,000 subscribers, and it was producing a weekly panel show distributed to 400 radio stations, as well as its own weekly panel-discussion programs carried by 128 commercial television stations.[74]

Besides the U.S. Chamber, there are thousands of state and local chambers of commerce and trade associations also engaged in public-relations and lobbying activities. The corporate and trade-association lobbying network community is "a network of well over 150,000 professionals,"[75] and its resources are related to corporate income, profits, and the protective value of public-relations and lobbying outlays. Corporate profits before taxes in 1985 were $295.5 billion. When the corporate community gets agitated about the political environment, as it did in the 1970s, it obviously has the wherewithal to meet the perceived threat. Corporate and trade-association image and issues advertising increased from $305 million in 1975 to $650 million in 1980.[76] So did direct-mail campaigns through dividend and other mail stuffers, the distribution of educational films, booklets and pamphlets, and outlays on initiatives and referendums, lobbying, and political and think-tank contributions. Aggregate corporate and trade-association political advertising and grass-roots outlays were estimated to have reached the billion-dollar-a-year level by 1978, and to have grown to $1.6 billion by 1984.[77]

To consolidate their preeminent position as sources, government and business-news promoters go to great pains to make things easy for news organizations. They provide the media organizations with facilities in which to gather; they give journalists advance copies of speeches and forthcoming reports; they schedule press conferences at hours well-geared to news deadlines;[78] they write press releases in usable language; and they carefully organize their press conferences and "photo opportunity" sessions.[79] It is the job of news officers "to meet the journalist's scheduled needs with material that their beat agency has generated at its own pace."[80]

In effect, the large bureaucracies of the powerful *subsidize* the mass media, and gain special access by their contribution to reducing the media's costs of acquiring the raw materials of, and producing, news. The large entities that provide this subsidy become "routine" news sources and have privileged access to the gates. Non-routine sources must struggle for access, and may be ignored by the arbitrary decision of the gatekeepers. It should also be noted that in the case of the largesse of the Pentagon and the State Department's Office of Public Diplomacy,[81] the subsidy is at the taxpayers' expense, so that, in effect, the citizenry pays to be propagandized in the interest of powerful groups such as military contractors and other sponsors of state terrorism.

Because of their services, continuous contact on the beat, and mutual dependency, the powerful can use personal relationships, threats, and rewards to further influence and coerce the media. The media may feel obligated to carry extremely dubious stories and mute criticism in order not to offend their sources and disturb a close relationship.[82] It is very difficult to call authorities on whom one depends for daily news liars, even if they tell whoppers. Critical sources may be avoided not only because of their lesser availability and higher cost of establishing credibility, but also because the primary sources may be offended and may even threaten the media using them.

Powerful sources may also use their prestige and importance to the media as a lever to deny critics access to the media: the Defense Department, for example, refused to participate in National Public Radio discussions of defense issues if experts from the Center for Defense Information were on the program; Elliott Abrams refused to appear on a program on human rights in Central America at the Kennedy School of Government, at Harvard University, unless the former ambassador, Robert White, was excluded as a participant;[83] Claire Sterling refused to participate in television-network shows on the Bulgarian Connection where her critics would appear.[84] In the last two of these cases, the authorities and brand-name experts were successful in monopolizing access by coercive threats.

Perhaps more important, powerful sources regularly take advantage of media routines and dependency to "manage" the media, to manipulate them into following a special agenda and framework (as we will show in detail in the chapters that follow).[85] Part of this management process consists of inundating the media with stories, which serve sometimes to foist a particular line and frame on the media (e.g., Nicaragua as illicitly supplying arms to the Salvadoran rebels), and at other times to help chase unwanted stories off the front page or out of the media altogether (the alleged delivery of MIGs to Nicaragua during the week of the 1984 Nicaraguan election). This strategy can be traced back at least as far as the Committee on Public Information, established to coordinate propaganda during World War I, which "discovered in 1917–18 that one of the best means of controlling news was flooding news channels with 'facts,' or what amounted to official information."[86]

The relation between power and sourcing extends beyond official and corporate provision of day-to-day news to shaping the supply of "experts." The dominance of official sources is weakened by the existence of highly respectable unofficial sources that give dissident views with great authority. This problem is alleviated by "co-opting the experts"[87]—i.e., putting them on the payroll as consultants, funding their research, and organizing think tanks that will hire them directly and help disseminate their messages. In this way bias may be structured, and the supply of experts may be skewed in the direction desired by the government and "the market."[88] As Henry Kissinger has pointed out, in this "age of the expert," the "constituency" of the expert is "those who have a vested interest in commonly held opinions; elaborating and defining its consensus at a high level has, after all, made him an expert."[89] It is therefore appropriate that this restructuring has taken place to allow the commonly held opinions (meaning those that are functional for elite interests) to continue to prevail.

This process of creating the needed body of experts has been carried out on a deliberate basis and a massive scale. Back in 1972, Judge Lewis Powell (later elevated to the Supreme Court) wrote a memo to the U.S. Chamber of Commerce urging business "to buy the top academic reputations in the country to add credibility to corporate studies and give business a stronger voice on the campuses."[90] One buys them, and assures that—in the words of Dr. Edwin Feulner, of the Heritage Foundation—the public-policy area "is awash with in-depth academic studies" that have the proper conclusions. Using the analogy of Procter & Gamble selling toothpaste, Feulner explained that "They sell it and resell it every day by keeping the product fresh in the consumer's mind." By the sales effort, including the dissemination of the correct ideas to "thousands of newspapers," it is possible to keep debate "within its proper perspective."[91]

In accordance with this formula, during the 1970s and early 1980s a string of institutions was created and old ones were activated to the end of propagandizing the corporate viewpoint. Many hundreds of intellectuals were brought to these institutions, where their work was funded and their outputs were disseminated to the media by a sophisticated propaganda effort.[92] The corporate funding and clear ideological purpose in the overall effort had no discernible effect on the credibility of the intellectuals so mobilized; on the contrary, the funding and pushing of their ideas catapaulted them into the press.

As an illustration of how the funded experts preempt space in the media, table 1-4 describes the "experts" on terrorism and defense issues who appeared on the "McNeil-Lehrer News Hour" in the course of a year in the mid-1980s. We can see that, excluding journalists, a majority of the participants (54 percent) were present or former government officials, and that the next highest category (15.7 percent) was drawn from conservative think tanks. The largest number of appearances in the latter category was supplied by the Georgetown Center for Strategic and International Studies (CSIS), an organization funded by conservative foundations and corporations, and providing a revolving door between the State Department and CIA and a nominally private organization.[93] On such issues as terrorism and the Bulgarian Connection, the CSIS has occupied space in the media that otherwise might have been filled by independent voices.[94]

The mass media themselves also provide "experts" who regularly echo the official view. John Barron and Claire Sterling are household names as authorities on the KGB and terrorism because the *Reader's Digest* has funded, published, and publicized their work; the Soviet defector Arkady Shevchenko became an expert on Soviet arms and intelligence because *Time,* ABC-TV, and the *New York Times* chose to feature him (despite his badly tarnished credentials).[95] By giving these purveyors of the preferred view a great deal of exposure, the media confer status and make them the obvious candidates for opinion and analysis.

Another class of experts whose prominence is largely a function of serviceability to power is former radicals who have come to "see the light." The motives that cause these individuals to switch gods, from Stalin (or Mao) to Reagan and free enterprise, is varied, but for the establishment media the reason for the change is simply that the ex-

TABLE 1-4

Experts on Terrorism and Defense on the "McNeil-Lehrer News Hour," January 14, 1985, to January 27, 1986*

CATEGORY OF EXPERT	NO.	%	NO. EXCLUDING JOURNALISTS	% EXCLUDING JOURNALISTS
Government official	24	20	24	27
Former government official	24	20	24	27
Conservative think tank	14	11.7	14	15.7
Academic	12	10	12	13.5
Journalist	31	25.8	—	—
Consultant	3	2.5	3	3.4
Foreign government official	5	4.2	5	5.6
Other	7	5.8	7	7.8
Totals	120	100	89	100

* This is a compilation of all appearances on the news hour concerning the Bulgarian Connection (3), the shooting down of the Korean airliner KAL 007 (5), and terrorism, defense, and arms control (33), from January 14, 1985, through January 27, 1986.

radicals have finally seen the error of their ways. In a country whose citizenry values acknowledgement of sin and repentance, the turncoats are an important class of repentant sinners. It is interesting to observe how the former sinners, whose previous work was of little interest or an object of ridicule to the mass media, are suddenly elevated to prominence and become authentic experts. We may recall how, during the McCarthy era, defectors and ex-Communists vied with one another in tales of the imminence of a Soviet invasion and other lurid stories.[96] They found that news coverage was a function of their trimming their accounts to the prevailing demand. The steady flow of ex-radicals from marginality to media attention shows that we are witnessing a durable method of providing experts who will say what the establishment wants said.[97]

1.4. FLAK AND THE ENFORCERS: THE FOURTH FILTER

"Flak" refers to negative responses to a media statement or program. It may take the form of letters, telegrams, phone calls, petitions, lawsuits, speeches and bills before Congress, and other modes of complaint, threat, and punitive action. It may be organized centrally or locally, or it may consist of the entirely independent actions of individuals.

If flak is produced on a large scale, or by individuals or groups with substantial resources, it can be both uncomfortable and costly to the media. Positions have to be defended within the organization and without, sometimes before legislatures and possibly even in courts. Advertisers may withdraw patronage. Television advertising is mainly of consumer goods that are readily subject to organized boycott. During the McCarthy years, many advertisers and radio and television stations were effectively coerced into quiescence and blacklisting of employees by the threats of determined Red hunters to boycott products. Advertisers are still concerned to avoid offending constituencies that might produce flak, and their demand for suitable programming is a continuing feature of the media environment.[98] If certain kinds of fact, position, or program are thought likely to elicit flak, this prospect can be a deterrent.

The ability to produce flak, and especially flak that is costly and threatening, is related to power. Serious flak has increased in close parallel with business's growing resentment of media criticism and the corporate offensive of the 1970s and 1980s. Flak from the powerful can be either direct or indirect. The direct would include letters or phone calls from the White House to Dan Rather or William Paley, or from the FCC to the television networks asking for documents used in putting together a program, or from irate officials of ad agencies or corporate sponsors to media officials asking for reply time or threatening retaliation.[99] The powerful can also work on the media indirectly by complaining to their own constituencies (stockholders, employees) about the media, by generating institutional advertising that does the same, and by funding right-wing monitoring or think-tank operations designed to attack the media. They may also fund political campaigns and help put into power conservative politicians who will more directly serve the interests of private power in curbing any deviationism in the media.

Along with its other political investments of the 1970s and 1980s, the corporate community sponsored the growth of institutions such as the American Legal Foundation, the Capital Legal Foundation, the Media Institute, the Center for Media and Public Affairs, and Accuracy in Media (AIM). These may be regarded as institutions organized for the specific purpose of producing flak. Another and older flak-producing machine with a broader design is Freedom House. The American Legal Foundation, organized in 1980, has specialized in Fairness Doctrine complaints and libel suits to aid "media victims." The Capital Legal Foundation, incorporated in 1977, was the Scaife vehicle for Westmoreland's $120-million libel suit against CBS.[100]

The Media Institute, organized in 1972 and funded by corporate-wealthy patrons, sponsors monitoring projects, conferences, and studies of the media. It has focused less heavily on media failings in foreign policy, concentrating more on media portrayals of economic issues and the business community, but its range of interests is broad. The main theme of its sponsored studies and conferences has been the failure of the media to portray business accurately and to give adequate weight to the business point of view,[101] but it underwrites works such as John Corry's exposé of the alleged left-wing bias of the mass media.[102] The chairman of the board of trustees of the institute in 1985 was Steven V. Seekins, the top public-relations officer of the American Medical Association; chairman of the National Advisory Council was Herbert Schmertz, of the Mobil Oil Corporation.

The Center for Media and Public Affairs, run by Linda and Robert Lichter, came into existence in the mid-1980s as a "non-profit, non-partisan" research institute, with warm accolades from Patrick Buchanan, Faith Whittlesey, and Ronald Reagan himself, who recognized the need for an objective and fair press. Their *Media Monitor* and research studies continue their earlier efforts to demonstrate the liberal bias and anti-business propensities of the mass media.[103]

AIM was formed in 1969, and it grew spectacularly in the 1970s. Its annual income rose from $5,000 in 1971 to $1.5 million in the early 1980s, with funding mainly from large corporations and the wealthy heirs and foundations of the corporate system. At least eight separate oil companies were contributors to AIM in the early 1980s, but the wide representation in sponsors from the corporate community is impressive.[104] The function of AIM is to harass the media and put pressure on them to follow the corporate agenda and a hard-line, right-wing foreign policy. It presses the media to join more enthusiastically in Red-scare bandwagons, and attacks them for alleged deficiencies whenever they fail to toe the line on foreign policy. It conditions the media to expect trouble (and cost increases) for violating right-wing standards of bias.[105]

Freedom House, which dates back to the early 1940s, has had interlocks with AIM, the World Anticommunist League, Resistance International, and U.S. government bodies such as Radio Free Europe and the CIA, and has long served as a virtual propaganda arm of the government and international right wing. It sent election monitors to the Rhodesian elections staged by Ian Smith in 1979 and found them "fair," whereas the 1980 elections won by Mugabe under British supervision it found dubious. Its election monitors also found the Salvadoran elections of 1982 admirable.[106] It has expended substantial resources in criticizing the media for insufficient sympathy with U.S. foreign-policy ventures and excessively harsh criticism of U.S. client states. Its most notable publication of this genre was Peter Braestrup's *Big Story*, which contended that the media's negative portrayal of the Tet offensive helped lose the war. The work is a travesty of scholarship, but more interesting is its premise: that the mass media not only should support any national venture abroad, but should do so with enthusiasm, such enterprises being by definition noble (see the extensive review of the Freedom House study in chapter 5 and appendix 3). In 1982, when the Reagan administration was having trouble containing media reporting of the systematic killing of civilians by the Salvadoran army, Freedom House came through with a denunciation of the "imbalance" in media reporting from El Salvador.[107]

Although the flak machines steadily attack the mass media, the media treat them well. They receive respectful attention, and their propagandistic role and links to a larger corporate program are rarely mentioned or analyzed. AIM head, Reed Irvine's diatribes are frequently published, and right-wing network flacks who regularly assail the "liberal media," such as Michael Ledeen,[108] are given Op-Ed column space, sympathetic reviewers, and a regular place on talk shows as experts. This reflects the power of the sponsors, including the well-entrenched position of the right wing in the mass media themselves.[109]

The producers of flak add to one another's strength and reinforce the command of political authority in its news-management activities. The government is a major producer of flak, regularly assailing, threatening, and "correcting" the media, trying to contain any deviations from the established line. News management itself is designed to produce flak. In the Reagan years, Mr. Reagan was put on television to exude charm to millions, many of whom berated the media when they dared to criticize the "Great Communicator."[110]

1.5. ANTICOMMUNISM AS A CONTROL MECHANISM

A final filter is the ideology of anticommunism. Communism as the ultimate evil has always been the specter haunting property owners, as it threatens the very root of their class position and superior status. The Soviet, Chinese, and Cuban revolutions were traumas to Western elites, and the ongoing conflicts and the well-publicized abuses of Communist states have contributed to elevating opposition to communism to a first principle of Western ideology and politics. This ideology helps mobilize the populace against an enemy, and because the concept is fuzzy it can be used against anybody advocating policies that threaten property interests or support accommodation with Communist states and radicalism. It therefore helps fragment the left and labor movements and serves as a political-control mechanism. If the triumph of communism is the worst imaginable result, the support of fascism abroad is justified as a lesser evil. Opposition to social democrats who are too soft on Communists and "play into their hands" is rationalized in similar terms.

Liberals at home, often accused of being pro-Communist or insufficiently anti-Communist, are kept continuously on the defensive in a cultural milieu in which anticommunism is the dominant religion. If they allow communism, or something that can be labeled communism, to triumph in the provinces while they are in office, the political costs are heavy. Most of them have fully internalized the religion anyway, but they are all under great pressure to demonstrate their anti-Communist credentials. This causes them to behave very much like reactionaries. Their occasional support of social democrats often breaks down where the latter are insufficiently harsh on their own indigenous radicals or on popular groups that are organizing among generally marginalized sectors. In his brief tenure in the Dominican Republic, Juan Bosch attacked corruption in the armed forces and government, began a land-reform program, undertook a major project for mass education of the populace, and maintained a remarkably open government and system of effective civil liberties. These policies threatened powerful internal vested interests, and the United States resented his independence and the extension of civil liberties to Communists and radicals. This was carrying democracy and pluralism too far. Kennedy was "extremely disappointed" in Bosch's rule, and the State Department "quickly soured on the first democratically elected Dominican President in over thirty years." Bosch's overthrow by the military after nine months in office had at least the tacit support of the United States.[111] Two years later, by contrast, the Johnson administration invaded the

Dominican Republic to make sure that Bosch did not resume power.

The Kennedy liberals were enthusiastic about the military coup and displacement of a populist government in Brazil in 1964.[112] A major spurt in the growth of neo-Fascist national-security states took place under Kennedy and Johnson. In the cases of the U.S. subversion of Guatemala, 1947–54, and the military attacks on Nicaragua, 1981–87, allegations of Communist links and a Communist threat caused many liberals to support counterrevolutionary intervention, while others lapsed into silence, paralyzed by the fear of being tarred with charges of infidelity to the national religion.

It should be noted that when anti-Communist fervor is aroused, the demand for serious evidence in support of claims of "communist" abuses is suspended, and charlatans can thrive as evidential sources. Defectors, informers, and assorted other opportunists move to center stage as "experts," and they remain there even after exposure as highly unreliable, if not downright liars.[113] Pascal Delwit and Jean-Michel Dewaele point out that in France, too, the ideologues of anticommunism "can do and say anything."[114] Analyzing the new status of Annie Kriegel and Pierre Daix, two former passionate Stalinists now possessed of a large and uncritical audience in France,[115] Delwit and Dewaele note:

> If we analyse their writings, we find all the classic reactions of people who have been disappointed in love. But no one dreams of criticising them for their past, even though it has marked them forever. They may well have been converted, but they have not changed. . . . no one notices the constants, even though they are glaringly obvious. Their best sellers prove, thanks to the support of the most indulgent and slothful critics anyone could hope for, that the public can be fooled. No one denounces or even notices the arrogance of both yesterday's eulogies and today's diatribes; no one cares that there is never any proof and that invective is used in place of analysis. Their inverted hyper-Stalinism—which takes the usual form of total manicheanism—is whitewashed simply because it is directed against Communism. The hysteria has not changed, but it gets a better welcome in its present guise.[116]

The anti-Communist control mechanism reaches through the system to exercise a profound influence on the mass media. In normal times as well as in periods of Red scares, issues tend to be framed in terms of a dichotomized world of Communist and anti-Communist powers, with gains and losses allocated to contesting sides, and rooting for "our side" considered an entirely legitimate news practice. It is the mass media that identify, create, and push into the limelight a Joe McCarthy, Arkady Shevchenko, and Claire Sterling and Robert Leiken, or an Annie Kriegel and Pierre Daix. The ideology and religion of anticommunism is a potent filter.

1.6. DICHOTOMIZATION AND PROPAGANDA CAMPAIGNS

The five filters narrow the range of news that passes through the gates, and even more sharply limit what can become "big news," subject to sustained news campaigns. By definition, news from primary establishment sources meets one major filter requirement and is readily accommodated by the mass media. Messages from and about dissidents and weak, unorganized individuals and groups, domestic and foreign, are at an initial disadvantage in sourcing costs and credibility, and they often do not comport with the ideology or interests of the gatekeepers and other powerful parties that influence the filtering process.[117]

Thus, for example, the torture of political prisoners and the attack on trade unions in Turkey will be pressed on the media only by human-rights activists and groups that have little political leverage. The U.S. government supported the Turkish martial-law government from its inception in 1980, and the U.S. business community has been warm toward regimes that profess fervent anticommunism, encourage foreign investment, repress unions, and loyally support U.S. foreign policy (a set of virtues that are frequently closely linked). Media that chose to feature Turkish violence against their own citizenry would have had to go to extra expense to find and check out information sources; they would elicit flak from government, business, and organized right-wing flak machines, and they might be looked upon with disfavor by the corporate community (including advertisers) for indulging in such a quixotic interest and crusade. They would tend to stand alone in focusing on victims that from the standpoint of dominant American interests were *unworthy*.[118]

In marked contrast, protest over political prisoners and the violation of the rights of trade unions in Poland was seen by the Reagan administration and business elites in 1981 as a noble cause, and, not coincidentally, as an opportunity to score political points. Many media leaders and syndicated columnists felt the same way. Thus information and strong opinions on human-rights violations in Poland could be obtained from official sources in Washington, and reliance on Polish dissidents would not elicit flak from the U.S. government or the flak machines. These victims would be generally acknowledged by the managers of the filters to be *worthy*. The mass media never explain *why* Andrei Sakharov is worthy and José Luis Massera, in Uruguay, is unworthy—the attention and general dichotomization occur "naturally" as a result of the working of the filters, but the result is the same as if a commissar had instructed the media: "Concentrate on the victims of enemy powers and forget about the victims of friends."[119]

Reports of the abuses of worthy victims not only pass through the filters; they may also become the basis of sustained propaganda campaigns. If the government or corporate community and the media feel that a story is useful as well as dramatic, they focus on it intensively and use it to enlighten the public. This was true, for example, of the shooting down by the Soviets of the Korean airliner KAL 007 in early September 1983, which permitted an extended campaign of denigration of an official enemy and greatly advanced Reagan administration arms plans. As Bernard Gwertzman noted complacently in the *New York Times* of August 31, 1984, U.S. officials "assert that worldwide criticism of the Soviet handling of the crisis has strengthened the United States in its relations with Moscow." In sharp contrast, the shooting down by Israel of a Libyan civilian airliner in February 1973 led to no outcry in the West, no denunciations for "cold-blooded murder,"[120] and no boycott. This difference in treatment was explained by the *New York Times* precisely on the grounds of utility: "No useful purpose is served by an acrimonious debate over the assignment of blame for the downing of a Libyan airliner in the Sinai peninsula last week."[121] There was a very "useful purpose" served by focusing on the Soviet act, and a massive propaganda campaign ensued.[122]

Propaganda campaigns in general have been closely attuned to elite interests. The Red scare of 1919–20 served well to abort the union-organizing drive that followed World War I in the steel and other industries. The Truman-McCarthy Red scare helped inaugurate the Cold War and the permanent war economy, and it also served to weaken the progressive coalition of the New Deal years. The chronic focus on the plight of Soviet dissidents, on enemy killings in Cambodia, and on the Bulgarian Connection helped weaken the Vietnam syndrome, justify a huge arms buildup and a more aggressive foreign policy, and divert attention from the upward redistribution of income that was the heart of Reagan's domestic economic program.[123] The recent propaganda-disinformation attacks on Nicaragua have been needed to avert eyes from the savagery of the war in El Salvador and to justify the escalating U.S. investment in counterrevolution in Central America.

Conversely, propaganda campaigns will *not* be mobilized where victimization, even though massive, sustained, and dramatic, fails to meet the test of utility to elite interests. Thus, while the focus on Cambodia in the Pol Pot era (and thereafter) was exceedingly serviceable, as Cambodia had fallen to the Communists and useful lessons could be drawn by attention to their victims, the numerous victims of the U.S. bombing *before* the Communist takeover were scrupulously ignored by the U.S. elite press. After Pol Pot's ouster by the Vietnamese, the United States quietly shifted support to this "worse than Hitler" villain, with little notice in the press, which adjusted once again to the national political agenda.[124] Attention to the Indonesian massacres of 1965–66, or the victims of the Indonesian invasion of East Timor from 1975 onward, would also be distinctly unhelpful as bases of media campaigns, because Indonesia is a U.S. ally and client that maintains an open door to Western investment, and because, in the case of East Timor, the United States bears major responsibility for the slaughter. The same is true of the victims of state terror in Chile and Guatemala, U.S. clients whose basic institutional structures, including the state terror system, were put in place and maintained by, or with crucial assistance from, U.S. power, and who remain U.S. client states. Propaganda campaigns on behalf of these victims would conflict with government-business-military interests and, in our model, would not be able to pass through the filtering system.[125]

Propaganda campaigns may be instituted either by the government or by one or more of the top media firms. The campaigns to discredit the government of Nicaragua, to support the Salvadoran elections as an exercise in legitimizing democracy, and to use the Soviet shooting down of the Korean airliner KAL 007 as a means of mobilizing public support for the arms buildup, were instituted and propelled by the government. The campaigns to publicize the crimes of Pol Pot and the alleged KGB plot to assassinate the pope were initiated by the *Reader's Digest*, with strong follow-up support from NBC-TV, the *New York Times*, and other major media companies.[126] Some propaganda campaigns are jointly initiated by government and media; all of them require the collaboration of the mass media. The secret of the unidirectionality of the politics of media propaganda campaigns is the multiple filter system discussed above: the mass media will allow any stories that are hurtful to large interests to peter out quickly, if they surface at all.[127]

For stories that are *useful*, the process will get under way with a series of government leaks, press conferences, white papers, etc., or with one or more of the mass media starting the ball rolling with such articles as Barron and Paul's "Murder of a Gentle Land" (Cambodia), or Claire Sterling's "The Plot to Kill the Pope," both in the *Reader's Digest*. If the other major media like the story, they will follow it up with their own versions, and the matter quickly becomes newsworthy by familiarity. If the articles are written in an assured and convincing style, are subject to no criticisms or alternative interpretations in the mass media, and command support by authority figures, the propaganda themes quickly become established as true even without real evidence. This tends to close out dissenting views even more comprehensively, as they would now conflict with an already established popular belief. This in turn opens up further opportunities for still more inflated claims, as these can be made without fear of serious repercussions. Similar wild assertions made in contradiction of official views would elicit powerful flak, so that such an inflation process would be controlled by the government and the market. No such protections exist with system-supportive claims; there, flak will tend to press the media to greater hysteria in the face of enemy evil. The media not only suspend critical judgment and investigative zeal, they compete to find ways of putting the newly established truth in a supportive light. Themes and facts—even careful and well-documented analyses—that are incompatible with the now institutionalized theme are suppressed or ignored. If the theme collapses of its own burden of fabrications, the mass media will quietly fold their tents and move on to another topic.[128]

Using a propaganda model, we would not only anticipate definitions of worth based on utility, and dichotomous attention based on the same criterion, we would also expect the news stories about worthy and unworthy victims (or enemy and friendly states) to differ in *quality*. That is, we would expect official sources of the United States and its client regimes to be used heavily—and uncritically—in connection with one's own abuses and those of friendly governments, while refugees and other dissident sources will be used in dealing with enemies.[129] We would anticipate the uncritical acceptance of certain premises in dealing with self and friends—such as that one's own state and leaders seek peace and democracy, oppose terrorism, and tell the truth—premises which will not be applied in treating enemy states. We would expect different criteria of evaluation to be employed, so that what is villainy in enemy states will be presented as an incidental background fact in the case of oneself and friends.[130] What is on the agenda in treating one case will be off the agenda in discussing the other.[131] We would also expect great investigatory zeal in the search for enemy villainy and the responsibility of high officials for abuses in enemy states, but diminished enterprise in examining such matters in connection with one's own and friendly states.

The quality of coverage should also be displayed more directly and crudely in placement, headlining, word usage, and other modes of mobilizing interest and outrage. In the opinion columns, we would anticipate sharp restraints on the range of opinion allowed expression. Our hypothesis is that worthy victims will be featured prominently and dramatically, that they will be humanized, and that their victimization will receive the detail and context in story construction that will generate reader interest and sympathetic emotion. In contrast, unworthy victims will merit only slight detail, minimal humanization, and little context that will excite and enrage.

Meanwhile, because of the power of establishment sources, the flak machines, and anti-Communist ideology, we would anticipate outcries that the worthy victims are being sorely neglected, that the unworthy are treated with excessive and uncritical generosity,[132] that the media's liberal, adversarial (if not subversive) hostility to government explains our difficulties in mustering support for the latest national venture in counterrevolutionary intervention.

In sum, a propaganda approach to media coverage suggests a systematic and highly political dichotomization in news coverage based on serviceability to important domestic power interests. This should be observable in dichotomized choices of story and in the volume and quality of coverage. In the chapters that follow we will see that such dichotomization in the mass media is massive and systematic: not only are choices for publicity and suppression comprehensible in terms of system advantage, but the modes of handling favored and inconvenient materials (placement, tone, context, fullness of treatment) differ in ways that serve political ends.

2

Worthy and Unworthy Victims

A PROPAGANDA SYSTEM WILL CONSISTENTLY PORTRAY PEOPLE abused in enemy states as *worthy* victims, whereas those treated with equal or greater severity by its own government or clients will be *unworthy.* The evidence of worth may be read from the extent and character of attention and indignation. We will show in this chapter that the U.S. mass media's practical definitions of worth are political in the extreme and fit well the expectations of a propaganda model. While this differential treatment occurs on a large scale, the media, intellectuals, and public are able to remain unconscious of the fact and maintain a high moral and self-righteous tone. This is evidence of an extremely effective propaganda system.

2.1. JERZY POPIELUSZKO VERSUS A HUNDRED RELIGIOUS VICTIMS IN LATIN AMERICA

A useful comparison can be made between the mass media's treatment of Jerzy Popieluszko, a Polish priest murdered by the Polish police in

October 1984, and the media's coverage of priests murdered within the U.S. sphere of influence. In our model, Popieluszko, murdered in an enemy state, will be a worthy victim, whereas priests murdered in our client states in Latin America will be unworthy. The former may be expected to elicit a propaganda outburst by the mass media; the latter will not generate sustained coverage.

2.1.1. Quantitative aspects of coverage.

Table 2-1 shows, on row 1, the coverage of Popieluszko's murder and the trial of his murderers by the *New York Times, Time* and *Newsweek,* and CBS News. Rows 2 through 5 summarize the coverage in the same media given to religious personnel murdered in Latin America by agents of U.S. client states:[1] Row 2 shows the coverage given seventy-two individuals in a list of Latin American religious "martyrs" named by Penny Lernoux in her book *Cry of the People*; row 3 describes media coverage of twenty-three priests, missionaries, and other religious workers murdered in Guatemala between January 1980 and February 1985. Row 4 summarizes the coverage of the murder of Archbishop Oscar Romero, of El Salvador, shot by an assassin in March 1980. Row 5 shows the level of media coverage of four U.S. women religious workers, murdered in El Salvador in December 1980.

The coverage of the Popieluszko murder not only dwarfs that of the unworthy victims, it constitutes a major episode of news management and propaganda. Nothing comparable can be found for victims within the free world.[2] It can be seen that the *New York Times* featured the Popieluszko case on its front page on ten different occasions, and the intensity of coverage assured that its readers would know who Popieluszko was, that he had been murdered, and that this sordid violence had occurred in a Communist state. By contrast, the public would not have seen mention of the names of Father Augusto Ramírez Monasterio, father superior of the Franciscan order in Guatemala, murdered in November 1983, or Father Miguel Ángel Montufar, a Guatemalan priest who disappeared in the same month that Popieluszko was killed in Poland, or literally dozens of other religious murder victims in the Latin American provinces, who were sometimes given substantial coverage in the local press of the countries in which the murders took place.

In fact, *none* of the extremely prominent victims of murder in Latin

America, including Archbishop Romero and the four American churchwomen, received anywhere near the attention accorded Popieluszko. We will show below that the *quality* of treatment of the worthy and unworthy victims also differed sharply. While the coverage of the worthy victim was generous with gory details and quoted expressions of outrage and demands for justice, the coverage of the unworthy victims was low-keyed, designed to keep the lid on emotions and evoking regretful and philosophical generalities on the omnipresence of violence and the inherent tragedy of human life. This qualitative difference is already apparent in placement and editorializing: ten front-page articles on Popieluszko is a statement about importance, as is the fact of three editorials denouncing the Poles, without a single editorial denunciation for the murderers of the unworthy victims.

By comparing rows 1 and 6 of table 2-1, we can see that for every media category the coverage of the worthy victim, Popieluszko, exceeded that of the entire set of one hundred unworthy victims taken together. We suspect that the coverage of Popieluszko may have exceeded that of all the many hundreds of religious victims murdered in Latin America since World War II, as the most prominent are included in our hundred. From the table we can also calculate the *relative* worthiness of the world's victims, as measured by the weight given them by the U.S. mass media. The worth of the victim Popieluszko is valued at somewhere between 137 and 179 times that of a victim in the U.S. client states;[3] or, looking at the matter in reverse, a priest murdered in Latin America is worth less than a hundredth of a priest murdered in Poland.

The claim is sometimes made that unworthy victims are so treated by the U.S. mass media because they are killed at a great distance, and are so unlike ourselves that they are easy to disregard.[4] Poland, however, is farther away than Central America, and its cultural and business links with the United States are not as great as those of Latin American countries in general. Three of the religious victims among the twenty-three murdered in Guatemala (row 3) were American citizens, a consideration that failed to light a fire under the media. Even the four American churchwomen raped and murdered by members of the Salvadoran National Guard failed to elicit attention comparable with that accorded Popieluszko. Their relative valuation by the *New York Times* was less than a tenth that of the Polish priest, and we will show later that the coverage of these American victims displayed considerably less outrage and passion than that of Popieluszko.[5]

The coverage of Popieluszko was somewhat inflated by the fact that his murderers were quickly tried, and in a trial that American reporters

TABLE 2-1

Mass-Media Coverage of Worthy and Unworthy Victims (1): A Murdered Polish Priest versus One Hundred Murdered Religious in Latin America

	NEW YORK TIMES								*TIME* and *NEWSWEEK*				*CBS NEWS*			
	Articles[1]		Column inches		Front-page articles		Editorials[1]		Articles[1]		Column inches		No. of news programs[1]		No. of evening news programs	
Victims	No.	% of row 1	No.	% of row 1	No.	% of row 1	No.	% of row 1	No.	% of row 1	No.	% of row 1	No.	% of row 1	No.	% of row 1
1. Jerzy Popieluszko, murdered on Oct. 19, 1984	78	(100)	1183.0	(100)	10	(100)	3	(100)	16	(100)	313.0	(100)	46	(100)	23	(100)
2. 72 religious victims in Latin America, 1964–78[2]	8	(10.3)	117.5	(9.9)	1	(10)	—	—	—	—	16	(5.1)	—[3]	—	—	—

3. 23 religious, murdered in Guatemala Jan. 1980–Feb. 1985[4]	7	(9.0)	66.5	(5.6)	—	—	—	—	2	(12.5)	34.0	(10.9)	2	(4.3)	2	(8.7)
4. Oscar Romero, murdered Mar. 18, 1980	16	(20.5)	219.0	(18.5)	4	(40)	—	—	3	(18.8)	86.5	(27.6)	13	(28.3)	4	(17.4)
5. 4 U.S. religious women, murdered in El Salvador, Dec. 2, 1980	26	(33.3)	201.5	(17.0)	3	(30)	—	—	5	(31.2)	111.0	(35.5)	22	(47.8)	10	(43.5)
6. Total of lines 2–5	57	(73.1)	604.5	(51.1)	8	(80)	—	—	10	(62.5)	247.5	(79.1)	37	(80.4)	16	(69.6)

1. The media coverage is for an 18-month period from the time of the first report of the victim's disappearance or murder.

2. Listed in Penny Lernoux, *Cry of the People* (New York: Doubleday, 1980), pp. 464–65. We have omitted the names of seven martyrs who had joined the guerrillas. Lernoux points out that her list is far from complete, and is composed of only the better-known victims.

3. The CBS News Index begins in 1975; our blank figure for this category does not cover earlier years.

4. This is a partial listing only, taken from tabulations of "Religious Killed or 'Disappeared' in Guatemala," put out periodically by CONFREGUA: *Conferencia de Religiosos de Guatemala.*

could freely report. Almost every murder of the Latin American victims was carried out by official or paramilitary forces in crimes that were never investigated or prosecuted under law, and were on occasion even subject to active official cover-ups (as we describe below in connection with Romero and the four churchwomen). Only in the case of the four murdered American women, in El Salvador, was there sufficient pressure to force some kind of investigation and legal process. As we will see, this legal process was barely noted by the mass media (in contrast with their intense interest in the Popieluszko trial), and the press did not comment upon or explore the significance of the fact that there was a relatively serious trial in "totalitarian" Poland, while state murders were being carried out on a daily basis without any investigations or trials of the murderers in a number of countries within the U.S. sphere of influence called "fledgling democracies."

2.1.2. Coverage of the Popieluszko case

Jerzy Popieluszko was an activist priest and a strong supporter of the Solidarity movement in Poland. In an effort to eliminate or intimidate him, members of the Polish secret police abducted him on October 19, 1984. He was beaten, bound, and gagged, and eventually thrown into a reservoir. His body was found several days later. In the furor that ensued, the police directly involved in the killing were quickly identified and were eventually tried and given stiff jail sentences. As we have seen, the level of attention given to the case in the United States was very great. The quality of coverage was also extremely well designed to score political points, and contrasts sharply with the quality of coverage of unworthy victims.

2.1.2(a). Fullness and reiteration of the details of the murder and the damage inflicted on the victim. The coverage of the Popieluszko murder was notable for the fullness of the details regarding his treatment by the police and the condition of the recovered body. What is more, these details were repeated at every opportunity. The condition of the body was described at its recovery, at the trial when the medical evidence was presented, and during the testimony of the perpetrators of the crime.[6] At the trial, the emotional strain and guilt manifested by the police officers were described time and again, interspersed with the description of how Popieluszko pleaded for his life, and evidence of the brutality of the act. Numerous unflattering photos of the policemen on trial were presented, adding dramatic detail in support of the image of police viciousness. In the courtroom, the guilty police sit, one with "a nervous tic on the right side of his face [that] caused his dark mustache to twitch uncontrollably," with "tear-filled testimony [that] gave the trial some of its most dramatic moments" (*Time*, Feb. 18, 1985). The police weep openly or bow their heads in the face of the grisly evidence. Popieluszko himself was humanized, with descriptions of his physical characteristics and personality that made him into something more than a distant victim.[7] In sum, the act of violence and its effects on Popieluszko were presented in such a way as to generate the maximum emotional impact on readers. The act was vicious and deserved the presentation it received. The acts against the unworthy victims were also vicious, but they were treated very differently.

2.1.2(b). Stress on indignation, shock, and demands for justice. In a large proportion of the articles on the Popieluszko murder there are quotations or assertions of outrage, indignation, profound shock, and mourning, and demands that justice be done. Steady and wholly sympathetic attention is given to demonstrators, mourners, weeping people, work stoppages, masses held in honor of the victim, and expressions of outrage, mainly by nonofficial sources. The population "continues to mourn," "public outrage mounted," the pope is deeply shaken, and even Jaruzelski condemns the action. The net effect of this day-in-day-out repetition of outrage and indignation was to call very forcible attention to a terrible injustice, to put the Polish government on the defensive, and, probably, to contribute to remedial action.

2.1.2(c). The search for responsibility at the top. In article after article, the U.S. media raised the question: how high up was the act known and approved? By our count, eighteen articles in the *New York Times* stressed the question of higher responsibility, often with aggressive headlines addressed to that point.[8] A number of articles bring in a Soviet link ("Lawyer Seemingly [*sic*] Implies a Soviet Link in Slaying of Priest" [Jan. 31, 1985]), and Michael Kaufman, of the *Times*, twice manages to drag in the plot to kill the pope, which the U.S. press, led by the *New York Times*, had been trying to tie in with the Soviets and Bulgarians.[9] These links to the Soviet Union and the Bulgarian Connection are established by finding someone who says what the reporter and his paper want to dredge up—in no case was there a trace of supportive evidence.

Time, *Newsweek* and CBS News played the same game of aggressively raising questions about "Hints of a Contract from the Top" *(Time)* and "Keeping the Lid on Murder" *(Newsweek)*, and *Time* raised questions about possible Soviet involvement as well as the Bulgarian Connection.

2.1.2(d). Conclusions and follow-up. The *New York Times* had three editorials on the Popieluszko case. In each it focused on the responsibility of the higher authorities and the fact that "A police state is especially responsible for the actions of its police" ("Murderous Poland," Oct. 30, 1984). It freely applied words like "thuggery," "shameless," and "crude" to the Polish state. The fact that police officers were quickly identified, tried, and convicted it attributed to the agitation at home and abroad that put a limit on villainy. This is a good point, and one that we stress throughout this book: villainy may be constrained by intense publicity. But we also stress the corresponding importance of a *refusal* to publicize and the leeway this gives murderous clients under the protection of the United States and its media, where the impact of publicity would be far greater.[10] The *Times* also fails to note the contrast between murderous Poland and murderous El Salvador—in the latter country, no murders of Salvadorans by the security forces or the death squads connected to them have ever resulted in a trial. The absence of such a comparison, as well as the failure of the *Times* to produce an editorial entitled "Murderous El Salvador," illustrates how a serviceable terrorism is protected in a propaganda mode.[11]

2.2. RUTILIO GRANDE AND THE UNWORTHY SEVENTY-TWO

As shown on table 2-1, the unworthy seventy-two on Penny Lernoux's list of martyrs were subject to a grand total of eight articles in the *New York Times,* one in *Newsweek,* and none in *Time,* and they were never mentioned on CBS News in the years of index coverage (1975–78). A total of seven names on the Lernoux list were mentioned in the eight *Times* articles, and two different ones were discussed in *Newsweek,* which means that sixty-three of the murders were blacked out entirely in these important media vehicles. None of the eight articles in the *New York Times* had any details or dramatic quality that might evoke sympathetic emotion. They described the murders as remote events in a distant world (see the *Times*'s description of the murder of Michael

Jerome Cypher, in table 2-2). But that is a matter of editorial choice. The drama is there for the asking—only the press concern is missing.[12]

TABLE 2-2

The Savageries Inflicted on Worthy and Unworthy Victims, as Depicted in the *New York Times*

WORTHY VICTIMS

***Jerzy Popieluszko,* a Polish priest, murdered on October 19, 1984.**

(1) Account at finding of body: "The sources who saw the priest's body on Tuesday, said it was badly bruised, indicating he had been beaten after he was kidnapped on a highway near the town of Torun. The autopsy also showed that Father Popieluszko had been gagged at the mouth and apparently tied with a rope from neck to feet so that if he struggled he would strangle himself, they said. The sources said they could not confirm reports quoting members of the slain priest's family as saying he had suffered injuries to his jaw and skull" (Dec. 29, 1984).

(2) Account at trial of murderers: "The film showed clearly that the priest's bent legs were tied to a noose around his neck in such a way that if he straightened them he would be strangled. The rope binding his hands had evidently come loose in the water. Several gags had also worked free and lay covering his clerical collar and the front of his cassock. From his legs hung a sack of rocks that, according to earlier testimony, had been carried all over Poland for the week that the three assailants were pursuing the priest. When the cameras were trained on the priest's face, the narration by a police officer at the reservoir declared that 'there are clear signs of beating.' This was confirmed by medical evidence offered Thursday by Dr. Maria Byrdy, a pathologist, who said Father Popieluszko had been struck more than a dozen times with a club" (Jan. 26, 1985).

UNWORTHY VICTIMS

***Michael Jerome Cypher,* an American priest murdered in Honduras.**

"The bodies were found in a dynamited well on an eastern Honduran estate . . ." (July 19, 1975). *Note:* There was no arrest or trial.

***Jaime Alcina,* a Spanish priest of the Catholic Action Workers movement, following his arrest in Chile:**

"Several days later a body with 10 bullet holes in the back was found in the Mapocho River. A Spanish consul identified the body as that of Father Alcina" (Oct. 1, 1973). *Note:* There was no arrest or trial.

***Archbishop Oscar Arnolfo Romero,* murdered in El Salvador on March 24, 1980:**

"Archbishop Romero was killed by a sniper who got out of a red car, apparently stood just inside the door of the Chapel of the Divine Providence Hospital, fired a single shot at the prelate and fled. The bullet struck the archbishop in the heart, according to a doctor at the hospital where the prelate was taken" (Mar. 25, 1980). *Note:* There was no arrest or trial.

***María Rosario Godoy de Cuevas,* secretary of the Mutual Support Group, murdered in Guatemala on April 4, 1985:**

"The body of the secretary of the Support Group for Families of the Detained and Disappeared in Guatemala was found Friday in a ravine nine miles south of Guatemala City, according to a spokesman for the group. The bodies of her brother and young son were also in the car" (Apr. 7, 1985, p. 5).* *Note:* There was no arrest or trial.

***Jean Donovan, Ita Ford, Dorothy Kazel, and Maura Clarke,* four American women murdered in El Salvador, December 4, 1980:**

(1) Account at the finding of the bodies:

"Witnesses who found the grave said it was about five feet deep. One woman had been shot in the face, another in the breast. Two of the women were found with their blood-stained underpants around their ankles" (Dec. 5, 1980).*

(2) Account at the trial of the murderers:

No description was given, although medical testimony was presented to the court; see text.

---

* For details that were not presented in this account, see the accompanying text.

The murder of one of the seventy-two, Father Rutilio Grande, was an important landmark in the escalation of violence in El Salvador and in its effect on the newly appointed conservative archbishop of San Salvador, Oscar Romero. Rutilio Grande was a Jesuit, the pastor of Aguilares, and a progressive who helped organize peasants in self-help groups. He was strongly opposed by the local landlords, police, and military commanders, but he was a national figure in the Salvadoran church and was a friend of the archbishop. Rutilio Grande was shot to death, along with a teenager and a seventy-two-year-old peasant, while on his way to Mass on March 12, 1977. According to a church autopsy, the bullets that riddled the priest were of the same caliber as the

Manzer guns used by the police. "By 'coincidence,' all telephone communications in the area were cut off within an hour of the triple assassination. Police patrols normally active in the region mysteriously disappeared."[13] Archbishop Romero wrote to the president of El Salvador, Arturo Armando Molina, urging a thorough investigation, which was promised. A week later, the church having established that it was probably police bullets that had killed the three victims, Romero wrote a harsher letter to Molina, noting the absence of a promised official report and pointing out that comments, "many of them unfavorable to your government," have been made. With continued inaction, Romero threatened to refuse church participation in any official government event unless the murders were investigated and the killers brought to justice. Romero's biographer writes:

> Six weeks later, the lawyer chosen by Romero to follow the case reported "an embarrassing and clear indifference toward the investigation on the part of state organizations." A suspect ordered arrested by a judge was living unconcernedly in El Paisnal, and no one had ordered the bodies exhumed and examined. The bullets are still in the graves.[14]

Rutilio Grande's murder followed a series of forcible expulsions of foreign clergy by the Molina government and several earlier murders of church personnel. Romero and the clergy deliberated at great length on their course of action in response to this escalation of the violence against them. They tried to get out their messages of concern, but many were not heard because of newspaper censorship. They finally decided to take dramatic action: temporary school closings, and implementation of the previously mentioned threat to refuse to support the government and other power groups on official occasions.

This entire package of murder and church response was hardly lacking in drama and newsworthiness. Yet murder, the confrontation of the desperate church with a repressive state, and the dramatic acts carried out to try to mobilize support in its self-defense were subject to a virtual blackout in the U.S. mass media. The murder of Rutilio Grande was mentioned in *Newsweek* ("Priests in Peril," Aug. 1, 1977), but it never once reached the audiences of the *New York Times, Time,* or CBS News. This was important in allowing the terror to go on unimpeded. To paraphrase the *New York Times* editorial on "murderous Poland": no publicity and agitation, no containment of terror.

2.3. ARCHBISHOP OSCAR ROMERO

The murder of Archbishop Oscar Romero, the highest Catholic church official in El Salvador, was "big news," and its political implications were enormous. At the time of his murder, Romero had become the foremost and most outspoken critic of the policy of repression by murder being carried out by the U.S.-supported military government. In his last sermon, he appealed to members of the army and security forces to refuse to kill their Salvadoran brethren, a call that enraged the officer corps trying to build a lower-class military that was willing to kill freely. Romero had been placed on right-wing death lists and received threats from the right wing, which from the beginning had been closely linked to the army and intelligence services.[15] Only a few weeks prior to his murder he had written a forceful letter to President Jimmy Carter opposing the imminent granting of U.S. aid to the junta as destructive of Salvadoran interests. The Carter administration had been so disturbed by Romero's opposition to its policies that it had secretly lobbied the pope to curb the archbishop.[16]

Romero, in short, was not merely an "unworthy" victim, he was an important activist in opposition to the local alliance of army and oligarchy and to U.S. policy in El Salvador. The U.S. media's news coverage of the archbishop's murder and its follow-up reflected well his threatening role, reaching new levels of dishonesty and propaganda service in their coverage of this and related events.

2.3.1. Details of the murder and public response

The details of the Romero murder provided by the U.S. mass media were concise (see table 2-2). While there were expressions of shock and distress, there were very few quotations and expressions of outrage by supporters of Romero. There were no statements or quotations suggesting that the murder was intolerable and that the guilty must be found and brought to justice. The *New York Times* had no editorial condemning, or even mentioning, the murder. It was quickly placed in the larger framework of alleged killings by both the left and the right that were deeply regretted by Salvadoran and U.S. officials.

2.3.2. The propaganda line: a reformist junta trying to contain the violence of right and left

The Salvadoran and U.S. governments contended at the time of Romero's murder that the killing going on in El Salvador was being done by extremists of the right and the left, not by the Salvadoran armed forces and their agents; and that the government was trying its best to contain the killings and carry out reforms. John Bushnell, of the State Department, stated before a House appropriations committee that "there is some misperception by those who follow the press that the government is itself repressive in El Salvador," when in fact the violence is "from the extreme right and the extreme left" and "the smallest part" of the killings come from the army and security forces.[17] This statement was a knowing lie,[18] contradicted by all independent evidence coming out of El Salvador and refuted by Archbishop Romero on an almost daily basis.[19] In his letter to Carter sent on February 17, 1980, the archbishop pointed out that aid to the junta had resulted in increasing repressive violence by the government, "amassing a total dead and wounded far higher than in the previous military regimes." And Romero explained to Carter that the idea that the junta was reformist was a myth, that "neither the junta nor the Christian Democrats govern the country," but, rather, power is in the hands of the army, serving itself and the oligarchy.[20]

What gave Bushnell's statement a certain credibility was the fact that there had been a "reformist coup" by young army officers in October 1979, and liberals and progressives entered the early junta. However, as Raymond Bonner points out,

> The young, progressive officers who carefully plotted the coup lost control of it as swiftly as they had executed it. Their ideals and objectives were subverted by senior, more conservative officers who had the backing of [U.S. Ambassador] Devine and the U.S. Embassy in El Salvador and key Carter administration officials in Washington.[21]

The progressive elements on the junta found themselves entirely without power, and gradually exited or were forced out, along with large numbers from the cabinet and administration. José Napoleón Duarte joined the junta in March to serve as a fig leaf and public-relations agent of the army, but all those who were not satisfied to serve in that role departed.[22]

Once the old-guard military had seized control from the progressive officers in October 1979, it began a general war of extermination against all progressive individuals and organizations in El Salvador. By the end of May, church sources reported 1,844 civilian deaths already in 1980, a figure that reached 10,000 by the end of the year, almost all at the hands of the government. A guerrilla war was *forced* on the center and left by the policy of unconstrained violence of the Carter-supported government. The government was not centrist and reformist—it was a military regime of the right, closely linked to the terrorist force ORDEN and the death squads, and it used them regularly as proxies. The paramilitary groups were not uncontrollable—they were doing what the army wanted them to do. The paramilitary forces and death squads of El Salvador had extensive interlocking relationships with the official military and security forces and their U.S. counterparts. There was a revolving door of personnel, close cooperation in sharing information, funding of the paramilitary groups by the official forces, and a division of labor between them. The paramilitary did jobs for which the official forces wished to disclaim responsibility.[23]

Although the paramilitary group ORDEN was formally abolished at the time of the October 1979 coup, it was secretly maintained and had a close relationship with the regular military establishment. According to one detailed account,

> The reformers had officially abolished ORDEN, the old information network. But . . . military officers suspicious of the young reformers secretly reestablished and expanded much of the old intelligence system into a grass-roots intelligence network that fed names of suspected subversives to military and paramilitary death squads. Four days after the coup, D'Aubuisson said in an interview, he was assigned by members of the high command to help reorganize ANSESAL [an intelligence communication network] inside a military compound under the chief of staff's office—out of the reach of civilians in the new junta.[24]

This secret assignment of D'Aubuisson was confirmed by junta member Colonel Jaime Abdul Gutiérrez, and then Deputy Defense Minister Colonel Nicholás Carranza.[25]

The U.S. mass media, however, followed the Bushnell formula virtually without deviation: there was a "civil war between extreme right and leftist groups" (*New York Times,* Feb. 25, 1980); the "seemingly well meaning but weak junta" was engaging in reforms but was unable to check the terror (*Time,* Apr. 7, 1980). The U.S. mass media had featured heavily the reformist character of the revolutionary junta, but they uniformly suppressed evidence of the powerlessness, frustrations, and early resignation of the progressives, and their replacement by civilians willing to serve as "front men" for state terror. Román Mayorga, an engineer and university professor who had been the unanimous choice of the original coup plotters, resigned on January 3, 1980, along with Guillermo Manuel Ungo "and at least 37 of the highest ranking government officials, including the heads of all government agencies."[26] But for the media, these events never happened, and the junta was still a "weak centrist government . . . beset by implacable extremes" (*New York Times* editorial, Apr. 28, 1980), not a right-wing government of massacre. Robin K. Andersen points out that

> None of the networks reported . . . the final resignation of the junta members. Even CBS, which had reported at length on the appointment of Román Mayorga, failed to report his resignation, or any of the others. For television news viewers, these political developments never happened. Television news coverage omitted every reference to this all-important political power struggle that could have accounted for the abuses that continued. . . . The civilian lack of control, and even their resignation, had no effect on the way in which the news characterized the junta; it continued to be labeled moderate.[27]

And the Salvadoran government has continued to be "moderate" and "centrist" up to today.

Other media suppressions aided in bolstering the myth of the neutral junta standing between the extreme right and the extreme left. On March 29, 1980, the *New York Times* carried a Reuters dispatch noting the resignation of three high Salvadoran officials, who, according to the article, "resigned last night in protest against the junta's inability to halt violence by leftist and rightist forces."[28] The preceding day, an AP dispatch recorded the same resignations, but without any explanation of the reasons for this. One of the resigning officials, Undersecretary of Agriculture Jorge Alberto Villacorta, issued a public statement saying that

> I resigned because I believed that it was useless to continue in a government not only incapable of putting an end to the violence, but a government which itself is generating the political violence through repression. . . . Recently, in one of the large estates taken over by the agrarian reform, uniformed members of the security

> forces accompanied by a masked person pointed out the directors of the self-management group and then these individuals were shot in front of their co-workers.[29]

It can be seen from the statement that the reference in the Reuter's dispatch to protest "against the junta's inability to halt violence by leftist and rightist forces" is a gross misrepresentation, and it is evident that an honest transmission of Villacorta's statement would have contradicted the propaganda line.

At Archbishop Romero's funeral, on March 30, 1980, where many thousands gathered to pay tribute, bomb explosions and gunfire killed some forty people and injured hundreds more. The version of the event provided by U.S. Ambassador Robert White and the Salvadoran government was that "armed terrorists of the ultra left sowed panic among the masses and did all they could to provoke the security forces into returning fire. But the discipline of the armed forces held."[30] Joseph Treaster's account in the *New York Times* quotes Duarte that the violence was from the left. It also quotes a junta statement that the army was strictly confined to its barracks, and Treaster says, "There was no sign of uniformed government forces in the plaza before or during the shooting." No other version of the facts is mentioned. However, a mimeographed statement on March 30, signed by twenty-two church leaders present at the funeral, claimed that the panic had been started by a bomb thrown from the national palace, followed by machine-gun and other shots coming from its second floor.[31] This account was suppressed by Treaster and was never mentioned in the *New York Times.*

In a follow-up article of April 7, 1980, Treaster repeats that on March 30 the junta ordered all military forces into their barracks, and that they obeyed "even though they knew leftists with weapons were pouring into the central plaza." Treaster asserts this government claim as fact, and he continues to suppress sources and evidence that contradict this government allegation. He also fails to explain why the leftists would indiscriminately shoot their own people paying homage to the archbishop.[32]

The title of Treaster's article of April 7, 1980, is "Slaying in Salvador Backfires on Rebels." The article reads as follows:

> The murder of Archbishop Oscar Arnulfo Romero two weeks ago and the killing of 30 at his funeral may have benefited, rather than hurt, the ruling civilian-military junta, in the view of many diplomats, businessmen and Government officials.
>
> The extreme right is being blamed for the killing of the Arch-

> bishop and the extreme left is being blamed for the shooting and bombing that turned the crowded central plaza into chaos as Archbishop Romero was being eulogized.
>
> "It's not so much that the junta gained," said Robert E. White, the United States Ambassador to El Salvador, "but that its opponents on the extreme right and left have lost prestige. The net result is a boost in prestige for the junta."

We may note how the title of the article transforms the murder of the leader of the dissident forces (and then of his followers at the funeral) from a moral issue deserving outrage into a question of political advantage, and turns that against the rebels. It would be hard to imagine the *New York Times* publishing an article on Popieluszko headed "Slaying in Poland Backfires on Solidarity Movement," featuring perhaps the playing up by the official press of demonstrator aggressiveness or violence. Note also how the question of identifying the killer of Romero, and the government's obligation to seek justice, has been pushed into the background. Finally, there is the statement that "the extreme left is being blamed" for the deaths in the plaza. Use of the passive voice allows Treaster to avoid specification of just who is blaming the extreme left. He mentions as his sources for the article as a whole "many diplomats, businessmen and Government officials"—he doesn't even pretend to have talked to ordinary Salvadorans or church representatives—but his only citation near the statement that "the extreme left is being blamed" is the then-U.S. ambassador, Robert White. By relying only on government handouts and carefully avoiding readily available conflicting evidence and alternative views, the *Times* once again found the means of applying the usual formula of a deadly right offsetting a deadly left, with the junta favored by the U.S. government once more placed in the middle—with enhanced prestige!

2.3.3. Misrepresentation of Romero's views

As we noted earlier, Romero was unequivocal in laying the blame for the violence in El Salvador on the army and security forces, and he viewed the left and popular groupings as victims provoked into self-defense by violence and injustice. The peoples' organizations, he told Carter, are "fighting to defend their most fundamental human rights" against a military establishment that "knows only how to repress the people and defend the interests of the Salvadorean oligarchy." And in his diary, Romero completely repudiated the idea that the army was reacting to somebody else's violence—the security forces are instruments "of a general program of annihilation of those on the left, who by themselves would not commit violence or further it were it not for social injustice that they want to do away with."[33] Thus Joseph Treaster's statement on the front page of the *New York Times* that Romero "had criticized both the extreme right and the extreme left for widespread killing and torture in El Salvador" (Mar. 31, 1980) is straightforward lying: Romero never accused the left of torture or widespread killing, he never equated the right and the left, and he was quite clear that the government (an agent of the right) was the primary killer. In this respect, Romero's perception, essentially the same as that *privately* conveyed to the press by the U.S. government, was grossly falsified in public by both the government and press.[34]

Interestingly, a year later, in an article marking the anniversary of the assassination of Archbishop Romero, Edward Schumacher, of the *Times,* noted that under Romero's successor, Archbishop Rivera y Damas, "the church has moved to a more centrist position in the civil war between the Government and the guerrillas."[35] Of course, if the church now takes a centrist position, as opposed to its position under Romero, this constitutes an admission that the theme played by Treaster and the *Times* a year previously of an even-handed Romero was a lie (which it was). Is it possible that the *Times* always finds the church in the middle and is lying one year later as well? The question must remain open, as his successor has been much more circumspect than Romero. The willingness of the right wing and the army to murder people like Romero might have affected Archbishop Rivera y Damas's ability to speak his mind freely and forced public caution. The point does not arise for Schumacher and the *Times.*[36]

2.3.4. The loss of interest in responsibility at the top

With Popieluszko, the media tried hard to establish that there was knowledge of and responsibility for the crime at higher levels of the Polish government. Soviet interest and possible involvement were also regularly invoked. With Romero, in contrast, no such questions were raised or pressed.

The media did note that Romero opposed aid to the Salvadoran junta (which Carter provided anyway), but they failed to convey the depth of his hostility to U.S. policy and the importance of his oppositional role (although it was far more threatening to U.S. policy than Popieluszko was to the Soviet Union). The press never mentioned the special emissary sent by Carter to the pope in an attempt to bring Romero into line, or the fact that the head of the Jesuit order in Central America was called to Rome, probably in response to this U.S. pressure.[37] The media also suppressed Romero's appeal to the military to refuse to kill, a fact that would have made much clearer how strongly opposed he was to the official policies, and how convenient his murder was to the rulers of El Salvador.

Although Romero was far and away the most important establishment figure aligned with the popular movements, the media pretended at first that the affiliation of his killers was a complete mystery. The *Washington Post* supposed an equal likelihood of a left- or right-wing source, and the *Miami Herald* noted on March 27 that "Both stood to benefit from any chaos his death might have created." (No American paper suggested that Popieluszko might have been murdered by Solidarity sympathizers to discredit the Polish government.) This foolishness was the minority position—the bulk of the press suggested that the killer was probably a rightist, but of obscure connection. The reliable Duarte suggested that the killing was too professional to be indigenous—it must have been a contract job from the outside. This view was dutifully repeated by the *New York Times*, *Time*, *Newsweek*, and CBS News.[38]

If, as seemed very likely, the killer was a Salvadoran rightist, or someone in their employ, what was his connection, if any, with the army and security forces? We saw earlier that the linkages between the death squads and the army were close: there was at least some degree of common command, shared operations, and mutual protection. Could the killer have been a member of the armed forces? Given the links of the army to the paramilitary forces, wasn't it likely that they knew who killed Romero? The U.S. mass media did not *raise*, let alone press, these questions. When D'Aubuisson's link to the murder became public knowledge, the media failed to make this a big issue, and his close relations to the official forces were not examined and discussed. This is evidence of a propaganda system at work.

Any possible *U.S.* connection to the crime was, of course, "far out," and could not be raised in the U.S. media. That we don't do this sort of thing is an ideological premise of the patriotic press, no matter what the facts of recent history tell us.[39] But still, the question might have been raised whether the environment that the United States was helping to create in El Salvador, training and aiding a murderous army whose violence had driven Romero to passionate opposition, made the United States indirectly guilty of the murder? The press never discussed this point either. The *Times* quotes Secretary of State Cyrus Vance on the murder: "Two weeks ago I wrote the Archbishop and said: 'We share a repugnance for the violence provoked by both extremes that is taking the lives of innocent people. We deplore the efforts of those seeking to silence the voices of reason and moderation with explosives, intimidation and murder.' "[40] The paper points out that the letter from Vance was in reply to Romero's appeal to cease supplying arms. The article failed to include the gist of Romero's argument, and it did not quote that part of Vance's letter that rejected the archbishop's appeal. The report also did not take note of Vance's serious misrepresentation of the archbishop's position when he says that "We *share* a repugnance [for] . . . both extremes"; Romero attributed the killings to the army and the right, not "both extremes." We may note also that while Romero was victimized by the very forces that Vance supported, and Romero's forecasts seem to be vindicated by his own murder, there is no hint in the account of any irony or criticism of Vance and his associates. Here the press cannot plead lack of knowledge. As later conceded, the media knew very well that the security forces were the source of the violence.

2.3.5. Murder unavenged—or triumphant

The assassins of Archbishop Romero were never "officially" discovered or prosecuted, and he joined the ranks of the tens of thousands of other Salvadorans murdered without justice being done. But in contrast with Popieluszko, the U.S. mass media seemed quite uninterested in who committed the act or in demanding just retribution.

Subsequently, a great deal of evidence became available showing that Roberto D'Aubuisson was at the center of a conspiracy to murder Romero. On the basis of numerous interviews with Arena party activists and U.S. officials, and examination of State Department cables, investigative reporters Craig Pyes and Laurie Becklund claimed in 1983 that D'Aubuisson had planned the assassination with a group of active-duty military officers, who drew straws for the honor of carrying out the murder.[41] Former ambassador Robert White, who had access to State Department cables and other inside information during his tenure in office, also stated before a congressional committee in February 1984 that "beyond any reasonable doubt" D'Aubuisson had "planned and ordered the assassination" of Archbishop Romero, and White gave details on the planning meeting and the subsequent execution of the trigger man to keep him quiet.[42] Further evidence of D'Aubuisson's involvement in the murder came to light with the confession of Roberto Santivánez, a former high official in Salvadoran intelligence. According to Santivánez, the murder of Romero was planned and carried out by D'Aubuisson with the aid of former national guardsmen of Somoza, but "under the protection of General García and Colonel Carranza."[43] Pyes's and Becklund's informants also indicated that D'Aubuisson was a subordinate and political ally of Carranza, who was the number two man in the Salvadoran military until his ouster under U.S. pressure in December 1980. Carranza then moved over to head the Treasury Police. D'Aubuisson also worked with the National Guard's G-2 central intelligence office while the guard was headed by General Eugenio Vides Casanova. Pyes and Becklund write that "During the time Vides commanded the Guard, active-duty military officers working with the G-2 were linked in State Department cables to the March 1980 assassination of Archbishop Oscar Arnulfo Romero. . . ."[44] Note that Vides Casanova became minister of defense, the post he still holds, under the Duarte government.

In short, there was substantial evidence concerning the identity of Romero's murderers, and there were significant links of the murders to the highest officials of the Salvadoran military establishment. In fact, a judicial investigation in El Salvador headed by Judge Atilio Ramírez quickly pointed a finger at D'Aubuisson and General Medrano, a U.S. protégé in El Salvador. But Ramírez soon fled the country after several threats and an attempt on his life, and active pursuit of the case in El Salvador ended. In exile, Judge Ramírez claimed that the criminal-investigation group of the police didn't arrive at the scene of the crime till four days after it was committed, and that neither the police nor the attorney general provided his court with any evidence. He concluded that there was "undoubtedly" a "kind of conspiracy to cover up the murder" from the very beginning.[45]

Needless to say, Judge Ramírez's testimony was not featured in the U.S. media, nor was the accumulating evidence of D'Aubuisson's involvement given significant play. It was back-page material at best, treated matter-of-factly and never put in a framework of indignation and outrage by the use of emotive language or by asking allies of Romero to comment on the evidence, and it never elicited strident demands for justice. To this day one will find no mention of the fact that the effective rulers of this "fledgling democracy" are military officers who were closely associated with D'Aubuisson and his cabal and may well have been implicated in the assassination.

After D'Aubuisson was caught in a raid on May 8, 1980, with documents showing that he was planning a coup and with evidence of his involvement in the murder of Romero, he was arrested and faced with the threat of trial and imprisonment. An assembly of the entire officer corps of the Salvadoran army—seven hundred strong—was quickly convened, and demanded his release. He was turned loose shortly thereafter, with the concurrence of the minister of defense.[46] The documents found in his possession dropped out of sight. The security forces also raided the legal-aid office of the archbishopric, removing all of their files bearing on the assassination. At the previously mentioned meeting of the Salvadoran officer corps, Colonel Adolfo Majano, the last of the reformers in the "reformist" junta of 1979, was denounced, and he quickly exited from the junta, to be replaced by yet another hard-liner. The army had expressed its solidarity with the hard-line–death-squad right, and the junta was adjusted to meet this new threat to the image of a reformist junta, with Duarte advanced to president, serving as a figurehead for the benefit of Congress and the media, to ensure that arms would flow to the killers.

The U.S. mass media gave little notice to this important display and consolidation of the power of the extreme right, and the semi-official vindication of the murderers of Archbishop Romero. This was telling evidence about the nature of power in El Salvador and the fictional quality of the claim that the government was centrist or reformist. Unbiased media would have featured and explained the meaning of this information. But these facts contradicted the Carter-Reagan mythology, so the media predictably remained silent about these events and continued to perpetuate the myth. On November 29, 1980, following the massacre of the leaders of the opposition in San Salvador, the *Times* suggested that there is "a severe challenge to the credibility" of the government, but there is no hint that the revolt of May 1980 had changed their view of April 28 that this was a "weak centrist government."

The media also adjusted nicely, then and later, to the rehabilitation of the probable murderer of Romero and his reintegration into the official power structure. As D'Aubuisson sought high office and eventually became president of the Salvadoran legislature, the U.S. mass media did not focus on his record as the probable organizer of the murder of Archbishop Romero and as the acknowledged leader of the death squads and a mass murderer. Even the open anti-Semitism of this Fascist was kept under the rug.[47] We would submit that if an anti-

Semite and professional assassin, who was suspected of having organized the murder of Popieluszko in Poland, ran for office and became head of the Polish legislature, there might have been a raised eyebrow or two in the U.S. media.

Throughout this period, media coverage adopted a central myth contrived by the government, and confined its reporting and interpretation to its basic premises: the "moderate government" that we support is plagued by the terrorism of the extremists of the left and right, and is unable to bring it under control. The U.S. government and the media understood very well that the violence was overwhelmingly the responsibility of both the U.S.-backed security forces, which were, and remain, the real power in the country, and the paramilitary network they created to terrorize the population. But this truth was inexpressible. To this day the media maintain the central myth of earlier years, long after having conceded quietly that it was a complete fabrication. Reporting on the prospects for peace in El Salvador, Lindsey Gruson comments that "Today, death squads of the right and left no longer terrorize the population into submission and silence," thanks to the success of President Duarte and his U.S. supporters in moving the country toward democracy—exactly as a propaganda model would predict.[48]

2.4. COVERAGE OF THE SALVADORAN NATIONAL GUARDS' MURDER OF THE FOUR U.S. CHURCHWOMEN AND ITS FOLLOW-UP

On December 2, 1980, four U.S. churchwomen working in El Salvador—Maura Clarke, Jean Donovan, Ita Ford, and Dorothy Kazel—were seized, raped, and murdered by members of the Salvadoran National Guard. This crime was extremely inconvenient to the Carter administration, which was supporting the Salvadoran junta as an alleged "reformist" government and trying to convince the public and Congress that that government was worthy of aid. While temporarily suspending military aid to El Salvador, the Carter administration sought a quick and low-keyed resolution of the case. It resumed aid at the drop of an announced rebel offensive, and—contrary to its promises—before there was any investigatory response by the Salvadoran government. A commission headed by William P. Rogers was quickly sent to El Salvador to inquire into the facts and offer U.S. aid in an investigation. The commission reported that it had "no evidence suggesting that any senior Salvadoran authorities were implicated in the murders themselves," but there is no indication that it ascertained this by any route beyond asking the authorities whether they were involved. The commission acknowledged that justice was not thriving in El Salvador,[49] but it proposed no independent investigation, merely urging the Salvadoran junta to pursue the case vigorously. It noted that the junta promised that the truth "would be pursued wherever it led anywhere in the country at any level."[50] Rogers was later to concede that perhaps he was a bit optimistic in expecting the Salvadoran junta to pursue the case seriously.[51]

With the arrival of the Reagan administration, the already badly compromised concern to find the culprits diminished further, and the dominance of the interest in protecting the client regime in El Salvador became still more overwhelming. It was quickly clear that the whole business could be forgotten—along with the thousands of Salvadorans already killed—except for the demands of public relations. The willingness to support any feasible cover-up was also quite evident. Secretary of State Alexander Haig stated before the House Committee on Foreign Affairs that the evidence "led one to believe" that the four women were killed trying to run a roadblock—a shameless lie that was soon acknowledged as such by the State Department.[52] The Reagan ambassador to the UN, Jeane Kirkpatrick, went Haig one better, suggesting that the four women were political activists for the "Frente"—as with Haig's statement, an outright lie—hinting quite broadly that they were fair game.[53]

Although Kirkpatrick also asserted that the Salvadoran government "unequivocally" was "not responsible" for the murders, evidence was soon available that showed that members of the National Guard had killed the four women. The administration then moved to the position that it was clear that the local guardsmen had "acted alone." This was asserted and reiterated despite the absence of any supportive investigation, and important leads suggesting the contrary were ignored. A propaganda model would expect that this preferred government explanation would be honored by the mass media, and that in contrast with the Popieluszko case, where useful points could be scored by searching for villainy at the top, the mass media would now be less eager to find that which their government was anxious to avoid.

The difference between the murder of the four women and the

thousands of others uninvestigated and unresolved in El Salvador was that the families of these victims were Americans and pressed the case, eventually succeeding in getting Congress to focus on these particular murders as a test case and political symbol. This forced these killings onto the political agenda. A trial and convictions were ultimately required as a condition for certification and aid to the military government of El Salvador. Both the Reagan administration and the Salvadoran military were thus obligated to "see justice done"—in this one instance. It took three-and-a-half years for justice to triumph in this one case, with a lid still kept on top-level involvement. It was a challenge to the mass media to present these murders, and the delayed and aborted outcome, in such a way as to keep indignation low and to downplay the quality of a system that murdered the women and had to be *forced* to find a set of low-level personnel guilty of the crime (which it took them years to do). The media met this challenge with flying colors.

2.4.1. Details of the savagery

The finding of Popieluszko's body was front-page news for the *New York Times*—in fact, the initial *failure* to find his body made the front page—and in all the media publications analyzed here, the details of his seizure, the disposition of his body, and the nature of his wounds were recounted extensively and with barely concealed relish (see table 2-2). These details were also repeated at every opportunity (and, most notably, at the trial). The finding of the bodies of the four women, by contrast, was a back-page item in the *Times*, and in all four of the media institutions in our sample the accounts of the violence done to the four murdered women were very succinct, omitted many details, and were not repeated after the initial disclosures. No attempt was made to reconstruct the scene with its agony and brutal violence, so that the drama conveyed in the accounts of Popieluszko's murder was entirely missing. The murder of the four churchwomen was made remote and impersonal.

The *Time* account, for example, after giving the names of the victims, says, "Two of the women had been raped before being shot in the back of the head." The *New York Times* account, shown in table 2-2, is also quite succinct. The Rogers Commission report pointed out that one of the victims had been shot through the back of the head with a weapon "that left exit wounds that destroyed her face." The Rogers report also noted that those present at the disinterment found "extensive" wounds and that "the bodies were also bruised." Raymond Bonner's account, in *Weakness and Deceit,* noted that

> In the crude grave, stacked on top of each other were the bodies of four women. The first hauled out of the hole was Jean Donovan, twenty-seven years old, a lay missionary from Cleveland. Her face had been blown away by a high calibre bullet that had been fired into the back of her head. Her pants were unzipped; her underwear twisted around her ankles. When area peasants found her, she was nude from the waist down. They had tried to replace the garments before burial. Then came Dorothy Kazel, a forty-year-old Ursuline nun also from Cleveland. At the bottom of the pit were Maryknoll nuns Ita Ford, forty, and Maura Clarke, forty-nine, both from New York. All the women had been executed at close range. The peasants who found the women said that one had her underpants stuffed in her mouth; another's had been tied over her eyes. All had been raped.

We may note the failure of *Time* and the *New York Times* to mention the bruises (which both of these publications mentioned and repeated, as regards Popieluszko); the failure to mention the destruction of Jean Donovan's face; the suppression of the degrading and degraded use of the nuns' underwear;[54] the failure to give the account of the peasants who found the bodies. These and other details given by Bonner and suppressed by *Time* and the *New York Times* (and also *Newsweek* and CBS News) add emotional force and poignancy to the scene. Such details are included for a Popieluszko, but not for four American women murdered by a U.S. client state. The Rogers report also pointed out that the forensic surgeons sent to the scene of the crime by the junta, at the urging of Ambassador Robert White, refused to perform an autopsy on the ground that no surgical masks were available. This touch, which would have cast the junta and its agents in a bad light, was also omitted from U.S. media accounts.

In the Popieluszko case, both the finding of the body *and the trial* were occasions for an aggressive portrayal of the details of the act of murder and the condition of the body. The mass-media reticence on such matters at the time of the finding of the bodies of the four women was exceeded by their restraint at the trial. Lydia Chavez, of the *New York Times,* who attended the trial, notes that there were eight hours of testimony and seven hours of argument that focused on the women's work in El Salvador "and on the details of their kidnappings and deaths," but her article gave no details whatsoever on the medical evidence.

2.4.2. Lack of indignation and insistent demands for justice

In the Popieluszko case, the press conveyed the impression of intolerable outrage that demanded immediate rectification. In the case of the murder of the four American women, while the media asserted and quoted government officials that this was a brutal and terrible act, it was not declared intolerable, and the media did not insist on (or quote people who demanded) justice. The media relied heavily on "senior officials" of the U.S. and Salvadoran governments, who expressed a more resigned view of the situation and were prepared to allow the Salvadoran system of justice to work things out. Correspondingly, the media also moved into a philosophical vein—the women, as *Time* points out, were "victims of the mindless, increasing violence" of El Salvador (Dec. 15, 1980). With Popieluszko, it was live government officials who committed the crime, not blind forces (that are hard to bring to book).

Even the funeral and memorial services for the women in the United States were not allowed to serve as an occasion for outrage and a demand for justice. For the most part, they were ignored and suppressed. The *New York Times* (Dec. 8, 1981) gave a tiny, back-page, UPI account of the memorial service for Sister Dorothy Kazel, featuring the apolitical statement by Bishop Anthony M. Pilla that "The life of a missionary has never been easy or glamorous."

We must consider, too, that as Ambassador Kirkpatrick indicated, the victims may have been asking for it. As *Newsweek* observed (Dec. 15, 1980), "The violence in El Salvador is likely to focus with increasing ferocity on the Roman Catholic Church. Many priests and nuns advocate reform, and some of them are militant leftists. Such sentiments mean trouble, even for more moderate members of the clergy." (Note here also the impersonality of "the violence"—nowhere in the article is there a suggestion that the U.S.-backed government initiated, and was doing the bulk of, the murdering.) In the case of Popieluszko, by contrast, the media never once suggested that he was a regrettable victim of escalating conflict between the state and rebellious forces (or between East and West). That situation was much simpler than the one in El Salvador: Popieluszko was murdered by officials of the state, and this was intolerable. The complexities and resort to philosophical inanities about unallocable "violence" are reserved for deaths in the provinces.

2.4.3. The lack of zeal in the search for villainy at the top

As we saw earlier, in the Popieluszko case the mass media eagerly, aggressively, and on a daily basis sought and pointed to evidence of top-level involvement in the killing. In the case of the killings of the four women, we can observe a completely different approach. Here the media found it extremely difficult to locate Salvadoran government involvement in the murders, even with evidence staring them in the face. Their investigatory zeal was modest, and they were happy to follow the leads of ("Trust me") Duarte and U.S. officials as the case unfolded. They played dumb. The Salvadoran army and security forces had been killing *Salvadorans*, in the same way they had killed the four women, for months. What is more, the churches with which the women were connected had been recently threatened by the army. More direct evidence was that local peasants had been forced to bury the bodies by the local military. But the media did not use this information to help them find the locus of the murders.

The initial line of the U.S. and Salvadoran governments was that there was no proof of military involvement, although the military's concealment of the bodies was not proper. A statement issued by the junta on December 8 claimed that the murderers were "terrorists of the extreme right,"[55] and Duarte reiterated this view to the press, which passed it along. In keeping with the government line, twenty days after the murders, the *New York Times* still spoke only of "unidentified assailants," although the leads to the National Guard were already plentiful, and it repeated the Rogers report finding that the security forces may have tried to "conceal the deaths" after the bodies had been found.[56]

Gradually, so much evidence seeped out to show that the women had been murdered by members of the National Guard that the involvement of government forces could no longer be evaded. A two-part process of "damage limitation" ensued, expounded by Salvadoran and U.S. officials and faithfully reflected in the media. One was a distinction between the government and the National Guard. In the Popieluszko case, the reader was never allowed to forget that the murdering police were part of the Polish government. In the case of the four American women, it was barely evident in the mass media that the killers had any connection with the Salvadoran government. This was in keeping with the basic myth, also consistently followed by the media, that the Salvadoran government was reformist and centrist, trying to control killings by extremists of the right and left.[57] This fabrication allowed a two-track system of massive killing by the army and its affiliates and simultaneous claims of regret by the reformers unable to control the extremists. This was reminiscent of the heyday of mass murder in Argentina, when the *New York Times* regularly portrayed the junta and people like the recently convicted General Videla as moderates "unable to control the right-wing extremists" who were killing people.[58]

The most important goal of the immediate damage-containment process was to stifle any serious investigation of the responsibility of the officials of the Salvadoran government. The Salvadoran strategy was foot-dragging from beginning to end, as the idea of convicting soldiers for killing anybody was contrary to Salvadoran practice, and, moreover, there is little doubt that the responsibility for the crime went high. The U.S. official strategy, once it was clear that the National Guard was responsible for the killing, was to get the low-level killers tried and convicted—necessary to vindicate the system of justice in El Salvador, at least to the extent of keeping the dollars flowing from Congress—while protecting the "reformers" at the top. On September 30, 1981, Ambassador Deane Hinton stated with assurance that the local national guardsmen "were acting on their own," although internal State Department documents of the time recognized that the Salvadoran investigation had been a joke, and other evidence existed suggesting top-level involvement.[59] Nonetheless, the official position was clear. To go along with the official line, the mass media had to stop investigating high-level involvement and even to suppress evidence emerging from other sources. And so they proceeded to do this.

After a two-month investigation of the murders, the reporter John Dinges filed a story through Pacific News Service that showed the murders to have been preplanned in some detail.[60] First, there were intercepted radio communications indicating military discussions of the arrival of the women at the airport, and other evidence of close surveillance of their flight plans, all suggesting a coordinated and extensive military operation. Second, a former deputy minister of planning described to Dinges a half-hour presentation by Salvadoran Defense Minister Guillermo García in the national palace, denouncing the nuns and priests in the very area of the murders and stating that something must be done, only two weeks prior to the murders.

In a remarkable feat of self-censorship, most of the mass media completely ignored the Dinges findings. Dinges's report appeared in the *Washington Post*, the *Los Angeles Times*, and some fifteen other papers, but not a word of it found its way into the *New York Times*, *Time*, *Newsweek*, or CBS News, and *its leads were not pursued* by any media. Instead, the media kept repeating the assurances of Duarte and U.S. officials that they were satisfied that the killings did not go beyond the local national guardsmen, and that the matter would be pursued diligently through proper legal channels.

In March 1984, Colonel Roberto Santivánez, a high official in Salvadoran intelligence, agreed to "talk" about the death-squad network in El Salvador, and his claims found their way onto CBS News and the front page of the *New York Times*.[61] Santivánez gave highly credible details about the murder of the four women, indicating that the act had been committed on the specific order of Colonel Oscar Edgardo Casanova, who was in charge of the zone in which the killings took place. Colonel Casanova was transferred to another assignment two weeks after the murder as part of the official cover-up. His first cousin Eugenio Vides Casanova, the minister of defense chosen by Duarte and head of the National Guard in December 1980, knew about the murder order by his cousin, as did Duarte. Although this crushing evidence implicated a high officer in the murder and the current minister of defense and Duarte in the cover-up, there was no follow-up to this story, no connection back to the Dinges story of high-level discussions of the need to do something about the religious workers—no editorials, no indignation, and no pressure for action.

In sum, the leads provided by Dinges, and the testimony of Santivánez, strongly suggest that the killing of the women was based on a high-level decision. The evidence is even clearer that middle-level officials of the government ordered the killing, and that the highest-level officials engaged in a continuing and systematic cover-up. In the Polish case, the evidence of top-level involvement was never forthcoming, but the issue was pursued by the U.S. mass media relentlessly. In the case of the four churchwomen, where the evidence of top-level involvement was abundant, the U.S. mass media failed to press the matter, or even to engage in the pursuit of obvious investigative leads.

We cannot describe here the full details of the failure of the Salvadoran process of justice, which never moved forward except under U.S. pressure and threats.[62] The mass media did at one point berate the Salvadoran government for "stonewalling" the investigation,[63] but the media entirely failed to capture the depth and scope of the stonewalling process, or to remark on its significance in this "fledgling democracy," and they generally transmitted Salvadoran and U.S. government claims about the state of the process without sarcasm or expressions of outrage. If they *had* given full details, the Salvadoran government would have been thoroughly discredited. Thus, the extensive evidence concerning official Salvadoran refusals to take action or to interrogate relevant witnesses, and concerning threats to witnesses, lawyers, and judges—which would have been aired with delight if applicable to a Polish investigation—were ignored.

A few illustrations of the Salvadoran proceedings will have to suffice here. Two years after the crime, for example,

> . . . the prosecutors expressed ignorance of the testimony [in the court record] of former guardsman César Valle Espinoza, dated August 9, 1982, which quotes Subsergeant Colindres Alemán as stating on December 2, 1980, that there were "superior orders" to apprehend the women. They were also ignorant of the statement of former National Guard Sergeant Dagoberto Martínez, taken by the FBI in Los Angeles, California, which establishes the existence of a cover-up of the crime as early as December 1980.[64]

A second illustration of the process: two of three judges assigned to the case resigned for fear of their lives. As we noted, Judge Ramírez, who was investigating the Romero murder, fled for the same reason. This line of evidence has cumulative weight, but it was never treated as a whole by the press (and was barely mentioned as individual items of back-page news). A third illustration: according to former ambassador Robert White, two national guardsmen who might have been able to link higher-ranking officers to the murders of the women were killed by military death squads, then listed as missing in action.[65] A final illustration: when the Salvadoran triggermen were finally assigned attorneys, one of the three, Salvador Antonio Ibarra, was prepared to defend the men seriously. His colleagues pressed Ibarra to abide by the statement that "the possibility of a cover-up had been thoroughly investigated" and rejected. He refused to go along with this request, with the consequence that on October 30, 1983, Ibarra was seized by the National Guard and tortured at its headquarters.[66] Released only under U.S. pressure, Ibarra fled the country, leaving the way clear for a lawyer team that would accept the notion that there had been a "thorough investigation" of top-level involvement. This last incident alone made it into the mass media in isolated and fleeting treatment; the others, and the package, were not featured in the free press.

The U.S. government also engaged in a systematic cover-up—of both the Salvadoran cover-up and the facts of the case. The U.S. mass media, while briefly noting the Salvadoran stonewalling, failed to call attention to the equally important lies and suppressions of their own government. As we have pointed out, both the Carter and Reagan administrations put protection of its client above the quest for justice for four U.S. citizens murdered by agents of that government. The U.S. government's stonewalling to protect its client took many forms. One was an active collaboration in the Salvadoran cover-up. Former National Guard sergeant Dagoberto Martínez was allowed to emigrate to the United States in December 1980, and although a subsequent interview by the FBI indicated that Martínez admitted knowledge of the perpetrators of the crime and a failure to report that information—in violation of Salvadoran law—no action was taken against him. U.S. officials also reiterated that there was no reason to believe that higher-level officials knew about the crime or participated in it, when they had clear knowledge of a cover-up and a refusal to investigate.[67] The State Department also regularly lied about the thoroughness of the investigation. Ambassador Hinton stated in public that national guardsman Pérez Nieto "was thoroughly interrogated and repeatedly denied that anyone superior to him had ordered him to watch the women." A State Department cable, however, describes Nieto's testimony as "incomplete, evasive, and uncooperative."[68]

A second form of official U.S. participation in the cover-up was a refusal to make public information on the Salvadoran investigation and evidence uncovered by the United States itself. The Rogers report was released belatedly, in a version that edited out the original report's statement about the sad state of the Salvadoran system of justice. In response to a growing chorus of criticism of the delays, Judge Harold R. Tyler was appointed by the U.S. government to carry out a further investigation. His report was kept under wraps for a long time, again apparently because it had some serious criticism of the Salvadoran judicial process that would have interfered with Reagan administration plans to claim progress every time such certification was required.[69] The families of the victims and their attorneys regularly found the U.S. government unwilling to release information on the case. The argument given was that the information was sensitive, and that releasing it would interfere with the legal process in El Salvador. As the Salvadoran process was a sick joke, moving only in response to U.S. threats, the official rationale was transparently fraudulent. Furthermore, Duarte was regularly making statements that the arrested guardsmen were surely guilty, and that nobody higher than them was involved, which blatantly prejudged the case. The only plausible rationale for the U.S. cover-up is that the administration wanted to minimize adverse publicity concerning the performance of its murderous client. Information on what was really going on, or its own internal analyses of the case or appraisals of the Salvadoran legal process, would make the client look bad. The administration hoped that the case would "go away," but until that happened, it wanted the publicity flow to be under its control.

Part of the reason the administration wanted control was to allow it to claim reasonable progress in the pursuit of the case whenever the military government was due for more money. As with other right-wing satellites, "improvement" is always found at money-crunch time. In its July 1982 certification report, the State Department found that "substantial progress" had been made in the case and predicted a trial in the fall of 1982. In early 1983, the certification report noted "significant developments" in the case. This manipulation of evidence to protect the flow of arms and money to the regime would not be easy with full disclosure—or with a critical and honest press.

This cover-up of the Salvadoran judicial process, even though four murdered American women were involved, did not arouse the press to indignation or satire, nor did it cause them to provide more than minimal coverage of the inquiry.

2.4.4. The trial—five national guardsmen for $19.4 million

The trial of the five immediate killers of the four women should have been presented in a Kafkaesque framework, but the U.S. media played it very straight. The trial took place three-and-a-half years after the acts of murder, despite the fact that the triggermen were immediately identified and despite enormous U.S. pressure. Two of three judges assigned to the case had resigned out of fear for their lives, and the only independent defense attorney had fled the country after a session of torture at National Guard headquarters. The defense at the trial made no effort to defend the men on the grounds of "orders from above," although this is a standard defense in such cases, and significant evidence was available for use in this instance. The mass media failed to note the point, although it suggests fear, a deal, or both, and although, as we saw in the Popieluszko case, the media are sometimes immensely alert to cover-ups. In March 1984, former intelligence officer Santivánez stated that the guardsmen knew that "If they don't name Casanova, they will get out of jail as soon as it is feasible."[70] This testimony was not referred to in the trial context—the media played dumb.

Like the Salvadoran elections of 1982 and 1984, this trial was thoroughly American in staging and motivation. As Ana Carrigan put it:

> Security in the courtroom was in the hands of a special Judicial Protection Unit, formed and trained in Glencoe, Alabama; the jurors were driven to the courtroom in the morning and returned to their homes after the verdict in bullet-proof American embassy vehicles; meals and camp beds were provided by the embassy so that if necessary the jurors and the staff of the court could sleep overnight within the protection of the guarded courthouse; and when the electricity failed, just as the prosecution began to make its presentation, light was restored by means of hurricane lamps delivered by embassy staff.[71]

The stakes were U.S. dollars. Congress had frozen $19.4 million pending the favorable outcome of the case. Within twenty-four hours of the decision, the State Department, announcing that justice had been done, released the money to the charge of Minister of Defense Vides Casanova, who had been head of the National Guard on December 4, 1980, when the murders took place, whose first cousin, according to Colonel Santivánez, had given the direct order to kill, and who had so effectively protected his cousin and stalled the prosecution of underlings for three-and-a-half years.

In conformity with the predictions of a propaganda model, the mass media failed entirely to capture the quality of this scene—the American omnipresence, the courtroom security, the failure of the defense to press the responsibility of the higher authorities, the role of Vides Casanova, the literal money transaction for justice *in this single case,* which dragged on for three-and-a-half years. *Newsweek* found the result a "remarkable achievement," in an article entitled "A Defeat for a Death Squad" (June 4, 1984), despite the fact that it was the National Guard that killed the women. The article does stress the difficulties in bringing and winning the case, and the possibility of a cover-up of higher-level personnel, but it does not use this information to point up the nature of the system being supported by the United States. It also closes out the discussion with reference to the Tyler report discounting high-level involvement, without quoting the report's acknowledgment of "some evidence supporting the involvement of higher-ups" or mentioning the report's admission of the limits of its information. No reference is made to Santivánez or the Dinges report: *Newsweek* sticks to an official source, and misreads it.

2.5. TWENTY-THREE RELIGIOUS VICTIMS IN GUATEMALA, 1980–85

The modern history of Guatemala was decisively shaped by the U.S.-organized invasion and overthrow of the democratically elected regime of Jacobo Arbenz in June 1954. Since that time, while Guatemala has remained securely within the U.S. sphere of influence, badly needed economic and social reforms were put off the agenda indefinitely, political democracy was stifled, and state terror was institutionalized and reached catastrophic levels in the late 1970s and early 1980s. Given the client status of Guatemala and the fact that the antidemocratic counter-revolution served important elite interests, a propaganda model suggests that its victims will be "unworthy," which should be reflected in both the quantity and quality of media attention. Furthermore, whereas victimization in Soviet client states like Poland and Czechoslovakia is regularly traced back to the Soviet occupations, a propaganda model would predict that the U.S. media will not explain the contemporary Guatemalan environment of state terror as a natural product of the U.S. intervention in 1954 (and thereafter). On the contrary, we would expect the United States to be portrayed as a benevolent and concerned by-stander, trying its very best to curb abuses of right and left extremists.

Before looking at the media's handling of Guatemala, however, let us step back for a brief review of the crucial period 1945–54 and its sequel to set the stage for an examination of the media's role in the 1980s. Arbenz and his predecessor, Juan Arévalo, led the first democratic system in Guatemalan history. During the decade of their rule, newspapers, social groups, unions, peasants, and political parties could organize without fear of repression or murder.[72] But this fragile democracy rested on a base of concentrated land ownership and foreign control of land and strategic facilities that was a constant threat to its independence and political freedom, as well as a human disaster. The struggle for unionization and land reform during the democratic decade was motivated in part by a desire to build a mass constituency that would provide an institutional base for democracy.[73] Each progressive move by both Arévalo and Arbenz was greeted with fierce hostility by the local oligarchy, the multinational corporate community, and the U.S. government.[74] "Communism" was found to be in control, or a threat, from the time trade unions were allowed to organize in 1947, and Arbenz's modest and effective land reform was the last straw.[75] With U.S. initiative, organization, funding, and direct psychological warfare and terror operations, a tiny mercenary army ousted Arbenz and installed an "anti-Communist" regime.

From 1954 to the present day, neither reform nor democracy, let alone radical change, has been possible in Guatemala. The main reason for this is that the forces into whose hands the United States delivered that country in 1954 "bitterly opposed any change that might affect, however slightly, their entrenched position,"[76] and they had learned from the 1945–54 lesson that democracy moves inexorably toward reform and threats to privilege in a system of extreme inequality. The very brief interludes of tentative openness after 1954 witnessed the quick emergence of protective organizations of urban workers and the peasantry, strikes, and reformist and radical parties and organizations. As Piero Gleijeses puts it, "in the last months of the Arana period [1970–74], the repression had acquired a more selective character, and on repeated occasions Laugerud [Arana's successor, 1974–78] refrained from 'settling' strikes by force."[77] But the feebleness of the reforms and the awakened hopes and pressures forced a further choice; and "given the nature of the regime," the wave of terror that followed "was the only logical choice" for the Guatemalan ruling class.[78]

Another reason for the failures of both reform and democracy has been ongoing U.S. influence. The U.S. establishment found the pluralism and democracy of the years 1945–54 intolerable, and it eventually ended that experiment.[79] In the succeeding thirty-two years of U.S. guidance, not only has Guatemala gradually become a terrorist state rarely matched in the scale of systematic murder of civilians, but its terrorist proclivities have increased markedly at strategic moments of escalated U.S. intervention. The first point was the invasion and counterrevolution of 1954, which reintroduced political murder and large-scale repression to Guatemala following the decade of democracy. The second followed the emergence of a small guerrilla movement in the early 1960s, when the United States began serious counterinsurgency (CI) training of the Guatemalan army. In 1966, a further small guerrilla movement brought the Green Berets and a major CI war in which 10,000 people were killed in pursuit of three or four hundred guerrillas. It was at this point that the "death squads" and "disappearances" made their appearance in Guatemala. The United States brought in police training in the 1970s, which was followed by the further institutionalization of violence. The "solution" to social problems in Guatemala, specifically attributable to the 1954 intervention and the form of U.S. assistance since that time, has been permanent state terror. With Guatemala, the United States invented the "counterinsurgency state."

The special role of the army in the counterinsurgency state gradually elevated its status and power, and eventually gave it the institutional capacity to rule Guatemala. As in many U.S. client states, the military used its power to carve out economic opportunities and to steal, directly or indirectly.[80] The terrorism, thievery, and autonomy of the Guatemalan military reached a temporary peak—later surpassed by Ríos Montt—during the reign of Lucas García (1978–82). This overlapped the brief interlude of the Carter human-rights policy, during which there was open criticism of the Guatemalan government and a brief and partial cutoff of arms supply from the United States under congressional pressure.[81] Even during the Carter years, however, relations with Guatemala were not hostile—it was as if a child in the family were naughty and briefly put in the corner. Part of the reason for the willingness of the Carter government to provide no new arms supplies was that the bad boy was in no danger. In El Salvador in 1980, by contrast, where the Carter administration saw the possibility of a left-wing victory, support was quickly forthcoming to a right-wing terror regime.

During the Reagan years, the number of civilians murdered in Guatemala ran into the tens of thousands, and disappearances and mutilated bodies were a daily occurrence.[82] Studies by Amnesty International (AI), Americas Watch (AW), and other human-rights monitors have documented a military machine run amok, with the indiscriminate killing of peasants (including vast numbers of women and children), the forcible relocation of hundreds of thousands of farmers and villagers into virtual concentration camps, and the enlistment of many hundreds of thousands in compulsory civil patrols.[83] Reagan, however, visiting Guatemala in December 1982, commented that head of state Ríos Montt was "totally committed to democracy" and was receiving a "bum rap" on human-rights abuses. Two months earlier, AI released its report describing sixty different Indian villages in which massacres of civilians took place in a three-month period, with the total killed exceeding 2,500.[84]

The Reagan policy toward Guatemala was, as with South Africa, "constructive engagement."[85] From the beginning, the administration strove to embrace and provide arms to the military governments. Ongoing mass murder was merely an inconvenience. One method by which the administration sought to rehabilitate our relations with the

Guatemala regimes was by continual lying about their human-rights record (with Reagan himself setting the standard). Stephen Bosworth, of the State Department, assured a House committee in July 1981 that the Lucas García government was successfully attacking the guerrillas "while taking care to protect innocent bystanders."[86] The State Department's Country Report on Human Rights for 1981 also found it impossible to determine who was doing all the killing in Guatemala, and disappearances were attributed to the "right" and the "left," but not to the government. Amnesty International, by contrast, in February 1981, gave detailed evidence that the thousands of murders were almost entirely governmental in origin, including those of the death squads, whose victims were targeted in an annex of Guatemala's national palace under the direct supervision of President Lucas García.[87]

With the overthrow of Lucas García, suddenly, as if by magic, the Reagan administration line altered, and Stephen Bosworth "could not emphasize strongly enough the favorable contrast between the current human rights situation in Guatemala and the situation last December. . . ." Melvyn Levitsky, deputy assistant secretary of state for human rights, told another congressional committee that "the United States cannot easily sustain a relationship with a government which engages in violence against its own people," as with the Lucas García regime.[88]

When Lucas García was in power, Bosworth found it a caring regime that protected the innocent, and the State Department couldn't determine that the government was doing any killing. With Lucas García ousted, the State Department discovered that he was an indiscriminate murderer and assumed a high moral tone about his behavior. That is, the State Department implicitly conceded that it was lying earlier and counted on the press not to point this out. Of course, the reason for the switch was to help make a favorable case for Lucas García's successor, Ríos Montt. Under Ríos Montt there was "a dramatic decline" in human-rights abuses, according to State Department spokesman John Hughes in January 1983. Ríos Montt is the one whom Reagan found to be getting a bum rap. But as we noted, Amnesty International found Ríos Montt to be another top-rank murderer, who appears to have exceeded his predecessor in civilian massacres.

When Ríos Montt was ousted in his turn, once again the State Department line shifted. It was admitted that things had been terrible under Ríos Montt in 1982, but *now* there was a dramatic improvement, and the government was showing "increased sensitivity to human rights questions."[89] It is evident that we have here a consistent pattern that may be formulated into a quasi-law: in the case of a terrorist state with which the administration wants "constructive engagement," things are always OK and improving; but when that regime is ousted, its record deteriorates ex post facto and looks most unfavorable compared with the humanistic and sensitive one now in power! This droll pattern of identical apologetics for each successor terrorist, and ex post denigration of the one ousted, is an Orwellian process that the Western press associates with totalitarian states, but it happens here. And it can only occur if the mass media are cooperative. They must be willing to downplay or ignore the large-scale murders going on in Guatemala in the first place. In that context, the serial apologetics, the lies defending each murderer, and the mind-boggling hypocrisy will hardly be newsworthy.

Given the U.S. role in originating and sustaining the Guatemalan counterinsurgency state, and the fact that that state is dedicated to blocking the growth of popular organizations (i.e., "anti-Communist" in Orwellian rhetoric) and has a strong U.S. business presence, a propaganda model would anticipate a lack of media interest in its "unworthy" victims and an evasion of the U.S. role in its evolution and practices. We would expect reports on Guatemala put out by Amnesty International and other human-rights groups to be downplayed or ignored, despite their spectacular data and horrifying stories. This is a strong test of the model, as the number of civilians murdered between 1978 and 1985 may have approached 100,000, with a style of killing reminiscent of Pol Pot. As AI pointed out in 1981:

> The bodies of the victims have been found piled up in ravines, dumped at roadsides or buried in mass graves. Thousands bore the scars of torture, and death had come to most by strangling with a garrotte, by being suffocated in rubber hoods or by being shot in the head.[90]

The expectations of a propaganda model are fully realized in this case. Referring to our table 2-1 comparison of media treatment of twenty-three religious victims in Guatemala with the coverage accorded Popieluszko, only four of the twenty-three were ever mentioned by name in our media sample, and the twenty-three taken together had approximately one-twentieth of the space in the *New York Times* that the newspaper of record gave to Popieluszko. In the case of the murder in Guatemala of the American priest Rev. Stanley Rother, the *New York Times* reported on August 5, 1981, in a tiny back-page article, that three men had been arrested for questioning in the shooting. What was the outcome of the arrests? Were the arrested persons tried? Readers of the *Times* will never know, and the Guatemalan government did not have to suffer the embarrassment and pressure of the press raising questions in this or any of the remaining twenty-two Guatemalan cases.

Along with the minuscule attention to the murder of Guatemalan priests, the details of the killings were brief, and no sense of outrage was generated or sustained.[91] The few lengthier articles never discuss the role of the 1954 coup and the long training and supply relationship of the United States to the Guatemalan police and army;[92] rather, they almost invariably put the killings in the format of a civil war with unexplained atrocities of extremists of the right and left (see "Archbishop Oscar Romero," p. 48). An AP dispatch in the *New York Times* of May 16, 1981, is entitled "Four Guatemalans Slain in Leftist-Rightist Rivalry." The article, which reports on the murder of one of our twenty-three priests, the Reverend Carlos Gálvez Galindo, says: "The attacks appeared to be related to the long struggle for power between leftists and rightists." A UPI dispatch in the *Times* of July 29, 1981, reporting on the murder of Rev. Stanley Rother, also relates the attack to "right-wing extremists"—not the Guatemalan government.

Time has Rother and his Guatemalan villagers "caught in the middle of an undeclared civil war. . . ."[93] *Time* never explains the roots of the civil war, nor the crucial role of the United States in refusing to allow peaceful social change and installing the institutions of permanent counterrevolution. *Time* does, in most unusual fashion, point out that the government was responsible for the "overwhelming majority" of the killings, and even more exceptionally, it cites Amnesty International's evidence that the paramilitary death squads are an arm of the government. But the article fails to give illustrations of the scope and quality of the murders, and retreats, as noted, to the civil-war rationale. Even more compromising is its framing of the U.S. policy debate. According to *Time*, "Yet Guatemala confronts the Reagan administration with one of its toughest foreign policy challenges: on one hand, the country is viewed as a victim of Cuban-sponsored insurgency, needing U.S. support; on the other, the government obviously violates human rights." The dichotomy offered by *Time* is a bit uneven: the Cuban sponsorship is a Cold War ploy for which no evidence has ever been given, but it provides a convenient propaganda framework that is regularly deployed by the State Department to divert attention from its support of mass murderers. *Time* thus elevates it to equality with a real and extremely serious charge—and without an honest citation even to a political hack. The "on the other hand" is, despite the "obviously," a gross understatement. The Reagan administration chose to support and provide regular apologetics for a genocidal government that was using a policy of massacre to destroy a purely indigenous revolt. The "challenge" for the

Reagan administration—quite different from that portrayed by *Time*—was how to *sell* the support of mass murder. *Time* did its little bit by unqualified transmission of the claim of a Cuban-based insurgency, which posed a serious dilemma for policy-making.

The holocaust years 1978–85 yielded a steady stream of documents by human-rights groups that provided dramatic evidence of a state terrorism in Guatemala approaching genocidal levels. Many of these documents had a huge potential for educating and arousing the public, but as a propaganda model would anticipate, they were treated in our media sample in a manner that minimized their informational value and capacity to create and mobilize public indignation. Using a selection of ten important reports on Guatemala by Amnesty International and Americas Watch issued in the years 1981–87, we could only find *mention* of four of them in our media sample.[94] None of these four made it to the first page, and none provided the basis for an editorial or the building up of a press campaign of sustained coverage and indignation. The spectacular AI report of 1981 on *"Disappearances": A Workbook*, describing a frightening development of state terrorism in the Nazi mold, was entirely ignored in our media sample, as was AI's March 1985 report on *"Disappearances" . . . under the Government of General Oscar Humberto Mejía Víctores*, which if publicized would have interfered with the media's portrayal of the Guatemalan elections of 1984–85 as exercises in legitimation (as described in the next chapter). AW's 1985 report on the Mutual Support Group was ignored, as was the 1987 study of human rights in Guatemala during Cerezo's first year. We return to the Mutual Support Group in the next section. We will see in the next chapter, too, that the media reported Cerezo's election in a framework of hopefulness and optimism, despite prior electoral experience in Guatemala and Cerezo's own expressed doubts about his ability to rule; the ignoring of AW's retrospective describing the actual results of Cerezo's presidency reflects the media's general failure to follow up on the effects of client state elections (as we show in chapter 3 with regard to El Salvador).

We described earlier the important Americas Watch study *Guatemala Revised: How the Reagan Administration Finds "Improvements" in Human Rights in Guatemala*, whose most striking and important theme was the ex post facto admission by the State Department that its apologetics for the *previous* general had been false. This illuminating document was ignored in our media sample, except for the *New York Times*, which gave it a three-inch article on page 7 under the benign title "Rights Group Faults U.S. on Guatemala Situation" (Sept. 24, 1985). The article describes the report as saying that the administration has refused to acknowledge major human-rights abuses in Guatemala, but it fails to mention the stress on the ex post facto tacit admission of lying. Mentioning this would, of course, suggest that the *Times*'s primary source for its "news" is thoroughly untrustworthy. The last paragraph of the article, which absorbs a quarter of the three inches devoted to this document, gives a State Department response to the AW report, which is that AW is "less a human rights organization than it is a political one." The brazen hypocrisy of this retort would have been clear and dramatic if the article had given the gist of AW's evidence that the administration was not merely an apologist for state terrorism in Guatemala, but was also demonstrably dishonest.

In its concern to protect the Guatemalan generals in their terroristic assault on the population, the Reagan administration took umbrage at organizations like Amnesty International and Americas Watch and mounted a systematic campaign in 1981 and 1982 to discredit them as left-wing and politically biased. In a letter dated September 15, 1982, directed to AI and the Washington Office on Latin America, Assistant Secretary of State Thomas Enders assailed the reporting of these organizations as one-sided and apologetic for the "ferocious" and "terrorist attacks"—of the guerrillas. Enders writes that

> No one would deny the possibility [*sic*] of units of the military, in contravention of stated policy, having been involved in violations of human rights. What is important is that since March 23 the Government of Guatemala has committed itself to a new course and has made significant progress.[95]

This amazing piece of apologetics for an army that was in the midst of slaughtering thousands of civilians was distributed within Guatemala as an official U.S. document, and its full text appeared in the Guatemalan press. AW states:

> We find this use of the letter unconscionable in light of the risks run by human rights investigators in a political climate like Guatemala's. It also appears to us to be further evidence that the State Department, like the Guatemalan government, admits no neutrals in the Guatemalan conflict; the bringer of bad news becomes, through this reasoning, part of the enemy, to be publicly discredited if possible.

Americas Watch also indicated that the State Department's substantive criticisms of AW and AI were not merely incompetent but, more important, were based largely on the assumed truthfulness of Guatemalan army claims (a form of gullibility displayed clearly in the statement by Enders quoted above).

As we discussed in chapter 1, the government is a primary flak producer as well as information source. This Guatemala episode is an important illustration of the government's efforts to silence competing sources of information. It is interesting that the *New York Times* never mentioned or criticized this sinister campaign, even though it was carried out in the context of a policy protecting mass murderers. We will see in the next chapter that *Time* magazine cooperated with the campaign, citing Americas Watch only once on Guatemala, but with the qualifying explanation that it is "a controversial group that is often accused of being too sympathetic to the left" (the State Department, on which *Time* relies very heavily, is never subject to any adjective suggesting any bias). The *Washington Post* (Dec. 4, 1982) had one back-page article by Terri Shaw, on the Enders letter, which features the State Department charges in the title—"Embassy Sees 'Disinformation' on Guatemala: U.S. Report Says Rights Groups are Used"—and in the text. The author allows the embassy claim that "the report never was meant to be made public" to stand unchallenged, and never refers to the threat posed to human-rights monitors by the release of such State Department charges. The human-rights groups are allowed to suggest a State Department intent to discredit, but the word "disinformation" is never applied to State Department allegations, and no serious examination of the content of those charges is provided. This superficial piece exhausts the sample media's coverage of this State Department campaign. The AW report *Human Rights in Guatemala: No Neutrals Allowed,* which discusses this campaign and the Enders letter, was never mentioned.

2.6. THE MUTUAL SUPPORT GROUP MURDERS IN GUATEMALA

Human-rights monitoring and protective agencies have had a very difficult time organizing and surviving in the "death-squad democracies" of El Salvador and Guatemala. Between October 1980 and March 1983, five officials of the Human Rights Commission of El Salvador were seized and murdered by the security forces. In accord with a propaganda model, these murders should have been of little interest to the U.S. mass media, and this expectation is borne out by evidence. As an illustrative comparison, the *New York Times* had a grand total of four back-page articles on these five murders,[96] whereas, during the same period, the *Times* had thirty-five articles on the Soviet human-rights activist Natan Sharansky, not all of them on the back pages. The proportionality of attention fits well our general propaganda-model analysis of the media's treatment of worthy and unworthy victims.

Guatemala has been even more inhospitable to human-rights organizations than El Salvador. Guatemalan Archbishop Monsignor Próspero Penados del Barrio asserted in 1984 that "It is impossible for a human rights office to exist in Guatemala at the present time."[97] "Disappearances" as an institutional form began in Guatemala in the mid-1960s and eventually reached levels unique in the Western Hemisphere, with the total estimated to be some 40,000.[98] Protest groups that have formed to seek information and legal redress have been consistently driven out of business by state-organized murder. The Association of University Students (AEU) sought information on the disappeared through the courts in the course of a brief opening in 1966, but after one sensational exposé of the police murder of twenty-eight leftists, the system closed down again. As McClintock points out, "In the next few years many AEU leaders and member law students were hunted down and killed."[99] In the 1970s, a Committee of the Relatives of the Disappeared was organized by the AEU, with headquarters in San Carlos National University. As Americas Watch points out, "It disbanded after plainsclothesmen walked into the University's legal aid center on March 10, 1974, and shot and killed its principal organizer, lawyer Edmundo Guerra Theilheimer, the center's director."[100] Another human-rights group, the National Commission for Human Rights, was created in the late 1970s by psychologist and journalist Irma Flaquer. Her son was murdered, and she herself "disappeared" on October 16, 1980.

According to the British Parliamentary Human Rights Group, in 1984 alone there were an average of one hundred political murders and over forty disappearances per month in Guatemala.[101] These figures are almost surely an underestimate, as only the disappearances that took place in and around Guatemala City received any publicity. The greater number of murders and disappearances occur among rural and Indian families who do not have the resources to complain and are more exposed to retaliation.

In this context of murder, fear, and the prior failure of all human-rights organizations, the Mutual Support Group, or GAM, was formed in June 1984. It was a product of the desperation felt by people seeking information on the whereabouts of disappeared relatives and willing to take serious risks to that end. Many of them had suffered enormous pain in frustrating searches and inquiries that never bore fruit. There is no legal redress in Guatemala, and nothing useful can be obtained by appeals to the police or courts of law. Mr. Hicho, looking for his disappeared daughter, saw some one hundred bodies in the months he spent at the morgue, and "seventy to seventy-five percent of them had been tortured."[102] Others took different painful routes in their search. In early 1985, one woman was told by an army officer that her husband was still alive, and that he would see to his return if she slept with him. She did so, and her husband turned up dead shortly thereafter.[103]

The intention of the organizers of GAM was to seek strength by collective action, and to use it to gather data and seek redress by petition and publicity. Their hope for survival and success rested, in part, on the fact that the chief of state, Mejía Víctores, was being built up by the Reagan administration as another "reformer," and the Reagan–Mejía Víctores team was trying to establish the appropriate "image" to induce Congress to loosen the purse strings. GAM also had support within Guatemala from Archbishop Penados del Barrio and other church groups and lay persons, although few felt able to speak up in the system of unconstrained state terror. Internationally, GAM received significant political support from progressive and humanitarian political parties and human-rights groups.

Thirty members of the newly organized GAM held a press conference in Guatemala City in June 1984, denouncing the disappearances and calling on the government "to intervene immediately in order to find our loved ones." In the latter part of June, and again in early August, masses were held in the Metropolitan Cathedral to express concern over the fate of the disappeared, with the initial services held by the university rector, Meyer Maldonado, and Archbishop Penados. A thousand people attended the August mass. On August 1, the group first met with General Mejía Víctores, at which time he promised to investigate the disappearances. In ads placed in the major newspapers on August 8 and 9, GAM put his promises on the public record. Subsequently the group began to call attention to the government's failure to follow through on the August 1 promises, and they moved gradually to other actions. In October 1984 they sponsored a march and mass for the disappeared at the cathedral—the first mass demonstration in Guatemala since May 1, 1980 (at which time protestors were seized on the streets and an estimated one hundred were assassinated, or disappeared).

The organization continued to grow, from the initial handful to 225 families in November 1984 and then to 1,300 in the spring of 1986. Most of the members were women, a large majority peasant women from the countryside. They were persistent. After initial petitions, requests, meetings, and marches, they began to make explicit accusations and "publicly charge elements of the national security forces as directly responsible for the capture and subsequent disappearance of our family members."[104] They asked for an investigation, an accounting, and justice. They appealed to the constituent assembly and began regular protests in downtown Guatemala City, banging pots and pans and, on occasion, peacefully occupying buildings.

Nothing, of course, was done in response to the GAM demands. The assembly had no powers anyway, but was too fearful even to pass a resolution of support. The military rulers toyed with GAM. In public, with the press on hand, Mejía Víctores would say, "I don't want to shirk responsibilities and something has to be done." But when the press was not there, he said, "It seems as though you are accusing me—and we don't have them [the disappeared]." "You have them," we said. "We don't have them," he replied.[105] The military rulers were getting annoyed, and phone threats, letters of warning, and open surveillance intensified. Two days after the exchange between Mejía Víctores and GAM, the tortured bodies of two disappeared associated with GAM members showed up, one placed in front of his house with his eyes gouged out and his face barely recognizable.

In a television interview on March 14, 1985, Mejía Víctores said that GAM was "being used by subversion, because if they have problems, solutions are being found, and they have been given every advantage to [solve these problems]."[106] A spate of newspaper headlines followed, stressing government warnings and allegations that GAM was being manipulated by subversives. In mid-March, General Mejía Víctores was asked on television what action the government would take against GAM. He replied, "You'll know it when you see it."[107]

On March 30, 1985, GAM leader Héctor Gómez Calito was seized, tortured, and murdered. (The six policemen who had come for him were themselves assassinated shortly after his death.)[108] He had been burned with a blowtorch, on the stomach and elsewhere, and beaten on the face so severely that his lips were swollen and his teeth were broken; his tongue had been cut out. Then, on April 4, another leader of GAM, María Rosario Godoy de Cuevas, her twenty-one-year-old brother, and her two-year-old son were picked up, tortured, and murdered. Her breasts had bite marks and her underclothing was bloody; her two-year-old son had had his fingernails pulled out.

On grounds of newsworthiness, the murders of the two GAM leaders, along with the brother and the child of one of them, would seem to deserve high-order attention. Their bravery was exceptional; the villainy they were opposing was extraordinary; the justice of their cause was unassailable; and the crimes they suffered were more savage than those undergone by Popieluszko. Most important of all, these were crimes for which we bear considerable responsibility, since they were perpetrated by clients who depend on our support, so that exposure and pressure could have a significant effect in safeguarding human rights. On the other hand, the Reagan administration was busily trying to enter into warmer and more supportive relations with the Guatemalan military regime and, as we described earlier, was going to great pains to put the regime in a favorable light. A propaganda model would anticipate that even these dramatic and horrifying murders would be treated in a low-key manner and quickly dropped by the mass media—that, unlike Popieluszko, there would be no sustained interest, no indignation capable of rousing the public (and disturbing the administration's plans). These expectations are fully vindicated by the record.

Table 2-3 compares media coverage of the Popieluszko case with that of the murders of the GAM leaders. It is immediately obvious that the treatment is radically different in the two cases. The GAM murders couldn't even make "the news" at *Time*, *Newsweek*, or CBS News. The *New York Times* never found these murders worthy of the front page or editorial comment, and we can see that the intensity of its coverage was slight. The first report of the quadruple murder was on April 7, 1985, in a tiny item on page 5 of the paper in which it is mentioned that the body of María Rosario Godoy de Cuevas was found in her car in a ravine, along with the bodies of her brother and her young son. In neither this item nor any succeeding article does the *Times* provide details on the condition of the bodies, or mention that the two-year-old child had his fingernails torn out.[109]

In other respects, too, the *Times* articles, all written by Stephen Kinzer, generally employ an apologetic framework. That is, they don't focus on the murders—who the victims were, the details of the violence, who did it, why, and the institutional structures and roots of organized murder of which these are an obvious part. With Popieluszko, these were *the* issues. Kinzer has little or nothing on the details of the GAM murders and very little on the victims and the experiences that brought them to GAM, and the question of who did it and what was being done (or not done) to bring the murderers to justice he hardly considers. Kinzer takes it for granted that the murders were committed by agents of the state, but he doesn't say this explicitly, or discuss the

TABLE 2-3

Mass-Media Coverage of Worthy and Unworthy Victims (2): A Murdered Polish Priest versus Two Murdered Officials of the Guatemalan Mutual Support Group

Victims	*NEW YORK TIMES*								*TIME* and *NEWSWEEK*				*CBS NEWS*			
	Articles[1]		Column Inches		Front-page articles		Editorials		Articles[1]		Column inches		No. of news programs[1]		No. of evening news	
	No.	% of row 1	No.	% of row 1	No.	% of row 1	No.	% of row 1	No.	% of row 1	No.	% of row 1	No.	% of row 1	No.	% of row 1
1. Jerzy Popieluszko, murdered on Oct. 19, 1984	78	(100)	1183.0	(100)	10	(100)	3	(100)	16	(100)	313.0	(100)	46	(100)	23	(100)
2. Héctor Orlando Gómez and María Rosario Godoy de Cuevas, murdered between Mar. 30 and Apr. 6, 1985 (along with a child, who was tortured)	5	(6.4)	80.0	(6.8)	—		—		—		—		—		—	

background, or provide a framework for evaluating the case. He looks "objectively" at the scene, quoting some of the GAM survivors in brief and rhetorical statements that are offset by quotes from the generals: they approved the formation of GAM (an ambiguous half-truth); they appointed an investigating committee that "found no evidence of secret detention centers in Guatemala" (no mention of the composition of the committee, no counter-evidence, and no mention of issues they may have overlooked—like disappeared who are murdered); and they deny any responsibility for the murder of Godoy, her brother, and her son, who they claim to have been victims of an auto accident. If Kinzer had given the details of the victims' injuries, this lie would have been exposed as such, and further questions would have suggested themselves.

In article after article, Kinzer repeats that the Mejía Víctores government has pledged to return to civilian rule shortly, which helps deflect attention from the ongoing killing and its causes, and from the GAM murders under discussion; he also does not tell us just what "civilian rule" would mean in a terrorist state in which, as he knows, the effective rulers would be the same military forces.[110] In the Popieluszko case, once it was established that the police had committed the murder, the media spent a great deal of space discussing the police apparatus and police methods, as well as attending to the responsibility of the people at higher levels for the murder. Kinzer doesn't discuss these questions at all. The structure of the Guatemalan murder machine and how it works would make a good story, and numerous details of its operations were available, but this did not fit the government agenda and the *Times* format. Similarly, the role of Mejía Víctores in the murder of the GAM leaders—recall his warnings just prior to the murders, and consider his virtually unlimited discretionary power to murder or protect the citizenry—is ignored. But once again, the links to the top in the case of unworthy victims do not fit the propaganda format. Kinzer does a nice job of making the GAM murders seem to be part of the natural background—regrettable but inevitable, part of the complex inheritance of a troubled country, and possibly, it is hoped, to be rectified when the new civilian government takes power.

In an attempt to gain support abroad, two of the remaining leaders of GAM, Nineth de García and Herlindo Hideo de Aquino, traveled to Europe in March and April 1986, after the inauguration of the elected civilian president, Christian Democrat Vinicio Cerezo. One of their most important messages was that killings and disappearances had not abated at all during the first three months of Cerezo's presidency, and that the death squads had actually reappeared and were active in

Guatemala City. Because of ill health, Nineth de García canceled her visits in Washington, D.C., and flew directly from Europe to Chicago, where she was scheduled to receive the key to the city from Mayor Harold Washington. As she went through customs in Chicago, however, the officials of the Immigration and Naturalization Service searched, interrogated, and harassed her for two hours, one of the customs officials calling her a subversive and a Communist. They also seized literature she carried and threatened to deport her, despite her intended brief stopover and valid visa. This intimidation had its effect, and Nineth de García flew directly to Guatemala. A friend attended the banquet in her place to accept the key presented by Mayor Washington.

This incident is revealing. It is unlikely that Sharansky or Walesa would be so treated by the INS, but if by some chance they were, the press outcry would be great.[111] When a press conference was held in Chicago by supporters of GAM to protest this outrage, the major media did not attend, and neither the press releases nor the follow-up letter from a congressional group signed by Senator Daniel Patrick Moynihan could break the silence. The convergence between Reagan administration policy toward Guatemala and media priorities was complete. (According to two organizers of the Chicago press conference, full information on this event was given Steve Greenhouse, the *New York Times*'s reporter in Chicago, but not a word about this incident appeared in the newspaper of record.)

A press release by the Guatemalan army on September 17, 1986, accused GAM of conducting

> . . . a black campaign of falsehood . . . insults and insolence directed at the military institution that exceed [the boundaries] of liberty and tolerance for free speech. The army cannot permit the insidiousness and truculence of GAM's maneuvers . . . that attempt to compromise the democratic international image of Guatemala.[112]

Although very similar threats preceded the murder of two leaders of GAM in March and April of 1984, the U.S. mass media entirely ignored this new information—despite strenuous efforts by GAM, the Guatemalan Human Rights Commission, and their allies to elicit publicity. As in the past, the unworthiness of these victims remains an essential ingredient in the Guatemalan army's continued freedom to kill.

3

Legitimizing versus Meaningless Third World Elections:

El Salvador
Guatemala
Nicaragua

THIRD WORLD ELECTIONS PROVIDE AN EXCELLENT TESTING ground for a propaganda model. Some elections are held in friendly client states to legitimize their rulers and regimes, whereas others are held in disfavored or enemy countries to legitimize *their* political systems. This natural dichotomization is strengthened by the fact that elections in the friendly client states are often held under U.S. sponsorship and with extensive U.S. management and public-relations support. Thus, in the Dominican Republic in 1966, and periodically thereafter, the United States organized what have been called "demonstration elections" in its client states, defined as those whose primary function is to convince the home population that the intervention is well intentioned, that the populace of the invaded and occupied country welcomes the intrusion, and that they are being given a democratic choice.[1]

The elections in El Salvador in 1982 and 1984 were true demonstration elections, and those held in Guatemala in 1984–85 were strongly supported by the United States for image-enhancing purposes. The election held in Nicaragua in 1984, by contrast, was intended to legitimize a government that the Reagan administration was striving to destabilize and overthrow. The U.S. government therefore went to great pains to cast the Nicaraguan election in an unfavorable light.

A propaganda model would anticipate mass-media support of the state perspective and agenda. That is, the favored elections will be found to legitimize, no matter what the facts; the disfavored election will be found deficient, farcical, and failing to legitimize—again, irrespective of facts. What makes this another strong test of a propaganda model is that the Salvadoran and Guatemalan elections of 1982 and 1984–85 were held under conditions of severe, ongoing state terror against the civilian population, whereas in Nicaragua this was not the case. To find the former elections legitimizing and the Nicaraguan election a farce, the media would have had to use different standards of evaluation in the two sets of cases, and, more specifically, it would have been necessary for them to avoid discussing state terror and other basic electoral conditions in the Salvadoran and Guatemalan elections. As we will see, the media fulfilled these requirements and met the needs of the state to a remarkable degree.

In order to demonstrate the applicability of a propaganda model in these cases, we will first describe the election-propaganda framework that the U.S. government tried to foist on the media; we will then review the basic electoral conditions under which elections were held in the three countries; and finally, we will examine how the U.S. mass media treated each of the three elections.

3.1. ELECTION-PROPAGANDA FRAMEWORKS

The U.S. government has employed a number of devices in its sponsored elections to put them in a favorable light. It has also had an identifiable agenda of issues that it wants stressed, as well as others it wants ignored or downplayed. Central to demonstration-election management has been the manipulation of symbols and agenda to give the favored election a positive image. The sponsor government tries to associate the election with the happy word "democracy" and the military regime it backs with support of the elections (and hence democracy). It emphasizes what a wonderful thing it is to be able to hold any election at all under conditions of internal conflict, and it makes it appear a moral triumph that the army has agreed to support the election (albeit reluctantly) and abide by its results.

The refusal of the rebel opposition to participate in the election is portrayed as a rejection of democracy and proof of its antidemocratic tendencies, although the very *plan* of the election involves the rebels' exclusion from the ballot.[2] The sponsor government also seizes upon any rebel statements urging nonparticipation or threatening to disrupt the election. These are used to transform the election into a dramatic struggle between, on the one side, the "born-again" democratic army and people struggling to vote for "peace," and, on the other, the rebels opposing democracy, peace, and the right to vote. Thus the dramatic denouement of the election is *voter turnout,* which measures the ability of the forces of democracy and peace (the army) to overcome rebel threats.

Official observers are dispatched to the election scene to assure its public-relations success. Nominally, their role is to see that the election is "fair." Their real function, however, is to provide the *appearance* of fairness by focusing on the government's agenda and by channeling press attention to a reliable source.[3] They testify to fairness on the basis of long lines, smiling faces, no beatings in their presence, and the assurances and enthusiasm of U.S. and client-state officials.[4] But these superficialities are entirely consistent with a staged fraud. Fairness depends on fundamental conditions established in advance, which are virtually impossible to ascertain under the brief, guided-tour conditions of official observers. Furthermore, official observers in sponsored elections rarely ask the relevant questions.[5] They are able to perform their public-relations function because the government chooses observers who are reliable supporters of its aims and publicizes their role, and the press gives them respectful attention.[6]

"Off the agenda" for the government in its own sponsored elections are all of the basic parameters that make an election meaningful or meaningless prior to the election-day proceedings. These include: (1) freedom of speech and assembly; (2) freedom of the press; (3) freedom to organize and maintain intermediate economic, social, and political groups (unions, peasant organizations, political clubs, student and teacher associations, etc.); (4) freedom to form political parties, organize members, put forward candidates, and campaign without fear of extreme violence; and (5) the absence of state terror and a climate of fear among the public. Also off the agenda is the election-day "coercion package" that may explain turnout in terms other than devotion to the army and its plans, including any legal requirement to vote, and explicit or implicit threats for *not* voting. Other issues that must be downplayed in conforming to the government propaganda format are the U.S. government's role in organizing and funding the election, the internal propaganda campaign waged to get out the vote, outright fraud, and the constraints on and threats to journalists covering the election.

Another issue off the government agenda is the *purpose* of the election. If its role is to influence the home population, spelling this out might arouse suspicions concerning its authenticity. In the case of the Vietnam election of 1967 and the El Salvador elections of 1982 and 1984, the purpose of the elections was not merely to placate the home public but also to mislead them on the ends sought. In both instances it was intimated that an election would contribute to a peaceable resolution to the conflict, whereas the intent was to clear the ground for intensified warfare. Nobody who proposed a peace option could appear as a serious candidate in Vietnam in 1967,[7] and as we describe below, there was no peace candidate at all in El Salvador in either 1982 or 1984, although the polls and reporters kept saying that peace was the primary concern of the electorate. This highlights both the fraudulence of these elections and the urgency that the intentions of the sponsor be kept under wraps.

In elections held in disfavored or enemy states, the U.S. government agenda is turned upside down. Elections are no longer equated with democracy, and U.S. officials no longer marvel at the election being held under adverse conditions. They do not commend the army for supporting the election and agreeing to abide by the results. On the contrary, the leverage the dominant party obtains by control of and support by the army is put forward in this case as compromising the integrity of the election. Rebel disruption is no longer proof that the opposition rejects democracy, and turnout is no longer the dramatic denouement of the struggle between a democratic army and its rebel opposition. *Now* the stress is on the hidden motives of the sponsors of the election, who are trying to legitimize themselves by this tricky device of a so-called election.

Most important, the agenda of factors relevant to appraising an election is altered. From the stress on the superficial—long lines and smiling faces of voters, the simple mechanics of election-day balloting, and the personalities of the candidates—attention is now shifted to the basic parameters that were off the agenda in the sponsored election. As noted by Secretary of State Shultz, "The important thing is that if there is to be an electoral process, it be observed not only at the moment when people vote, but in all the preliminary aspects that make an election meaningful." Spelling this out further, Shultz mentioned explicitly that for elections to be meaningful, "rival political groups" must be allowed "to form themselves and have access to people, to have the right of assembly, to have access to the media."[8] These remarks were made apropos of the 1984 *Nicaraguan* election. No congresspersons or media commentators raised any question about whether these criteria should perhaps be applied to the Salvadoran or Guatemalan elections scheduled during the same year.

In brief, the government used a well-nigh perfect system of Orwellian doublethink: forgetting a criterion "that has become inconvenient, and then, when it becomes necessary again, . . . draw[ing] it back from oblivion for just so long as it is needed."[9] It even acknowledges this fact: a senior U.S. official told members of the Latin American Studies Association (LASA) observing the Nicaraguan election:

> The United States is not obliged to apply the same standard of judgment to a country whose government is avowedly hostile to the U.S. as for a country like El Salvador, where it is not. These people [the Sandinistas] could bring about a situation in Central America which could pose a threat to U.S. security. That allows us to change our yardstick.[10]

But while a government may employ a blatant double standard, media which adhere to minimal standards of objectivity and are not themselves part of a propaganda system would apply a single standard. Did the mass media of the United States follow a single standard in dealing with the elections in El Salvador, Guatemala, and Nicaragua, or did they follow their government's agenda in order to put the Salvadoran and Guatemalan elections in a favorable light and to denigrate the one held in Nicaragua?

3.2. BASIC ELECTORAL CONDITIONS IN EL SALVADOR, GUATEMALA, AND NICARAGUA, 1982–85

All three of these countries, in which elections were held in the years 1982–85, were in the midst of serious conflict: Nicaragua was being subjected to regular border incursions by the U.S.-organized and supplied contras. El Salvador was in the midst of a combination civil conflict and externally (U.S.) organized and funded counterinsurgency war. Guatemala, as we noted earlier, had evolved into a counterinsurgency state, with permanent warfare to keep the majority of Indians and other peasants in their place, and violent repression was structured into the heart of the political system.

Despite the common feature of ongoing conflict, however, electoral conditions were far more favorable in Nicaragua than in El Salvador and Guatemala, for several reasons. First, and crucially important, in the latter countries, at the time of the elections the army was still engaged in mass slaughter of the civilian population, with the toll in the tens of thousands in each country and the killing often carried out with extreme sadism. Nothing remotely similar was true in Nicaragua. These facts, which are not controversial among people with a minimal concern for reality, immediately establish a fundamental distinction with regard to the electoral climate. In countries that are being subject to the terror of a rampaging murder machine, supported or run by a foreign power, electoral conditions are fatally compromised in advance, a point that the media would recognize at once if we were considering the sphere of influence of some official enemy.[11]

A further—and related—distinction was that the ruling Sandinista government was a popular government, which strove to serve majority needs and could therefore *afford* to allow greater freedom of speech and organization. The LASA report on the Nicaraguan election notes that their program "implies redistribution of access to wealth and public services. The state will use its power to guarantee fulfillment of the basic needs of the majority population." The "logic of the majority," the report continues, also implies the involvement of "very large numbers of people in the decisions that affect their lives."[12] Qualified observers conclude that the Nicaraguan government pursued this logic, although this fact is excluded from the free press. After citing the World Bank's observation that "Governments . . . vary greatly in the commitment of their political leadership to improving the condition of the people and encouraging their active participation in the development process," Dianna Melrose, of the charitable development agency Oxfam, states that "From Oxfam's experience of working in seventy-six developing countries, Nicaragua was to prove exceptional in the strength of that Government commitment."[13] The Salvadoran and Guatemalan governments, by contrast, were ruled by elites that had been struggling desperately for decades to avoid the very kinds of reforms the Sandinistas were implementing. Extreme repression was the longstanding method of control of the majority in El Salvador and Guatemala, with vigorous and unceasing U.S. support. The aim of this repression was to keep the populace apathetic and to destroy popular organizations that might lay the basis for meaningful democracy. The

Sandinistas were engaged in mobilizing the majority and involving them in political life, which they could afford to do because their programs were intended to serve the general population.

A third factor affecting electoral conditions was that in El Salvador and Guatemala the conflict was internal, and violence against the majority was integral to the struggle. In Nicaragua, the conflict was one involving an externally sponsored aggression that had very limited internal support. The Sandinistas could appeal to nationalist sentiments, easily mobilized against Yankee-organized terrorism. The Salvadoran and Guatemalan governments could hardly do the same—the Salvadoran government especially had to contend with a negative nationalist reaction to obvious foreign (i.e., U.S.) domination and manipulation of its affairs, a fact that reached the level of absurdity when Duarte, visiting Washington in the fall of 1987, made himself an object of ridicule throughout Latin America by promptly kissing the American flag. While the Sandinistas did increasingly crack down on internal supporters of the contras as the conflict intensified, by the standards the United States usually applies to this region dissenters were dealt with remarkably benignly in Nicaragua.[14] In El Salvador and Guatemala, the ruling elites could not afford such toleration, and repression by large-scale terror had long been institutionalized in these states.

A fourth factor making for a more benign electoral environment in Nicaragua, paradoxically, was U.S. hostility and the power of its propaganda machine. Every arrest or act of harassment in Nicaragua was publicized and transformed into evidence of the sinister quality of the Sandinista government in the free press of the United States. Meanwhile, as we described in chapter 2, the Guatemalan and Salvadoran regimes could indulge in torture, rape, mutilation, and murder on a daily and massive basis without invoking remotely proportional attention, indignation, or inferences about the quality of these regimes. In the context, the Nicaraguan government was under intense pressure to toe the mark, whereas the U.S. satellites were free to murder at will without serious political cost.

Let us examine briefly how El Salvador, Guatemala, and Nicaragua compared in the individual categories of conditions of a free election, before we turn to the media treatment of these issues.

3.2.1. Free speech and assembly.

In El Salvador, the right to free speech and free assembly was legally suspended under a state-of-siege order of March 7, 1980. Decree No.

507 of December 3, 1980, essentially destroyed the judicial system, permitting the armed forces to hold citizens without charge or evidence for 180 days. Under these rulings, in the thirty months before the March 1982 election, and prior to the 1984 elections, many thousands of civilians were seized, imprisoned, tortured, raped, and murdered outside of legal processes for alleged "subversive" actions and thoughts. The state of siege was lifted in early 1982 solely for the six parties contesting the election, and it was lifted entirely ten days before the election for all Salvadorans—although, unfortunately, the citizenry was not informed of this fact until after the election was over and state-of-siege conditions were reimposed.[15] The practice of exposing mutilated bodies for the edification of the citizenry became institutionalized in the early 1980s in El Salvador. We described in chapter 2 the difficulty the U.S. government had in getting underlings jailed, tried, and convicted for the murder of four American citizens, even under intense U.S. pressure. The people of El Salvador had no protection whatsoever from the state terrorists, apart from that afforded by the guerrilla army in the regions under their control. The threat of extreme violence by the state against dissident speech was acute in El Salvador in 1982 and 1984, and was incompatible with a free election.

In Guatemala, similarly, during 1984 and 1985, and for many years before, the actions of the armed forces against alleged subversives was entirely outside the rule of law. Thousands were seized, tortured, and killed without warrant and without any individual right to hearing or trial. As in El Salvador, mutilation and exposure of the tortured bodies became commonplace in the late 1970s and the 1980s.[16] The courts were dominated by the military, as the latter would simply not execute or obey a court order of which they disapproved, and the judges were not inclined to challenge the military for reasons of dependency or fear. Even Viscount Colville of Culross, the special rapporteur of the UN General Assembly who has been a notorious apologist for the Guatemalan regime, after pointing out that over eighty members of the judiciary, court staff, and legal profession had been murdered in the early 1980s and that many others were threatened, says that "Such events make their mark and cannot quickly be mitigated."[17] Two illustrations of the lack of court autonomy may be noted here: in May 1983, Ricardo Sagastume Vidaure, then president of the supreme court, was simply removed by military order for attempting to bring military personnel under the jurisdiction of the legal system.[18] On July 19, 1984, Colonel Djalmi Domínguez, head of public relations for the army, told the newspaper *Prensa Libre* that the army wouldn't tolerate its members being taken to court on any charges.[19]

In the early 1980s, following the mass killings and village destruction of 1980–83, vast numbers of peasants were resettled in "model villages" and other places under army control, and over 800,000 males were made obligatory members of civil patrols with military functions under close army surveillance. According to the British parliamentary group that visited Guatemala in 1984, "The civilian patrol system is implemented by terror, and designed also to sow terror. . . . People who do anything out of the ordinary come under immediate suspicion and are taken by the patrols to the army's *destacamiento.* Interrogation will be done by the army, but the killing of murdered suspects [is] often by the civilian patrols."[20] Bishops Taylor and O'Brien, representing the Roman Catholic Bishops' Conferences of Scotland and England-Wales respectively, reported after their visit to Guatemala in 1984 that

> The civilian population is under almost total control by a heavy army and police presence throughout the country, which we were able to observe. There is also a nationwide network of civil defense patrols, military commissioners and informers, and "model villages" serving in some cases as internment camps for the Indian population from the areas of conflict. Much of Guatemala resembles a country under military occupation. One of our informants summed up the situation by saying that the military had established a system of "structural control."[21]

The InterAmerican Commission on Human Rights, following an on-site visit in May 1985, also found that freedom of speech and assembly did not exist in Guatemala:

> The right of assembly and freedom of association, considered in Articles 15 and 16 of the American Convention, are also restricted and curtailed, because existing security measures in the Development Poles and the strict supervision of the Civil Defense Patrols inhibit residents from taking part in any social, ideological, cultural or other assemblies or associations. All such meetings, when they do occur, are subject to surveillance, supervision and control by the authorities, so they do not enjoy the freedom implied by such rights.[22]

Public demonstrations were permissible in Guatemala during the 1984–85 elections, with three days' advance notice and approval of the military authorities. In the Guatemalan context, however, this grant of rights was not meaningful. The delegation of the International Human

Rights Law Group and the Washington Office on Latin America noted that whatever the election guarantees,

> the military and civil defense patrols and the climate of fear also made it difficult for many Guatemalans to organize and assemble. One local observer said that years of terror and oppression against local organizations had demobilized the whole rural population: "Four CUC [peasant league] members were killed in this village alone. Now it would be very difficult to organize any kind of group." Civil patrols, police and army checkpoints on highways, and the need for travel permits for residents of the model villages impeded free movement. In the rural areas the civil patrols discouraged gatherings because people feared being reported.[23]

It was noted by many observers of the Guatemalan elections that although the big issues in that country were land distribution and reform and human rights, no political candidates discussed or advocated either land reform, or restructuring the military and forcing an accounting of tens of thousands of "disappearances." One Christian Democratic adviser explained to the law group that "We Christian Democrats haven't raised such issues because this isn't the moment to start a confrontation with either the army or the private sector."[24]

In short, despite the "momentary improvement in the conditions of free speech" that occurred during the election campaign, Guatemala did not meet the first condition of a free election. The rural masses were under army discipline and traumatized by mass killings and the absence of any vestige of rule of law, and the candidates were unable to raise openly the fundamental issues of the society.

Free speech and rights of assembly were constrained in Nicaragua in 1984 by social pressures and threats and by a state of siege that had been terminated some six months prior to the November 1984 election. Very important differences existed, however, between the Nicaraguan constraints and those prevailing in El Salvador and Guatemala. Most important, in Nicaragua the army and police did not regularly seize alleged subversives, and torture and murder them. Mutilated bodies have not been put on public display as a part of the system of public education. What the law group called the "constant, overt political terror" in Guatemala, based on "numerous documented massacres of whole villages," and what the former Salvadoran official Leonel Gómez called the state of "fearful passivity" prevalent in El Salvador, did not apply to Nicaragua. In Nicaragua, in 1984, dissidents were able to speak freely without fear of murder, and the LASA group noted that "Every member of our delegation was approached at least once by an irate citizen as we walked around Managua and other cities. Several of these encounters turned into heated arguments between the individual who had approached us and passers-by who joined the discussion. . . . These people did not feel intimidated."[25]

Freedom of assembly in Nicaragua was somewhat limited by harassment, but, once again, it was not ruled out by state terror, as was the case in El Salvador and Guatemala. The LASA delegation examined in detail the charges of Sandinista harassment of opposition-group meetings and found them largely unfounded, concluding that the contesting parties "were able to hold the vast majority of their rallies unimpeded by pro-FSLN demonstrations. . . ."[26]

Our conclusion is that the first basic condition of a free election was partially met in Nicaragua, but was not met at all in El Salvador and Guatemala.

3.2.2. Freedom of the press.

In El Salvador, the only substantial newspapers critical of the government, *La Crónica del Pueblo* and *El Independiente*—neither by any means radical papers—were closed in July 1980 and January 1981, respectively, the first because its top editor and two employees were murdered and mutilated by the security forces, the second because the army arrested its personnel and destroyed its plant. The church paper and radio station were repeatedly shut down by bombing attacks. No paper or station representing the principal opposition has been able to operate except clandestinely. Over thirty journalists have been murdered in El Salvador since the revolutionary junta took power. An intensified campaign against the press occurred just prior to the 1982 election. On March 10, a death list of thirty-five journalists was circulated by a "death squad," and on March 18 the mutilated bodies of four Dutch journalists were recovered.[27] None of the murders of journalists in El Salvador was ever "solved"—they were essentially murders carried out under the auspices of the state.

In Guatemala, forty-eight journalists were murdered between 1978 and 1985,[28] and many others have been kidnapped and threatened. These killings, kidnappings, and threats have been a primary means of control of the media. As in El Salvador, nobody has yet been apprehended and tried for any of these crimes, which must be viewed as murders carried out by the state or with state approval. There are no papers or radio or television stations in Guatemala that express the views of the rebels or the majority Indian population or the lower classes in general. "At most, the variants reflect shades of strictly conservative thinking."[29] Given the extreme climate of fear, and threats for stepping out of line, even the conservative press is cautious and engages in continuous self-censorship. All the central topics that should be debated in this terrorized society are carefully avoided.[30]

In Nicaragua, once again, there have been no reported deaths of journalists by state terrorists, nor even threats of personal violence. In 1984, the majority of the fifty-odd radio stations were privately owned, and some of them provided their own news programs; four other independent producers supplied radio news programs without prior censorship. Foreign radio and television from commercial and U.S. propaganda sources broadcasting from Costa Rica, Honduras, and elsewhere were of growing importance in 1984.[31] Two of the three newspapers were privately owned, one supportive of the government but critical of specific programs and actions, the other violently hostile. The latter, *La Prensa,* which represented the small, ultraconservative minority and supported the contras and a foreign-sponsored invasion of the country, was allowed to operate throughout the 1984 election, although it was censored. The censorship still allowed the paper to publish manifestos of opposition groups and a pastoral letter critical of the regime. No comparable paper has been allowed to exist aboveground, even briefly, in El Salvador and Guatemala.

There is no doubt that the media in Nicaragua have been under government constraint, with censorship and periodic emergency controls that seriously encroached on freedom of the press.[32] It should be noted, however, that Nicaragua is under foreign attack and in a state of serious warfare. John S. Nichols points out that under the U.S. Espionage Act of 1917, over one hundred publications were banned from the mails, and hundreds of people were jailed for allegedly interfering with military recruitment. Furthermore,

> Given that the United States was a relatively mature and homogenous political system during World War I and was not particularly threatened by the fighting, the range of public discussion tolerated in Nicaragua during the first five years of the revolution was remarkable. Despite assertions by President Reagan, IAPA, and others that the control of the Nicaraguan media was virtually totalitarian, the diversity of ownership and opinion was unusual for a Third World country, particularly one at war.[33]

Our conclusion is that the condition of freedom of the press necessary for a free election was clearly absent in El Salvador and Guatemala, and that it was partially met in Nicaragua.

3.2.3. Freedom of organization of intermediate groups.

Perhaps the most important fact about El Salvador in the two years prior to the election of March 1982 was the decimation of popular and private organizations that could pose any kind of challenge to the army and oligarchy. As we noted in chapter 2, this was the main thrust of policy of the revolutionary junta from late 1979 onward, and thousands of leaders were murdered and numerous organizations were destroyed or driven underground. The teachers' union was decimated by several hundred murders; the university was occupied, looted, and closed down by the army; organized student and professional groups were destroyed by arrests and killings, and even the peasant union sponsored by the AFL-CIO (i.e., supporters of the regime) had some one hundred of its organizers and leaders murdered between October 1979 and the election of March 1982.[34]

In Guatemala, too, intermediate organizations such as peasant and trade unions, teacher and student groups, and professional organizations have been regularly attacked by the armed forces since 1954. The process of demobilization of institutions threatening the dominant elites culminated in the early 1980s, when by government proclamation "illicit association" was made punishable by law. All groups "which follow, or are subordinated to, any totalitarian system of ideology" (evidently an exception is made of the Guatemalan armed forces and the national-security ideology) are illicit. Only the armed forces determine when illicitness occurs. If General Mejía Víctores finds the GAM mothers to be agents of subversion, they may be killed (see chapter 2). Unions, peasant groups, student and professional organizations have grown up periodically in Guatemala, only to be crushed by systematic murder as soon as their demands were pressed with any vigor. The 1984–85 elections followed the greatest era of mass murder in modern Guatemalan history—under the regimes of Lucas García, Ríos Montt, and Mejía Víctores. Union membership in 1985 was below its 1950 level, and other urban groups were decimated or inactive; the peasant majority was totally demobilized and under the tight control and surveillance of the military.

In Nicaragua, again the contrast with the two U.S. clients is marked. Under Sandinista management there was a spurt in union and peasant organization. A deliberate attempt was made to mobilize the population to participate in decision-making at the local level and to interact with higher-level leaders. Oxfam compliments the Nicaraguan government highly for this effort, as we pointed out earlier.

There is legitimate debate over the extent to which the grass-roots and other organizations sponsored by the ruling FSLN are independent, and whether they might not be a vehicle for both state propaganda and coercion. Oxfam America and its parent organization in London clearly find them constructive. Luis Héctor Serra contends that the grass-roots organizations are relatively autonomous, and that their close relationship to the leadership of the FSLN "did not obstruct their capacity to express the concerns of their members at the local level."[35] He concludes that the popular organizations were "profoundly democratic" in their effects of involving the populace in decision-making and educating them on the possibilities of participation in public life.[36] The difference with the organization of the Guatemalan peasantry in "poles of development," where the essence of the organization was, quite openly, military control by terror and enforced *nonparticipation,* is quite dramatic, whatever one's general assessment of the FSLN popular organizations may be.

We conclude that on the third basic condition for a free election, El Salvador and Guatemala did not qualify in the years 1984–85; Nicaragua did, at least to a significant degree.[37]

3.2.4. Freedom to organize parties, field candidates, and campaign for office

No party of the left could organize and present candidates in the 1982 and 1984 elections in El Salvador. The Democratic Front (FDR) had been quickly driven underground. Five of its top leaders were seized in El Salvador in November 1980 by official and paramilitary forces, and were tortured, mutilated, and killed. A year before the March 1982 election, the army published a list of 138 "traitors," which included virtually all politicians of the left and left-center. Colonel Gutiérrez, a powerful member of the junta, had stated forcefully that the FDR could not participate in the election because it was a "front" for the guerrillas. The invitation to the FDR and the FMLN to lay down their arms and compete in the election was thus fraudulent, a fact confirmed by the admission of the U.S. embassy that the FDR could not safely campaign in El Salvador, with the accompanying suggestion that they might do so by means of videotapes sent in from outside the country's borders![38] Subsequently, even Duarte, the preferred candidate of the United States, was unable to campaign outside San Salvador in 1982 for fear of murder, and scores of Christian Democratic politicans were killed in the years 1980–84.[39] In short, not only radical but even pro-U.S., mildly reformist parties could not escape decimation by political murder during those years.

It should also be emphasized that no party could organize and run candidates in El Salvador that put high priority on terminating the war by negotiations with the rebels. What makes this especially important is that reporters and observers were unanimous in 1982 that the main thing the public wanted out of the election was peace. The propaganda formula for getting out the vote in 1982 was "ballots versus bullets," with the implication that ballots were a possible route to a reduction in the use of bullets. If, in fact, no peace candidate was eligible to run, the election was a fraud for this reason alone.

Defenders of these elections have argued that there was a substantial difference between the candidates, especially between D'Aubuisson and Duarte, so that voters had a meaningful choice.[40] But D'Aubuisson and Duarte did not disagree on the central issue of interest to the Salvadoran people—whether to fight to win, or to strive for a negotiated settlement with the rebels. Both were members of the war party, with only tactical differences. Although Duarte made occasional demagogic claims that he would talk with the rebels and bring about peace, he never spelled out a peace-making agenda, never went beyond suggesting "dialogue" (as opposed to "negotiations," which imply the possibility of substantive concessions), and never departed from the position that the rebels should lay down their arms and participate in the new "democracy" that Duarte and the army had established.

Duarte joined the junta at a moment of severe crisis in March 1980, when all the progressive civilians had left and immediately after the murder of the Christian Democratic attorney-general, Mario Zamora, by the newly prospering death squads. It was clear that the army and affiliated death squads had embarked on a policy of large-scale massacre. Duarte provided the fig leaf and apologetics that the army needed for the second *matanza.*[41] We believe that Duarte never would have received U.S. support and protection, and could not have survived in El Salvador, unless he had made it clear that he was in basic accord with the aims of the U.S. administration and the Salvadoran army. From

1980 onward, Duarte always accepted fully the pursuit of a military solution and no compromise with "the subversives" (a phrase that Duarte uses continually, just as do the army and death-squad leaders). As Raymond Bonner points out,

> The repression in 1980 reached a magnitude surpassed only by the [first] *matanza* and was far worse than anything imagined under General Romero. . . . By the end of the year the number [murdered] had reached at least 9,000. Every day mutilated bodies, missing arms or heads, were found: behind shopping centers; stuffed in burlap bags and left on dusty rural roads; hurled over cliffs into ravines.[42]

And through all of this, Duarte not only provided the facade of "reform," he regularly complimented the army for its loyal service. In a letter published in the *Miami Herald* on November 9, 1981, Duarte wrote that

> The armed forces are waging a heroic battle against a cruel and pitiless enemy supported by great resources of ideological aggression. This goes parallel with armed aggression. . . . This would be one more prey in the conquest plan in the Central American region that Moscow has designed to pursue. Immediately after that its greatest reward would be the North American nation. . . .

In brief, the Salvadoran public was never offered the option that the press itself acknowledged the voters craved.

In Guatemala, as in El Salvador, no parties of the left participated in the 1984 election for a constituent assembly, and only one crippled party made a tentative but wholly ineffectual foray in the 1985 presidential election.[43] The main guerrilla movements were, of course, outside the electoral orbit. Their leaders would have been killed if apprehended, but they would not have participated anyway without a drastic alteration in basic social and electoral conditions.[44] Even a centrist party like the Christian Democrats had suffered scores of murders in the years 1980–83, and the current president of Guatemala, the Christian Democrat Vinicio Cerezo, survived three known assassination attempts. No seriously left party could have qualified in 1984–85 under the laws of "illicit association" mentioned earlier.

The peasant majority was not represented or spoken for by any candidate. The Guatemalan Human Rights Commission, an organization not able to function within Guatemala, has pointed out that national political parties that speak for major groups like the working class or indigenous people "do not exist and . . . as a result, these sectors are institutionally excluded from the political system."[45] Americas Watch states that one of the civil-patrol system's functions is "to provide vigilance and control of the local population, preventing any form of independent political organization."[46] This exclusion of the peasantry from any political opportunity was reflected in two ways in the 1984–85 elections. One was that in registering for the election, only 3 percent of the electorate signed up as members of political parties. Another, more compelling, is that no candidate in the election urged land reform, although this was one of the two central issues in Guatemala (the other being unconstrained army murder, also not an issue in the election, given the understanding on all sides that the army will remain the ruling force, whoever gains office).

As with Duarte in El Salvador, the presence of Vinicio Cerezo as a candidate, and as the eventual winner in the 1985 election, raises the question of whether, despite the constraints on the left, Cerezo did not really offer a significant option to the voting public. Cerezo differentiated himself from his electoral rivals, especially toward the end of the campaign and the runoff, by expressing compassion for the masses and a determination to make changes in the human-rights picture and mass poverty. He occasionally mentioned the need for structural reform, although he was not specific and stressed that the first requirement was to reestablish civilian control. He was quite clear, however, that if he were elected, his power would be nominal at first and would have to be enlarged while he was in office:

> The election will not bring automatic transfer of real power to the president. There will be a handover of *formal* power. What are my chances of consolidating that power? Fifty-fifty.[47]

During the election campaign, Cerezo never straightforwardly addressed the question of land reform, and news reports in Guatemala suggested that he had promised the landowners' lobby that land reform was not on his agenda.[48] Similarly, he did not promise any legal action against those who had murdered thousands, nor did he say that he would dismantle the counterinsurgency state. There would seem to have been at least a tacit understanding between Cerezo and the military that he would protect them against prosecution and preserve their power and relative autonomy; in fact, he could not do otherwise and survive.[49] In the year and a half that has elapsed since he took office,

Cerezo has made no meaningful move toward land reform, has supported the army vigorously against any accounting, and has made no move to dismantle the civil patrols, the development poles, and other features of institutionalized terror.[50] The human-rights situation in Guatemala "remains terrible,"[51] although improved (but partly because higher rates of killing are no longer deemed beneficial). The poor, for whom he expressed so much compassion during the electoral campaign, have suffered further losses in real income, as Cerezo's "reforms" have accommodated the demands of the army and oligarchy. He is on very poor terms with the Mutual Support Group. Thus, the postelection pattern shows that Cerezo, in part by prior agreement but more decisively by structural constraints, has been entirely unable to serve his mass constituency. In the 1984–85 election, Cerezo gave the Guatemalan people an opportunity to vote for a man of seeming goodwill and good intentions, but one unable to respond to democratic demands opposed by the *real* rulers of the state.

In Nicaragua, in 1984, the spectrum of candidates was much wider than in El Salvador, Guatemala, or, for that matter, the United States.[52] The Conservative Democratic party and the Independent Liberal party both issued strong calls for respect for private property, reduced government control of the economy, elimination of press and other controls, and a foreign policy of greater nonalignment and accommodation. Both were able to denounce the Sandinistas for the war and to call for depoliticization of the army and negotiations with the contras. Arturo Cruz, after lengthy negotiations with representatives of the government, chose not to run in the 1984 election. But this was a voluntary act of Cruz (albeit under heavy U.S. pressure),[53] in contrast with the position of the left in El Salvador and Guatemala, and was not based on physical threats to his person or limits on his access to the populace.[54]

The FSLN had a strong advantage over the opposition parties as the party in power, defending the country from foreign attack and having mobilized the population for their own projects of development. The LASA group felt that much of the incumbency advantage of the FSLN was characteristic of governments everywhere, and concluded:

> It seems clear that the FSLN took substantial advantage of its incumbent position and, in some ways, abused it. However, the abuses of incumbency do not appear to have been systematic; and neither the nature of the abuses nor their frequency was such as to cripple the opposition parties' campaigns or to cast doubt on

> the fundamental validity of the electoral process. . . . Generally speaking, in this campaign the FSLN did little more to take advantage of its incumbency than incumbent parties everywhere (including the United States) routinely do, and considerably *less* than ruling parties in other Latin American countries traditionally have done.[55]

We would conclude that the ability of candidates to qualify and run, and the range of options, was substantially greater in Nicaragua than in El Salvador and Guatemala. Furthermore, as all major political groups of the left were off the ballot by threat of violence in the latter two cases, those elections fail to meet still another basic electoral condition.

3.2.5. Absence of state terror and a climate of fear

During the years 1980–84 the death squads worked freely in El Salvador, in close coordination with the army and security forces. The average rate of killings of civilians in the thirty months prior to the 1982 election was approximately seven hundred per month. Many of these victims were raped, tortured, and mutilated. All of this was done with complete impunity, and only the murder of four American women elicited—by dint of congressional pressure—any kind of legal action. Even William Doherty of the American Institute for Free Labor Development—a longtime supporter of U.S. policy in El Salvador—asserted before a congressional committee that there was no system of justice operative in that country, while Leonel Gómez, a former land-reform official in El Salvador, told the same committee a bit later that state terror had put the population in a state of "fearful passivity."[56]

In Guatemala, too, the endemic fear based on years of unconstrained and continuing army violence was a dominant fact of national life. According to Americas Watch, writing in early 1985,

> Torture, killings, and disappearances continue at an extraordinary rate, and millions of peasants remain under the strict scrutiny and control of the government through the use of civil patrols and "model villages." Guatemala remains, in short, a nation of prisoners.[57]

The law group described Guatemala in 1985 as "a country where the greater part of the people live in permanent fear."[58]

In the case of Nicaragua, we repeat the central fact that differentiates it from the U.S. client states: in 1984 its government was not murdering civilians.[59] The main fear of ordinary citizens in Nicaragua was of violence by the contras and the United States.

Our conclusion is that the fifth condition for a free election was met in Nicaragua, but not in El Salvador and Guatemala. And our overall finding is that neither El Salvador nor Guatemala met *any* of the five basic conditions of a free election, whereas Nicaragua met some of them well, others to a lesser extent.

3.3. THE COERCION PACKAGES IN EL SALVADOR, GUATEMALA, AND NICARAGUA

As we noted, in the U.S. government's sponsored elections, voter turnout is interpreted as public support for the election and its sponsors. In disapproved elections (here, Nicaragua), this frame is abandoned, and voter turnout is either ignored or declared meaningless because of limited options or coercive threats by the authorities. But the question of coercive threats should clearly be raised in all cases where this is a potential problem. As we have just described, the elections in El Salvador were held under conditions of military rule where mass killings of "subversives" had taken place and a climate of fear had been established. If the government then sponsors an election and the local military authorities urge people to vote, a significant part of the vote should be assumed to be a result of built-in coercion. A propaganda model would anticipate that the U.S. mass media make no such assumption, and they did not.

In El Salvador in 1982 and 1984, voting was also required by law. The law stipulated that failure to vote was to be penalized by a specific monetary assessment, and it also called on local authorities to check out whether voters did in fact vote. This could be done because at the time of voting one's identification card (ID, *cédula*) was stamped, acknowledging the casting of a vote. Anybody stopped by the army and police would have to show the ID card, which would quickly indicate whether the individual had carried out his or her patriotic duty. Just prior to the March 1982 election, Minister of Defense García warned the population in the San Salvador newspapers that the failure to vote would be regarded as an act of treason. And in the 1984 election, "Advertising by the government and military prior to the elections stressed the obligation to vote rather than the freedom to vote."[60] Given the climate of fear, the voting requirement, the ID stamp, the army warning, and the army record in handling "traitors," it is evident that the coercive element in generating turnout in Salvadoran elections has been large. This is supported by queries made by independent observers on the reasons why Salvadorans voted.[61]

In Guatemala, as in El Salvador, voting was required by law; nonvoters were subject to a fine of five *quetzales* ($1.25). Also, as in El Salvador, newspaper ads sponsored by the army asserted that it was treasonous to fail to vote or to vote null or blank.[62] The law group reported that "many" people expressed fears that nonvoting would subject them to reprisals, and after the military threats in the week before the election there was "a widespread belief that failure to vote would be punishable by more than the five-*quetzal* fine stipulated by law."[63]

In Nicaragua, while registration was obligatory, *voting was not required by law.* Voter-registration cards presented on election day were retained by election officials, so that the failure to vote as evidenced by the lack of a validated voter credential could not be used as the basis of reprisals.[64] Most of the voters appeared to LASA observers to be voting under no coercive threat—they did not have to vote by law; they were urged to vote but not threatened with the designation of "traitors" for not voting; there were no obvious means of identifying nonvoters; and the government did not kill dissidents, in contrast to the normal practice in El Salvador and Guatemala.

In sum, Nicaragua did not have a potent coercion package at work to help get out the vote—as did the Salvadoran and Guatemalan governments.

3.4. EL SALVADOR: HOW THE U.S. MEDIA TRANSFORMED A "DERANGED KILLING MACHINE" INTO THE PROTECTOR OF AN INCIPIENT DEMOCRACY

In reporting on the 1982 Salvadoran election, the U.S. mass media closely followed the government agenda. The personalities of the candidates, the long lines waiting to vote, alleged rebel disruption, and "turnout" were heavily featured.[65] As Jack Spence pointed out, "every media outlet, particularly the networks, cast the election-day story in a framework of voting in the midst of extensive guerrilla violence at polling places."[66] Warren Hoge and Richard Meislin, of the *New York Times*, repeated day after day that the rebels were threatening disruption, Hoge asserting that "The elections have taken on a significance beyond their outcome because leftist guerrillas mounted a campaign to disrupt them and discourage voters from going to the polls."[67] This is a precise statement of the government's propaganda frame. But Hoge and Meislin never once cited a rebel source vowing disruption, and nobody else did, either. On election day no voters were killed or polling stations attacked, and the general level of rebel military activity was below average. In short, the disruption claims were falsifications of both plans and election-day results, but as they fit the patriotic agenda they were given prominence, repeated frequently, and used to establish the contest between the forces of good and evil.[68] At the election-day close, Dan Rather exclaimed, "A triumph! A million people to the polls." Rather did not regard it as a triumph that the Sandinistas got 700,000 people to the polls—a higher proportion of the population, and without a voting requirement. The propaganda frame of the government gave turnout high importance in the Salvadoran election but none in the Nicaraguan election, and Rather followed like a good lap dog.

Neither Rather nor any other media analyst on or before March 30, 1982, noted that voting was required by law in El Salvador, and not one mentioned the warning by the defense minister, General Guillermo García, in the San Salvador newspapers that nonvoting was treasonous.[69] The basic parameters were entirely off the media agenda. The destruction of *La Crónica* and *El Independiente* and the murder of twenty-six journalists prior to the election were unmentioned in discussing the election's quality and meaning.[70] The army and its allies had been killing civilians on a massive scale in El Salvador, for many months before (and into) March 1982. Would this not create a climate of fear and, in conjunction with a state of siege, somewhat encumber free debate and free choice? The point was rarely even hinted at in the mass media.

Could candidates run freely and campaign without fear of murder? Could the rebels qualify and run? After all, if it was a civil war, the rebels were clearly the "main opposition." Again, the mass media played dumb. They pretended that this exclusion was not important, or that it represented a willful boycott by the rebels rather than a refusal based on conditions unfavorable to a free election and a blatantly stacked deck. Neither the March 1981 death list nor the Gutierrez statement that the FDR would not be permitted to run were mentioned by the mass media in our sample. They never once suggested that the election *plan* was to create an electoral environment of extreme coercion and bias in which the rebels could not run, and then use this for the dramatic game of disruption and triumphant turnout. That the military agreed to the election because it couldn't lose was never suggested by these media.

The role of the army was summarized by Warren Hoge in the *New York Times:*

> Is the military playing any role in the election? Members of the military are not allowed to vote, and the armed forces are pledged to protect voters from violence and to respect the outcome of the contest.[71]

We may note that the army's mass killing of civilians and systematic destruction and demobilization of virtually all popular organizations in El Salvador over the preceding thirty months, which bears on what Secretary of State Shultz referred to as the "preliminary aspects that make an election mean something," is not part of the army's "role" for Hoge and the *Times.* Hoge repeats the Salvadoran army's pledge, not only taking it at face value, but never suggesting that it (and the election itself) was meaningless in a terror state where the "main opposition" was off the ballot and only the war parties were able to field candidates. In the propaganda framework, the security forces of client states "protect elections";[72] only those of enemy states interfere with the freedom of its citizens to vote without constraint.

As noted earlier, observers and reporters in El Salvador all agreed that the populace was most eager for an end to the war, and government propaganda even stressed that voting was an important vehicle to that end—the public was urged to substitute "ballots for bullets." But no peace party was on the Salvadoran ballot. And after the election was over, the war went on, and the death squads continued to flourish. This is in accordance with the hypothesis that the real purpose of the election was to placate the home population of the United States and render them willing to fund more war and terror. It is a poor fit to the hypothesis that the people of El Salvador had a free choice. An honest press would point up the failure of the election to substitute "ballots for bullets." The mass media of the United States did not raise the issue.

Nor did the experience of 1982 and its aftermath affect the media's willingness to follow the patriotic agenda once again in 1984. We will return to this below in a statistical comparison of the *New York Times*'s coverage of the Salvadoran and Nicaraguan elections.

3.5. "FIRST STEP: GUATEMALA OPTS FOR MODERATION"[73]

The U.S. government was less deeply involved in the Guatemalan elections of 1984 and 1985 than it was in those held in El Salvador, but, as we saw in chapter 2, the Reagan administration went to great pains to put a favorable gloss on the murderous regimes of Lucas García, Ríos Montt, and Mejía Víctores, and to attempt to reintegrate them fully into the free-world alliance.[74] It encouraged the 1984–85 elections, provided advisory and financial support for election management, and gave public-relations assistance and sent official observers to help put the election in a favorable light. There was little effort made to disguise the fact that the purpose of the election, from the standpoint of the Reagan administration and the ruling army, was to alter the international "image" of Guatemala in order to facilitate aid and loans.

With the administration supporting the new look, but without the intensity of commitment and propaganda backup brought to bear in El Salvador, and given the steady stream of reports of ongoing mass murder in Guatemala, a propaganda model would anticipate a media response that put the Guatemalan elections in a favorable light, but with qualifications. There was, in fact, far less coverage than of the Salvadoran election; what there was had a little more "balance," but the apologetic framework was still overwhelmingly dominant.

A telling manifestation of bias was the media's ready acceptance of the Guatemalan elections as meaningful, even though they were admittedly for image-making, in a context of long-standing army rule and massacre, and despite new institutional arrangements in the countryside—the massive relocations of the population, the "model villages," and the civil-defense patrols—that were, on their face, incompatible with a free election. In an enemy state where an election was held under comparable conditions, it would be designated a meaningless public-relations exercise.[75] In the case of Guatemala, however, the civil patrols and ongoing massacres were rarely mentioned, sources that addressed these matters were ignored, and the overall tone of the news was cautiously hopeful and optimistic. It was the consensus that the 1984 election for a constituent assembly was "encouraging" and an important first step, and that the 1985 presidential election "*ended* [emphasis added] more than 30 years of military domination" (*Newsweek*, Jan. 17, 1986). Dan Rather, on CBS News, reported that Cerezo became Guatemala's "first civilian leader after thirty years of almost uninterrupted military rule" (Dec. 9, 1985). This is ambiguous, but the implication, directly asserted by *Newsweek*, is that Cerezo, not the army, *rules*. Julio Méndez Montenegro was a civilian president from 1966 to 1970, but he did not rule, and he was eventually discredited by the fact that he presided over a huge escalation of army violence. Given the earlier experience, the fact that the generals had made it clear that the civilian government was "a project" of the military,[76] and Cerezo's own expressed reservations about his power, objective news reporting would have been careful about an alleged *ending* of military rule.

As in the case of El Salvador, the murderous rule of the Guatemalan generals did not delegitimize them for the U.S. mass media nor suggest any possible justice to the rebel cause. *Time* noted (Feb. 27, 1984) that a leftist insurgency "poses a permanent challenge to the regime," but it did not inquire into the roots of this insurgency or suggest that its leaders constituted a "main opposition" whose ability to run would be an "acid test" of election integrity (as they pronounced in Nicaragua). *Time* also did not observe that the regime poses a permanent challenge to the survival of its population. The mass murders of the Guatemalan state were even semi-justified by the unquestioned need to quell insurgents—"Much of the killing," says *Time*, "is linked to Mejía's success against the insurgents." The phrase "linked to" is an apologetic euphemism to obscure the fact that Mejía's "success" was based on the mass murder of men, women, and children in literally hundreds of destroyed villages.[77] Mejía has a "mixed record," with the mass murder offset by "improvements in some important areas" (the State Department, quoted by *Time*). Mejía, says *Time*, "won support because he has kept the promises he made after seizing power." *Time* never explains how it determined that Mejía "won support," or from whom, other than the U.S. State Department. Was the press then free to speak out? Did a system of justice come into being?

In chapter 2 we summarized Americas Watch's demonstration that the Reagan administration made serial adjustments in its apologetics for each successive Guatemalan terrorist general, *with a lagged, tacit acknowledgment that it had previously been lying.* This has no influence whatsoever on *Time*'s treatment of State Department pronouncements as authentic truth—the standard from which other claims may be evaluated. Thus *Time* says that "Americas Watch, a controversial group that is often accused of being too sympathetic to the left, called Guatemala 'a nation of prisoners.' " *Time* doesn't independently evaluate the quality of sources—the State Department is unchallenged because it expounds the official and patriotic truth. Americas Watch is denigrated (and only rarely cited, even with a dismissing put-down) because it challenges official propaganda. *Pravda* could hardly be more subservient to state demands than *Time* in its coverage of demonstration elections.[78]

The mass media's sourcing on the Guatemalan election was confined almost entirely to U.S. officials and official observers, the most prominent Guatemalan political candidates, and generals. Spokespersons for the insurgents—what in Nicaragua would be labeled the "main opposition"—the smaller parties, spokespersons for popular organizations, the churches, human-rights groups, and ordinary citizens, were essentially ignored by the media. *Time, Newsweek* and CBS News almost never talked to ordinary citizens or spokespersons for the insurgents. Stephen Kinzer, in the *Times,* had only one citation to a rebel source in several dozen articles on Guatemala during the election periods, although on election day in 1984 he did speak with a number of ordinary citizens (who gave a much less optimistic view than Kinzer's usual sources).

The restricted menu of media sources flows from and reinforces the media's propensity to adopt a patriotic agenda. U.S. government officials and observers are always optimistic and hopeful in their statements about sponsored elections. The leading contestant politicians are also moderately optimistic, as they have a good chance of acquiring at least nominal power. They do, however, express occasional doubts about whether the army will relinquish power. This allows the election drama to assume a slightly different character from that in El Salvador, where it was the democratic army "protecting the election" versus the undemocratic rebels who refused to lay down their arms and participate. In Guatemala, the frame was: Will the generals keep their promise to stay in the barracks? The triumph is that they *do* stay in the barracks—a civilian president takes office and now "rules." The media then quickly drop the subject, so that whether the army really does relinquish power to the civilian leaders is never checked out (just as the "peace" sought by the populace in El Salvador was never considered in retrospect). In Poland, in January 1947, and Nicaragua, in 1984, and in enemy states generally, the focus was on the *substance* of power, and the extent to which that power shaped the electoral results in advance, as by limiting the ability of important constituencies to run for office and compete effectively. Not so for Guatemala.

If the mass media had enlarged their sources, fundamental conditions would have assumed greater prominence. For example, before both the July 1, 1984, and December 1985 elections in Guatemala, the Guatemala Bishops' Conference issued pastoral statements that suggested in no uncertain terms and with detailed arguments that conditions in the country were incompatible with a free election. Its pastoral letter of June 8, 1984, focused on the civil-defense patrols as "susceptible to manipulation," and it discussed the disappearances, "insatiable corruption," and the fact that sociopolitical structures are "not capable of promoting the welfare of the whole society."[79] Stephen Kinzer mentioned this report in a *Times* news article of July 22, 1984, but his reference is made *after* the election of July 1, and Kinzer did not use it to frame the discussion of electoral conditions and to arrive at an assessment of the quality of the election. Furthermore, his summary of the twenty-seven-page report, that it "denounced torture, electoral fraud, concentration of wealth and 'massacres of entire families,'" ignores the quite specific critique of the conditions bearing on an election. *Time* mentioned this pastoral letter briefly; *Newsweek* and CBS News never mentioned it.

In connection with the 1985 election, the bishops put forth another powerful statement, once again questioning whether an election can be meaningful in "a situation close to slavery and desperation."[80] They point out that the civil-defense patrols, the "ideology of national security," and hunger and impoverishment are not conducive to serious elections:

> In order that the longed-for results be obtained, there must be not only the freedom at the moment of casting one's vote, but also a whole series of particular social, political and economic conditions which are, unfortunately, not happening in Guatemala. In effect there still persist in Guatemala harsh violence, lack of respect for human rights and the breaking of basic laws. It is a fact that any citizen pressured, terrorized or threatened is not fully able to exercise his/her right to vote or to be elected conscientiously.

This letter was not mentioned in the major media or anywhere else, to our knowledge, although the bishops are conservative, credible, and one of the few organized bodies in Guatemala not crushed by state terror.

There were other dissenting voices in Guatemala—politicians of the lesser parties, union officials, human-rights groups, lawyers, and jurists—who spoke out occasionally on the limits to free electoral conditions in Guatemala. And there were events of note that threw a powerful light on the subject. Most of these were blacked out in the U.S. mass media. For example,[81] on July 4, 1984, the Guatemalan Human Rights Commission issued a statement in Mexico saying that the election's meaning should be viewed in the context of three important facts: namely, that the requirements for a meaningful election stipulated by the United Nations in a March 14 statement had not been met; that the left had been excluded from participation in the election; and that 115 persons had been murdered or disappeared in the thirty days prior to the election of July 1. This statement, and the facts cited by the commission, were ignored in the U.S. press.

Consider also the following facts: On May 3, General Oscar Mejía Víctores removed Ricardo Sagastume Vidaure from his position as president of the judiciary and the supreme court. On April 11, the judiciary had issued writs of habeas corpus on behalf of 157 kidnapped individuals, and Sagastume had protested to Mejía Víctores over the difficulty in proceeding against military abuses. On May 4, Acisco Valladares Molina, head of the Populist party, noted that Sagastume had been "fired like a simple subordinate." On May 8, a communiqué from the Guatemalan bar association stated that in Guatemala there is no rule of law, as demonstrated by the constant violation of human rights and uncontrolled exercise of arbitrary power. By May 8, at least sixteen judicary officials, including supreme court and court of appeals magistrates, had resigned in protest at Sagustume's removal.

Stephen Kinzer never discussed any of these events, or their meaning, in the *Times,* nor did any of his colleagues elsewhere in the mass media. This is in accord with our hypothesis that in elections held in client states, fundamental electoral conditions, such as the presence or absence of the rule of law, are off the agenda. The point applies to other relevant structural conditions. Thus, while Kinzer occasionally mentioned the civil-defense patrols, he never described them and their operations in any detail or tied them in with other institutional structures of control, and he failed to relate them in a systematic way to army power. The numerous reports on these coercive institutions and their terrorist role by Amnesty International, Americas Watch, and the British Parliamentary Human Rights Group were almost never cited by Kinzer in providing facts relevant to the Guatemalan elections. Although the constituent assembly elected in 1984 produced a new constitution, Kinzer never once discussed the nature of this instrument, which validated the special army role and structural constraints on freedom of the press.

Kinzer was reporting news in a way that fit the *Times*'s editorial position and the U.S. government agenda. The *Times* editorial frame was that "The military, in power for most of 31 years, has honored its promise to permit the free election of a civilian president."[82] Kinzer's news articles of the same period convey the same message—one of them is entitled "After 30 Years Democracy Gets a Chance in Guatemala" (Nov. 10, 1985)—which accurately summarizes the contents, although they contain an undercurrent of reserved final judgment. That central message was false, however, if the basic conditions of a free election were not met, if the army's power remained unimpaired, and if these were confirmed in a written constitution that allows the army freedom from the rule of law and a license to kill without constraint from the nominal "democracy."[83] Kinzer could only convey this false message by ignoring the Sagastume case, the institutional arrangements of the counterinsurgency state, the ongoing murders, and the omnipresent fear—i.e., the basic conditions of a free election—and by laying stress instead on expressions of hope, orderliness of the election processes, and army promises—i.e., the government's propaganda agenda in a demonstration election.

In what must be one of the low points of his journalistic career, in an article of December 27, 1985 ("Guatemala Vote Heartens Nicaragua Parties"), Kinzer even implies that the Guatemala election establishes an electoral model for Nicaragua. He describes a Cerezo visit to Nicaragua, in which Kinzer features the encouragement Cerezo gives to the dissident parties that perhaps the power of the Sandinistas can be broken by patience (implying that Cerezo had broken the power of the army in Guatemala and was in full command). The article closes with a quote from an opposition figure: "Ortega is now the last President in Central America who wears a military uniform, and the contrast is going to be evident." Nowhere in the article does Kinzer point out that army power can not be read from whether the head of state wears a uniform, or that the rule of the army in Guatemala has not yet been overcome. He does not refer to the fact that the Guatemalan army has killed tens of thousands of ordinary civilians. Nor does he show any recognition of the fact that the election held in Nicaragua was much more open than that held in Guatemala. On the contrary, this is a fact that the media, including the *New York Times,* explicitly and consistently deny, in accordance with state imperatives.

As in the case of El Salvador, the U.S. mass media never suggested that the exclusion of the Guatemalan insurgent groups rendered the Guatemalan election meaningless. Kinzer several times mentioned with extreme brevity that the left was off the ballot, but he never asked anybody to discuss the meaning of this in terms of the options available to the various segments of society. As coauthor of an important book on this topic, Kinzer is well aware of the facts.[84] The vast majority of Guatemalans are very poor, and they have been entirely excluded from political participation or representation since 1954. The insurgency grew out of the parlous condition and exploitation of that mass, and the absence of any possibility of a democratic process to alleviate injustice and misery. The ruling army had allowed only parties to run and civilians to hold office who agreed, tacitly or explicitly, to keep off the policy agenda all matters of central concern to the impoverished majority. There is no way to measure the strength of popular support for the insurgents, but in light of the fact that they espouse programs well oriented to the interests of the general population and have been able to maintain an insurgency without significant external aid, and that the army response has been a war against virtually the entire rural population, the rebel claim to be a "main opposition" would appear to be stronger than that of Arturo Cruz and his upper-class Nicaraguan associates. And if the rebels—or any candidates who would threaten the army and oligarchy in ways appealing to the majority—cannot qualify in a Guatemalan election, is it not essentially fraudulent? This was strongly suggested in both 1984 and 1985 by the Guatemalan Bishops' Conference, but this respectable source, in contrast with Arturo Cruz and Robert Leiken, is blacked out. As with El Salvador, the election was not evaluated, either in advance or in retrospect, on the basis of whether or not the fundamental requirements of a free election were met. For the U.S. government, the insurgents were not a main opposition, Guatemalan state terror was merely a public-relations inconvenience, and the elections were fair. The mass media's treatment of the Guatemalan election reflected well this government propaganda agenda.

3.6. NICARAGUA: MEDIA SERVICE IN THE DELEGITIMIZING PROCESS

In contrast with the Salvadoran and Guatemalan cases, the Reagan administration was intent on discrediting the Nicaraguan election, which threatened to legitimize the Sandinista government and thus weaken the case for U.S. funding of a terrorist army. The administration had been berating the Sandinistas for failing to hold an election, but the actual holding of one was inconvenient. From the inception of Nicaraguan planning for the election, therefore, the administration began to express doubts about its quality. And just as it devoted itself to creating a positive image of the two client-state elections, so it expended substantial resources to depict the Nicaraguan election in the worst possible light. The media dutifully followed course, as a propaganda model predicts.

The mass media failed to call attention to the cynicism of first assailing Nicaragua for failing to hold an election, and then striving to have the election either postponed or discredited.[85] *Time* even cites the absence of "official delegations [of observers] from the major western democracies" (Nov. 19, 1984), as if this were evidence of something discreditable in the election, rather than as a reflection of U.S. power. There were 450-odd foreign observers in attendance at the Nicaraguan election, some with superb credentials, observing more freely and at greater length than the official U.S. observers in El Salvador and Guatemala. *Time* and the rest of the mass media paid no attention to them.[86]

Stephen Kinzer's use of observers is noteworthy. In the case of Nicaragua, he completely ignored the unofficial observers—many exceedingly well qualified to observe, as we have noted—and he even ignored the official Dutch government team, drawn from the center-right and highly apologetic about atrocities in El Salvador, which observed both the Salvadoran and the Nicaraguan elections and concluded that the elections in Nicaragua "were more open than in El Salvador, in the sense that more people were able to take part; that the opposition did not fear for their lives"; and that "the legitimation of the regime is thus confirmed."[87] In Guatemala, by contrast, he cited the official observer report in both the 1984 and 1985 elections, despite their great bias and superficiality (see the report discussed in appendix 1). In the 1984 Guatemala election, Kinzer did refer to the report of the unofficial Human Rights Law Group that we cited earlier, quoting their statement that the voting process was "procedurally correct," but neglecting to note here and elsewhere their numerous statements to the effect that "the greater part of the population lives in permanent fear" (p. 4), so that "procedural correctness" has little meaning.

With no U.S.-government–designated official observers available in Nicaragua, the media relied even more heavily than usual on U.S. government handouts. It is enlightening to compare this conduited propaganda of the mass media with the findings of foreign-observer teams on the scene in Nicaragua. For the purpose of this comparison, which follows, we will use two such reports. One, that of the Irish Inter-Party Parliamentary Delegation, is *The Elections in Nicaragua, November 1984*. The delegation was composed of four individuals, three from right-wing or moderate-right political parties, who spent seventeen days in Nicaragua at the time of the election. We will also use as a basis of comparison of media coverage the previously cited report of the 15-member delegation sent by the Latin American Studies Association (LASA), half of whom had had "substantial field experience" in Nicaragua itself. This delegation spent eight days in Nicaragua before the election, traveled in a rented bus, determined their own itinerary, and "spoke with anyone who we chose to approach (as well as numerous people who spontaneously approached us)."[88]

3.6.1. Tone of negativism and apathy

Time magazine hardly attempts to hide the fact that it takes its cues from Washington. It quotes John Hughes, then a public-relations man for the State Department (and previously, and subsequently, a columnist for the *Christian Science Monitor*): "It was not a very good election. . . . It was just a piece of theatre for the Sandinistas."[89] *Time* follows this cue with a series of denigrating strokes: "The Sandinistas win, as expected. . . . The Nicaraguan election mood was one of indifference. . . . The outcome was never in doubt. . . . Something of an anticlimax" (all in the issue of November 19, 1984). In an earlier article (October 29), *Time* indulged in the same negative refrain: "A campaign without suspense," voters "too apathetic to go to the polls at all" (this was a forecast dredged up well before the election). In both articles, "fear" was also featured heavily. In the Salvadoran election, *Time*'s tone was different: "There was no denying the remarkable sense of occasion" (i.e., the Reagan administration had a big public-relations investment in the election); "hundreds of thousands . . . braved the threats, and sometimes the bullets, of the Marxist-led [FMLN] to join long serpentine polling lines for the country's much awaited presidential elections" (Apr. 9, 1984).[90] In Guatemala too, "Some 1.8 million voters braved four-hour polling lines, tropical rainstorms and a bewildering array of political choices to cast ballots in their country's most open and fraud-free elections in more than a decade" (July 16, 1984). There is never apathy or fear of *government* force in *Time*'s renditions of demonstration elections.

Stephen Kinzer, in the *Times,* also took a far less kindly view of the election in Nicaragua than of those in Guatemala, giving enormous attention to election opponents like the U.S. candidate Arturo Cruz (whereas in Guatemala he almost completely ignored the small parties, union protesters, rebels, and human-rights groups), and finding more people voting out of fear than he did in Guatemala, a remarkable discovery given the circumstances in the two countries.[91] He focuses steadily on the Sandinistas' efforts to get out the vote, the fact that the election result is a foregone conclusion, claims of the breaking up of election rallies, and allegations of unfairness and withdrawals by the opposition. As with *Time,* the voters are "philosophical," "enthusiasm for the election was not universal," and "there was little visible enthusiasm." Kinzer did not compare the electoral modalities, range of options, or other basic conditions in Nicaragua and Guatemala (or El Salvador). In short, he discussed different questions in his news reporting on the elections in Nicaragua and Guatemala, adhering closely to the propaganda frame.[92]

On the alleged negativism and apathy, both the Irish and LASA delegations noted that voting was not required in Nicaragua and was entirely secret. Therefore, as the Irish delegation pointed out, the low rate of abstention is more meaningful and "invalidates predictions that large sectors of the population were opposed to the election. Furthermore, the percentage of spoiled votes (7.4 percent) is comparable to any European election in a country with a highly literate population" (p. 7). They also note that

> Speaking with one old man, awaiting his turn to vote in a rural polling station, one member of the delegation inquired: "What difference do you see between this and any other election in which you voted?" He replied: "Everything." "In what way?" He simply shrugged: "Everything is different."

The U.S. media never located anybody like this old man. The Irish delegation also pointed out that

> Some observers from other countries suggested that the people did not appear enthusiastic as they went to the polls. This is not surprising as people stood in long queues waiting patiently their turn to go behind the curtain to mark their ballot paper. One member of the delegation who had the opportunity to observe voters in the American election just two days later, noted no greater enthusiasm for standing in queues there!

It is our belief that the invariable enthusiasm and optimism found by the U.S. mass media in client-state elections, and the apathy and negativism found in elections in states disfavored by the U.S. administration, has nothing to do with electoral realities and must be explained entirely by an imposed propaganda agenda and the filtering out of contrary opinion and information.

3.6.2. Ignoring the superior quality of the Nicaraguan election

In the propaganda format, a great deal of attention is paid to the mechanical properties of elections in client states, but not in states whose elections are being denigrated. This was true in the cases under discussion. *Time* (Apr. 9, 1984) described in detail the elaborate electoral preparations in El Salvador, the "tamper-proof" procedures, the use of transparent Lucite ballot boxes, and the indelible-ink marking and stamping of ID cards. It turned out, however, that the high-tech, computerized voting procedures weren't understood by the population, more than half of whom were illiterate. At no point did *Time,* or its media colleagues, raise any question about the importance of improving literacy as a necessary prelude to an election; nor did they suggest that the Lucite boxes might compromise the secrecy of the vote, or that the stamped ID card might be a coercive instrument helping to explain turnout.

Nicaragua went to great pains to provide for election secrecy, and for an easy and intelligible system of voting. For one thing, they had a massive literacy campaign before the election, making electoral printed matter generally accessible. Both the Irish and LASA delegations mention this as an electoral plus. Nicaragua also put a high priority on getting a complete registration list and getting the voters registered. The Irish delegation noted that "Recent elections in other Central American countries such as El Salvador and Guatemala did not introduce such measures, and there was considerable debate concerning the validity of their registers, which were based on out-of-date census figures, incomplete official registers of population changes, and other sources" (p. 5). Nicaragua also deliberately avoided transparent ballot boxes, ID stamping, and any other mechanism that would allow the authorities to identify whether or how somebody had voted. LASA points out that

> The ballots were also printed on heavy opaque white paper. The contrast with Somoza-era elections is striking. The Somozas used translucent ballots, so virtually everyone assumed that their ballot was not secret. The same problem occurred in the 1984 elections in El Salvador, where thin-paper ballots were deposited in transparent ballot boxes. The vote in Nicaragua in 1984 was truly a *secret* ballot (p. 14).

In Nicaragua, also, there was proportional voting, which made it possible for the smaller parties to obtain legislative representation. Parties could also qualify quite easily to participate in the election. In Guatemala, 4,000 signatures were needed to qualify in 1984, a large number and not easy for dissident parties to collect in a society with daily political murders.

Stephen Kinzer and his associates never mentioned these differences. More generally, the substantial merits of the Nicaraguan elections were never contrasted with the procedures in the U.S. client states, a comparison that would have been most revealing and that would have thoroughly undermined the Reagan agenda to which the media were committed in their reporting of the election. *Time,* as noted, mentions the compromised Salvadoran procedures as if they were meritorious. The *Times* mentioned the transparent voting boxes in El Salvador only once (Richard Meislin, on March 25, 1984), repeating without question the official line that the purpose of the translucent boxes was to prevent fraud. Any other possibility is unmentioned. *Newsweek* and CBS News ignored these matters.

3.6.3. Rebel disruption into the black hole; turnout no longer an index of triumph of democracy

In the Salvadoran election, rebel disruption was a central feature of the government's propaganda frame. Because the rebels opposed the election, voting by the people proved their rejection of the rebels and approval of the army. Turnout was the index of democratic triumph and rebel defeat. As we saw, the mass media followed this frame without question. In the case of Nicaragua, the propaganda format was reversed—the rebels were the good guys, and the election held by the bad guys was condemned in advance. Rebel opposition to the election—and efforts at disruption—did not make voting and a large turnout a repudiation of the rebels and approval of the Sandinistas.

The U.S. mass media once again followed the government agenda, *even though it meant an exact reversal of the standards they had applied in the Salvadoran election.* The contras and their supporters urged the public not to vote, and interfered with the election process with at least as much vigor as (and with more killings than) the rebels in El Salvador. Furthermore, voting was more assuredly secret and the citizens were not required to vote, or to have ID cards stamped indicating that they had. And the Sandinistas did not kill ordinary citizens on a daily basis, as was true in the "death-squad democracies." Thus turnout was far more meaningful in the Nicaraguan election than in the ones held in El Salvador and Guatemala—the public was free to abstain as well as to vote for opposition parties.

The U.S. mass media disposed of this problem mainly by massive suppression. They simply ignored the contra-U.S. campaign for abstention, waged with threats and attacks on polling places and election workers; and they buried the fact of an effectively secret vote and the right *not* to vote,[93] just as, in parallel, they had inflated rebel disruption efforts in El Salvador in 1982 and 1984 and buried the voting *requirement* and other pressures to vote.

Although the *New York Times* had gone out of its way to focus on the "challenge" of rebel opposition and alleged disruption as giving turnout special meaning in the Salvadoran election of 1982,[94] Stephen Kinzer never once mentioned that the contras attacked a number of polling stations and had issued radio appeals for abstention.[95] For Kinzer, neither these facts nor the U.S. campaign to discredit were seen as posing a "challenge" that made turnout meaningful in Nicaragua.

The Irish delegation pointed out that "The Parties of the Democratic Coordinating Committee [based in the business community] opposed the voter registration, and called for a boycott of this process" (p. 5), and it noted that eleven polling stations were closed down by counterrevolutionary activities (p. 7). The public voted in large numbers "despite the possible dangers involved," which suggested to the Irish delegation that turnout was significant and "showed how important the election was to the people" (p. 6). LASA pointed out the various ways in which the "main opposition" called for voter abstention, and cited the radio warnings broadcast into the country from Costa Rica threatening that voters would be killed by the contras (pp. 16, 28). LASA also pointed out that "voter turnout was heavy," with "more enthusiasm among voters in low-income areas than in more affluent neighborhoods."[96] Like *Time,* LASA notes that the turnout did not quite realize the expectations of FSLN officials, but unlike *Time,*

LASA points out that the rate of participation achieved "compares very favorably with the rates achieved in 11 other recent Latin American elections, as well as the 1984 U.S. presidential election . . ." (p. 16).[97]

In sum, the two observer reports discuss rebel disruption in Nicaragua, turnout, and the meaning of that turnout. The U.S. mass media, which had featured these matters heavily in reference to the Salvadoran election—where they fitted the government's propaganda agenda—found them entirely unnewsworthy as regards Nicaragua.

3.6.4. The revived sensitivity to coercion

As we described earlier, the "coercion package" was off the agenda for the U.S. government and mass media in addressing the Salvadoran and Guatemalan elections. So was the element of fear engendered by mass murder and the absence of any rule of law in these U.S. client states. Coercion and fear were back on the agenda, however, for Nicaragua. This revival was illustrated with amazing dishonesty and hypocrisy in *Time*, which had never mentioned fear and pressures from the government as factors possibly explaining turnout in the U.S.-sponsored elections, even after the murder of 50,000 civilians. In Nicaragua, however, the "pugnacious" Sandinistas had "an awesome monopoly of force," and getting them to "relax their grip," which was "essential for free electoral competition," was extremely dubious. *Time*'s Central American correspondent George Russell even located a "Latin American diplomat" who says, "You can't have democracy where there is no personal liberty at all" (Oct. 8 and May 14, 1984). Russell and *Time* had never found the Salvadoran government "pugnacious," with any "awesome monopoly of force," or as having a "grip" that needed relaxing for electoral competition, and personal liberty was never mentioned as lacking or even pertinent to Salvadoran elections. For the Nicaraguan election, however, *Time* found that "The pressure to participate was high: many citizens feared they would lose precious rationing cards." Further, "the government had made it clear that it considered failure to vote a counterrevolutionary stance." Later, quoting Daniel Ortega, "All Nicaraguans who are Nicaraguans are going to vote. The only ones who are not going to vote are sellouts" (Nov. 19, 1984).

As we pointed out earlier, both the Guatemalan and Salvadoran army warned the public that voting was required by law and that nonvoting was treasonous. These statements were more precisely *warn-*

ings, whereas Ortega's was an insult but not a clear threat. Ortega's was the only such statement of its kind reported, and *Time*'s statement that the government "made it clear" that nonvoting was "counterrevolutionary" is doubly dishonest—the statement was not clearly a warning, and "counterrevolutionary" is an invidious word concocted by *Time.* The official government position *as expressed in the law* was that Nicaraguans did not have to vote. *Time* suppresses this fact. It suppresses the secrecy of the ballot and absence of a checkable ID card, so that there would have been no way to implement a threat even if one had been made. It suppresses the fact that the Nicaraguan army did not regularly murder even "counterrevolutionaries," whereas the Salvadoran and Guatemalan armies murdered numerous people who weren't "revolutionaries" but were somehow in the way. In short, propaganda could hardly be more brazen.

Time's alleged "fact," that "many" people feared the removal of the rationing card, is contested by LASA, which states that "in our interviews in many neighborhoods in several cities, we found no evidence that ration cards were being held back or withdrawn . . . for *any* reason." They note that there were five reports filed with the supreme electoral council alleging intimidation by threat of withdrawal of ration cards, "but none of these allegations were sustained upon investigation" (p. 27). *Time* does not indicate the source of its evidence and fails to provide a single illustration of the "many" cases.

We noted earlier that Stephen Kinzer cited more claims of coercion in the Nicaraguan than the Guatemalan elections, a remarkable journalistic achievement, given the unchallenged facts about the actual scale and character of repression in the two states. His playing down of state terror in Guatemala as a basic factor affecting the quality of the election in all its dimensions—the ability of candidates to run, freedom of speech and press, the existence of intermediate groups, endemic fear, and the meaning of turnout—amounts to massive deceit. His Nicaraguan coverage also involved large-scale misrepresentation. He did not point out the *absence* of mass killings, and he failed to mention the absence of a coercion package—no transparent boxes, no requirement that an ID card be stamped, and no legal obligation to vote. Kinzer's one notice of the voting requirement in his fourteen articles on the election amounts to serious deception—he quotes a voter as follows: " 'I've always voted because it is always required,' he said. 'Of course, the law says one thing, but after a while one realizes that voting is part of patriotism, and patriotism leads to long life.' "[98] Kinzer's source implies but doesn't say directly that voting is not legally required in Nicaragua, and this murky statement—the closest Kinzer ever comes to acknowledging the absence of a voting requirement—is counterbalanced by his respondent's suggestion that voting may be based on some kind of threat.

Both the Irish and LASA delegations stressed the superior protection of secrecy in the balloting, which, in LASA's words, was "meticulously designed to minimize the potential for abuses" (p. 15). They also emphasized the fact that voting was not required by law, and that, contrary to the U.S. government propaganda expounded by *Time* and other media entities, the coercive elements in getting out the vote were small. Human-rights abuses by the government that contribute to an environment of fear, LASA pointed out, were "on a very small scale" when "compared to other nations in the region . . ." (p. 28). In fact, they note that fear in Nicaragua is directed more to the United States and the contras than to the government in Managua.

3.6.5. The "main opposition" to the fore

As we saw, in El Salvador and Guatemala, the fact that the insurgents were off the ballot did not faze the U.S. media one bit. Neither did Duarte's acknowledgment in 1981 that "the masses were with the guerrillas" when he joined the junta a year earlier (which would clearly make them a "main opposition").[99] Nor were the media affected by the army's murder of the opposition leadership in both El Salvador and Guatemala. In El Salvador, the exclusion of the rebels was part of the U.S. government's electoral plan; they were, therefore, not a "main opposition," and the debarment and even murder of their leaders did not compromise election quality. In the Nicaraguan case, in sharp contrast, the U.S. government worked with a different frame—the exclusion of its sponsored rebels and any other candidates was a serious matter that threatened the quality of the election. The media followed like good little doggies (lap- rather than watch-).

The central dramatic propaganda line for the Nicaraguan election pressed by U.S. officials was the alleged struggle of Arturo Cruz to induce the Sandinistas to create an open system in which he would be able to compete fairly, the failure of the "Marxists-Leninists" to make adequate concessions, Cruz's refusal to compete, and the subsequent "exclusion" of the "main opposition." Cruz, however, was a "main opposition" only in the propaganda construct of the U.S. government and mass media. A longtime expatriate (who now concedes that he was on the CIA payroll), with no mass base in Nicaragua, Cruz would almost certainly have done poorly in a free election.[100] There is good reason to believe that Cruz never intended to run, but that he and his sponsors had held out this possibility precisely to allow the propaganda frame to be used effectively.[101]

The mass media focused on the Cruz drama heavily and uncritically. Cruz was given enormous play: he was continually referred to as the "main opposition" or "leading opponent" of the ruling party (without any supporting evidence), and his candidacy was made "an acid test of the Sandinistas' democratic intentions" (*Time,* Oct. 29, 1984). For the *Times,* the election would be a "sham" without Cruz (editorial, Oct. 7, 1984), and its news columns placed "main opposition" Cruz on center stage, from which vantage point he could regularly denounce the proceedings as a "farce" or sham.[102] The *Times* did have one good back-page article that provided evidence that Cruz had not intended to run or would not have been allowed to run by his closest Nicaraguan allies and U.S. officials, and that his function was, as we stated, to discredit the election by pretending to be interested, thus capturing press attention.[103] But this low-keyed article stood alone and did not alter the unremitting focus on the alleged exclusion of this alleged main opposition as the centerpiece of the Nicaraguan election drama.

In focusing on an alleged "main opposition" in Nicaragua, which voluntarily chose not to run, while ignoring a *real* main opposition in El Salvador, excluded by force and plan, the mass media simply adopted without question the government's propaganda framework. Sources that would speak to the condition of the "main opposition" in El Salvador and the significance of its exclusion—both Salvadorans and foreign observers—were simply ignored.[104] In the case of the Nicaraguan election, in contrast, Cruz and U.S. government officials were given the floor to present their themes, which were transmitted on a daily basis with no accompanying notice of their possible falsity and manipulative intent, in perfect accord with the expectations of a propaganda model.

The Reagan administration not only dangled Cruz before the media, it tried hard to induce or bribe other candidates in the Nicaraguan election to withdraw in order to fulfil the prophecy of a meaningless election. The brazenness of this intervention by a great power was remarkable, but the U.S. media gave it minimal attention. They never denounced it as antidemocratic, they failed to link it to Cruz's campaign (with its suggestion of a larger effort to discredit by boycott), and they never suggested that voter "turnout" was more meaningful given the active U.S. campaign to discredit the election. On October 31, 1984,

Stephen Kinzer noted that senior U.S. officials confirmed accounts of "regular contacts" with the Nicaraguan parties. Kinzer's article is headlined "Nicaraguan Parties Cite Sandinista and U.S. Pressure," the headline and article itself equating the government's aid to, and agreements with, its own political parties with U.S. intervention to get the Nicaraguan parties to boycott the election! CBS, *Newsweek*, and *Time* ignored the U.S. bribe program entirely. *Time* gave great emphasis to the number of candidates and the withdrawal of several, but it never once mentioned that this was helped along by U.S. connivance, bribes, and pressure. It even quotes without comment the State Department fabrication that "it did not try to influence the outcome of the election" (Nov. 19, 1984). All substantive evidence is placed in the black hole. In the same article, *Time* asserts that "the U.S. had pushed hard for elections in which all parties felt free to participate," a fabrication of considerable audacity.

As regards the scope of electoral options in Nicaragua, the Irish delegation noted that "The [political parties] law guarantees participation to political parties of all ideologies," an interesting point validated by a range of political opinion in the contesting parties far wider than that found in El Salvador and Guatemala (or the United States).

LASA states that "No major political tendency in Nicaragua was denied access to the electoral process in 1984" (p. 18). This, of course, could not be said of El Salvador and Guatemala. These important features of the Nicaraguan law and practice were not mentioned in the U.S. media or compared with those of the client states.

The Irish delegation stressed two facts about Cruz as the "main opposition." First,

> The delegation found no evidence that these parties [the three small Cruz-related parties that boycotted the election] had wide support within the country. Speaking with many political figures, including representatives of the legitimate opposition parties, it became clear that the intention of Arturo Cruz to stand for election was dubious from the start. . . . While considerable coverage was given to these parties in the international press, members of the delegation found that their impact among the population was scant and few people supported their policies (p. 7).

Second, the Irish delegation stressed the fact that the populace was free *not* to vote or to spoil votes, and the low level of both, "despite the abstentionism promoted by" the Cruz parties, deflated their claims to any serious support (p. 7). The LASA report reached similar conclusions, based on an extensive review of the evidence, namely: (1) that "circumstantial evidence" indicates the strong probability that Cruz had no intention of running, and (2) that he had no mass base and would have been badly beaten.

In retrospect, Kinzer concedes the fact, although with the customary propaganda twist. He writes that "Ortega's landslide victory was never in doubt," because "the opposition was splintered" (and, as he fails to observe, had no popular base, in contrast to the well-organized Sandinista party), and "because the Sandinistas controlled the electoral machinery." Neither he nor anyone else has offered a particle of evidence that Sandinista control over the electoral machinery made the elections a sham, or to contest the conclusion of the LASA delegation that "the FSLN did little more to take advantage of its incumbency than incumbent parties everywhere (including the United States) routinely do." A few days earlier, Kinzer had quoted Arturo Cruz as observing that the Sandinistas deserve credit for having overthrown Somoza and "having broken barriers in Nicaragua that had to be broken, and that is irreversible," because "the Sandinistas were working in the catacombs while we in the traditional opposition were out of touch with the rising expectations of the masses." As Kinzer knows, but will not write, the same was true at the time of the 1984 elections, which is why the Sandinista victory was never in doubt. This deceitful dismissal of the 1984 elections is one of Kinzer's many contributions to the media campaign to contrast the "elected presidents" of the four Central American "democracies" with the Sandinista dictator Ortega, not an elected president by U.S. government imprimatur. The specific context was the massive media campaign to attribute the failures of the Guatemala City peace agreement of August 1987 to the Sandinistas, in accordance with Reagan administration priorities, on the eve of the crucial congressional vote on renewed contra aid.[105]

LASA also stresses the fact that Cruz—effectively representing the contras, a segment of the local business community, and the United States—could have run in the Nicaraguan election, with excellent funding, ample media access, and without fear of being murdered. Even without Cruz the contras had an electoral voice. LASA notes that

> We know of no election in Latin America (or elsewhere) in which groups advocating the violent overthrow of an incumbent government have themselves been incorporated into the electoral process, particularly when these groups have been openly supported by a foreign power. The *contras* nevertheless had a voice in the 1984 election campaign. Two of the Coordinadora-affiliated par-

> ties, the PSD and the PLC, supported their inclusion in the elections. And while denying that they represented the *contras*, Arturo Cruz and the Coordinadora seemed to endorse and promote their cause, both within Nicaragua and abroad (p. 18).

LASA also discusses in some detail the U.S. intervention in the election, noting the terrorizing overflights by U.S. planes during the election campaign, and considering at some length the U.S. efforts to induce the withdrawal of candidates. LASA reported the claims by both Liberal and Conservative party figures that the United States offered specific and large sums of money to get candidates to withdraw from the election.

3.6.6. The concern over freedom of the press and assembly

Not only the rights of any and all candidates to run for public office, but other basic conditions that had been off the agenda in El Salvador and Guatemala were of deep concern to the U.S. government and mass media in reference to Nicaragua. The *New York Times, Time, Newsweek*, and CBS News all put great stress on the trials and tribulations of *La Prensa*,[106] although during the Salvadoran election none of them had even mentioned the destruction by physical violence and murder of *La Crónica* and *El Independiente*, or the toll of murdered journalists. Mob violence allegedly organized by the government, and the threat of the neighborhood defense committees, were featured by *Time* in Nicaragua, whereas ORDEN and the death squads in El Salvador and Guatemala it had never mentioned as pertinent to election quality. Basic conditions of a free election were not only back on the media agenda, but there were strong suggestions that Nicaragua was failing to meet these conditions. These suggestions were based almost entirely on quotes from U.S. officials and Cruz and his allies in Nicaragua. The media never gave evidence of having actually looked into these matters for themselves or tapped independent sources of evidence.

Richard Wagner, on CBS News (Nov. 3, 1984), citing as usual Arturo Cruz as the "strongest opposition," also mobilizes a single Nicaraguan citizen (no doubt selected at random) who says: "How can this be free elections [*sic*] when we don't have freedom of speech, freedom of the press?" Wagner says that "In addition to censorship" there were food shortages, a deteriorated transportation system, an unpopular draft, and church opposition, so that "it becomes apparent why a free and open election is not in the cards." The cynicism in failing to raise the question of *why* there are food shortages and a deteriorated transportation system in Nicaragua is remarkable. Wagner also misses another distinction between Nicaragua and El Salvador; the former has an "unpopular draft," whereas in the terror state of El Salvador there is no draft—instead there is press-ganging of young men into the army from the slums, refugee camps, and rural areas, while the young sons of the wealthy live the high life in San Salvador and Miami (much the same is true in Guatemala and Honduras). Wagner's double standard is also remarkable. In El Salvador in 1982 and 1984 there was far more severe censorship (including outright murder), food shortages, a deteriorating transport system, and church opposition—and more pertinent, a complete exclusion of the "main opposition" and massive state terror—but these didn't make it apparent to CBS News that a free and open election was not in the cards in that U.S.-sponsored election.[107]

The Irish delegation and LASA, especially the latter, addressed these issues, gave evidence of having examined them seriously, and came up with conclusions sharply at odds with the U.S. government–media portrayals. LASA provided an extensive discussion of the Sandinista defense committees and the scope of the *turba* violence and interference with freedom of assembly, concluding that the total number of disruptive incidents reported was "quite small," and that the most serious occurred before the official campaign began. "In spite of Daniel Ortega's unfortunate statement on these disruptions, there is no evidence that the FSLN had a coherent strategy of stimulating or orchestrating them" (p. 24). As regards the defense committees, LASA concluded that they did not seem to be functioning as a spying network and that there was no serious evidence that they were a force making for intimidation (p. 27). LASA makes two additional points ignored by the free press. One is that the electoral commission "placed paid advertisements in the press urging citizens to respect the rights of all political parties to hold rallies without interference" (p. 24). The second is that the Cruz rallies that were disrupted were held in violation of the electoral law, which requires permits for campaign rallies and promises police protection. "In other words, given their decision not to register, Cruz and the Coordinadora were deliberately campaigning outside of the legal framework of protections which had been created by the electoral law" (p. 25). LASA also compares the violence in the Nicaraguan election with that elsewhere in the area and in the Nicaraguan context, concluding that "compared to other nations in the region and in the face of a war against the contras, such abuses are on a very small scale" (p. 28).

LASA also discussed freedom of the press, which it regards as one of the election's most troublesome features. It considers the imposition of press censorship to have been damaging to the election's quality and credibility, even though the argument of the Sandinistas, that a country at war "can't allow a newspaper which is the instrument of the enemy to publish its opinions freely" (Sergio Ramírez), is viewed as not wholly unreasonable. Nevertheless, while the censorship was also somewhat arbitrary and legalistic, LASA concluded that "The opposition could and did get its message out" (p. 26). And the finding overall was that the Nicaraguan election "by Latin American standards was a model of probity and fairness" (p. 32).

The U.S. mass media did not concur, but it is striking how they avoid comparisons and data. The way in which the media can denounce restrictions on freedom of the press in Nicaragua after having totally ignored the question in El Salvador, where restrictions were far more severe, is remarkable. This process of dichotomization is so internalized that the writers use the double standard within the same article, apparently unaware of their own bias. In an article in the *New York Times* of March 12, 1984, "Clear Choices in Salvador, Murky Plans in Nicaragua," Hedrick Smith regards the choices as "clear" in El Salvador, whereas in Nicaragua the problem is whether in an election the Sandinistas will "give up significant power and control." Multiple parties from the far right to the center-right in El Salvador demonstrate clear choices, but a variety of parties from right to far left in Nicaragua didn't cause Smith to perceive real choices there, although he didn't explain why. It apparently never occurs to Smith that there is an issue of whether the army and United States "will give up power and control" (and their determination to fight to victory) by the electoral route in El Salvador.

Are there essential freedoms and absence of coercion in El Salvador that are necessary for a truly free election? Hedrick Smith talks about substantive electoral conditions *only* in Nicaragua. He provides extensive detail on the trials of *La Prensa,* press censorship, the Sandinista monopoly of power, and limits allegedly imposed on opposition candidates in Nicaragua. Not a word, however, on death-squad and army murders of civilians in El Salvador or the Draconian laws of the state of siege. How many journalists have been killed in El Salvador? Papers closed? Radio stations blown up? Union leaders and political figures murdered? These questions are off the agenda in U.S.-staged elections, and Hedrick Smith ignores them. As a de facto spokesman for his government, the *Times* commentator uses doublethink with as much insouciance as Reagan and Shultz.

3.7. QUANTITATIVE EVIDENCE OF SYSTEMATIC MEDIA BIAS

To demonstrate more rigorously the structural bias in media coverage of Third World elections, tables 3-1, 3-2, and 3-3 compare the topics mentioned in the *New York Times* in its articles on the Nicaraguan and Salvadoran elections of 1984. The tables are organized according to the U.S. government agenda described earlier. The elements in the upper part of the tables are the approved issues—rebel disruption, personalities, election mechanics, etc.—that the government wishes to stress in its sponsored elections. Below the line are the basic conditions and other negative elements that are off the agenda in sponsored elections. Our hypothesis is that the media will follow the agenda, stressing personalities and other elements above the line in sponsored elections and playing down basic conditions, whereas in elections like that in Nicaragua the agenda will be reversed—the stress will be placed on basic conditions.

TABLE 3-1

Topics Included and Excluded in the *New York Times*'s Coverage of the Salvadoran Election of March 25, 1984*

TOPICS	NUMBER OF ARTICLES DEALING WITH TOPIC	PERCENTAGE OF ARTICLES DEALING WITH TOPIC
Those compatible with the U.S. government's agenda for the Salvadoran election:		
1. Democratic purpose and hopes	6	21.4
2. Rebel disruption	15	53.6

TOPICS	NUMBER OF ARTICLES DEALING WITH TOPIC	PERCENTAGE OF ARTICLES DEALING WITH TOPIC
3. Turnout	7	25.0
4. Election mechanics	9	32.1
5. Personalities and political infighting	10	35.7
6. Official reflections on the election	10	35.7
7. The army as protector of the election	5	17.9
Those incompatible with the U.S. government's agenda for the Salvadoran election:		
8. The public-relations purpose	3	10.7
9. U.S. investment in the election	2	7.1
10. Fraud in the 1982 election	0	0
11. The existence of free speech and assembly—legal state of siege	1	3.6
12. Freedom of the press	0	0
13. Organizational freedom	0	0
14. Limits on the ability of candidates to qualify and campaign	0	0
15. Prior state terror and climate of fear	3	10.7
16. Power of armed forces, links to candidates and parties, as possible negative factor	1	3.6
17. Legal obligation to vote	4	14.3
18. Legal penalties for nonvoting	2	7.1
19. Marking of voters' fingers	1	3.6
20. Stamping identification cards	2	7.1
21. Legal requirement that authorities check within 10 days, that voters have voted	0	0
22. Possible nonlegal threat to nonvoters from death squads and security forces	0	0

TOPICS	NUMBER OF ARTICLES DEALING WITH TOPIC	PERCENTAGE OF ARTICLES DEALING WITH TOPIC
23. Use of transparent voting urns	1	3.6
24. Legal right of the security forces to an armed presence at voting stations	0	0

* Based on a study of the 28 articles on the El Salvador election that appeared in the *New York Times* between Feb. 1 and Mar. 30, 1984.

TABLE 3-2

Topics Included and Excluded in the *New York Times*'s Coverage of the Nicaraguan Election Planned for November 4, 1984*

TOPICS	NUMBER OF ARTICLES DEALING WITH TOPIC	PERCENTAGE OF ARTICLES DEALING WITH TOPIC
Those compatible with the U.S. government's agenda for the Nicaraguan election: (Of the 7 items in table 3-1, all are blanks except one.)		
1. Election mechanics	3	37.5
Those incompatible with the U.S. government's agenda for the Nicaraguan election:**		
2. The public-relations purpose	3	37.5
3. Free speech	2	25.0
4. Freedom of the press	6	75.0
5. Organizational freedom	4	50.0

TOPICS	NUMBER OF ARTICLES DEALING WITH TOPIC	PERCENTAGE OF ARTICLES DEALING WITH TOPIC
6. Ability of candidates to qualify and run	5	62.5
7. Power of the armed forces, link to state, as negative factor	3	37.5

* Based on a study of the 8 articles on the forthcoming Nicaraguan election that appeared in the *New York Times* between Feb. 1 and Mar. 30, 1984.

** Many of the topics listed in Table 3-1 under this subheading are not relevant to the Nicaraguan election—all that are covered in the articles examined are listed here.

TABLE 3-3

Topics Included and Excluded in the *New York Times*'s Coverage of the Nicaraguan Election of November 4, 1984*

TOPICS	NUMBER OF ARTICLES DEALING WITH TOPIC	PERCENTAGE OF ARTICLES DEALING WITH TOPIC
Those compatible with the U.S. government's agenda for the Nicaraguan election:		
1. Democratic purpose and hopes	1	4.8
2. Rebel disruption	0	0
3. Turnout	5	23.8
4. Election mechanics	0	0
5. Personalities and political infighting	3	14.3
6. Official reflections on the election	3	14.3
7. The army as protector of the election	0	0

TOPICS	NUMBER OF ARTICLES DEALING WITH TOPIC	PERCENTAGE OF ARTICLES DEALING WITH TOPIC
Those incompatible with the U.S. government's agenda for the Nicaraguan election:		
8. The public-relations purpose	7	33.3
9. Sandinista investment in the election	2	9.5
10. Fraud in prior elections	NA	NA
11. Free speech and assembly	8	38.1
12. Freedom of the press	6	28.6
13. Organizational freedom	2	9.5
14. Limits on the ability of candidates to qualify and campaign	11	52.4
15. Prior state terror and climate of fear	3	14.3
16. Control of armed forces by government	3	14.3
17. Legal obligation to vote	NA	4.8
18. Legal penalties for nonvoting	NA	NA
19. Marking of voters' fingers	1	NA
20. Stamping identification cards	NA	NA
21. Legal requirement to check voting	NA	NA
22. Nonlegal threat to nonvoters	1	4.8
23. Use of transparent voting urns	NA	NA
24. Security force presence at voting stations	NA	NA

* Based on a study of 21 news articles appearing between Sept. 5 and Nov. 6, 1984.

NA = Not Applicable

It can readily be seen in table 3-1 that in the Salvadoran election the *Times*'s news coverage dealt heavily with subjects above the line and neglected the basic conditions that make an election meaningful in advance. We can observe how the *Times* totally ignores the question of freedom of the press, organizational freedom, and limits on the ability of candidates to run.[108] Table 3-2 shows how the *Times* treated the forthcoming Nicaraguan election in the same two-month period covered in table 3-1. It is evident that the paper focuses heavily on the fundamental conditions of a free election, i.e., on topics that it was entirely ignoring while addressing the Salvadoran election. Table 3-3 shows the breakdown of topics covered by the *Times* during the Nicaraguan election later in the year. Again, although the differences are less marked than the ones in tables 3-1 and 3-2, the substantial attention to basic conditions in the Nicaraguan case is clear, reflecting editorial news choices that follow a patriotic agenda. As the basic conditions for a free election were superior in Nicaragua and the coercive elements less acute, the emphasis on basic conditions only in the Nicaraguan case is even more clearly evidence of systematic bias.

3.8. THE MIG CRISIS STAGED DURING NICARAGUA'S ELECTION WEEK

As *Newsweek* pointed out on November 19, 1984, "The story of the freighter [to Nicaragua, allegedly carrying MIGs] first broke during the election-night coverage," but at no point does *Newsweek* (or *Time*, the *Times*, or CBS News) suggest that the timing was deliberate. The *Times*, in its extensive coverage of the MIGs that weren't there, at one point quotes a Nicaraguan official who suggests that the crisis was purely a public-relations operation, but that exhausts the *Times*'s exploration of this point. Although the MIGs weren't there, and the timing was perfect for diverting attention from a successful election that the Reagan adminstration had been attempting to discredit, the elite media asked no questions, even in retrospect. The administration claimed that when the freighter was loaded, satellite observation was blocked so that the cargo was unknown. The mass media presented this as fact, making no effort to evaluate the claim.

What the media chose to focus on was administration assessments of what it might do *if* MIGs were in fact being delivered. This allowed the whole frame of discourse to shift to the assumption that the *Nicaraguans* had *done* something (and something intolerable, to boot). *Newsweek*, in a retrospective article entitled "The MIGs That Weren't There," had a lead head: "To bring in high-performance craft indicates that they are contemplating being a threat to their neighbors." The fact that the MIGs *weren't* brought in, as stated in the article's very title—that this was a concoction of U.S. officials—doesn't interfere with imputing an intention to the Nicaraguans based on a nonexistent fact. The assertion that they were contemplating being a threat, as opposed to defending themselves against a proxy invasion, is also a patriotic editorial judgment. *Newsweek* also says in the text that "All sides appeared to be playing a very clumsy and very dangerous game." This is an intriguing form of evenhandedness. A person who, admittedly, had been falsely accused of robbery by an assailant is alleged to be "playing a dangerous game," along with the attacker who is also the bearer of false witness.[109]

In the middle of an article on the Nicaraguan election, *Time* inserts the government claim that a ship carrying crates of the type used to transport MIG-21s was due at a Nicaraguan port. *Time* never questions a government propaganda ploy, no matter how blatant, and it offers a retrospective only when the government tacitly concedes it had deliberately deceived. Like *Newsweek* and the *Times, Time* allows the government to set the agenda with a public-relations statement: *if* the Nicaraguans did this, it would be a challenge to the United States. How then would we react, what are our policy options, etc. The truth of the claim and the likelihood that this is a manipulative ploy to help remove the unwanted elections from attention are not discussed; and, naturally, the fact that this is part of a policy of aggression against a tiny victim is never raised.

The only credits in the media coverage of the MIG crisis go to CBS News. On November 6, Dan Rather gave the straight administration "news" that MIGs might be on their way and that a strategic option to destroy them was under consideration. On November 7 and 8, however, perhaps out of a recognition that it had once again been "used," CBS gave substantial coverage to Nicaraguan Foreign Minister Miguel D'Escoto's rebuttal, which allowed him to point out the absurdity of the Nicaraguan "threat," the tie-in of the MIG claims to the Nicaraguan election, and the U.S. refusal to go along with the Contadora peace proposals.

The MIG ploy was, nevertheless, entirely successful. A tone of crisis was manufactured, and "options" against the hypothetical Sandinista "threat" were placed at the center of public attention. The Nicaraguan election was not discussed. LASA points out that "The final results of Nicaragua's election were not even reported by most of the international media. They were literally buried under an avalanche of alarmist news reports" (p. 31). LASA concludes that the Nicaraguan electoral process was manipulated, as the U.S. government claims, but by the U.S. government itself in its efforts to discredit an election that it did not want to take place. The Salvadoran and Guatemalan elections successfully legitimized the U.S.-backed regimes, at least for American elite opinion. The far more honest Nicaraguan election failed to accomplish this, thanks to the loyal service of the media.

3.9. THE ROLE OF OFFICIAL "OBSERVERS" IN REINFORCING A PROPAGANDA LINE

Official observers provide a perfect example of the use of government-controlled "experts" and "pseudo-events" to attract media attention and channel it in the direction of the propaganda line. And they regularly succeed in doing this in demonstration elections, no matter how brief their stay and foolish their comments (see appendix 1). The media take it for granted that official observers are newsworthy: they are notables, their selection by the government from "reputable" institutions adds to their credibility, and their observations will have effects on opinion and policy. This rationale is in the nature of a self-fulfilling prophecy; they have effects only because the media accord them attention. As the official observers reliably commend the elections as fair without the slightest attention to basic conditions, the media's regular use of these observers for comments on election quality violates norms of substantive objectivity in the same manner as the use of any straight government handout by the *Times* or *Pravda*.[110]

The Nicaraguan election was remarkable for the number of foreign observers and observer teams. We pointed out earlier that *Time* mentioned 450 foreign observers, but the magazine failed to cite any one of them (relying instead, and characteristically, on State Department handouts). As we saw, the State Department was able to get the media to follow its agenda, even though this involved them in a blatant reversal of the criteria they had employed the same year in El Salvador and Guatemala. It was also able to induce the media to disregard the outcome of the Nicaraguan election, with the help of the diversionary MIG ploy. The media also allowed major lies to be institutionalized—for example, that coercion was greater and pluralistic choices less in the Nicaraguan than in the Salvadoran and Guatemalan elections, and that the latter were legitimizing in a substantive sense, in contrast with Nicaragua.

These propaganda lies could not have been perpetrated if such reports as those of the Irish delegation and LASA had been accorded proper weight. LASA actually contacted the major mass-media outlets and tried to interest them in doing a story on their report. LASA was turned down by every major outlet. The LASA report is probably the best-documented and most closely reasoned observer report ever written. Its authors are far and away the most qualified group ever to write such a report, half with field experience in Nicaragua, and the document was an official report of the major scholarly organization that deals with Central America. The authors represent a variety of opinions, on balance liberal but revealing a strong critical capability (and in no sense biased, as are the official observer teams to whom the media accord much attention). Their report covers every issue of importance and openly confronts and weighs evidence. If one reads the LASA report, and then the accounts of the Nicaraguan election in *Time, Newsweek,* and the *New York Times,* it is not so much the difference in conclusions that is striking but the difference in depth, balance, and objectivity. LASA offers serious history and context, a full account of the organization of the election, and a full discussion of each relevant issue with comparisons to other elections. We believe that an important reason the mass media failed to use LASA as a source of information was that its report contradicts in every way the propaganda claims which the media were disseminating daily and uncritically. Thus its very credibility, objectivity, and quality were disturbing, and necessitated that it be bypassed by institutions serving a propaganda function.

3.10. CONCLUDING NOTE

As we have seen, electoral conditions in Nicaragua in 1984 were far more favorable than in El Salvador and Guatemala, and the observer team of LASA found the election in Nicaragua to have been "a model of probity and fairness" by Latin American standards.[111] In El Salvador and Guatemala, *none* of the five basic preconditions of a free election was met. In both of these countries, state-sponsored terror, including the public exposure of mutilated bodies, had ravaged the civilian population up to the very day of the elections. In both, voting was required by law, and the populace was obliged to have ID cards signed, testifying that they had voted. In both, the main rebel opposition was off the ballot by law, by credible threat of violence, and by plan. Nevertheless, in exact accord with the propaganda line of the state, the U.S. mass media found the large turnouts in these countries to be triumphs of democratic choice, the elections legitimizing, and "fledgling democracies" thus created. This was accomplished in large part by the media's simply refusing to examine the basic conditions of a genuinely free election and their application to these client-state elections. Only for the Nicaraguan election did the media look at matters such as freedom of the press, and they did this with conspicuous dishonesty. Despite its superiority on every substantive count, the Nicaraguan election was found by the media to have been a sham and to have failed to legitimize.

Given the earlier similar performance of the mass media in the cases of the U.S.-sponsored elections in the Dominican Republic in 1966 and Vietnam in 1967, we offer the tentative generalization that the U.S. mass media will *always* find a Third World election sponsored by their own government a "step toward democracy," and an election held in a country that their government is busily destabilizing a farce and a sham. This is, of course, what a propaganda model would predict, although the degree of subservience to state interests in the cases we have examined was extraordinary, given the absence of overt coercion. The "filters" yield a propaganda result that a totalitarian state would be hard put to surpass.

Having perpetrated a successful fraud in the interests of the state, the media proceeded, in subsequent years, to reinforce the imagery established by their deception. Guatemala and El Salvador were "new democracies" with "elected presidents." Nicaragua, in contrast, is a Marxist-Leninist dictatorship that does not have an "elected president" and would never permit elections unless compelled to do so by U.S. force. On December 1, 1987, the *New York Times,* in an editorial urging the administration not to betray Haitian Democrats by "shrugging off impoverished and anarchic Haiti as a hopeless case," states that doing so "would undermine Washington's protestations about the need for free elections in Nicaragua." The wording is murky, and the remarks on Haiti characteristically ignore Washington's support of the Duvalierists who made the elections a mockery, but it is clear that the *Times* accepts the Reagan line that free elections were not held in Nicaragua in 1984 and that the U.S. goal is to bring about free elections. This line is based on major falsifications, but in keeping with their propaganda function, the *Times* as well as the other major media find Big Brother's portrayal of elections in Central America to be true, by hook or by crook.

As we stressed earlier, the media's adherence to the state propaganda line is extremely functional. Just as the government of Guatemala could kill scores of thousands without major repercussion because the media recognized that these were "unworthy" victims, so today aid to state terrorists in El Salvador and Guatemala, and the funding of contra attacks on "soft targets" in Nicaragua, depend heavily on continued media recognition of "worth" and an appropriate legitimization and delegitimization. As their government sponsors terror in all three states (as well as in Honduras), we may fairly say that the U.S. mass media, despite their righteous self-image as opponents of something called terrorism, serve in fact as loyal agents of terrorism.

4

The KGB-Bulgarian Plot to Kill the Pope:

Free-Market Disinformation as "News"

In the case of the Salvadoran, Guatemalan, and Nicaraguan elections, the government was the moving force in providing the suitable frames of analysis and relevant facts, with the mass media's role mainly that of channeling information and assuring that the government's agenda was not seriously challenged. With the shooting of the pope, in May 1981, and the eventual charges of a KGB-Bulgarian plot, the mass media played a much larger role in originating the claims and in keeping the pot boiling from inception to conclusion of the case.[1]

In many ways, however, the process was similar. A dominant frame was eventually produced that interpreted the shooting of the pope in a manner especially helpful to then-current elite demands. A campaign quickly ensued in which the serviceable propaganda line was instilled in the public mind by repetition. Alternative frames were ignored, and sources inclined toward other ways of looking at the issue were excluded from the mass media. Facts were selected that fit the dominant frame; others were passed by even if they bore on the validity of its premises.[2] At the same time, the dominant sources, who had been allowed to monopolize mass-media space, complained bitterly that their voices could not be heard over the din of Soviet propaganda. When the legal proceeding brought against the Bulgarians in Italy was lost after a lengthy trial, this was rationalized by the media as far as could be done. No serious retrospectives were entertained, and, without resolving the contradictions, the story was then dropped.

What makes the Bulgarian Connection so apt an illustration of the value of a propaganda model is that there was no credible case for a Bulgarian Connection from the very beginning, and long before the Rome trial it had taken on a truly comic aspect. But the mass media played it straight to the bitter end. An analogous sequence carried out in Moscow, with the West as the target—with a half-crazed criminal, after seventeen months in a Soviet prison and some friendly sessions with the KGB and a prosecutor, implicating employees of the American embassy in a conspiracy to murder, and subsequently changing his testimony on a daily basis—would have been hooted off the stage in the West without anyone even bothering to look at alleged evidence. The Bulgarian Connection, however, although no less absurd, met the criterion of utility.

The case began when Mehmet Ali Agca shot and seriously injured Pope John Paul II in St. Peter's Square on May 13, 1981. Agca was a Turkish rightist and assassin long associated with the Gray Wolves, an affiliate of the extreme right-wing Nationalist Action party. Initial Western news reports pointed out that Agca was a wanted criminal who had escaped from a Turkish prison in 1979, and that his durable political affiliations had been with the Fascist right. His motives in shooting the pope were unclear. Agca's friends were violently anti-Communist, so that, at first, pinning the crime on the East seemed unpromising.

Two factors allowed a KGB-Bulgarian plot to be developed. The first was that in his travels through Europe in the Gray Wolves underground, which carried him through twelve different countries, Agca had stayed for a period in Bulgaria. Turkish drug dealers, who had connections with the Gray Wolves, also participated in the drug trade in Bulgaria. There were, therefore, some "links" between Agca and Bulgarians, minimal facts that would eventually be put to good use.

The second factor was Western elite needs and the closely associated flare-up of a carefully stoked anti-Communist fervor in the West. At the first meeting of the Jonathan Institute, in Jerusalem, in July 1979, at which a large Western political and media contingent were present (including Claire Sterling, George Will, George Bush, and Robert Moss),[3] the main theme pressed by Israeli Prime Minister Menahem Begin in his opening address, and by many others at the conference, was the importance and utility of pressing the terrorism issue and of tying terrorism to the Soviet Union.[4] Claire Sterling did this in her 1981 volume *The Terror Network*, which became the bible of the Reagan administration and the international right wing, and elevated Sterling to the status of number one mass-media expert on that subject. Terrorism and Soviet evil were the centerpieces of the Reagan administration's propaganda campaign that began in 1981, designed to support its planned arms increase, placement of new missiles in Europe, and interventionist policies in the Third World. Thus the shooting of the pope by Agca in May 1981 occurred at a time when important Western interests were looking for ways to tie the Soviet Union to "international terrorism."[5]

4.1. THE STERLING-HENZE-KALB MODEL

Although the initial media reaction to the shooting was that the roots of the act would seem to lie in Turkish right-wing ideology and politics, some rightists immediately seized the opportunity to locate the origins of the plot in the Soviet bloc. Only six days after the assassination attempt, the Italian secret-service organization SISMI issued a document which claimed that the attack had been announced by a Soviet official at a meeting of the Warsaw Pact powers in Bucharest, Romania, and that Agca had been trained in the Soviet Union. Subsequently, this "information" was shown to have been fabricated by SISMI or one of its intelligence sources, but it entered the stream of allegations about the plot in a book published in West Germany and via further citations and leaks.[6]

The *Reader's Digest* saw the propaganda opportunity presented by the assassination attempt quite early, and hired both Paul Henze, a longtime CIA officer and propaganda specialist, and Claire Sterling to investigate the topic. Sterling's September 1982 article in the *Reader's Digest*, "The Plot to Kill the Pope," was the most important initiator of the Bulgarian Connection, and its ideas and those of Paul Henze formed the basis for the NBC-TV program "The Man Who Shot the Pope—A Study in Terrorism," narrated by Marvin Kalb and first aired on September 21, 1982.

The Sterling-Henze-Kalb (SHK) model, in which Agca was an agent of the Bulgarians (and, indirectly, of the Soviet Union), quickly became the dominant frame of the mass media, through the great outreach of the *Reader's Digest* and the NBC-TV program (which was repeated in revised form in January 1983), and the ready, even eager, acceptance of this view by the other mainstream media.[7] The mass media in our sample—*Newsweek*, *Time*, the *New York Times*, and CBS News—all accepted and used the SHK model from the beginning, and retained that loyalty to the end of the Rome trial in March 1986. In the process they excluded alternative views and a great deal of inconvenient fact. With the *Reader's Digest*, the *Wall Street Journal*, the *Christian Science Monitor*, and NBC-TV also firmly adhering to the SHK line, it quickly established a dominant position throughout the mainstream media.

In the balance of this and the following two sections, we will describe the SHK model, discuss its weaknesses, and outline an alternative frame explaining Agca's confession implicating the Bulgarians, which the media ignored. We will then turn to a closer examination of the media's gullible reception of the SHK view and its fit to a propaganda model.

The SHK model had the following essential elements:

1. Motive. In Sterling's *Reader's Digest* article, the preeminent motive in the assassination attempt was a Soviet desire to weaken NATO, to be accomplished by implicating a Turk in the assassination of the pope: "The Turk was there at St. Peter's to signal Christendom that Islamic Turkey was an alien and vaguely sinister country that did not belong in NATO." This motive was accompanied (and soon supplanted) by the contention that the shooting was to help quell the Solidarity movement in Poland by removing its most important supporter. At one point Paul Henze suggested that the intent of the KGB was perhaps merely to "wing" the pope, not kill him, as a warning, as in a James Bond movie. The costs and risks to the Soviet bloc of such a venture were never discussed by Sterling, Henze, or Kalb.

2. The proof of Soviet and Bulgarian involvement. Before Agca's confession and his identification of Bulgarians in November 1982, the evidence on which SHK relied was confined to the fact that Agca had stayed in Bulgaria in the summer of 1980, and that Turkish drug traders with links to the Gray Wolves did business in Bulgaria. In November 1982, Agca named three Bulgarians as his alleged accomplices and claimed to have been hired by the Bulgarians to do the job. He offered no credible evidence and named no witnesses to any dealings with Bulgarians, so that the new "evidence" was simply Agca's assertions, after seventeen months in an Italian prison.

3. The ideological assumptions. As the case looked extremely thin, especially before Agca's new confession of November 1982, the gaps were filled by ideological assumptions: This is the kind of thing the Soviets do. The Soviet Union and Bulgaria have been actively striving to "destabilize" Turkey.[8] If there is no hard evidence it is because the Soviets are consummate professionals who cover their tracks and maintain "plausible deniability." The KGB hired Agca in Turkey and caused him to use a rightist cover to obscure the fact that he was a KGB agent. Although Agca traveled through eleven other countries, his stay in Bulgaria was crucial because Bulgaria is a totalitarian state and the police know everything; therefore they knew who Agca was, and they must have been using him for their own purposes.[9]

4.2. PROBLEMS WITH THE STERLING-HENZE-KALB MODEL

The basic Sterling-Henze-Kalb model suffered from a complete absence of credible evidence, a reliance on ideological premises, and internal inconsistencies. As problems arose, the grounds were shifted, sometimes with a complete reversal of argument.[10]

An initial problem for the model was the Bulgarian-Soviet motive. In this connection, we should note the extreme foolishness of Sterling's original suggestion that the Eastern bloc went to the trouble of locating a Turkish Fascist to shoot the pope in order to make Turkey look bad, and thereby to loosen its ties to NATO. That such a loosened tie would follow from a Turkish Fascist shooting the pope is not sensible, nor is it likely that the conservative Soviet leadership would indulge in such a fanciful plan even if it had a greater probability of "success."[11] This theory assumed that Agca would be caught and identified as a Turk, but that he wouldn't reveal that he had been hired by the Bulgarians and the Soviets. Subsequently, Sterling suggested that Agca was supposed to have been shot in the square to assure his silence. The amazingly incompetent KGB failed to accomplish this simple task. SHK also maintained at various points that Agca may not even have known who hired him, so he couldn't implicate the East. Later, when Agca claimed that he had been heavily involved with Bulgarians in Rome, Sterling and Henze lapsed into silence on the failure of the KGB to maintain a semblance of plausible deniability.

SHK finally settled firmly on the idea that quelling the Polish Solidarity movement was the real Soviet-Bulgarian motive. But this theory is as implausible as its predecessor, when we take account of timing and elementary cost-benefit analysis. Agca was allegedly recruited in Turkey long before Solidarity existed. In a variant Sterling version of the timing of his recruitment, Agca was hired by the Bulgarians in July 1980, which was still prior to the Gdansk shipyard strike, and thus before Solidarity appeared a credible threat to Soviet control. The risks and costs of an assassination attempt would seem heavy—and, in fact, the costs to the Soviet Union and Bulgaria were severe based merely on the widespread belief in their involvement, even in the absence of credible evidence. The supposed benefits from the act are also not plausible. The assassination of the pope, especially if blamed on the Soviet Union, would infuriate and unify the Poles and strengthen their opposition to a Soviet-dominated regime. And the further costs in damaged relations with Western Europe—which were extremely important to the Soviet Union in 1981, with the gas pipeline being negotiated and with the placement of new U.S. missiles in Western Europe a major Soviet concern—would seem to militate against taking foolish risks.[12]

A second problem with the SHK model is that Agca had threatened to kill the pope in 1979 at the time of a papal visit to Turkey—again, long before Solidarity existed. This suggests that Agca and the Turkish right had their own grievances against the pope and a rationale for assassinating him that was independent of any Soviet influence. It was partly for this reason that SHK argue that Agca was recruited by the Soviet Union in Turkey before the pope's visit there, setting him up for the later attack. But not only is this pure speculation unsupported by a trace of evidence, it fails to explain why the entire Fascist press, not just Agca, assailed the pope's visit in 1979. Was the entire Fascist right serving Soviet ends? The only time this issue was ever raised in the mass media, on the "McNeil-Lehrer News Hour" of January 5, 1983, Paul Henze stated in no uncertain terms that "there was no [press] opposition" to the pope's visit in 1979. The Turkish journalist Ugur Mumcu, however, assembled a large collection of citations from the Turkish rightist press of the time to demonstrate that Henze's statement was false.[13]

A third problem for the SHK model was that Agca was a committed rightist, and therefore not a likely candidate for service to the Communist powers (although perhaps amenable to fingering them as co-conspirators in a prison context). SHK strove mightily to make Agca out to be a rootless mercenary, but the best they could come up with was the fact that Agca didn't seem to have been registered as a member of the Gray Wolves.[14] But all his friends, associates, and affiliations from high school days onward were Gray Wolves, and in his travels through Europe up to the time of his May 13, 1981, rendezvous, he moved solely through the Gray Wolves network. While in prison, Agca addressed a letter to Alparslan Turkes, the leader of the Nationalist Action Party of Turkey, expressing his continued commitment and loyalty. This letter was bothersome to Sterling and Henze as it is inconsistent with their depiction of Agca as apolitical, and Sterling dismissed it without argument as a "laughably clumsy forgery." A problem, however, is that Agca's letter was introduced as evidence in a trial in Ankara by the Turkish military authorities, usually adequate proof for Sterling of authenticity. She doesn't mention this fact or examine their case. Ugur Mumcu devotes five pages of his book *Agca Dossier* to a detailed account of the Turkes letter, describing the great pains the authorities took, including tapping outside experts, to establish its authenticity. The conclusion on all sides was that the letter was genuine.

A fourth problem with the SHK model is the notion that because of the efficiency of the Bulgarian secret police, Agca's presence in Sofia must have been known to them, and he must therefore have been on their payroll. This assumed efficiency is an ideological assumption unsupported by any evidence and contradicted by actual Bulgarian and Soviet performance. There is no evidence that the Bulgarians ever identified Agca, who was using a false passport. Furthermore, the contention that the Bulgarian police know everything was refuted in important testimony during the Rome trial on September 22, 1985, when Gray Wolves official Abdullah Catli stated that many Gray Wolves preferred to traverse Bulgaria because it was easy to hide in the large flow of Turkish immigrant traffic through that country.

A fifth problem for the SHK model was the fact that Agca seems to have gotten his gun through the Gray Wolves network, not from the Bulgarians, who presumably could have slipped it to him quite easily in Rome. In her *Reader's Digest* article, Sterling traced Agca's gun to Horst Grillmaier, an Austrian gun dealer who, according to Sterling, had fled behind the Iron Curtain after May 13, 1981, to avoid questioning in the West. It turned out later, however, that Grillmaier was a former Nazi who specialized in supplying right-wing gun buyers; that he had not disappeared behind the Iron Curtain at all; and that the gun had proceeded through a number of intermediaries, to be transmitted to Agca by a Gray Wolves friend. Sterling handles the disintegration of the original Grillmaier line by simply shifting to a new conspiratorial ground: the clever Bulgarians had Agca purchase a gun through a known Fascist to strengthen the case that Agca was a right-winger who could not possibly be connected to the Communist powers.

A final *set* of problems for the SHK model lies in the extraordinary level of incompetence and gross violations of the principles of plausible deniability that it attributes to the Bulgarian and Soviet secret police—features that coexist uneasily with the superspy image invoked elsewhere in the model. At various points, SHK contended that the Soviets and Bulgarians were professionals who could afford to go after the pope because they would never be implicated themselves. But hiring Agca, a wanted criminal and a mentally unbalanced rightist, would appear extremely foolish, as the cover would quickly be blown in the likely event that he was caught. In Sterling's initial tale, the KGB *wanted* him to be caught—or at least to have his body identified—to discredit Turkey. With the shift to weakening Solidarity as the motive, the threat of disclosure of Bulgarian-Soviet involvement would seem very serious. Yet the Bulgarians and KGB hired Agca and then failed to kill him. Another anomaly was bringing Agca to Sofia for instructions. If he had already been recruited in Turkey, wouldn't bringing him to Sofia be a foolish compromising of his carefully prepared "cover"? If so, doesn't his visit to Sofia constitute an argument *against* Soviet and Bulgarian involvement?

While Agca's November 1982 confession that he had Bulgarian co-conspirators made the Bulgarian Connection instantly "true" for the Western media, it wreaked havoc with the SHK model and with the logic of "plausible deniability." If, as Agca confessed, the Bulgarians connived with him in Rome, escorted him to St. Peter's Square to plan the attack, entertained him at their apartments, and participated in the attack itself, what happens to the logic of the "cover"?

4.3. AN ALTERNATIVE MODEL

An alternative explanation of the Bulgarian Connection can be derived from the questions the U.S. press would surely have raised if an analogous scenario had occurred in Moscow, in which Agca, who had briefly visited the United States on his travels, and has been in a Soviet prison for seventeen months after having shot a high Soviet official, now confesses that three U.S. embassy members were his co-conspirators. In this case, the U.S. press would have paid close attention to the convenience of the confession to Soviet propaganda needs, to the seventeen-month delay in the naming of Americans, and to the obvious possibility that Agca had been encouraged or coerced into revising his story. They would have focused intently on Agca's prison conditions, his visitors there, his amenability to a "deal" with his captors, and any evidence in his statements or from other sources that he had been coached. The fact that Agca had visited the United States, among twelve countries, would not be considered strong evidence of CIA involvement, and the press might even have pointed out that a minimally competent CIA would not have brought Agca to Washington for instructions in the first place.

The alternative model would take the same fact that SHK start out with—Agca's stay in Sofia, Bulgaria—but interpret it differently. That visit violates principles of plausible deniability and would be especially foolish if the KGB had already recruited Agca in Turkey. On the other hand, it provides a Western propaganda system with the necessary tie between Agca's terrorist attack in Rome and the Soviet bloc. The *convenience* of Agca's confession—to Socialist leader Craxi, to the Christian Democrats and neo-Fascists in Italy, and to Reagan searching for a tie-in between "international terrorism" and the Soviet Union—is also crystal clear, and would immediately suggest to an objective press the possibility that this "demand" might have elicited an appropriate "supply" from the imprisoned Agca. The lag in Agca's naming of any Bulgarians—seventeen months after he entered an Italian prison and seven months after he had agreed to "cooperate" with the investigating magistrate, Ilario Martella—is also highly suggestive. Why did it take him so long to name his co-conspirators? Sterling tried to explain this on the ground that Agca had hopes that the Bulgarians would "spring him" and gave them time; his successive elaborations of claims and subsequent retractions she explained in terms of Agca's "signaling" to his alleged partners. This complex and speculative attempt to rationalize inconvenient facts is not necessary; a very straightforward explanation based on Agca's character and affiliations and the inducements known to have been offered to him (described below) does quite nicely.[15] Furthermore, Sterling's explanation does not account for the fact that Agca failed to provide serious evidence late in the trial, long after it was clear that the Bulgarians had not responded to his alleged signals.

Another suggestive feature of Agca's confession is that it *followed* the creation and wide media distribution of the SHK model. During the course of the investigation of the plot, it was revealed that the imprisoned Agca had access to newspapers, radio, and television, among other modes of personal communication with the outside world. It was also brought out in the investigation that Agca's "desire for personal publicity seems unquenchable. . . . At one point in the Italian investigation, he abruptly clammed up when the magistrates refused his demand that journalists be present as he 'confessed.' "[16] Agca was interrogated about a possible Bulgarian connection long before his confession, and was surely aware that his interrogators would be quite pleased to have him produce one. And by the fall of 1982 one was being provided to him in the press and on the screen every day.

We mentioned earlier that the Italian secret-service agency SISMI had actually distributed a piece of disinformation tying the Soviets to the assassination attempt within days of the attack. At the time of the shooting, SISMI was headed by General Giuseppe Santovito, a member of the extreme right-wing organization Propaganda Due (P-2), and SISMI and the other intelligence agencies were heavily infiltrated with P-2 members. A P-2 scandal broke in Italy in March 1981, and by August Santovito had been forced to leave SISMI, but the rightist grip on this organization was by no means broken.

An important feature of Italian politics in the period from 1966 through 1981 was the protection given by the intelligence services to right-wing terror, under a program designated the "strategy of tension."[17] One aspect of this strategy was the carrying out of right-wing terrorist attacks, which were then attributed to the left, frequently with the help of forged documents and planted informers committing perjury. The point of the strategy was to polarize society, discredit the left, and set the stage for a rightist coup. Many P-2 members in the armed forces and intelligence services took part in implementing this program, and many others were sympathetic to its aims. In July 1984, an Italian parliamentary commission published its final report on the P-2 conspiracy, and it and its accompanying volumes of hearings pointed up the politicization of the intelligence services, their frequent use of techniques of disinformation, and their connivance with and protection of right-wing terror. In July 1985 a Bologna court issued a decision in which it named SISMI and its officers as having engaged in numerous forgeries, and also in having collaborated in covering up the Bologna terrorist bombing of 1980.[18]

SISMI participated in a five-hour interrogation of Agca in December 1981, exploring his link to "international terrorism." Investigating Judge Martella acknowledges in his long investigative report that he had spoken to Agca about the possibility of a commuted sentence if he "cooperated," and the Italian press quoted Agca's lawyer's report of the terms of proposed deals that had been offered to Agca.[19] There were also a variety of reports in the European and dissident media of pressures applied to Agca while in prison. A London *Sunday Times* team pointed out in May 1983 that the secret services "visited Agca and warned him that once his solitary confinement was over, 'the authorities could no longer guarantee his safety.' "[20] According to Orsen Oymen, a Turkish expert on the case, the Catholic chaplain in Agca's prison, Father Mariano Santini, had frequent access to Agca and was one of those who pressed him to cooperate with the authorities.[21] There is some possible confirmation of Santini's pressure tactics in a letter which Agca addressed to the Vatican, dated September 24, 1982, which complained bitterly of threats to his life emanating from a Vatican emissary.

During the course of the Rome trial, Giovanni Pandico, the principal Italian state witness in the trial of Mafia leaders in Naples and an associate of Raphael Cutolo, a Mafia leader who had been in Ascoli Piceno prison with Agca, claimed in an interview (and subsequently before the court) that Agca had been coerced, persuaded and coached to implicate the Bulgarians by Cutolo, Santini, and others. Pandico claimed that Cutolo himself had been coerced into working on Agca by threats to himself, and that former SISMI officials Giuseppi Musumeci and Francesco Pazienza were key initiators of the plot. One of the important individuals accused by Pandico, Francesco Pazienza, while denying the charges, gave his own detailed account of who in SISMI *had* participated in persuading Agca to talk.

From the inception of the case, there were points suggesting that Agca was coached while in prison. After his long (and unexplained) silence, Agca identified the Bulgarians in a photo album allegedly shown to him for the first time on November 9, 1982. But in a speech before the Italian parliament, the minister of defense, Lelio Lagorio, stated that Agca had identified the Bulgarians in September of 1982. This discrepancy has never been explained, but that Agca saw these photos for the first time on November 9 is not believable.[22] A key element in Agca's testimony was his claim to have visited the apartment of Sergei Antonov, one of the Bulgarians arrested in the "plot," and to have met his wife and daughter, which was supported by many fine details regarding Antonov's hobbies and the characteristics of his apartment. The defense, however, was able to show that one feature of Antonov's apartment mentioned by Agca was in error, although characteristic of the other apartments in Antonov's building, which suggests that Agca had been supplied information based on observation of other apartments. More important, the defense was able to establish that at the time of Agca's visit at which he met Mrs. Antonov, she was out of the country. Following newspaper publicity given these defense contentions, on June 28, 1983, Agca retracted his claims that he had visited the apartment and met Antonov's family. The details he had given about apartment and family then became inexplicable, except on the supposition that Agca had been fed information while in prison. In a number of other instances Agca provided information that bore strong suspicion of having been provided by officials and agents of the court or the police. The London *Sunday Times* reporters, who interviewed one of the accused Bulgarians in Sofia, wrote that "When asked by Martella in Bulgaria whether he had any salient physical features, Vassilev said that he had a mole on his left cheek. In a *subsequent* confession, as Vassilev points out, 'Agca described my mole in *the very same words* which I used in describing it here.' "[23]

During the course of the Rome trial in 1985–86, no trace was ever found of the money that Agca claimed he had received from the Bulgarians. The car that Agca indicated the Bulgarians had used to escort him around Rome was never located. No witness was ever found who saw him in his many supposed encounters with Bulgarians. His gun was transferred to him through the Turkish Gray Wolves network, and there was no shortage of evidence of his meetings with members of the Gray Wolves in Western Europe. The note that was found on Agca's person on May 13, 1981, did not mention any collaborators, and suggested a loose timetable for the assassination attempt and a planned railroad trip to Naples.

In sum, it is highly probable that Agca was offered a deal to talk, and that it was made clear to him that the people with power over his well-being wanted him to implicate the Bulgarians and the Soviet Union in the assassination attempt. He had access to the SHK model even before he confessed. His confession was therefore suspect from the start, and an "alternative model" of inducement-pressure coaching was plausible and relevant, from the Agca's first implication of Bulgarians. This model became more cogent over time as Agca retracted strategic claims, and as no confirming evidence of a Bulgarian Connection was produced. By the same token, the SHK model, implausible from the beginning, became even less tenable.

4.4. THE MASS MEDIA'S UNCRITICAL ACCEPTANCE OF THE BULGARIAN CONNECTION

Despite the implausibility of the SHK claim that Agca had been hired by the Bulgarians and the KGB to shoot the pope, and although it was sustained by argument that amounted to sheer humbuggery, the Bulgarian Connection met the standard of utility. In this case, therefore, as a propaganda model would anticipate, the U.S. mass media accepted the SHK model as valid, ignored the alternative model, and participated in a classic propaganda campaign that got the message of Bulgarian-Soviet guilt over to the public. Some members of the mass media helped originate the claim of a Bulgarian Connection, while others participated only in disseminating the SHK line (and excluding alternative views and inconvenient information).

The campaign began with Sterling's *Reader's Digest* article of September 1982, which was closely followed by the NBC-TV program of September 21, 1982. The outreach of these two statements asserting a Bulgarian Connection was great, and they were widely reported upon in the rest of the media in the form of a summary of their claims, with virtually no questions raised about their validity. With Agca's November 1982 naming of Bulgarians, the mass media began to report the Bulgarian Connection intensively. This reporting was carried out exclusively within the frame of the SHK model, and for most of the mass media no serious departures from this model occurred through the conclusion of the Rome trial in March 1986.[24]

Agca's naming of the Bulgarians was the key fact that generated news coverage, providing the basis for reiterated details about the Bulgarians, explanations of the Bulgarian (and Soviet) motive, and speculation about the political implications of the charges, if confirmed. A major characteristic of these news reports was their sheer superficiality, with the charges never seriously examined but merely regurgitated and elaborated with odd facts and opinion, and with no departures from the SHK frame (and no hints of the possible relevance of an alternative frame). The charges constituted a form of vindication of the SHK model if taken at face value and presented superficially—i.e., if the media presentations never considered political convenience, prison conditions, possible deals, plausible deniability, etc. And this procedure—a reiteration of Agca claims, supplemented by extremely superficial pro-plot speculation—was the principal modality by which the mass media accepted and pushed the propaganda line.

Newsweek provides a prototype of news coverage within the SHK framework in its article of January 3, 1983, "The Plot to Kill Pope John Paul II." The Bulgarian-Soviet motive as portrayed by SHK is reiterated through quotes from congenial sources—"a precautionary and alternative solution to the invasion of Poland"—while nobody is quoted discussing costs and benefits, the nature of the Soviet leadership, or *Western* benefits from Agca's confession.[25] In fact, *Newsweek* suggests that this charging of the Soviet bloc with the assassination attempt is a painful embarrassment to Western governments (parroting the SHK line on this point). *Newsweek* nowhere discusses the seventeen-month lag in Agca's confession or his prison conditions, nor does it report in this (or any later) article the claims and information noted in the London *Sunday Times* and the Italian press about inducements or coercive threats that might have been applied to Agca while in custody.

Agca's evidence is given credibility by *Newsweek* through several devices: repeating his claims several times as the core of the story; stressing in two separate sequences investigative judge Martella's alleged honesty, integrity, conscientiousness, etc.; quoting from Italian officials who say they "have the evidence" that "Agca operated in close contact with the Bulgarians"; asserting that "all the evidence suggests" that Agca is "not crazy." But most important is the previously mentioned refusal to discuss the premises of the SHK framework or to use an alternative frame.

Newsweek swallows intact a series of SHK ideological assumptions, such as that "investigators [read "Paul Henze"] now think" Agca was probably using the Gray Wolves as a cover; Bulgaria and the Soviet Union have long been trying "to destabilize Turkey through terrorism" (quoting Henze directly); in Sofia, Agca's presence "must have come to the attention of the Bulgarian secret police" (duplicating the frequent SHK error of forgetting their claim that Agca had already been recruited for the papal assassination attempt in Turkey, as well as erroneously assuming that the Bulgarian secret police can easily identify Turks passing through their country). *Newsweek* states as established fact that "Agca had help from a huge set of Bulgarians," although it provides no evidence for this except assertions by Agca, Italian officials, and Paul Henze. It reports Agca's numerous transactions with Bulgarians in Rome without mentioning the problem of plausible deniability and without batting an eyelash at the sheer foolishness of the scenario. This *Newsweek* article is nonetheless powerful, with its reiteration of many details, its confidently asserted plots and subplots, its quotes from many authorities supporting the charges, and its seeming openness and occasional mention of lack of full proof—but it is a piece of uncritical propaganda that confines itself strictly within the SHK frame, with the exception of the single phrase cited earlier.

Initially, the other major media performed quite uniformly in the same mold—uncritical, trivial, working solely within the bounds of the SHK model, and entirely bypassing all the hard but obvious questions raised by the "alternative" model. Of the thirty-two news articles on, or closely related to, the plot that appeared in the *New York Times* between November 1, 1982, and January 31, 1983, twelve had no news content whatever but were reports of somebody's opinion or speculation about the case—or refusal to speculate about the issue. (The *Times* carried one news article whose sole content was that President Reagan had "no comment" on the case.) More typical was the front-page article by Henry Kamm, "Bonn is Fearful of Bulgaria Tie with Terrorists" (Dec. 12, 1982), or Bernard Gwertzman's "U.S. Intrigued But Uncertain on a Bulgarian Tie" (Dec. 26, 1982). In "news report" after news report, unnamed individuals are "intrigued," their interest is "piqued," evidence is said to be "not wholly convincing," or "final proof is still lacking." Four of the news articles in the *Times* were on peripheral subjects such as smuggling in Bulgaria or papal-Soviet relations. Of the sixteen more direct news items, *only one* covered a solid news fact—namely, Antonov's arrest in Rome. The other fifteen news items were trivia, such as Kamm's "Bulgarians Regret Tarnished Image" (Jan. 27, 1983), or another Kamm piece entitled "Italian Judge Inspects Apartment of Suspect in Bulgarian Case" (Jan. 12, 1983). All of these expressions of opinion, doubts, interest, suppositions, and minor detail served to produce a lot of smoke—which kept the issue of possible Soviet involvement before the public. They steered quite clear of substantive issues that bore on motives, quality of evidence, and Turkish and Italian context.

During the years that followed, to the end of the trial in March 1986, the mass media, with only minor exceptions, adhered closely and uncritically to the SHK framework.[26] They not only failed to press alternative questions, they also refused to examine closely the premises, logic, or evidence supporting the SHK case. Part of the reason for this was the media's extraordinary reliance on Sterling and Henze as sources (and Kalb's position as a news reporter on NBC-TV), and their unwillingness to ask these sources probing questions.

4.5. BIASED SOURCING

Sterling and Henze, and to a lesser extent Michael Ledeen, dominated perceptions of the Bulgarian Connection in the U.S. mass media to a remarkable degree. Moreover, they affected the course of events in Italy, as their version of Bulgarian guilt was aired in the Italian media before Agca named the Bulgarians and may have influenced Martella as well.[27] Sterling and Henze dominated media coverage by virtue of the very wide distribution of their articles and books on the case, and by their extensive and uncritical use as experts by the elite press, news magazines, and television news and talk shows.[28] Sterling, in addition to her *Reader's Digest* article, had three substantial pieces in the *Wall Street Journal* and several articles in the *New York Times.* Her views were given repeated airing on CBS News, without rebuttal. Henze accounted for twelve of the fourteen articles on the Bulgarian Connection case in the *Christian Science Monitor* between September 1982 and May 1985, and his articles were used widely elsewhere. The only opinion piece on the Bulgarian Connection that appeared in the *Philadelphia Inquirer* during that same period was by Michael Ledeen. Sterling, Henze, and Ledeen together accounted for 76 percent of the time in three shows on the subject on the "McNeil-Lehrer News Hour." No tough questions were asked of them on these shows, and no dissident voices were heard, perhaps because Sterling and Henze refused to appear on television shows (or in college debates) with people who opposed their views, and Henze insisted on approving in advance any questions to be asked. Thus their initial dominance was further enhanced by coercive tactics.[29]

If we ask the deeper question of why these experts should predominate in the first place, we believe the answer must be found in the power of their sponsors and the congeniality of their views to the corporate community and the mainstream media. Their messages passed quite easily through the filters of a propaganda system. Sterling was funded and published by *Reader's Digest,* which gave her enormous outreach and immediate brand-name recognition. The conservative network is fond of Sterling, so their large stable of columnists and think-tank affiliates, like the Georgetown Center for Strategic and International Studies (CSIS) and the American Enterprise Institute, pushes her views. The Reagan administration was also delighted with Sterling—despite her frequent denunciations of the CIA and the State Department for their cowardice in failing to pursue terrorism and the Bulgarian Connection with sufficient aggressiveness!—and so were the *New York Times, Time, Newsweek,* CBS News, and many others. Sterling was the outstanding popular expositor of the theme urged upon the conferees at the Jonathan Institute meeting of July 1979 and advocated by the Reagan administration team anxious to create a moral environment for an arms race and global support of counterrevolutionary freedom fighters.[30] Henze, an old CIA hand and protégé of Zbigniew Brzezinski, was also funded by the *Reader's Digest,* and Ledeen was affiliated with both the CSIS and the Reagan political team. If the media transmit literal lies by this Big Three—which they did frequently—the flak machines remain silent. As one network official told one of the authors, if a critic of the Bulgarian Connection were allowed on the air, the official would "have to make sure that every *i* was dotted and *t* crossed; but with Sterling, there were no problems."

Again in conformity with a propaganda model, it was of no apparent concern to the mass media that Sterling, Henze, and Ledeen were exceptionally biased sources, immune to the rules of evidence and, in fact, agents of disinformation. We discussed earlier Sterling's dismissal of Agca's commitment to Turkes and her handling of Agca's gun, and similar cases could be cited in large number.[31] Sterling's *Terror Network* is notable for its gullibility in accepting at face value claims fed her by Israeli, South African, and Argentinian secret police, and, most notably, the Czech Stalinist defector, Jan Sejna,[32] whose evidence for a Soviet terror network came from a document forged by the CIA to test Sejna's integrity![33] A remarkable feature of Sterling's *Time of the Assassins* and other writings on the Bulgarian Connection is her reiterated belief that the Reagan administration and CIA dragged their feet in pursuing the Red plot because of their interest in détente.[34] And despite her phenomenal sales and uncritical reception in the U.S. media, Sterling bemoaned the "accepted position, the socially indispensable position . . . if you care to move in certain circles and if you care to be accepted at your job professionally" in the West, of doubting the Bulgarian Connection, which she attributed to the success of the KGB in pushing a forty-page booklet on the plot by Soviet journalist Iona Andronov.[35]

These evidences of charlatanry did not impair Sterling's credibility with the U.S. mass media—in fact, the *New York Times* allowed her front-page space and a regular role as a reporter of *news* on the Bulgarian connection. By doing this, the *Times* guaranteed that editorial policy would control the news fit to print. This was displayed fully in Sterling's front-page news story of prosecutor Albano's report on June 10, 1984. The most important *new* information in that report—that on June 28, 1983, Agca had retracted a substantial part of his evidence against the Bulgarians—was omitted from Sterling's story, although she coyly suggested that some undescribed points had been retracted that were already "corroborated." This was seriously misleading. Agca's having visited Antonov's apartment and met with his family was never corroborated, and the details he gave on these matters had previously been cited by Sterling and Henze as crucial corroboration of his general claims. His retraction thus led to the important question of how Agca had learned details about Antonov's apartment without having been there. This issue was never seriously addressed in the *New York Times*.[36]

Paul Henze was a longtime CIA official who had been head of the CIA station in Turkey and a specialist in propaganda. Former Turkish head of state Bulent Ecevit even accused Henze of helping destabilize Turkey during his term of operations there.[37] Henze never refers in his "news" articles to his active participation in Turkish affairs as a CIA official. His writings are notable for their consistent apologetics for military rule in Turkey, for their dishonesty,[38] and for the fact that Henze openly disdains the use of rules of evidence in proving Soviet villainy.[39]

Michael Ledeen, as we saw in chapter 1, contends that the mass media believe Qaddafi more readily than the U.S. government, and focus more heavily on the victims of state terror in U.S. client states (Indonesia in East Timor, and Guatemala?) than in enemy and radical states (Cambodia and Poland?). Again, such absurdities do not reduce Ledeen's access to the mass media as an expert on the Bulgarian Connection, or on anything else.[40]

The mass media not only allowed these disinformation sources to prevail, they protected them against disclosures that would reveal their dubious credentials. That Henze was a longtime CIA official was almost never mentioned in the press (never, to our knowledge, on television), and his consistent apologetics for the Turkish military regime and frequent lies were never disclosed. In Sterling's case, her numerous errors of fact, foolish arguments, and wilder political opinions were not disclosed to readers of the *New York Times*, *Time*, or *Newsweek*, or watchers of CBS News or the "McNeil-Lehrer News Hour," and even "newsworthy" matters bearing on her qualifications were ignored. For example, Sterling's numerous attacks on the murdered French activist-radical Henry Curiel resulted in suits for slander brought against her in Paris. The *New York Times* has never mentioned these slander suits, which would put Sterling in a bad light not only because she lost them in whole or part, but also because of the insight they provide concerning her sources and methods. Sterling had gotten much of her information from a French journalist, George Suffert, who was a conduit for French and South African intelligence, and who had obligingly placed the African National Congress at the top of his list of "terrorist" organizations. In her *Terror Network*, Sterling strongly intimates that Curiel was a KGB agent, but the French court, on the basis of documents provided by French intelligence, found no support for this claim. Sterling retreated to the defense that her insinuation of Curiel's KGB connection was merely a "hypothesis" rather than an assertion of fact. The case, in short, showed that she was a conduit of disinformation, quite prepared to slander a murdered radical on the basis of claims by extreme right-wing disinformation sources.

Michael Ledeen, a neoconservative activist and disinformationist, with ready access to the *Times*, has also received its close protection. His book *Grave New World* was reviewed in the *Times* by William Griffith, a *Reader's Digest* "roving editor" and right-wing MIT political scientist who found Ledeen's version of the Bulgarian Connection entirely convincing.[41] Ledeen was deeply involved with Francesco Pazienza in the "Billygate" affair and had numerous contacts with Italian intelligence and the Italian extreme right. The Italian Fascist and head of P-2, Licio Gelli, hiding in Uruguay, instructed one of his accomplices to convey a manuscript to Ledeen. Pazienza claimed (and SISMI head Santovito confirmed) that Ledeen was a member of the Italian intelligence agency SISMI, with code number Z-3. Ledeen received over $100,000 from SISMI for services rendered, including the supplying of stale U.S. intelligence reports that SISMI then passed off as its own. Ledeen funneled this money into a Bermuda bank account. His manipulative activities in Italy were on such a scale that in the summer of 1984 a newly appointed head of SISMI told the Italian parliament that Ledeen was a "meddler" and *persona non grata* in Italy.[42] None of these points was ever disclosed in the *Times*.[43]

4.6. THE PROPAGANDA AGENDA: QUESTIONS UNASKED, SOURCES UNTAPPED

There is a close linkage among sources used, frames of reference, and agendas of the newsworthy. When the mass media chose to use Sterling, Henze, and Ledeen heavily, they simultaneously adopted a frame of reference in which the Bulgarians and Soviets were presumed guilty, Agca was an apolitical mercenary, and justice was being promoted by diligent Judge Martella in free-world Italy. In the propaganda campaign that ensued, hard questions about the quality of the SHK model were simply not asked, and alternative sources and frames were ignored.

A distinction between matters on and off the agenda, such as we used in the previous chapter, is once again applicable and illuminating. "On the agenda" are statements by Agca and Martella about Agca's latest claims and proofs of Bulgarian involvement, Brzezinski's opinion on whether the Bulgarians are likely to have engaged in such an escapade (they were), or Judy Woodruff's question to Paul Henze as to whether the Soviets "would have any notion, any desire to try this again" (they do this kind of thing all the time—just got a little careless here because "they had got away with so much in Italy").[44] As in the Third World election cases described in chapter 3, the media prefer to focus on superficial detail about the participants and opinions within a narrow range of establishment views (plus bluff denials by Bulgarian and Soviet officials), along with each development supporting the accepted case (a defector's accusations, a further Agca confession, an investigator's or prosecutor's report, and leaks of alleged claims or expected new developments), whatever its credibility.

"Off the agenda" are arguments and facts that would call into question the validity of the basic SHK model, and those relating to the "alternative model" (which *starts* with the question of why Agca confessed so late and the likelihood that he was encouraged and pressed to talk). We will run through only a few of the important questions and points of evidence that the mass media put off the agenda.

The basic SHK model rested its case on the Soviet motive, Agca's stay in Sofia, and the high professionalism of the Soviet and Bulgarian secret police, which made it likely that they were manipulating Agca if he stopped off in Bulgaria. Only the ABC "20/20" program of May 12, 1983, explored the Soviet motive in any depth, despite the constant mass-media reiteration of the SHK line. ABC went to the trouble of asking the Vatican about the validity of Marvin Kalb's claim that the pope had written a note threatening to resign and to return to Poland to lead the resistance to any Soviet invasion. Cardinal John Krol, speaking for the Vatican, said that "Not only was there not such a letter, but such a letter directly from the Pope to Brezhnev would have been a total departure from all normal procedures. In no way could you conceive of the Holy Father saying, 'I would resign.' " ABC's information from the Vatican too was that the pope's *spoken* message to Brezhnev was conciliatory. This spectacular repudiation of an important element in the SHK case was unreported in the rest of the media, and simply died with the ABC broadcast. And any balancing of supposed gains against the costs and risks to the Soviet Union in sponsoring Agca was simply not undertaken in the mass media.

None of them stopped to evaluate Agca's 1979 letter threatening to kill the pope on his earlier visit to Turkey. Sterling's ludicrous claim that the KGB hired a Turk to kill the pope in order to damage Turkey's relation to NATO was never discussed. The question of the authenticity of Agca's letter to Turkes, which bears on Agca's political commitments (and thus another SHK premise), was never discussed in the U.S. mass media. During the trial, Abdullah Catli's statement that Bulgaria was a preferred Gray Wolves route to Europe because of the relative ease of hiding in the heavy Turkish traffic—which directly contradicts the SHK claim that the Bulgarian secret police know everything, and that Agca's stay in Sofia must therefore have been by Bulgarian official plan—was never picked up in the U.S. mass media's coverage of the Rome trial.

The most striking deficiencies of the mass media's handling of the basic SHK claims, however, was their remarkable naïveté in the face of the pseudoscientific speculations of SHK and the *accumulating* violations of elementary principles of plausible deniability. The preposterous SHK claims—without a vestige of evidence—that Agca had been recruited by the KGB in Turkey for future work, and that he took on the appearance of a right-winger as a "cover," were not ridiculed, and were not evaluated when presented as purported truth.[45] There was never any discussion in the mass media of the fact that the thesis of prior recruitment and careful cultivation of Agca's cover in Turkey was flatly inconsistent with the claim that he was brought to Sofia for a lengthy stay for instructions. With regard to Agca's alleged open dealings with Bulgarians in Rome, the mass media simply refused to discuss the fact that the alleged professionalism and use of the right-wing Turk as a "cover" had disappeared.

As regards the alternative model, and the likelihood that Agca had been encouraged and coached, here also the mass media refused to explore these dissonant possibilities. They simply would not examine and discuss the *convenience* of the newly discovered plot for so many Western interests; the huge time lag in the naming of Bulgarians; Agca's prison conditions and prison contacts; reports of meetings, offers, and threats to Agca to induce him to talk; and the compromised character of the Italian police and intelligence agencies. This involved the media in the suppression of important documents.

As one important instance, the July 12, 1984, Italian *Report of the Parliamentary Commission on the Masonic Lodge P-2* describes in great detail the penetration of this massive neo-Fascist conspiracy into the military establishment, secret services, press, and judiciary, among others. This report was newsworthy in its own right, but it also had a bearing on the Bulgarian Connection case, as it addressed characteristics of Italian institutions that were directly involved in making and prosecuting the case against the Bulgarians. The *New York Times, Time, Newsweek,* and CBS Evening News never mentioned the publication of this report.

As a second major illustration, one year later, in July 1985, the Criminal Court of Rome handed down a *Judgment in the Matter of Francesco Pazienza et al.,* which described repeated corrupt behavior by officials of the Italian secret-service agency SISMI, including the forgery and planting of documents. These officials were also charged with involvement in a cover-up of the agents carrying out the 1980 Bologna railway-station massacre, the kind of terrorist connection that attracts frenetic mass-media attention when attributable to suitable villains. As we noted earlier, SISMI officials had visited Agca in prison and SISMI had issued a forged document implicating the Soviet Union in the shooting of the pope on May 19, 1981, only six days after the assassination attempt. This forgery was never mentioned in the *Times, Time,* and *Newsweek,* or on CBS News, and the July 1985 court decision was barely mentioned in a back-page article of the *Times.*

These blackouts are of materials that suggest a corrupt Italian process and the possibility that Agca was persuaded and coached to pin the plot on the East. A propaganda system exploiting the alleged Bulgarian Connection will naturally avoid such documents.

Agca's extremely loose prison conditions and the numerous claims in the Italian and dissident U.S. press of visits by Italian intelligence personnel were also virtually unmentioned by the U.S. mass media throughout 1982 and 1983. In June 1983, Diana Johnstone, the foreign editor of the newspaper *In These Times* submitted on Op-Ed column to the *New York Times* and the *Philadelphia Inquirer* that summarized the evidence and claims of intelligence-agency visits, the reported threats to Agca that his open and pleasant prison conditions might be terminated if he remained uncooperative, and Martella's proposed deal with Agca. This Op-Ed offering was rejected, and no commentary or news along these lines was permitted to surface in the *Times* or the *Philadelphia Inquirer*—or elsewhere, to our knowledge. Several years later, in an article in the *New York Times* of June 17, 1985, referring to Pandico's detailed description of how Agca was coached in prison, John Tagliabue describes Agca's prison as "notoriously porous." But the *Times* had never mentioned this notorious fact before, or considered it in any way relevant to the case.

When Agca identified the Bulgarians in November 1982, the integrity of the Italian investigative-judicial process in pursuing the case was already badly compromised for a wide variety of reasons,[46] but the U.S. mass media weren't interested. Nor were they interested in the strange circumstances of the famous Antonov photo, widely circulated in the Western press, which shows Antonov very clearly and in a remarkable likeness watching the scene at St. Peter's Square on May 13, 1981. This photo, Martella eventually claimed, was not of Antonov but an American tourist. But this tourist, who apparently looked exactly like Antonov, has never been located, and the film from which this shot was taken has unaccountably disappeared.[47] Agca's alterations in his claims about the Bulgarians, with Martella generously allowing him to change his recollections about the timing of events on May 13 whenever Bulgarian counter-evidence was too strong, failed to attract the media's attention.[48] Agca's June 28, 1983, retraction of his claim that he had visited Antonov's apartment and met his family was not mentioned in the mass media until a full year after the event, and even then suggested to the press no very serious problems with the case or with Martella's investigative work.[49] How could Agca know details about Antonov's apartment if he had never been there? An honest press would have pursued this relentlessly. The *New York Times,* with Sterling as its reporter, suppressed the issue.[50] The rest of the press simply wasn't interested.

The media also weren't interested in Orsen Oymen's finding that the Vatican had gone to some pains to try to implicate the Bulgarians, or the trial disclosure that the West German authorities had tried to bribe Gray Wolves member Oral Celik to come to West Germany and confirm Agca's claims. Pandico's and Pazienza's insider claims of Mafia and SISMI involvement in getting Agca to talk were also given only the slightest attention, and this accumulating mass of materials on the Italian process was never brought together for a reassessment.

Perhaps the most blatant case of willful ignorance concerned the Italian fixer and former member of SISMI, Francesco Pazienza. Wanted for several crimes, Pazienza had fled Italy, and in 1985 he resided in exile in New York City. Eventually he was seized and held there by the Immigration and Naturalization Service. Pazienza had been a partner of Michael Ledeen in the "Billygate" affair in Italy, and retained his connection after Ledeen became General Haig's right-hand man in Italy in the early days of the Reagan presidency. Pazienza had also been a close associate of SISMI head Giuseppe Santovito. From 1983 onward it was alleged in the Italian press that Pazienza had been involved in getting Agca to talk, and he himself eventually made detailed accusations of coaching by elements of SISMI. Although Pazienza was readily available for interviews in a New York City jail, the *New York Times* ignored him. Our hypothesis is that they did this because if they had talked to him it would have been difficult to avoid discussing his connections with Ledeen and Sterling (both *Times* sources and under *Times* protection). This would not have reflected well on the quality of the paper's sourcing. Pazienza's story would also have highlighted the *Times*'s suppression of facts concerning the corruption of SISMI and raised questions about coaching. This would have disturbed the propaganda line.

The trial in Rome was awkward for the Western media, as Agca quickly declared himself to be Jesus and, more important, failed to produce any supportive evidence backing up his claims of Bulgarian involvement. The diligent and extensive court investigation found numerous Gray Wolves links to Agca in the period just up to his assassination attempt, but no witness to his (allegedly) numerous meetings with Bulgarians in Rome, no money, no car, and, in the end, no conviction. As we have pointed out, in addition to the already available evidence of atrocious prison practice in dealing with Agca, and the 1981 meetings with intelligence officials and Martella's offer, there was a steady accumulation of claims and evidence of pressures on Agca to implicate the Bulgarians. But, despite this evidence and the failure to convict the Bulgarians after a lengthy investigation and trial, the mass media of the West never provided any serious reevaluations of the case. Almost uniformly they hid behind the fact that an Italian court dismissed the case for lack of evidence rather than demonstrated innocence. They never hinted at the possibility that an Italian court and jury might still be biased against the Eastern bloc and protective of the powerful Western interests that had supported the Bulgarian Connection so energetically.

The mass media also never looked back at their own earlier claims and those of the disinformationists to see how they had stood up to the test of accumulated evidence. On January 3, 1983, *Newsweek* had quoted an Italian official who said that "we have substantial evidence . . . [that] Agca operated in close contact with the Bulgarians," and the *New York Times* editorialized on October 20, 1984, that "Agca's accounts of meetings with Bulgarian officials are verifiable in important details." If there was "substantial evidence" and "verifiable" details long before the trial, why was this evidence not produced in the courtroom? Why, after an enormous further investigative effort was there still not enough evidence to sustain a conviction? The U.S. mass media didn't even try to answer these questions. This would mean asking serious questions about the validity of the SHK model and considering alternatives, which the media have never been prepared to do. For them, the alternative model, plausible from the beginning and, by March 1986, based on a great deal of evidence, was still the "Bulgarian view." The questions raised by the "Bulgarian view," we believe, would have been applied by the U.S. mass media to analogous facts in a Moscow setting. This means that the view actually employed by the media from beginning to end was a "U.S. government view," as suggested by a propaganda model. That this was true even after the trial ended we show in a detailed analysis in appendix 3, "Tagliabue's Finale on the Bulgarian Connection: A Case Study in Bias."

5

The Indochina Wars (I): Vietnam

MEDIA COVERAGE OF THE U.S. WARS IN INDOCHINA HAS ENgendered a good deal of bitter controversy, some close analysis of several specific incidents, and a few general studies.[1] It is widely held that the media "lost the war" by exposing the general population to its horrors and by unfair, incompetent, and biased coverage reflecting the "adversary culture" of the sixties. The media's reporting of the Tet offensive has served as the prime example of this hostility to established power, which, it has been argued, undermines democratic institutions and should be curbed, either by the media themselves or by the state.

A propaganda model leads to different expectations. On its assumptions, we would expect media coverage and interpretation of the war to take for granted that the United States intervened in the service of generous ideals, with the goal of defending South Vietnam from aggression and terrorism and in the interest of democracy and self-determination. With regard to the second-level debate on the performance of the media, a propaganda model leads us to expect that there would be no condemnation of the media for uncritical acceptance of the doctrine of

U.S. benevolence and for adherence to the official line on all central issues, or even awareness of these characteristics of media performance. Rather, given that the U.S. government did not attain all of its objectives in Indochina, the issue would be whether the media are to be faulted for undermining the noble cause by adopting too "adversarial" a stance and departing thereby from fairness and objectivity.

We shall see that all of these expectations are amply fulfilled.

5.1. THE BOUNDS OF CONTROVERSY

"For the first time in history," Robert Elegant writes, "the outcome of a war was determined not in the battlefield, but on the printed page, and above all, on the television screen," leading to the defeat of the United States in Vietnam. The belief that the media, particularly television, were responsible for U.S. government failures is widely expressed. It was endorsed by the right-wing media-monitoring organization Accuracy in Media in its hour-long "Vietnam Op/Ed" aired by public television in response to its own thirteen-part series on the war.[2] According to a more "moderate" expression of this view, the media had become a "notable new source of national power" by 1970 as part of a general "excess of democracy," contributing to "the reduction of governmental authority" at home and a resulting "decline in the influence of democracy abroad." "Broader interests of society and government" require that if journalists do not impose "standards of professionalism," "the alternative could well be regulation by the government" to the end of "restoring a balance between government and media."[3] Freedom House Executive-Director Leonard Sussman, commenting on *Big Story,* the study of media coverage of the Tet offensive sponsored by Freedom House, describes the "adversarial aspect" of the press-government relation as "normal," presupposing without argument that it has been demonstrated, but asks: "Must free institutions be overthrown because of the very freedom they sustain?"[4] John Roche proceeds further still, calling for congressional investigation of "the workings of these private governments" who distorted the record in pursuit of their "anti-Johnson mission," although he fears Congress is too "terrified of the media" and their awesome power to take on this necessary task.[5]

New York Times television critic John Corry defends the media as merely "unmindful," not "unpatriotic" as the harsher critics claim. They are not "anti-American," despite their adversarial stance; rather, "they reflect a powerful element of the journalistic-literary-political culture," where "the left wins battles . . . by default" because "its ideas make up the moral and intellectual framework for a large part of the culture," and "television becomes an accomplice of the left when it allows the culture to influence its news judgments," as in his view it regularly does.[6]

Media spokespersons, meanwhile, defend their commitment to independence while conceding that they may err through excessive zeal in calling the government to account in vigorous pursuit of their role as watchdog.

Within the mainstream, the debate is largely framed within the bounds illustrated by the PBS-AIM interchange broadcast on the public television network. AIM's "Vietnam Op/Ed" accused PBS of "deliberate misrepresentation" and other sins, while the producers of the documentary defended its accuracy. A dozen commentators, ranging from extreme hawks to mild critics of the war such as General Douglas Kinnard, added their thoughts.[7] The program concluded with a studio wrap-up featuring three "intelligent citizens": Colonel Harry Summers of the Army War College, a hawkish critic of the tactics of the war; Peter Braestrup, one of the harshest critics of media war coverage; and Huynh Sanh Thong, speaking for what the moderator called "the South Vietnamese community," meaning the exile community.

The hypothesis advanced by the propaganda model, excluded from debate as unthinkable, is that in dealing with the American wars in Indochina, the media were indeed "unmindful," but highly "patriotic" in the special and misleading sense that they kept—and keep—closely to the perspective of official Washington and the closely related corporate elite, in conformity to the general "journalistic-literary-political culture" from which "the left" (meaning dissident opinion that questions jingoist assumptions) is virtually excluded. The propaganda model predicts that this should be generally true not only of the choice of topics covered and the way they are covered, but also, and far more crucially, of the general background of presuppositions within which the issues are framed and the news presented. Insofar as there is debate among dominant elites, it will be reflected within the media, which in this narrow sense may adopt an "adversarial stance" with regard to those holding office, reflecting elite dissatisfaction with current policy. Otherwise the media will depart from the elite consensus only rarely and in limited ways. Even when large parts of the general public break free of the premises of the doctrinal system, as finally happened during the Indochina wars, real understanding based upon an alternative conception of the evolving history can be developed only with considerable effort by the most diligent and skeptical. And such understanding as can be reached through serious and often individual effort will be difficult to sustain or apply elsewhere, an extremely important matter for those who are truly concerned with democracy at home and "the influence of democracy abroad," in the real sense of these words.

These conclusions concerning media conformism are accepted in part by mainstream critics of the media. Thus Leonard Sussman, of Freedom House, observes that "U.S. intervention in 1965 enjoyed near-total . . . editorial support."[8] The "intervention" in 1965 included the deployment of U.S. combat forces in Vietnam, the regular bombing of North Vietnam, and the bombing of South Vietnam at triple the scale in a program of "unlimited aerial warfare inside the country at the price of literally pounding the place to bits."[9] It is a highly significant fact that neither then, nor before, was there any detectable questioning of the righteousness of the American cause in Vietnam, or of the necessity to proceed to full-scale "intervention." By that time, of course, only questions of tactics and costs remained open, and further discussion in the mainstream media was largely limited to these narrow issues. While dissent and domestic controversy became a focus of media coverage from 1965, the actual views of dissidents and resisters were virtually excluded. These individuals were presented primarily as a threat to order, and while their tactics might be discussed, their views were not: "The antiwar movement stood at the bottom of the media's hierarchy of legitimate political actors," Daniel Hallin concludes from his survey of television coverage (the print media were hardly different), "and its access to the news and influence over it were still more limited."[10] All exactly as the propaganda model predicts.

As the war progressed, elite opinion gradually shifted to the belief that the U.S. intervention was a "tragic mistake" that was proving too costly, thus enlarging the domain of debate to include a range of tactical questions hitherto excluded. Expressible opinion in the media broadened to accommodate these judgments, but the righteousness of the cause and nobility of intent were rarely subject to question. Rather, editorials explained that the "idealistic motives" of "the political and military commands" who "conceive[d] their role quite honestly as that of liberators and allies in the cause of freedom . . . had little chance to prevail against local leaders skilled in the art of manipulating their foreign protectors."[11] "Our Vietnamese" were too corrupt and we were too weak and too naive to resist their manipulations, while "their Vietnamese" were too wily and vicious. How could American idealism cope with such unfavorable conditions? At the war's end, the liberal media could voice the lament that "the high hopes and wishful idealism with which the American nation had been born . . . had been chastened by the failure of America to work its will in Indochina."[12] But no conflict can be perceived between "wishful idealism" and the commitment to "work our will" in foreign lands, a comment that holds of "the culture" more broadly.

As for direct reporting, the major charge of the influential Freedom House study of the Tet offensive, echoed by others who condemn the media for their overly "adversarial" stance, is that reporting was too "pessimistic." We return to the facts, but consideration of the logic of the charge shows that even if accurate, it would be quite consistent with a propaganda model. There was, no doubt, increased pessimism within the German general staff after Stalingrad. Similarly, Soviet elites openly expressed concern over the wisdom of "the defense of Afghanistan" and its costs, and some might have been "overly pessimistic" about the likelihood of success in this endeavor. But in neither case do we interpret these reactions as a departure from service to the national cause as defined by the state authorities. The Freedom House charge tacitly but clearly presupposes that the media must not only accept the framework of government propaganda, but must be upbeat and enthusiastic about the prospects for success in a cause that is assumed without discussion to be honorable and just.

This basic assumption endures throughout, and provides the basic framework for discussion and news reports. The harshest critics within the mainstream media, as well as what Corry calls "the culture," held that the war began with "blundering efforts to do good," although "by 1969" (that is, a year after corporate America had largely concluded that this enterprise should be liquidated) it had become "clear to most of the world—and most Americans—that the intervention had been a disastrous mistake," and that it was a "delusion" to attempt to build "a nation on the American model in South Vietnam"; the argument against the war "was that the United States had misunderstood the cultural and political forces at work in Indochina—that it was in a position where it could not impose a solution except at a price too costly to itself" (Anthony Lewis).[13] Stanley Karnow's highly praised companion volume to the PBS television series describes the American war as "a failed crusade" undertaken for aims that were "noble" although "illusory" and "motivated by the loftiest intentions": specifically, the commitment "to defend South Vietnam's independence."[14]

Within "the culture," it would be difficult to find harsher critics of U.S. Asia policy than John King Fairbank, the dean of American China scholarship, or Harvard government professor Stanley Hoffmann, or *Dissent* editor Irving Howe. In his presidential address to the American Historical Association in December 1968, Fairbank characterized the U.S. involvement, which he termed a "disaster," as the result of "an excess of righteousness and disinterested benevolence," an "error" based on misunderstanding. Howe explained that "we opposed the war because we believed, as Stanley Hoffman [*sic*] has written, that 'Washington could "save" the people of South Vietnam and Cambodia from Communism only at a cost that made a mockery of the word "save."' " Hoffmann explains later that our efforts in "supporting the South Vietnamese" were "undermined" by the way the war was fought, while the means adopted to "deter the North Vietnamese from further infiltration" were "never sufficient"; and sufficient means, "had the United States been willing to commit them, would have created for the United States real external dangers with potential adversaries and in relations with allies." Again, we find not the slightest recognition that the familiar pieties of state propaganda might be subject to some question.[15]

In its 1985 tenth-anniversary retrospective on the Vietnam war, *Foreign Affairs* presents both the hawk and the dove positions. Representing the more dovish view, David Fromkin and James Chace assert without argument that "the American decision to intervene in Indochina was predicated on the view that the United States has a duty to look beyond its purely national interests," and that, pursuant to its "global responsibilities," the United States must "serve the interests of mankind." "As a moral matter we were right to choose the lesser of two evils" and to oppose "communist aggression" by the Vietnamese in Vietnam, but on the "practical side" it was "wrong" because "our side was likely to lose." The moral imperatives of our service "to the interests of mankind" do not, however, require that we intervene to overthrow governments that are slaughtering their own populations, such as the Indonesian government we supported in 1965, or our Guatemalan and Salvadoran clients of the 1980s. On the contrary, they observe, the success of our Indonesian allies in destroying the domestic political opposition by violence in 1965 was a respectable achievement that should have led us to reconsider our Vietnam policy. They cite Lyndon Johnson's national security adviser, McGeorge Bundy, who feels in retrospect that "our effort" in Vietnam was "excessive" after 1965, when "a new anti-communist government took power in Indonesia and destroyed the communist party [the only mass-based political party] in that country . . .," incidentally slaughtering several hundred thousand people, mostly landless peasants, and thus "securing" Indonesia in accord with our "global responsibilities" and "serving the interests of mankind."[16]

Fromkin and Chace define "opponents of the war"—meaning, presumably, critics whose views merit serious consideration—as those who "did not believe that 'whipping' the enemy [North Vietnam] was enough, so long as the enemy refused to submit or surrender." The media, they say, "brought home to the American people how little effective control over the population had been purchased by all of General Westmoreland's victories," thus strengthening the "opponents of the war," dissatisfied by our inability to gain "effective control over the population." "The media cannot be blamed for pointing out the problem, and if General Westmoreland knew the answer to it, perhaps he should have revealed it to the public."

Outside of those committed to "the cause," although possibly skeptical about its feasibility or the means employed, there are only those whom McGeorge Bundy once described as "wild men in the wings," referring to people who dared to question the decisions of the "first team" that was determining U.S. policy in Vietnam.[17]

Quite generally, insofar as the debate over the war could reach the mainstream during the war or since, it was bounded on the one side by the "hawks," who felt that with sufficient dedication the United States could succeed in "defending South Vietnam," "controlling the population," and thus establishing "American-style democracy" there,[18] and on the other side by the "doves," who doubted that success could be achieved in these noble aims at reasonable cost[19]—later, there arrived the "owls," who observed the proceedings judiciously without succumbing to the illusions of either extreme of this wrenching controversy. Reporting and interpretation of the facts were framed in accordance with these principles.

5.2. "THE WILD MEN IN THE WINGS"

As the elite consensus eroded in the late 1960s, criticism of the "noble cause" on grounds of its lack of success became more acceptable, and the category of "wild men in the wings" narrowed to those who opposed the war on grounds of principle—the same grounds on which they opposed the Soviet invasions of Hungary, Czechoslovakia, and, later, Afghanistan. Let us consider how superpower intervention would be presented from a point of view that permits aggression to be understood as aggression.

In the case of Soviet intervention, there is no serious controversy. True, the Soviet Union has security concerns in Eastern Europe, including states that collaborated with the Nazis in an attack on the Soviet Union that practically destroyed it a generation ago and now serve as a buffer to a rearmed West Germany that is part of a hostile and threatening military alliance. True, Afghanistan borders areas of the Soviet Union where the population could be inflamed by a radical Islamic fundamentalist revival, and the rebels, openly supported by bitter enemies of the Soviet Union, are undoubtedly terrorists committed to harsh oppression and religious fanaticism who carry out violent acts inside the Soviet Union itself and have been attacking Afghanistan from Pakistani bases since 1973, six years before the Soviet invasion.[20] But none of these complexities bear on the fact that the Soviet Union invaded Czechoslovakia, Hungary, and Afghanistan, holds Poland in a firm grip, etc. True, the Russians were invited into Afghanistan in 1979, but as the London *Economist* accurately observed, "an invader is an invader unless invited in by a government with some claim to legitimacy,"[21] and the government that the Soviet Union installed to invite it in plainly lacked any such claim.

None of these matters elicit serious controversy, nor should they. The Soviet invasion of Afghanistan, like earlier cases of Soviet intervention in the region occupied by the Red Army as it drove out the Nazis during World War II, are described as aggression, and the facts are reported in these terms. The United Nations has repeatedly condemned the Soviet aggression in Afghanistan and regularly investigates and denounces the crimes they have committed. Western reporters cover the war from the standpoint of the rebels defending their country from foreign attack, entering Afghanistan with them from their Pakistani sanctuaries. Official Soviet pronouncements are treated not merely with skepticism but with disdain.

In the case of the U.S. intervention in Indochina, no such interpretation has ever been conceivable, apart from "the wild men in the wings," although it is at least as well grounded as the standard, and obviously correct, interpretation of the Soviet aggression in Afghanistan. Furthermore, the reporting practice of journalists and commentators is also radically different in the two cases. We put off for a moment the more significant issue of how the war is understood, focusing first on the narrower question of journalistic practice.

In sharp contrast to the Soviet aggression, it was standard practice throughout the Indochina war for journalists to report Washington pronouncements as fact, even in the extreme case when official statements were known to be false. Furthermore, this practice persisted through the period when the media had allegedly had become "a notable new source of national power" threatening government authority. To mention only one typical case from the year in which, we are to understand, this status had been definitively attained (see p. 170), in March 1970 the media reported a North Vietnamese invasion of Laos on the basis of a speech by President Nixon announcing that North Vietnamese forces in Laos had suddenly risen from 50,000 to 67,000. Nixon's comment came immediately after the U.S. military attaché in Vientiane had presented his standard briefing citing the lower figure—a source of much private amusement among the press corps in Vientiane, as one of us witnessed at first hand—but the presidential fabrication was reported as fact. The lower figure was also fraudulent, although this fact was never reported.[22] Throughout the Indochina wars, when official statements were questioned, it was generally on the basis of U.S. military sources in the field, so that reporting and analysis remained well within the bounds set by U.S. power.[23]

Only very rarely did U.S. reporters make any effort to see the war from the point of view of "the enemy"—the peasants of South Vietnam, Laos, or later Cambodia—or to accompany the military forces of "the enemy" resisting the U.S. assault. Such evidence as was available was ignored or dismissed. In reporting the war in Afghanistan, it is considered essential and proper to observe it from the standpoint of the victims. In the case of Indochina, it was the American invaders who were regarded as the victims of the "aggression" of the Vietnamese, and the war was reported from their point of view, just as subsequent commentary, including cinema, views the war from this perspective.

Refugee testimony, which could have provided much insight into the nature of the war, was also regularly ignored. The enemy of the U.S. government was the enemy of the press, which could not even refer to them by their own name: they were the "Viet Cong," a derogatory term of U.S.-Saigon propaganda, not the National Liberation Front, a phrase "never used without quotation marks" by American reporters,[24] who regularly referred to "Communist aggression" (E. W. Kenworthy) by the South Vietnamese in South Vietnam and Communist efforts "to subvert this country" (David Halberstam)[25]—their country, then under the rule of a U.S.-imposed client regime.

To a substantial extent, the war was reported from Washington. In late 1970, when the process of elite defection was well under way, *Los Angeles Times* Washington correspondent Jules Witcover described the Washington scene during the earlier years:

> While the press corps in those years diligently reported what the government said about Vietnam, and questioned the inconsistencies as they arose, too few sought out opposing viewpoints and expertise until too late, when events and the prominence of the Vietnam dissent could no longer be ignored. In coverage of the war, the press corps' job narrowed down to three basic tasks—reporting what the government said, finding out whether it was true, and assessing whether the policy enunciated worked. The group did a highly professional job on the first task. But it fell down on the second and third, and there is strong evidence the reason is too many reporters sought the answers in all three categories from the same basic source—the government.[26]

The search for "opposing viewpoints" as things went wrong was also extremely narrow, limited to the domain of tactics—that is, limited to the question of "whether the policy enunciated worked," viewed entirely from the standpoint of U.S. interests, and with official premises taken as given.

Furthermore, the U.S. war was openly supported by U.S. allies, some of whom sent combat forces (Australia, Thailand, South Korea), while others enriched themselves through their participation in the destruction of Indochina. For Japan and South Korea, this participation contributed significantly to their "take-off" to the status of major economic powers, while Canada and Western Europe also profited from their support for the U.S. operations. In contrast to the Soviet invasion of Afghanistan, the United Nations never condemned the U.S. "intervention," nor did it investigate or denounce the crimes committed in the course of U.S. military operations, a reflection of U.S. world power and influence. These facts notwithstanding, it is common practice to denounce the UN and world opinion for its "double standard" in condemning the U.S. "intervention" in defense of South Vietnam while ignoring the Soviet invasion of Afghanistan, regularly described as "genocidal," a term never used in the mainstream media with regard to the United States in Indochina.

At the time of the full-scale U.S. invasion of Vietnam, in 1965, when there was as yet no debate over the righteousness of the already massive "intervention," the United States had not yet succeeded in establishing a government able or willing to "invite it in." It appears that the United States simply *moved in* without even the formalities of request or acquiescence by a supposedly sovereign government. Nevertheless, at the dovish extreme of U.S. journalism, Tom Wicker, explaining his view that "the United States has no historic or God-given mission to bring democracy to other nations," observes that the matter is different in the case of the "maintenance of freedom" where it already exists:

> U.S. support for a democratic regime that is being attacked or subverted by repressive forces of the left or right might well be justified if invited—although, *as in Vietnam,* the "freedom" being defended may be minimal and the cost may be astronomical.[27]

As a dissident commentator, Wicker recognizes that the "freedom" we were defending in Vietnam was minimal and that the cost proved too high. But the doctrine that we were "invited in" remains sacrosanct, and the idea that we were "defending" nothing beyond our right to impose our will by violence is completely beyond the range of the thinkable. We might ask how we would characterize the Soviet media if the harshest condemnation of the war in Afghanistan that could be expressed in the year 2000 is that Soviet support for the democratic regime in Afghanistan that invited the Russians in might be justified, although the "freedom" that the Soviets were defending was perhaps minimal and the cost was far too high.

Let us now turn to "the wild men in the wings" who adopt the principles universally accepted in the case of Soviet aggression when they approach the U.S. wars in Indochina. The basic facts are not in doubt. By the late 1940s, U.S. authorities took for granted that in backing France's effort to reconquer its Indochina colonies after World War II, they were opposing the forces of Vietnamese nationalism represented by the Viet Minh, led by Ho Chi Minh. In 1947, the State Department noted that Ho had established himself as "the symbol of nationalism and the struggle for freedom to the overwhelming majority of the population."[28] By September 1948, the department deplored "our inability to suggest any practicable solution of the Indochina problem" in the light of "the unpleasant fact that Communist Ho Chi Minh is the strongest and perhaps the ablest figure in Indochina and that any suggested solution which excludes him is an expedient of uncertain outcome," the Communists under Ho having "capture[d] control of the nationalist movement," while the U.S. "long-term objective" was "to eliminate so far as possible Communist influence in Indochina."[29] Nonetheless, the United States supported the cause of France against Vietnam, covering some 80 percent of the cost of the war at the end and contemplating a direct U.S. attack, had France agreed.

When the French withdrew, in 1954, the United States at once turned to the task of subverting the Geneva agreements that laid the groundwork for unification of Vietnam with countrywide elections by 1956, establishing a client state in South Vietnam (the GVN) that controlled its population with substantial violence and rejected the terms of the Geneva political settlement, with U.S. support. State terrorism evoked renewed resistance, and by 1959, Viet Minh cadres in the South, who were being decimated by U.S.-organized state terror, received authorization to use violence in self-defense, threatening the quick collapse of the U.S.-imposed regime, which by then had killed tens of thousands of people and alienated much of the peasantry as well as urban elites. The Vietnam correspondent for the *London Times* and the *Economist,* David Hotham, wrote in 1959 that the Diem regime imposed by the United States

> has crushed all opposition of every kind, however anti-Communist it might be. He has been able to do this, simply and solely because of the massive dollar aid he has had from across the Pacific, which kept in power a man who, by all the laws of human and political affairs, would long ago have fallen. Diem's main supporters are to be found in North America, not in Free Vietnam. . . .[30]

The leading U.S. government specialist on Vietnamese Communism, Douglas Pike, whose denunciations of the "Viet Cong" often reached the level of hysteria, conceded that the NLF "maintained that its contest with the GVN and the United States should be fought out at the political level and that the use of massed military might was in itself illegitimate," until forced by the United States and its clients "to use counterforce to survive."[31]

The Kennedy administration escalated the war in South Vietnam, engaging U.S. military forces directly in bombing, defoliation, and "advising" combat troops from 1961 to 1962 as part of an effort to drive several million people into concentration camps ("strategic hamlets") in which they could be "protected" behind barbed wire and armed guard from the guerrillas whom, the United States conceded, they were willingly supporting. Douglas Pike assessed indigenous support for the NLF at about 50 percent of the population at the time—which is more than George Washington could have claimed—while the United States could rally virtually no indigenous support. He explained that political options were hopeless, since the NLF was the only "truly mass-based political party in South Vietnam," and no one, "with the possible exception of the Buddhists, thought themselves equal in size and power to risk entering a coalition, fearing that if they did the whale [the NLF] would swallow the minnow." As for the Buddhists, the United States regarded them "as equivalent to card-carrying Communists" (Ambassador Henry Cabot Lodge), and later backed the use of force to destroy their political movement, to ensure that no independent political force would remain, since no such force could be controlled.[32] In a highly regarded military history and moral tract in justification of the American war, Guenter Lewy describes the purpose of the U.S. air operations of the early 1960s, which involved "indiscriminate killing" and "took a heavy toll of essentially innocent men, women and children," in a manner that Orwell would have appreciated: villages in "open zones" were "subjected to random bombardment by artillery and aircraft so as to drive the inhabitants into the safety of the strategic hamlets."[33]

It was conceded on all sides that the government imposed by the United States lacked any significant popular support. The experienced U.S. pacification chief John Paul Vann, widely regarded as the U.S. official most knowledgeable about the situation in South Vietnam, wrote in 1965 that

> A popular political base for the Government of South Vietnam does not now exist. . . . The existing government is oriented toward the exploitation of the rural and lower class urban populations. It is, in fact, a continuation of the French colonial system of government with upper class Vietnamese replacing the French. . . . The dissatisfaction of the agrarian population . . . is expressed largely through alliance with the NLF.[34]

Virtually all parties concerned, apart from the United States, were making serious efforts in the early 1960s to avoid an impending war by neutralizing South Vietnam, Laos, and Cambodia—the official stand of the National Liberation Front, the "Viet Cong" of U.S. propaganda, essentially the southern branch of the Viet Minh. But the United States was committed to preventing any political settlement.

Unable to develop any political base in the south, the U.S. government proceeded to expand the war. It was able to do this by continually manipulating the political scene in South Vietnam to assure the attainment of its objective: continued fighting until an anti-Communist regime, susceptible to American will, was established in the South. Ambassador Lodge observed in January 1964 that "It is obvious that the generals are all we have got."[35] And we would keep replacing them until we got the right ones, "right" meaning that they were willing to follow orders and fight, not negotiate. One of Diem's early replacements told newsmen that he found out that he was going to be the next head of state only when his U.S. adviser "told me that a coup d'état was planned in Saigon and that I was to become President. . . ." General Maxwell Taylor spoke quite frankly about the need of "establishing some reasonably satisfactory government," replacing it if we are not satisfied, either with civilians, or with "a military dictatorship."[36]

It should be noted in this connection that after the long-standing U.S. manipulation of governments in its client state had finally succeeded in its aim, and the United States had placed in power two former French collaborators, Ky and Thieu, whose sole qualification for rule was that they met the U.S. condition of willingness to fight and evade political settlement, the U.S. media continued to pretend that the government of South Vietnam was a free choice of the South Vietnamese people.[37] Thus the *New York Times* commented editorially on June 4, 1966, that "Washington cannot shape the political future in Saigon, but it can continue to urge a search for unity among all the South Vietnamese political factions pending the September elections." In fact, the rulers at the moment had been imposed by the United States, the election was a U.S. idea, and—needless to say—the South Vietnamese who constituted the only "truly mass-based political party in South Vietnam" (Pike, referring to the NLF) were not considered one of the "South Vietnamese political factions." As for the "unity" sought by the United States, it was intended solely to provide a base for prosecution of the U.S. war. As that goal could be accomplished only by suppression of all popular movements, later in 1966 the military junta, with U.S. approval and direct assistance, crushed by force the largest non-Communist group, the organized Buddhists, thereby clearing the ground for durable rule by Thieu and Ky. Despite all of this, the U.S. media did not point out that any basis for a free election had been destroyed, and that the unelected government was maintained in power solely because its aims were identical to those of the U.S. administration—that is, that it was a classic example of a puppet government.[38] On the contrary, the junta never ceased to be the leaders of free and independent South Vietnam, the word "puppet" being reserved for agents of enemy states.

Returning to the expanding U.S. war, efforts to obtain congressional support succeeded with the August 7, 1964 resolution, after the Tonkin Gulf incident, authorizing the president "to take all necessary measures to repel any armed attack against the forces of the United States and to prevent further aggression" by the Vietnamese in Vietnam, "a virtual blank check in waging the war for the Administration."[39]

The United States invaded outright in early 1965, also initiating the regular bombing of North Vietnam in the hope that Hanoi would use its influence to call off the southern resistance, and to justify the escalation of the attack against the South, which required something beyond the "internal aggression" by the NLF within South Vietnam that UN Ambassador Adlai Stevenson identified as the problem we faced.[40] By the time of the U.S. land invasion in 1965, over 150,000 people had been killed in South Vietnam, according to figures cited by Bernard Fall, most of them "under the crushing weight of American armor, napalm, jet bombers and finally vomiting gases," or victims of the state terrorism of the U.S.-installed regimes.[41] From January 1965, the United States also employed Korean mercenaries, some 300,000 in all, who carried out brutal atrocities in the South. The first regular North Vietnamese unit, a four-hundred-man battalion, was thought to have been detected in border areas of the south in late April 1965; until the Tet offensive in January 1968, according to Pentagon sources, North Vietnamese units, mainly drawing U.S. forces away from populated centers, were at about the level of Korean and Thai mercenaries who were terrorizing South Vietnam, all vastly outnumbered by the U.S. forces.

By 1967, the war had reached such a level of devastation that, in Fall's words, "Vietnam as a cultural and historic entity . . . is threatened with extinction . . . [as] . . . the countryside literally dies under the blows of the largest military machine ever unleashed on an area of this size."[42] The strategy of destroying South Vietnam was generally considered a success. Harvard professor and government adviser Samuel Huntington concluded that "In an absent-minded way the United States in Vietnam may well have stumbled upon the answer to 'wars of national liberation,' " namely, "forced-draft urbanization and mobilization" by violence so extreme as "to produce a massive migration from countryside to city," thus "undercutting" the Maoist strategy of organizing the peasant population (over 80 percent of the population when these techniques were initiated) and undermining the Viet Cong, "a powerful force which cannot be dislodged from its constituency so long as the constituency continues to exist."[43]

The Tet offensive of January 1968, conducted almost entirely by South Vietnamese NLF forces in cities and towns throughout the country, convinced U.S. elites that the war was proving too costly to the United States, and that strategy should shift toward a more "capital-intensive" operation with reliance on an indigenous mercenary army (in the technical sense of the phrase) and gradual withdrawal of the U.S. forces, which were by then suffering a severe loss of morale, a matter of growing concern to military authorities. U.S. forces undertook a post-Tet "accelerated pacification campaign," in actuality a mass-murder operation that demolished the NLF and much of what was left of the peasant society while killing tens of thousands and extending the destruction of the country. Much of North Vietnam, particularly the southern region, was turned into a moonscape, and Laos was battered under the heaviest bombing in history, including the peasant society of northern Laos where, the U.S. government conceded, the bombing had no relation to its war in South Vietnam. The United States bombed and invaded Cambodia, destroying much of the countryside and mobilizing embittered peasants to the cause of the Khmer Rouge, previously a marginal force. By the war's end, the death toll in Indochina may have reached four million or more,[44] and the land and societies were utterly devastated. Subsequent U.S. policy has sought to prevent any recovery from this cataclysm by refusing reparations, aid, and trade, and blocking assistance from other sources—although not all aid: U.S. aid to the Khmer Rouge in the 1980s appears to have run to many millions.[45]

Applying the principles that we rightly adopt in the case of Soviet aggression, the conclusion seems obvious. The United States attacked South Vietnam, arguably by 1962 and unquestionably by 1965, expanding its aggression to all of Indochina with lethal and long-term effects. Media coverage or other commentary on these events that does not begin by recognizing these essential facts is mere apologetics for terrorism and murderous aggression. The United States was "defending South Vietnam" in the same sense in which the Soviet Union is "defending Afghanistan."

But from the point of view of the media, or "the culture," there is no such event in history as the U.S. attack against South Vietnam and the rest of Indochina. One would be hard put to find even an single reference within the mainstream to any such event, or any recognition that history could possibly be viewed from this perspective—just as *Pravda,* presumably, records no such event as the Soviet invasion of Afghanistan, only the defense of Afghanistan against "bandits" supported by the CIA. Even at the peak period of peace-movement activism there was virtually no opposition to the war within the intellectual culture on the grounds that aggression is wrong[46]—the grounds universally adopted in the case of the Soviet invasion of Czechoslovakia in 1968—for a very simple reason: the fact of U.S. aggression was unrecognized. There was much debate during the war over whether the North Vietnamese were guilty of aggression in Vietnam, and as we have seen, even the South Vietnamese were condemned for "internal aggression" (Adlai Stevenson); but there was *no discussion* of whether the United States was guilty of aggression in its direct attack against South Vietnam, then all of Indochina. These intriguing facts reflect the overwhelming dominance of the state propaganda system and its ability to set the terms of thought and discussion, even for those who believe themselves to be taking an "adversarial stance." As for the media, departures from these doctrinal principles were negligible; indeed, they may well have been literally zero in the vast coverage and commentary on the war, while it was in progress or since.

In a revealing article entitled "Lessons of Running Viets' War," published in August 1987, Stanley Karnow, a veteran Asia correspondent and author of a highly regarded liberal history of the Vietnam War, argues that the United States erred in Vietnam because it allowed the Vietnamese people to depend too heavily on us.[47] Reciprocally, the South Vietnamese people also "allowed themselves to be lulled into a complacent sense of dependency on the United States," thinking we wouldn't back down, not realizing that small clients are expendable. The South Vietnamese people who fought the U.S. invasion are never mentioned, or considered to be "South Vietnamese" within Karnow's patriotic frame, although they constituted the majority of the population and the only serious political force, according to U.S. specialists and officials on the scene, and despite the fact that the U.S.-selected faction repeatedly stressed that "Frankly, we are not strong enough now to compete with the communists on a purely political basis."[48] A Soviet Karnow would no doubt express similar concern in retrospect that the Soviet Union allowed the "Afghans" to rely too heavily on Soviet power.

By the standards we rightly apply to the actions of the Soviet Union or other official enemies, there is nothing further that need be said about the media and Indochina. Any further discussion is on a par with the minor question of whether *Pravda* reports facts accurately about "the Soviet defense of Afghanistan." Adopting the Freedom House–Trilateral Commission perspective, a Communist party functionary might criticize *Pravda* for excessive pessimism or for too adversarial a stance, contributing to the eventual loss of the war and the takeover of Afghanistan by feudalist elements committed to terrorism, horrifying repression of women, religious fanaticism, plans to "march on Jerusalem," etc. Or if he found that the reporting was sufficiently upbeat and not too distorted, he might laud *Pravda* for its accuracy and objectivity. But all of this would be nonsense, whatever is discovered; serious evaluation of the media is effectively over when we discover that the basic principle of state propaganda—the principle that the USSR is defending Afghanistan from terrorist attack—is adopted as the unquestioned framework for further reporting and discussion. The same is true in the case of U.S. aggression in Indochina.

We cannot quite say that the propaganda model is verified in the case of the Indochina wars, since it fails to predict such extraordinary, far-reaching, and exceptionless subservience to the state propaganda system. The fact that this judgment is correct—as it plainly is—is startling enough. Even more revealing with regard to Western intellectual culture is that the simple facts cannot be perceived, and their import lies far beyond the bounds of the thinkable.

Nevertheless, let us pursue the narrow question of media coverage of Indochina, bearing in mind that we are now turning to relatively minor matters, having taken note of a central and quite devastating criticism: the media's pervasive, docile, and unthinking acceptance of a set of patriotic assumptions at such a level as to make further commentary of secondary significance, at best.

5.3. THE EARLY STAGES: A CLOSER LOOK

The "first Indochina war," fought by the French and their client forces and largely supplied by the United States, came to an end with the Geneva Accords of 1954, which established a partition at the 17th parallel pending reunification through elections within two years. The United States pledged not to obstruct these arrangements.

The Geneva settlement was quickly undermined by the United States and its client regime because it was taken for granted on all sides that elections would lead to a unified Vietnam under Viet Minh rule. "American intelligence sources were unanimous that Diem [the U.S.-imposed client] would lose any national election," George Kahin concludes from a close inspection of the available record. The Viet Minh had agreed to the Geneva decision for regroupment of its forces well to the north of territories it controlled on the basis of "the assurance that the struggle for the control of Vietnam would be transferred from the military to the political level, a realm in which the Vietminh leaders knew their superiority over the French and their Vietnamese collaborators was even greater than it was militarily. . . . For the Vietminh, this was the heart of the Geneva Agreements."[49]

The secret U.S. response to the perceived disaster of Geneva was a plan to resort to military action (including attacks on China if deemed necessary) in the event of "local Communist subversion or rebellion not constituting armed attack," in explicit violation of the UN Charter, which limits the use of force to self-defense in the event of "armed attack" until the UN Security Council is able to respond. This crucial decision, misrepresented beyond recognition in the *Pentagon Papers* history and generally ignored, also recommended operations against China, "covert operations on a large and effective scale" throughout Indochina (including North Vietnam), remilitarization of Japan, development of Thailand "as the focal point for U.S. covert and psychological operations in Southeast Asia," etc.[50] Defense Secretary Robert McNamara observed in a memorandum for President Johnson that "Only the U.S. presence after 1954 held the south together . . . and enabled Diem to refuse to go through with the 1954 provision calling for nationwide free elections in 1956."[51]

Surveying the media during this period, Howard Elterman observes that "during a six-month period in 1955 and 1956, there was virtually no news coverage" about the U.S. policy of undermining the Geneva Accords in the *New York Times* and the three newsweeklies. Communist charges to this effect were occasionally mentioned on back pages but dismissed as propaganda—accurate propaganda, in fact. When the evasion of elections was conceded, it was justified on the basis of Communist terror and regimentation. The *Times* (June 2, 1956) described Vietnam as a country "divided into the Communist regime in the north and a democratic government in the south"—namely, the murderous and corrupt Diem dictatorship. *Newsweek* denounced the "wide infiltration in South Vietnam" in support of the "implacable purpose" of the Viet Minh, while *U.S. News & World Report* condemned Ho Chi Minh for "plotting new Red aggression in Southeast Asia."[52]

More generally, through 1956 "the press insured that the reading public would view the war as a struggle between Communism and the Free World," Susan Welch observes on the basis of her survey of several leading journals. Ho Chi Minh and the Viet Minh were presented as "merely agents of Moscow and Peking whose primary means of gaining support was through terror and force (although occasional mention was made of their nationalist appeal)," while France was "a gallant ally . . . fighting alongside the United States to preserve liberty and justice in Asia," a cause carried on by the United States alone after Geneva. State doctrine was "never challenged" by editors or columnists. The liberal press showed particular enthusiasm for the cause, and "News stories also reinforced the preconceptions of the Administration," because "the press relied almost completely on Administration sources for information which was reported." Although coverage of Indochina was limited, apart from a peak in 1954, and faded still further afterwards, "the terms of the future debate over U.S. policy were being hardened into usage by the press."[53]

With peaceful settlement successfully deterred, the United States and its client regime turned to the task of internal repression, killing tens of thousands and imprisoning tens of thousands more.[54] Diem supporter and adviser Joseph Buttinger describes "massive expeditions" in 1956 that destroyed villages, with hundreds or thousands of peasants killed and tens of thousands arrested by soldiers in regions "controlled by the Communists without the slightest use of force," facts that "were kept secret from the American people"—and still are.[55]

The main target of the repression was the anti-French resistance, the Viet Minh, which was virtually decimated by the late 1950s. The reasons for the resort to violence were simple and have been amply documented.[56] Recourse to violence was the only feasible response to the successes of the Viet Minh, reconstituted as the National Liberation Front (NLF), in organizing the peasantry, which left the United States only one option: to shift the struggle away from the political arena, where it was weak, to the arena of violence, where it was strong. Despite the U.S.-organized terror, the Communist party continued to advocate political action. The outline of strategy for the coming year sent to the South in late 1958 still called for political struggle without the use of arms.[57] As Jeffrey Race documents, when the Communist party finally authorized the use of violence in self-defense in 1959 in response to pleas from the southern Viet Minh, the slaughter could no longer proceed unimpeded, and government authority quickly collapsed. Nevertheless, ". . . the government terrorized far more than did the revolutionary movement—for example, by liquidations of former Vietminh by artillery and ground attacks on 'communist villages,' and by roundups of 'communist sympathizers.' "

The fundamental source of strength for the revolutionary movement, Race continues, was the appeal of its constructive programs—for example, the land-reform program, which "achieved a far broader distribution of land than did the government program, and without the killing and terror which is associated in the minds of Western readers with communist practices in land reform." On the contrary, "the principal violence was brought about not by the Party but by the government, in its attempts to reinstall the landlords"—the usual pattern, in fact, although not "in the minds of Western readers." The lowest economic strata benefited the most from the redistributive policies implemented. Authority was decentralized and placed in the hands of local people, in contrast to the rule of the U.S. client regime, perceived as "outside forces" by major segments of the local population: "what attracted people to the revolutionary movement was that it represented a new society in which there would be an individual *redistribution* of values, including power and status as well as material possessions." In Long An province, near Saigon, which Race studied intensively, the NLF had become dominant in the early 1960s, while the government apparatus and its armed forces dissolved without violent conflict, undermined by NLF organizing and propaganda. By late 1964, parts of the province were declared a free-strike zone, and by early 1965, "revolutionary forces had gained victory in nearly all the rural areas of Long An."[58]

The first units of the "North Vietnamese aggressors" entered the province at the time of the 1968 Tet offensive. In fact, up to summer 1969, when the post-Tet accelerated pacification campaign had succeeded in decimating the indigenous resistance, U.S. sources reported about eight hundred North Vietnamese "against an estimated total of 49,000 Vietcong soldiers and support troops" in the entire Mekong Delta.[59]

This picture and what it entails was essentially invisible to the American public, and it is so remote from news coverage that sampling of the record is beside the point. The same remains true today outside of the specialist and dissident literature.

The context of McNamara's observation cited earlier on the crucial U.S. role in blocking the election and unification provisions after Geneva was the "growth of antiwar and neutralist sentiment in the Saigon-controlled areas" in 1964. This came at a time when virtually all Vietnamese factions, along with international opinion generally, were seeking a political solution among Vietnamese that would head off the impending war to which the United States was committed because of its recognition that it had no political base in South Vietnam.[60]

The United States overturned the Diem regime in 1963 because of its ineptitude in conducting the war, as well as because of fears that it was moving toward a negotiated settlement with the NLF. There were few illusions about popular support for the U.S. efforts to maintain and extend the military struggle. As for the generals, who are "all we have got," as Ambassador Lodge recognized in January 1964, U.S. policymakers knew little about them. William Bundy, soon to become assistant secretary of state for Far Eastern affairs, later commented that "Actually no one on our side knew what the new people were thinking at all. . . . Our requirements were really very simple—we wanted any government which would continue to fight." The generals, however, did not want to continue to fight. Rather, along with the prime minister installed as a civilian cover for the military regime, they "wanted to move as rapidly as possible towards transferring the struggle for power in the South from the military to the political level," leading to "a negotiated agreement among the Vietnamese parties themselves, without American intervention." They saw the NLF "as preponderantly noncommunist in membership" and largely independent of Hanoi's control, and regarded a political settlement among South Vietnamese as feasible in essential agreement with the official NLF program.[61]

But none of this was acceptable to the United States. President Johnson explained to Ambassador Lodge that his mission was "knocking down the idea of neutralization wherever it rears its ugly head," because neutralism, as Ambassador Maxwell Taylor observed, "appeared to mean throwing the internal political situation open and thus inviting Communist participation" in a democratic process, here—as always—intolerable to the United States unless the right outcome is first determined by establishing a proper distribution of force.[62] Ambassador Taylor feared as the worst outcome a government that would "continue to seek a broadened consensus" and would thus "become susceptible to an accommodation with the liberation front." After the war ended, senior Pentagon legal adviser Paul Warnke observed critically in retrospect that "For the United States to 'compromise' and permit the indigenous forces of Vietnam to work their own way would be to condone the demise of the anti-Communist regime we had supported in Saigon for twenty years."

UN Secretary-General U Thant initiated a negotiation effort in the fall of 1964, with the support of Moscow and Hanoi and in accord with the consensus of Vietnamese as well as others, but it was rebuffed by Washington. As for the media, "It was not until after the die had been cast—not until March 9, 1965, after the United States had mounted its sustained air war against the North and landed the first U.S. ground forces in Vietnam—that *The New York Times* reported U Thant's 1964 efforts."[63]

The U.S. position throughout was that "after, *but only after,* we have established a clear pattern of pressure," could peaceful means be considered (William Bundy, Aug. 11, 1964; his emphasis). First violence, then—perhaps—recourse to the peaceful means required by international law and the supreme law of the land. The elections provision of the Geneva Accords had been officially described in a 1961 State Department white paper as "a well-laid trap" that the United States had skillfully evaded, and planners were in no mood to fall into such a "trap" in 1964, until the use of violence had secured their objectives.[64] Increasingly, U.S. planners turned to the policy of expanding the war to the North in the hope that this would compensate for their political weakness.

No such conception of the evolving events, and their meaning, was ever made accessible through the mainstream media, which kept to the official line that the United States was pursuing limited measures "to strengthen South Vietnam against attack by the Communists," supporting South Vietnam "against Communist aggression."[65]

In the *New York Times* version, the United States was leading "the free world's fight to contain aggressive Communism" (Robert Trumbull), defending South Vietnam "against the proxy armies of Soviet Russia—North and South Vietnamese guerrillas" (Hanson Baldwin), just as the French had fought "a seven-and-a-half-year struggle" against "foreign-inspired and supplied Communists." In early 1965, President Johnson decided "to step up resistance to Vietcong infiltration in South Vietnam" (Tom Wicker); the Vietcong "infiltrate" in their own country, while we "resist" this aggression. Since the South Vietnamese guerrillas were "trying to subvert this country" (David Halberstam), it was natural that the *Times* supported the strategic-hamlet program as necessary despite the coercion and brutality; it was "conducted as humanely as possible" to offer the peasants "better protection against the Communists" (Halberstam, Homer Bigart). The peasant support for the South Vietnamese "aggressors" and the reasons for it were ignored. Hallin comments that in the entire *New York Times* coverage from 1961 through September 1963, he found two "extremely brief" references to land tenure.[66]

While the print media did on occasion reflect the perceptions and opinions of American military officers in the field, arousing much irate condemnation thereby for their anti-Americanism and "negative reporting," television was more obedient. Thus "the head of the Pentagon's public-affairs office was able to assure Kennedy that the [NBC] network had been persuaded that it would be 'against the interest of the United States' to show its coverage of 'rough treatment by South Vietnamese soldiers to Viet-Cong prisoners, with a U.S. Army captain appearing in this sequence.' NBC's news director undertook to withhold this film's scheduled appearance on the Huntley-Brinkley show, and to keep it on the shelf so far as any other programs were concerned."[67]

Until the expansion of the war in 1965 began to provoke some concern, the NLF and DRV were "treated almost exclusively as an arm of international Communism," Hallin found in his analysis of the *Times*'s coverage. "The term *civil war* began to be used in 1965" and "the term *aggression* began to appear sometimes in quotation marks"—referring, of course, to Vietnamese aggression in Vietnam, the concept of American aggression being unimaginable, then or since. But concern over Vietnamese "aggression" never abated, as when James Reston discussed "the main point": "How, then, is this aggression by subversion to be stopped?"—referring to aggression by Vietnamese against the American invaders and their clients. Similarly, on television, even more conformist than the print media, Peter Jennings, showing Pentagon films on U.S. air attacks, commented that "This is the shape of things to come for Communist aggression in Vietnam," while NBC's Jack Perkins, reporting an air-force attack that wiped out a "village unabashedly advertising itself with signs and flags as a Vietcong village," justified the attack as necessary: "The whole village had turned on the Americans, so the whole village was being destroyed." It is taken for granted that the Americans had every right to be marauding in a region of Vietnam where "Everything in this area for years was Vietcong." A television report on Operation Attleboro described the fighting as raging "once again to preserve democracy."[68]

Summarizing, from the late 1940s, the United States supported the French war of conquest; overturned the political settlement arranged at Geneva in 1954; established a terrorist client regime in the southern section of the country divided by foreign (i.e., U.S.) force; moved on to open aggression against South Vietnam by 1962 and worked desperately to prevent the political settlement sought by Vietnamese on all sides; and then invaded outright in 1965, initiating an air and ground war that devastated Indochina. Throughout this period, the media presented the U.S. intervention entirely within the framework predicted by a propaganda model.

There are, of course, those who demand still higher standards of loyalty to the state, and for them, the fact that critical perceptions of American military officers in the field sometimes reached public attention is an intolerable "adversarial stance" reflecting the left-wing proclivities of "the culture." Putting this interesting perspective to the side, as far as this period is concerned we may dismiss the conception that the media "lost the war," although it would be quite accurate to conclude that they encouraged the United States to enter and pursue a war of aggression, which they later were to regard as "a tragedy," or "a blunder," while never acknowledging their fundamental contribution to rallying public support for the policies that they were ultimately to deplore. Given the conformism and obedience of the media during this crucial period, when the basis for U.S. aggression was firmly and irrevocably laid, it is small wonder that public concern was so slight, and that opposition was so negligible as to be entirely without significance. Only the most ardent researcher could have developed a moderately clear understanding of what was taking place in Indochina.

Public attitudes after the bombing of North Vietnam in February

1965, in "reprisal" for an attack on U.S. military installations by the "Viet Cong," are therefore hardly surprising. Asked "Who do you think is behind the attacks by the Viet Cong?" 53 percent blamed the Chinese Communists and 26 percent blamed North Vietnam, while 7 percent said, "Civil war."[69] In no identifiable sector of American opinion would it have been possible even to ask the obvious question that would receive an easy and accurate answer in the case of the Soviet invasion of Afghanistan: "Why do you think the southern resistance is attacking U.S. military installations in South Vietnam?" In fact, even at the peak of peace-movement activities—or today, many years later, when it should be possible to observe the plain facts with some detachment—it would be quite impossible to raise this simple and obvious question, or to answer it, within the mainstream media and most of "the culture."

In this dismal record we see very clearly the consequences of mindless media obedience in a state with enormous resources of violence.

5.4. REPORTING ON THE WAR

As the U.S. invasion mounted in scale and intensity, Indochina was flooded with war correspondents, many of whom reported what they saw and heard with honesty and courage. With rare exceptions, however, they gave an account of the war as perceived by the U.S. military on the ground or as offered in press briefings. In the home offices, Washington's version prevailed until elite divisions within the United States expanded the range of tactical debate.

Reporters often did not conceal atrocities committed by the U.S. military forces, although they did not appear to perceive them as atrocities and surely did not express the horror and outrage that would have been manifest if others were the perpetrators, and the United States or its clients the victims.[70] Malcolm Browne quotes a U.S. official who describes B-52 strikes in the South as "the most lucrative raids made at any time during the war":

> Every single bomb crater is surrounded with bodies, wrecked equipment and dazed and bleeding people. At one such hole there were 40 or 50 men, all in green North Vietnamese uniforms but without their weapons, lying around in an obvious state of shock. We sent in helicopter gunships, which quickly put them out of their misery.[71]

The Geneva conventions require that "members of armed forces who have laid down their arms and those placed *hors de combat* by sickness, wounds, detention, or any other cause, shall in all circumstances be treated humanely"; and there are no limits to the horror expressed, until today, over Communist treatment of U.S. pilots captured during the air operations that leveled much of North Vietnam. But the victims that the *New York Times* is describing are Vietnamese carrying out aggression against Americans in Vietnam, so no such scruples are in order, and none were expressed.

Similarly, there was little reaction when B-52 raids in "the populous [Mekong] delta" were reported in 1965, with unknown numbers of civilian casualties and hordes of refugees fleeing to government-controlled areas "because they could no longer bear the continuous bombings."[72] The victims fell under the category of "the unfortunate accidental loss of life incurred by the efforts of American military forces to help the South Vietnamese repel the incursion of North Vietnam and its partisans," as explained by Sidney Hook while condemning Bertrand Russell because he "plays up" these meritorious actions "as deliberate American atrocities."[73] No doubt one can find similar remarks today in *Pravda* in commentary on Afghanistan by other commissars who are much admired as leading humanitarians because they courageously condemn the crimes of the United States and its allies in Soviet journals.

Not only was there no reaction to these and subsequent atrocities, but there was also no attempt to place them in the context of what had immediately preceded—that is, to make them intelligible. Indeed, there was little awareness of the background, because the media were so closely wedded to U.S. government goals and perceptions that they never sought to learn the facts. As the war progressed, ample evidence became available from U.S. government sources to explain why the United States had been forced to resort to violence in "the populous delta," as elsewhere, as we described in the preceding section. But such materials, inconsistent with the preferred image of the United States defending South Vietnam from Communist terror and aggression, had little impact on news reporting or commentary, except for occasional illustration of the difficulties faced by the United States in pursuing its noble cause.

The reason for the U.S. resort to violence was overwhelmingly clear by the time of the outright U.S. invasion in 1965, and would have been no less clear before had any serious effort been made to determine the facts. As noted above, the United States was compelled by the political and social successes of the southern Viet Minh (NLF, "Viet Cong") to shift the struggle away from the political arena, where it was weak, to the arena of violence, where it was strong, a typical response to a classic dilemma.

It is in this context that we can understand the resort to B-52 raids in "the populous delta" and elsewhere to destroy the civilian base of the indigenous enemy, expanding the failed efforts of the strategic-hamlet program and earlier terror. The U.S. media continued to report the subsequent atrocities, but from the standpoint of the aggressors. One had to turn to the foreign press to find reports from zones held by the South Vietnamese enemy—for example, those of the pro-Western correspondent Katsuichi Honda, who reported in the Japanese press in the fall of 1967 from the Mekong Delta, describing attacks against undefended villages by gunboats in the Mekong River and helicopter gunships "firing away at random at farmhouses," "using the farmers for targets as if in a hunting mood": "They are hunting Asians. . . . This whimsical firing would explain the reason why the surgical wards in every hospital in the towns of the Mekong delta were full of wounded." His reports were available only to readers of antiwar literature, not the "objective" media, which had no interest in how the war might appear from the standpoint of the Vietnamese victims of the attack by the United States and the local forces it established.[74]

The media continued to observe and discuss atrocities blandly, not considering them as controversial or as raising any moral issue—in fact, not regarding them as atrocities at all, although we detect no such reserve with regard to the violence of official enemies. The respected columnist Joseph Harsch describes the frustrations of an American pilot dropping bombs "into a leafy jungle" with "no visible result" and without "the satisfaction of knowing what he achieved":

> A hit on a big hydroelectric dam is another matter. There is a huge explosion visible from anywhere above. The dam can be seen to fall. The water can be seen to pour through the breach and drown out huge areas of farm land, and villages, in its path. The pilot who takes out a hydroelectric dam gets back home with a feeling of accomplishment. Novels are written and films are made of such exploits. . . . The bombing which takes out the dam will flood villages, drown people, destroy crops, and knock out some electric power. . . . Bombing the dam would hurt people.[75]

Nevertheless, it is better to bomb trucks, he concludes, although there would plainly be no moral barrier to the much more satisfying alternative rejected on tactical grounds.

In the South, bombing of dikes and virtually limitless destruction was an uncontroversial tactic, as in the Batangan Peninsula, where 12,000 peasants (including, it appears, the remnants of the My Lai massacre) were forced from their homes in an American ground sweep in January 1969 and shipped off to a waterless camp near Quang Ngai over which floated a banner saying: "We thank you for liberating us from Communist terror." The *Times* reported that the refugees had lived "in caves and bunkers for many months" because "heavy American bombing and artillery and naval shelling" had destroyed their homes, as well as a dike that was "blasted by American jets to deprive the North Vietnamese [*sic*] of a food supply." It was left unrepaired, so that two years later "the salt water of the South China Sea continues to submerge the fields where rice once grew." The reason, according to an American official, is that the people "were written off as communists," and for the same reason the region was left in ruins: "the hills that overlook the flooded paddies, once scattered with huts, are . . . filled with bomb fragments, mines and unexploded artillery shells," and "B-52 craters nearly 20 feet deep pock the hills."[76]

Bombing of dikes in the North, occasionally reported,[77] *was* controversial, as was the bombing of North Vietnam generally. The reason is that the cost to the United States might be high because of a potential Chinese or Soviet response, regarded as a serious and dangerous possibility, or because of the impact on international opinion.[78] But these questions did not arise in the case of U.S. terror against the South Vietnamese, which therefore proceeded without notable concern or, it seems, much in the way of planning. In the *Pentagon Papers,* we find extensive discussion and debate over the escalation of the bombing against the North, while there is virtually nothing about the far more destructive bombing, defoliation, destruction of vast areas by Rome plows, etc., in South Vietnam, where we were "saving" the population from "aggression." With regard to South Vietnam, the planning record is limited to the question of deployment of U.S. troops, which again raised potential costs to the United States.[79]

The most notable exception to the easy tolerance of atrocities perpetrated against South Vietnamese was the My Lai massacre, in March 1968, reported at once by the NLF among other massacres that are still not acknowledged or discussed. Details were disclosed in Paris in June 1968, but neglected by the media until November 1969 despite extensive efforts by helicopter gunner Ronald Ridenhour to publicize the story, which finally broke through to the general public, thanks to the persistence of Seymour Hersh, at the time of a massive demonstration in Washington, when media attention was focused on antiwar protest. The massacre was a footnote to the post-Tet accelerated pacification campaign, and minor in context. More revealing was the massacre at nearby My Khe, with ninety civilians reported dead, discovered by the Peers Panel inquiry into the My Lai massacre; proceedings against the officer in charge were dismissed on the grounds that this was merely a normal operation in which a village was destroyed and its population murdered or forcibly relocated, a decision that tells us all we need to know about the American war in South Vietnam, but that passed without comment.[80]

While the nation agonized about the sentencing of Lieutenant William Calley for his part in the My Lai massacre, a new ground sweep in the same area drove some 16,000 peasants from their homes, and a year later the camp where the My Lai remnants were relocated in this operation was largely destroyed by air and artillery bombardment, the destruction attributed to the Viet Cong.[81] These events too passed with little notice, and no calls for an inquiry—reasonably enough, since these too were normal and routine operations.

Medical workers at the nearby Canadian-run hospital reported that they knew of the My Lai massacre at once but gave it little attention because it was not out of the ordinary in a province (Quang Ngai) that had been virtually destroyed by U.S. military operations. The highest-ranking officer to have faced court-martial charges for the massacre, Colonel Oran Henderson, stated that "every unit of brigade size has its Mylai hidden some place," although "every unit doesn't have a Ridenhour" to expose what had happened.[82] Knowledgeable elements of the peace movement also gave the My Lai massacre no special notice, for the same reasons.

The reasons why this particular massacre became a cause célèbre were explained by *Newsweek*'s Saigon bureau chief Kevin Buckley, referring to Operation Wheeler Wallawa, with 10,000 enemy reported killed, including the victims of My Lai, who were listed in the official body count:

> An examination of that whole operation would have revealed the incident at My Lai to be a particularly gruesome application of a wider policy which had the same effect in many places at many times. Of course, the blame for that could not have been dumped on a stumblebum lieutenant. Calley was an aberration, but "Wheeler Wallawa" was not.

The real issue concerning this operation, Buckley cabled to the U.S. office of *Newsweek*, was not the "indiscriminate use of firepower," as is often alleged. Rather, "it is charges of quite discriminating use—as a matter of policy, in populated areas," as in this operation or many others, among them Operation Speedy Express, with thousands of civilians murdered and many others driven to refugee and prison camps by such devices as B-52 raids targeted specifically on villages.

An experienced U.S. official, cited by Buckley, compared My Lai to the exploits of the U.S. Ninth Infantry Division in a range of similar operations:

> The actions of the 9th Division in inflicting civilian casualties were worse. The sum total of what the 9th did was overwhelming. In sum, the horror was worse than My Lai. But with the 9th, the civilian casualties came in dribbles and were pieced out over a long time. And most of them were inflicted from the air and at night. Also, they were sanctioned by the command's insistence on high body counts.... The result was an inevitable outcome of the unit's command policy.[83]

In short, the My Lai massacre was ignored when it occurred, and the substantial attention given to it later is a more subtle form of cover-up of atrocities. An honest accounting, inconceivable in the media or "the culture" generally, would have placed the responsibility far higher than Lieutenant Calley, but it was more convenient to focus attention on the actions of semi-crazed GI's in a gruesome combat situation with every Vietnamese civilian a threatening enemy. My Lai did not prompt the media generally—there were some individual exceptions—to take a deeper look at the nature of the war, or to display an interest in reports of similar events in nearby areas that suggested its unexceptional character. This particular massacre was made exceptional by an arbitrary cutoff of attention and refusal to investigate beyond narrowly circumscribed limits. The limited but dramatized attention to My Lai was even used to demonstrate the conscience of America, in the face of enemy provocations. Thus a 1973 *New York Times* report from My Lai describes the "battered Batangan peninsula," an area where the inhabitants were "generally supporters of the Vietcong," now demolished by U.S. bombardment and ground operations: "big guns fire into the peninsula as they have again and again over the eight years that American, South Korean and South Vietnamese forces have been trying *to make it safe.*" The report quotes villagers who accuse the Americans of having killed many people here: "They are in no position to appreciate what the name My Lai *means to Americans,*" the reporter adds thoughtfully.[84]

The standard critique of the media for having "lost the war" identifies television as the major culprit. Television analyst Edward Jay Epstein formulates the standard view as follows:

> Over the past 10 years, almost nightly, Americans have witnessed the war in Vietnam, on television. Never before in history has a nation allowed its citizens to view uncensored scenes of combat, destruction and atrocities in their living rooms, in living color. Since television has become the principal—and most believed—source of news for most Americans, it is generally assumed that the constant exposure of this war on television was instrumental in shaping public opinion. It has become almost a truism, and the standard rhetoric of television executives, to say that television, by showing the terrible truth of the war, caused the disillusionment of Americans with the war. . . . This has also been the dominant view of those governing the Nation during the war years. . . . Depending on whether the appraisal has come from hawk or dove, television has thus been either blamed or applauded for the disillusionment of the American public with the war.[85]

There have been several studies of the matter, suggesting a rather different picture. We will return to some of these issues in discussing the coverage of the Tet offensive, but we should observe that there are some rather serious questions about the standard formulations. Suppose that some Soviet investigators were to conduct an inquiry into coverage of the war in Afghanistan to determine whether *Pravda* should be blamed or applauded for the disillusionment of the Soviet public with the war? Would we consider such an inquiry to be meaningful without consideration of both the costs and the justice of the venture?

Epstein notes an obvious "logical problem" with the standard view: for the first six years of television coverage, from 1962 and increasingly through 1967, "the American public *did* approve of the war in Vietnam" according to polls. Furthermore, in a 1967 Harris poll for *Newsweek*, "64 per cent of the nation wide sample said that television's coverage made them *more* supportive of the American effort, and only 26 per cent said that it had intensified their opposition," leading the journal to conclude that "TV has encouraged a decisive majority of viewers to support the war."

Epstein's review of his and other surveys of television newscasts and commentary during this period explains why this should have been the case. "Up until 1965," he writes, "the network anchor men seemed unanimous in support of American objectives in Vietnam," and most described themselves as "hawks" until the end, while the most notable "dove," Walter Cronkite, applauded "the courageous decision that Communism's advance must be stopped in Asia" in 1965 and later endorsed the initial U.S. commitment "to stop Communist aggression wherever it raises its head." In fact, at no time during the war or since has there been any detectable departure from unqualified acceptance of the U.S. government propaganda framework; as in the print media, controversy was limited to tactical questions and the problem of costs, almost exclusively the cost to the United States.

The network anchormen not only accepted the framework of interpretation formulated by the state authorities, but also were optimistic about the successes achieved in the U.S. war of defense against Vietnamese aggression in Vietnam. Epstein cites work by George Baily, who concludes: "The results in this study demonstrate the combat reports and the government statements generally gave the impression that the Americans were in control, on the offense and holding the initiative, at least until Tet of 1968," a picture accepted by the network anchormen. Television "focused on [the] progress" of the American ground forces, supporting this picture with "film, supplied by the Pentagon, that showed the bombing of the North" and "suggesting that the Americans were also rebuilding South Vietnam"—while they were systematically destroying it, as could be deduced inferentially from scattered evidence for which no context or interpretation was provided. NBC's "Huntley-Brinkley Report" described "the American forces in Vietnam as 'builders' rather than destroyers," a "central truth" that "needs underscoring."

What made this especially deceptive and hypocritical was the fact, noted earlier, that the most advanced and cruel forms of devastation and killing—such as the free use of napalm, defoliants, and Rome plows—were used with few constraints in the *South,* because its population was voiceless, in contrast with the North, where international publicity and political complications threatened, so that at least visible areas around the major urban centers were spared.[86]

As for news coverage, "all three networks had definite policies about showing graphic film of wounded American soldiers or suffering Vietnamese civilians," Epstein observes. "Producers of the NBC and ABC evening-news programs said that they ordered editors to delete excessively grisly or detailed shots," and CBS had similar policies, which, according to former CBS News president Fred W. Friendly, "helped shield the audience from the true horror of the war." "The relative bloodlessness of the war depicted on television helps to explain why only a minority in the Lou Harris–Newsweek poll said that television increased their dissatisfaction with the war"; such coverage yielded an impression, Epstein adds, of "a clean, effective technological war," which was "rudely shaken at Tet in 1968." As noted earlier, NBC withdrew television clips showing harsh treatment of Viet Cong prisoners at the request of the Kennedy administration.

Throughout this period, furthermore, "television coverage focused almost exclusively on the American effort." There were few interviews with GVN military or civilian leaders, "and the Vietcong and North Vietnamese were almost nonexistent on American television newscasts."

There was one famous exception to the sanitizing of the war, an August 5, 1965, CBS report by Morley Safer showing U.S. Marines burning huts in the village of Cam Ne with cigarette lighters, which elicited "a semiofficial campaign" by the Pentagon "to discredit the television story and vilify the correspondent as 'unpatriotic.' " But surveys of television newscasts by Epstein and Wisconsin Professor Lawrence Lichty show that "instances shown on TV of American brutality toward the South Vietnamese, such as Cam Ne, 'could be counted on one hand' [Lichty]," "even though hundreds of South Vietnamese villages were destroyed during this period." "The Cam Ne story is famous for being the exception to the rule."

Returning soldiers told a different story, and it became increasingly clear, although not through the medium of television, that the war was bloody and brutal, leading to "disillusionment"—and among a large sector of the general population, increasingly "out of control," a much stronger and more appropriate reaction.

But, Epstein continues, "the televised picture of gradual progress in the war was abruptly shattered by the Communist [Tet] offensive" in January–February 1968, when the military lost its "control over the movements of the press," who could step outside their hotels and find "themselves willy-nilly in the midst of bloody fighting." For this brief moment, correspondents sent on-the-spot reports that were aired in place of "the usual carefully edited view of an orderly, controlled war," and the policy of "shield[ing] American viewers from the grisly close-ups of wounded Americans, body bags and death" briefly collapsed, though newscasts continued to be edited in home offices as "too strong," in the words of NBC producer Robert Northshield. This coverage convinced Walter Cronkite that the war had become "a bloody stalemate," in a controversial report to which we will return.

The Tet offensive convinced U.S. elites that the war was becoming too costly to the United States, and the government shifted toward the policy of "Vietnamization," large-scale massacre operations to destroy the indigenous resistance and its civilian base, expansion of the war in Laos and Cambodia, and the commencement of negotiations with North Vietnam. "Accordingly, the networks again changed the focus of their coverage, this time from the battlefields in Vietnam to the negotiation tables in Paris. . . . The 'story' was now the negotiations, not the fighting," Northshield explained, adding that "combat stories seemed like a contradiction and would confuse the audience." "Similar decisions were made at the other networks," Epstein adds, as all "altered their coverage in late 1969 from combat pieces to stories about the 'Vietnamization' of the war" and the negotiations in Paris. The post-Tet accelerated pacification campaign, one of the most crucial and murderous operations in the U.S. war against South Vietnam, received little attention.

Epstein believes that "there is a marked difference between the coverage of the formative years of the war (1962–1967) and the later years (when the antiwar movement was at its height)." "Up until 1968, television coverage was controlled to a large extent by the American military, and generally it reflected a controlled American initiative which seemed to be winning the countryside and decimating the Vietcong. The searchlight rarely focused on related questions, such as the sufferings of Vietnamese civilians." During the Tet offensive, the focus changed to Americans "shown on the defensive, endangered and helplessly frustrated," then to "the story of the American withdrawal" as "negotiations began at the end of 1968." The differences, however, are misleading. Apart from the live coverage during the Tet offensive, there is very little departure from the principle that the war must be viewed from the standpoint determined by official Washington doctrine—a standpoint that broadened in scope after Tet, as tactical disagreements arose within elite circles.

In his survey of network newscasts from 1965 through the January 1973 peace treaty, Daniel Hallin reaches similar conclusions. Until the Tet offensive, television coverage was "lopsidedly favorable to American policy in Vietnam," well beyond even the "remarkably docile" print media. Like Epstein, he notes the "dramatic" change after Tet, "part of a larger change, a response to as well as a cause of the unhappiness with the war that was developing at many levels, from the halls of the Pentagon, to Main Street, U.S.A. and the fire bases of Quang Tri province"—and, much more crucially, the unhappiness that had become quite significant by 1968 among business elites, leading to the changes in U.S. government policy already discussed. "Before Tet, editorial comments by television journalists ran nearly four to one in favor of administration policy; after Tet, two to one against," reflecting divisions in the "establishment itself." He quotes *New York Times* editor Max Frankel, who said in an interview that "we're an establishment institution, and whenever your natural constituency changes, then naturally you will too." The same was true of television, and it is hardly surprising—and quite in accord with the propaganda model—that its fervent loyalty to the administration changed when "the establishment bastards have bailed out," as Lyndon Johnson put it bitterly after the "Wise Men" advised him in March 1968 to abandon hope of military victory and to de-escalate the conflict, in the wake of the Tet offensive.[87]

Television typically presented events in terms of "a kind of morality play, . . . a dramatic contrast between good, represented by the American peace offensive [in 1966], and evil, represented by Hanoi." Reporting was relatively bloodless, focusing on the successes of "the 'good guys': American boys in action," regularly depicted as "brave men," "the greatest men in the world," "heroes," exuding competence, humanity, and high morale as they fight against "Communist aggression" in the "battle for democracy," and "win hearts and minds" by caring for sick and injured civilians after a village "was burned and blasted to death"—properly, because ammunition had been found there, which "was enough proof of its being used by the Vietcong" (Greg Harris, NBC-TV, Oct. 27, 1967). The issue of racism "was apparently too sensitive to touch," Hallin adds, noting that he found no "comment on the hostility that many American soldiers felt towards all Vietnamese, . . . a prominent theme in veterans' recollections of the war."

The focus of coverage was the Americans: soldiers bravely defending Vietnam, medics caring for the wounded, pacification officials rebuilding after the damage for which Communist terror bore responsibility. "Our South Vietnamese" were virtually ignored, with virtually nothing on political, economic, or social affairs, and "the peasant figured in the news mainly as a victim and prize of the conflict." The political opposition in Vietnam was portrayed with considerable hostility, "like the antiwar movement at home." They were "forces of anarchy . . . on the march" (Walter Cronkite, CBS-TV, Mar. 31, 1966). The utterly fraudulent elections were portrayed as a triumph as democracy, courageously carried out in defiance of the disruptive attacks of "Vietcong terrorists."[88]

Civilian casualties were downplayed, or regarded as unavoidable side consequences of "a job that had to be done," raising no moral question. Observing an air strike on a village of "unabashed" Viet Cong supporters after a column of American soldiers had drawn fire, NBC's Jack

Perkins commented: "There was no discriminating one house from another. There couldn't be, and there did not need to be. The whole village had turned on the Americans, so the whole village was being destroyed," as is only right and just. In a follow-up on the Cam Ne incident, Dan Rather offers a comment that Hallin cites as an example of "a muckraking tone," the harshest he presents: the marines are holding Cam Ne

> by force, not through the pacification program . . . [which] hasn't taken hold in Cam Ne. And until it does take hold here and a lot of other places in South Vietnam, nobody can feel very good about this dirty little war.

In short, as long as there is still resistance to American violence, we cannot feel good about proceeding with our necessary chores; such comments as these presumably account for Rather's reputation among the "doves" as a courageous opponent of the war, and among the "hawks" as a dangerous leftist. Walter Cronkite reported "an urgent plea from the Vietcong for medical and surgical supplies" to the International Red Cross, "an indication that our bombing raids and infantry sweeps are taking a heavy toll of all kinds of *Red equipment.*"[89]

Reporting of civilian casualties rose from 1966 to a peak in early 1968, then declined sharply as the United States turned to the murderous accelerated pacification campaign, which Hallin does not discuss, presumably because it was largely ignored by television, which had shifted attention to the negotiating tables in Paris in accordance with Washington priorities. The coverage rose again in 1972, when casualties could be attributed to a North Vietnamese offensive and the U.S. "response." In a 1971 CBS documentary entitled "The Changing War in Indochina," Charles Collingwood reported the progress of the pacification campaign in Kien Hoa Province in the Mekong Delta—"once an NLF stronghold," Hallin observes. This province had been the target of Operation Speedy Express in early 1969, one of the most brutal American operations of the war in an area that had been organized under NLF control with no known North Vietnamese presence, conquered through the "awesome firepower" of the Ninth Division. This included air strikes using napalm, high explosives, and anti-personnel bombs, B-52 bombing, and artillery shelling "around the clock" at a level that "it is impossible to reckon," with armed helicopters "scouring the landscape from the air night and day" and accounting for "many and perhaps most of the enemy kills"—about 11,000 according to the U.S. command, with 748 weapons captured, a fair indication of who was killed.[90] Collingwood was pleased to observe progress in pacification, although there was still "Indian country" beyond. "This is almost like St. Louis on the move into the frontier," his companion, a U.S. government adviser replied, in a reference that is more accurate than he probably knew.[91]

In contrast to the heroic and humane image of the American soldiers defending democracy, the NLF and North Vietnamese were portrayed in "an almost perfectly one-dimensional image . . . as cruel, ruthless and fanatical." Of twelve positive comments by journalists that he found throughout the war, Hallin remarks, "10 concerned the effectiveness of enemy forces: this was the only element of television's image of the enemy that changed substantially" in the course of the post-Tet shift, mirroring establishment qualms about the prospects for the success of American arms. "What did not change was the dark picture of evil." When U.S. forces burned villages, this was a necessity because they provided cover and support for the Viet Cong. The results of B-52 saturation bombing were a "tragedy of war." But when a North Vietnamese artillery shell hit an orphanage in An Hoa in October 1970, ABC's George Watson commented with horror: "No one was prepared for the massacre, the irrational murder that the North Vietnamese inflicted on An Hoa." Although civilian casualties were overwhelmingly the result of U.S. firepower, attribution of responsibility by television was weighted by a 10 to 7 ratio to the account of the enemy; its "calculated *policy* of terror" contrasted with the unfortunate but legitimate side-effects of U.S. operations. Even military operations of the enemy were "terrorism." Reporting on a Viet Cong ambush of an American patrol, ABC's Peter Jennings recounted "another of those small but [and here he paused a moment for dramatic effect] harrowing VC butcheries" (October, 1965). The North Vietnamese and Viet Cong were portrayed as "savage," "brutal," "murderous," "fanatical," "suicidal," "halfcrazed," mere vermin in areas that were "Communist infested" or "Vietcong infested," and thus had to be cleansed by the American liberators.[92]

The style and technique are familiar in state propaganda of all varieties.

Overall, Hallin concludes from his survey, television never veered from the official interpretation of the war as "a struggle to defend democracy against aggression." In the early years, it was taken for granted that

> we would surely win, not only because we were more powerful but because the right was clearly on our side. Television held this view

> strongly, perhaps more strongly than the public itself. It didn't work out that way, and eventually television brought the bad news. But it never explained *why*: it never reexamined the assumptions about the nature of the war it had helped to propagate in the early years. So to the public, the bad news must have seemed nearly as incomprehensible as an earlier "American defeat" in Asia: the "loss" of China.

Attribution of the American failure by the public to "treason" or "lack of American will" caused by the failure of the media to support our just cause with sufficient fervor is, therefore, "hardly surprising."[93]

This may well explain why the public has apparently been willing to accept the tales about media treachery. But among the educated elites, the explanation may lie elsewhere: in a totalitarian cast of mind that regards even the actual level of media subservience to the state as inadequate and a threat to order and privilege by the "forces of anarchy . . . on the march."

5.5. SOME CRUCIAL EVENTS OF THE WAR

5.5.1. The Tonkin Gulf incident

By mid-1964, there was a growing consensus among Vietnamese in favor of a negotiated political settlement, while the United States was maneuvering with increasing desperation to evade what internal documents describe as "premature negotiations." The reason, as frankly explained, was that the United States was politically isolated, in opposition to the NLF, the non-Communist opposition, and even the generals. It was therefore regarded as necessary to expand the war to the North to "obtain [the DRV's] cooperation in bringing an end to the Viet Cong insurgency" and to "persuade or force the DRV to stop its aid to the Viet Cong and use its directive powers to make the Viet Cong desist" (Ambassador Maxwell Taylor). Intelligence, meanwhile, concluded that "the basic elements of Communist strength in South Vietnam remain indigenous."[94]

U.S.-run military operations against North Vietnam began on February 1, 1964 (OPLAN-34A), using South Vietnamese and "third-country" mercenaries, "presumably mostly Nationalist Chinese," according to Kahin. These operations were officially "designed to result in substantial destruction, economic loss, and harassment."[95] On July 30–31, Saigon Navy vessels attacked North Vietnamese islands, eliciting an official DRV protest to the International Control Commission on July 31. The U.S. destroyer *Maddox,* conducting an electronic espionage operation in that general area, entered the twelve-mile zone regarded by North Vietnam as its territorial waters on August 2. The *Maddox* was challenged by North Vietnamese patrol boats, fired "warning shots," and was hit by a single bullet in the ensuing battle, in which the patrol boats were damaged or destroyed by the destroyer and U.S. aircraft. On August 3, Secretary of State Dean Rusk sent a (secret) cable to Ambassador Taylor, stating that "We believe that present Op Plan 34 A activities are beginning to rattle Hanoi, and Maddox incident is directly related to their efforts to resist these activities." The *Maddox* was returned to the area along with the destroyer *Turner Joy* on August 3, and on August 3 and 4 Saigon naval vessels bombarded North Vietnamese coastal facilities, "quite possibly one that the destroyer's electronic surveillance had activated and located," Kahin observes. There was some indication that the U.S. destroyers might have come under attack by North Vietnamese patrol boats on August 4, although Captain John Herrick of the *Maddox* was unsure, and radioed that reports "appear very doubtful" and that there were "No actual sightings by Maddox," recommending "complete evaluation before any further action." Subsequent evidence indicates that almost certainly no attack took place.[96]

On August 5, President Johnson publicly denounced the "open aggression on the high seas against the United States of America" by the North Vietnamese, while the DRV and China stated that "the so-called second Tonkin Gulf incident of 4 August never occurred" (Chinese government statement). On August 5, U.S. planes bombed North Vietnamese installations and destroyed North Vietnamese patrol boats. After testimony by Defense Secretary Robert McNamara in which he falsely claimed that the *Maddox* "was operating in international waters, was carrying out a routine patrol of the type we carry out all over the world at all times," Congress passed a resolution authorizing the president to "take all necessary measures to repel any armed attack against the forces of the United States and to prevent further aggression" (416 to 0 in the House, Wayne Morse and Ernest Gruening alone in opposition in the Senate). This August 7 resolution was subsequently exploited as the basis for the escalation of the U.S. attack against Vietnam.[97]

"The Gulf of Tonkin incident," Hallin observes, "was a classic of Cold War news management. . . . On virtually every important point, the reporting of the two Gulf of Tonkin incidents . . . was either misleading or simply false"—and in accordance with the needs of the U.S. executive at that crucial moment. The *New York Times* had reported sabotage missions against the North as recently as July 23, and reported Hanoi's August 2 protest of an attack on North Vietnamese villages by Laotian Air Force planes, but neither the *Times* nor the *Washington Post* mentioned these facts "either at the time of the incidents or in the weeks that followed, aside from inconspicuous sidebars on Hanoi's 'allegations' [which were accurate, but dismissed] and a passing reference" in a column by James Reston. The reporting was "objective" in that it correctly reported U.S. government statements, raising no question about them, presenting no relevant background, and marginally citing Communist denials while proceeding to report the events as Washington wished them to be perceived.[98]

In subsequent weeks, the *Times* published a number of brief references to what was "charged" or "asserted" in the generally accurate reports from North Vietnam, which were rejected and dismissed by reporters while front-page stories and headlines presented the false Washington version as fact, with much speculation about Hanoi's motives in sending a few patrol boats to attack the mighty U.S. Seventh Fleet. The relevant background continued to be ignored or buried with marginal references in back pages. The criticism by Senator Morse was barely mentioned, and dismissed. There was no hint of administration doubts that the August 4 incident had even taken place.[99]

The newsweeklies adhered still more rigidly to the government propaganda line, even providing vivid and dramatic accounts of the August 4 incident, which apparently never took place. The accurate criticism by Senators Gruening and Morse received a few lines, dismissed as "predictable" responses by the "irascible" Morse. There was no interest in their charge that the Tonkin Gulf resolution had been predated, also dismissed by the *Times* without inquiry. North Vietnamese and Chinese reactions were dismissed as "bluster" by Communists who "boiled with hatred and hostility toward the U.S." *(Newsweek)* and "propaganda blasts" *(U.S. News & World Report)*. None of the weeklies considered the possibility that U.S. actions might have provoked the August 2 incident, or that there were doubts in Washington about the August 4 attack, although some of the relevant facts had been briefly noted (e.g., *Time,* July 31, noting missions inside North Vietnam by parachuted sabotage teams). The U.S. government version was simply adopted as unquestioned truth, with no further discussion or inquiry necessary.[100]

There were ample grounds at the time for suspicion about the U.S. government version. The foreign press was able to see that serious questions arose. *Le Monde* presented public statements on all sides and an analysis of what the public record indicated. "Neither the *Times* nor the *Post* made any such analysis of the record," simply taking the false Washington version to be correct and dismissing the accurate Communist "allegations" with a bare mention.[101] In London, the *New Statesman* covered the U.S. and Chinese versions, including the (accurate) Chinese account of the U.S.-Saigon actions that preceded the incidents and the charge that the first was provoked by Washington while the second never occurred, and concluding that "the incidents in Vietnam do not seem quite as simple as the initial headlines indicated" (a substantial understatement). In the United States, the left-wing *National Guardian,* with five major articles, and *I.F. Stone's Weekly* provided the most extensive, careful, and accurate account of the events. In contrast to the fevered rhetoric of the mainstream newsweeklies, the *National Guardian* simply described the facts that were available, asking whether the August 2 "skirmish" had been provoked and whether the "alleged" August 4 incident had taken place. The relevant background and Communist versions were accurately presented, with appropriate questions raised. Wayne Morse's commentary was given ample coverage, as were South Vietnamese General Ky's statements on sabotage missions in North Vietnam. *I.F. Stone's Weekly* also reported the facts accurately, adding relevant background ignored by the major media.[102]

In summary, the national media, overcome by jingoist passion, failed to provide even minimally adequate coverage of this crucial event, although appropriate skepticism would have been aroused in the mind of the reader of the foreign or "alternative" media, or the reader with the sophistication to treat the media as a disinformation system disguising a reality that can perhaps be ascertained with sufficient energy and dedication. The *Pentagon Papers* analyst describes these events as "an important firebreak," noting that "the Tonkin Gulf Resolution set U.S. public support for virtually any action."[103]

The willingness of the media to serve as a vehicle for government propaganda helped impel the country toward what they were later to regard as "the tragedy" of Vietnam. The reaction of Congress and the public laid the basis for the outright invasion of early 1965, providing support for the planners who were secretly concerned that the NLF was continuing "to seek a political settlement favorable to the communists" through the device of "neutralism" and "a coalition government" (Maxwell Taylor, Aug. 10, 1964), and who warned about "Saigon and Vientiane hanky panky with Reds" (John McNaughton, October 1964)—that is, moves toward a political settlement—in accordance with the NLF program as described by intelligence: "to seek victory through a 'neutralist coalition' rather than by force of arms."[104] When the United States extended the war in early 1965 to try to salvage its position in the South, the media continued to offer total support, in accordance with "the guiding principle of American foreign policy since 1945" as outlined by the distinguished liberal commentator of the *New York Times* James Reston,

> that no state shall use military force or the threat of military force to achieve its political objectives. And the companion of this principle has been that the United States would use its influence and its power, when necessary and where it could be effective, against any state that defied this principle,

which was "at stake in Vietnam," where "the United States is now challenging the Communist effort to seek power by the more cunning technique of military subversion."[105]

In the Orwellian world of American journalism, the attempt to seek a political settlement by peaceful means is the use of "military force," and the use of military force by the United States to block a political settlement is a noble action in defense of the "guiding principle" that the use of military force is illegitimate.

The United States then proceeded to fight a long and brutal war to try to achieve its objectives in Vietnam, demolishing much of Indochina in the process and leaving a legacy that may never be overcome. Finally, in January 1973, the United States formally accepted a peace treaty that was virtually identical with the Vietnamese consensus it overturned by violence in 1964, except that by that time, the indigenous NLF had been effectively demolished and little remained in Indochina outside of North Vietnam, laying the basis for North Vietnamese domination of Indochina, exactly as had been predicted, long before, by "the wild men in the wings." The media bear a major responsibility for these tragic events, coverage of the Tonkin Gulf incident with its congressional "blank check" for further aggression serving as a notable example.

5.5.2. The Tet offensive

Media coverage of the Tet offensive has been the centerpiece of the critique of the media for "losing the war" by their incompetent reporting and their anti-government bias reflecting their passion for confronting authority. The authoritative "proof" of this contention was provided in the two-volume Freedom House study by Peter Braestrup. Conducted over a six-year period with a wide range of distinguished participants and consultants, and support acknowledged from some two dozen corporations and labor unions, this study was hailed as a "monumental" work by Don Oberdorfer in a *Washington Post* magazine cover story on the tenth anniversary of the offensive, with the title: "Tet: The Turning Point: How a 'Big Event' on Television Can Change Our Minds." Professor John P. Roche, of the Fletcher School of Law and Diplomacy of Tufts University, "intellectual-in-residence" for the Johnson administration, described the Freedom House study as "one of the major pieces of investigative reporting and first-rate scholarship of the past quarter century," a "meticulous case-study of media incompetence, if not malevolence." In a relatively critical discussion in the *Times*'s Sunday book review, Edwin Diamond praises this "painstakingly thorough study of how the Vietnam war was presented to the American public by its leading image makers," a "highfalutin' epistemological quest" by a "conscientious . . . reporter-analyst" that raises profound questions about "how do we know what we know," revealing "the biases introduced by standard journalistic assumptions and organizational practices" that contributed to undermining the U.S. position in Vietnam among the general public and Congress. Similarly, Charles Mohr reports that in a conference of "aging hawks and doves" on the tenth anniversary of the Tet offensive at the University of North Carolina, "Journalism came in for some strong criticism and only a rather muted defense." The criticism was by Braestrup, who "expounded gently the theme of his recent book," *Big Story,* and the hawks in attendance, "while some of the reporters there demurred only softly." The study is regularly cited by historians, without qualification, as the standard work on media reporting of the Tet offensive, "in some respects as important as the battle itself," here "analysed in depth" (R. B. Smith).[106]

Oberdorfer too accepts the conclusions of the study as proven: it was the " 'Big Event' on television" that changed our minds about the war. The only commentary he cites, even obliquely, accepts this judgment (Roche and others unnamed). Within the mainstream more generally, it is assumed with little question that this remarkable scholarly contribution made its case, though one may debate whether it revealed "malevolence" or deeper problems of "standard journalistic assumptions and organizational practices," reflecting perhaps the "adversarial stance" of the media with regard to established power.

Braestrup claims to have shown that the reporting of the Tet offensive is "an extreme case" of the "unsatisfactory" performance of the media: "Rarely has contemporary crisis-journalism turned out, in retrospect, to have veered so widely from reality" by presenting "a portrait of defeat for the allies"—"allies" being the term regularly used to refer to the U.S. invaders, the local forces they organized, and the largely mercenary forces they introduced to support U.S. military operations in Indochina, and a term chosen to exploit the favorable connotations provided by World War II, when "the allies" fought "the Axis." "To have portrayed such a setback for one side [them] as a defeat for the other [us]—in a major crisis abroad—cannot be counted as a triumph for American journalism," which "shouted that the patient was dying, then weeks later began to whisper that he somehow seemed to be recovering—whispers apparently not heard amid the clamorous domestic reaction to the initial shouts," with television the worst offender. The whispers began "about late February," he asserts. These journalistic failures, Braestrup concludes, reflect "the more volatile journalistic style—spurred by managerial exhortation or complaisance—that has become so popular since the late 1960s," accompanied with "an often mindless readiness to seek out conflict, to believe the worst of the government or of authority in general, and on that basis to divide up the actors on any issue into the 'good' and the 'bad.' " The "bad actors" include the U.S. forces in Vietnam, the "military-industrial complex," and the CIA, among others, while "the good" in the eyes of the media are presumably the Communists, who, Braestrup argues sardonically throughout, were consistently overpraised and protected. The prospect, he foresees, "is for a continuation of the current volatile styles, always with the dark possibility that, if the managers do not themselves take action, then outsiders—the courts, the Federal Communications Commission, or Congress—will seek to apply remedies of their own," a proposal taken up in Roche's call for a congressional inquiry and the subsequent warnings of the Trilateral Commission, cited earlier (*Big Story*, I, 705ff.)

The Braestrup–Freedom House thesis has two essential components: (1) coverage of the Tet offensive illustrates media incompetence and their "adversarial stance"; (2) by their portrayal of an American victory as a defeat, the media bear responsibility for the loss of American resolve and the subsequent American defeat in Vietnam. It is the second component of the thesis that carries the dramatic impact, and that has permitted it to set much of the agenda for subsequent discussion of the fourth estate and the dangers that its new-found power and "sixties' style" of "mindless" hatred of authority pose for the very survival of free institutions and democracy.

The first component of the thesis is commonly accepted even by those who deny the second. Thus, rejecting "the stab-in-the-back thesis," George Herring nevertheless observes: "That the media was hostile to the war and to Johnson seems clear, and much of the reporting of Tet was misleading"; these "distortions of the media" may have contributed to "growing popular discontent" with the war and "public anxiety," Herring adds, but these were not the operative factors in Johnson's decision to de-escalate and seek negotiations after Tet.[107]

An analysis of the facts and the argument demonstrates that neither component of the Freedom House thesis is tenable. The second, as we shall see, is conceded in the Freedom House study to be false with regard to public opinion, and the straw at which they then grasp will plainly not bear the weight. As for the first component, on the narrow question of professional competence in reporting the facts available under trying and confused circumstances, the performance of the media was acceptable if not outstanding, and compares quite favorably to the internal reporting of the American military authorities and U.S. intelligence, insofar as these are available. But when we turn to broader questions of the sort discussed earlier—that is, if we evaluate the media by the standards that we would properly apply to reporting, say, on the Soviet invasion of Afghanistan—we see that indeed they can be faulted in precisely the terms anticipated by the propaganda model. The very example selected as providing the strongest grounds for their accusations by Freedom House and other critics from the jingoist right wing of the political spectrum actually happens to demonstrate the precise opposite of what is alleged—namely, it provides yet another striking illustration of the subservience of the media to the state propaganda system.[108]

The Freedom House study itself provides ample documentation to establish these conclusions, and to refute its own specific allegations point by point. Given the major role that this study and the thesis it allegedly established has played in recent ideology, we will give some attention to the chasm that lies between its interpretation and summaries, on the one hand, and the documentary record that it (in part) presents, on the other.[109] The comments and summaries often seriously misrepresent the contents of the documents described or are outright falsifications. The analysis, laced with bitter sarcasm throughout, is thoroughly undermined when compared with the actual documents. When the countless errors and careless and inaccurate comments are corrected, nothing remains of the Freedom House case. The sardonic reference to "straw man journalism," "CBS exclusives" and the like, referring to alleged misdeeds of the media, is misplaced; case by case, we find, instead, "Freedom House exclusives."

Before proceeding to details, we should take careful note of the background assumptions that guide this inquiry. As we noted, for Braestrup and Freedom House, the "allies" are the United States, the South Vietnamese client government, and the various South Korean, Thai, Australian, Chinese Nationalist, and other forces (largely mercenary) mobilized by the United States. The "South Vietnamese" include our client government and the armed forces organized, supplied, trained, and directed by the United States, but exclude the indigenous NLF and its supporters, although the U.S. government never had the slightest doubt, and its specialists do not hesitate to concede, that the client regime had little support while its opponents in South Vietnam constituted so powerful a *political* force that any peaceful settlement was unthinkable. That the United States has a right to conduct military operations in South Vietnam to uproot the NLF and destroy the peasant society in which it was based, that its goals are democracy and self-determination, and that its forces "protect" and "bring security" to South Vietnamese peasants are principles taken for granted in the Braestrup–Freedom House version, where no patriotic assumption or cliché is ever challenged—or even noticed, so deeply rooted are these doctrines. Correspondingly, the fact that the media coverage surveyed is framed entirely within these patriotic premises passes unnoticed. The Freedom House inquiry cannot perceive fundamental bias favorable to the state because all of the premises of state doctrine are taken as given. There is "mindlessness" here, as Braestrup observes, although it is not quite what he perceives; rather, we find that Braestrup "mindlessly" adopts what we referred to in chapter 3 as a patriotic agenda, even more so than the media he condemns. And as we described in chapter 1, the function of such "flak machines" as Freedom House is to ensure that the press stays within the bounds of this patriotic agenda.

The Tet offensive of January 1968 began on January 21 with a siege by North Vietnamese (NVA) regulars of a U.S. military base at Khe Sanh, near the 17th parallel. It was soon apparent that the purpose was to draw U.S. forces away from populated centers, and the siege succeeded in this aim, as General Westmoreland rushed combat forces to the northern areas. On January 31, all major cities and thirty-six of forty-four provincial capitals, along with numerous other towns, came under simultaneous attack by southern NLF resistance forces ("Viet Cong"), along with some NVA elements. The effects are succinctly summarized by Wallace Thies in his scholarly study of the U.S. strategy of "coercing Hanoi":

> . . . although U.S. military commanders would later claim that the offensive had been anticipated and that the heavy casualties suffered by the attackers had resulted in a great victory for the Allies, the offensive was in fact a military setback for the American side. To meet the threat in the northern provinces and forestall a Dien Bien Phu–type defeat at Khe Sanh, half of all U.S. maneuver battalions in South Vietnam were deployed in I Corps [in the north]; the rest, along with the bulk of the combat-ready ARVN [GVN, Government of (South) Vietnam] units, were tied down defending the cities against the possibility of a second wave of attacks. As a result, the countryside went by default to the NLF, the pacification program was left in a shambles, and whatever losses the DRV / VC [North Vietnamese / Viet Cong] forces did suffer in the initial assaults were largely offset by the unimpeded recruiting that they conducted in the rural areas in the weeks that followed.[110]

International Voluntary Services (IVS), which had a close familiarity with the situation in rural areas, withdrew most of its field workers in early 1968 because of "security conditions." A volunteer reported in February: "The number of locations at which we can safely place a volunteer have significantly decreased in recent months"; another added that "we all knew that security in the countryside was getting worse and worse," contrary to the optimistic evaluations of the U.S. high command and Washington, which were relayed with little skepticism by the media in the pre-Tet period. A South Vietnamese senator estimated that after Tet, the government controlled "only one third of the country," the remaining two-thirds being in the hands of the NLF, an estimate consistent with U.S. intelligence reports.[111]

The Tet offensive left Washington in a state of "troubled confusion and uncertainty," Undersecretary of the Air Force Townsend Hoopes observed, and "performed the curious service of fully revealing the doubters and dissenters to each other, in a lightning flash," within the Pentagon. While General Westmoreland persisted with the optimistic assessments that had been undermined by this dramatic demonstration that the NLF remained firmly rooted in the South despite the devastating American attack on the rural society, the reaction in official Washington circles was quite different. Summarizing the impact in Washington, George Herring observes that in private,

> Johnson and his advisers were shocked by the suddenness and magnitude of the offensive . . . and intelligence estimates were much more pessimistic than Westmoreland. . . . An "air of gloom" hung over White House discussions, [General Maxwell] Taylor later observed, and [Chairman of the Joint Chiefs of Staff] General [Earle] Wheeler likened the mood to that following the first Battle of Bull Run.[112]

General Wheeler reported that "to a large extent the VC now control the countryside," the situation being particularly bad in the Mekong Delta, and the Pentagon systems-analysis group concluded that "our control of the countryside and the defense of the urban areas is now essentially at pre-August 1965 levels," when the U.S. war was being lost, according to General Westmoreland. A U.S. government military-historical summary of the offensive in the Mekong Delta, completed in April 1968, concluded that "The Tet offensive in IV Corps had a devastating effect on the Revolutionary Development [pacification] Program." As we shall see, these internal assessments are considerably more "pessimistic" than those of the media that are denounced for the crime of excessive pessimism by Freedom House standards.

We might incidentally note that in IV Corps (including the Mekong Delta), there were "no regular North Vietnam units" according to Defense Secretary McNamara; the Freedom House study states that "In the southernmost Delta, it was an ARVN-Vietcong [actually, U.S.-Vietcong] guerrilla struggle," and more generally, Hanoi "had yet to commit sizable (multi-division) forces in sustained, concerted attacks" anywhere in South Vietnam (I, 24).[113] These assessments are what motivated the mass-slaughter campaign carried out in the rural areas of the delta and elsewhere in the post-Tet accelerated pacification campaign, discussed earlier.

Even before the Tet offensive, Defense Secretary McNamara had privately concluded that military victory was an unreasonable objective and that the course of the war should be changed. Clark Clifford, who was brought in to replace him after Tet, had long shared such doubts, and they were reinforced by the evidence available to him and by the conclusions of the "Wise Men" whom Johnson called in to assess the situation.[114] Dean Acheson, who headed this group of longtime hawks drawn from business and political elites, agreed with Clifford's pessimism and "advised Johnson to scale down ground operations, reduce the bombing, and seek every means of terminating hostilities without abandoning South Vietnam." The "Wise Men," "after full briefings from diplomatic and military officials, confirmed Acheson's findings . . . the consensus, as summed up by one of the participants, was that 'there are no military conclusions in this war—or any military end in the future,' " so that "Johnson should therefore de-escalate the conflict."[115]

Notice that at this point some rather serious problems arise concerning the second component of the Freedom House thesis: that the misdeeds of the media caused the public to oppose the war, undermining government resolve and leading to U.S. failure in its (by definition, benevolent) aims. To establish the "stab-in-the-back" component of the Freedom House thesis, it is necessary to show that public opinion was swayed toward opposition to the war by media coverage, and that the media and public opinion were a significant factor in the shift of government policy. Neither claim can be sustained.

With regard to the course of public opinion, the Freedom House study decisively refutes its own thesis. It includes a chapter on public opinion polls by Burns Roper, which demonstrates, as Braestrup concedes, that "there is no available evidence of a direct relationship between the dominant media themes in early 1968 and changes in American mass public opinion vis-à-vis the Vietnam war itself," but rather a continuing "slow drift toward the dove side" after an initial wave of support for the president and "frustration and anger at the foe" during the Tet offensive. A closer examination of their own data undermines the Freedom House thesis even more thoroughly. The early response to the Tet offensive, during the period when media incompetence and unwarranted pessimism were allegedly at their height, was "an increase in the belligerency of the American public"; "the immediate reaction of the U.S. public was to favor stiffened resistance [that is, U.S. resistance to an attack by South Vietnamese in South Vietnam] and intensified U.S. effort." The major sentiment aroused was "Bomb the hell out of them." In later February and March, when the media, in the Freedom House version, were beginning to "whisper" the true story of American victory, "there developed a decided negative reaction to the President's handling of the war and the war itself, and a distinct opposition to more aggressive U.S. military action." In early February 1968, when the impact of the alleged media "distortions" and "pessimism" reached its peak, public opinion shifted toward the "hawks." Public opinion returned to the pre-Tet figures by late February, when the media were allegedly correcting their earlier errors. By April, after the offensive had ended and the "errors" had been overcome (albeit in a "whisper"), there was a sharp shift toward the "doves." By April–May–June, measurements had returned to pre-Tet levels. "When looked at on this broader time scale, the Tet offensive appears merely to have caused a minor ripple in a steadily changing attitude toward our involvement in the war," a shift toward the position of the doves after an initial shift toward the hawks during the period of media "pessimism." Tet was just "one more incident" that "reminded the public that the war was not going well—that the confident predictions out of Washington had to be taken with a grain of salt—and that helped move public opinion in the antiwar direction in which it had been moving for nearly three years. . . ."[116]

Faced with this thorough refutation of one essential component of their thesis, without which the thesis loses all significance even if the residue were tenable, the Freedom House analysts retreat to the position that although the public was unaffected by the perverse behavior of the media, there was an effect "on the nation's 'leadership segment' " (Burns)—a safer claim, since, as they concede, no data are available. The director of the Freedom House study, Leonard Sussman, concludes that "the Tet offensive, as portrayed in the media, appeared to have had a far greater effect on political Washington and the Administration itself than on the U.S. population's sentiment on the war" (I, xxxiv). The media failures, in short, left the public unaffected or even more supportive of the war while they misled the government—along with presidential adviser Clark Clifford, the "Wise Men" from the corporate, political, and military elites including former top-level military commanders, and such media addicts as Dean Acheson, Henry Cabot Lodge, McGeorge Bundy, Douglas Dillon, Robert Murphy, etc. We are asked to believe that their decision to move toward disengagement in a situation that they perceived as one of stalemate was based not on military briefings, intelligence reports, and all the information available at the highest level to official Washington, but on watching the evening news with Walter Cronkite.[117]

In short, we can dismiss out of hand the second component of the Freedom House thesis, the component that had dramatic impact and continuing influence within the post-Vietnam "right turn" among elites and that has set the agenda for subsequent discussion about the "adversarial stance" of the media and its grim consequences. We are left with the conclusion that the media were either irrelevant, or that they continued to operate within the general confines of the approved ideological system, thus refuting the first component of the thesis as well. All that remains of the Freedom House story is the possibility that the media were incompetent (even malevolent), but ineffectual. Notice that the Freedom House thesis here faces the same "logical problem" noted earlier with regard to the charges concerning television: if television is as influential as claimed, then the evidence shows that through 1967 it "encouraged a decisive majority of viewers to support the war."

To evaluate the remaining shreds of the Freedom House thesis, let us continue with the record of the Tet offensive, now asking whether the media did in fact distort it in their zealous—although utterly ineffectual—efforts to undermine authority.

With lavish use of firepower, U.S. forces succeeded in regaining control of the towns and cities. The city of Hué, which had been conquered from its own population by GVN troops with American assistance several months earlier in a desperate U.S. effort to prevent the growth of popular movements calling for democracy and a negotiated political settlement,[118] was 80 percent destroyed by bombing and shelling, which left 2,000 civilians buried in the "smashed ruins," according to U.S. Air Force Undersecretary Townsend Hoopes; the marines listed "Communist losses" at over 5,000, while Hoopes states that a "sizable part" of the Communist force of 1,000 men who captured the city escaped, allowing a determination of who constituted the "Communist losses." U.S. AID in May estimated that some 4,000 civilians were left dead in the ruins of the city, most of them victims of U.S. firepower.[119]

In the Mekong Delta, "Artillery and air strikes leveled half of My Tho, a city of 80,000, and the provincial capital of Ben Tre [Kien Hoa Province, later devastated in the post-Tet terror campaign; see p. 204], with 140,000 inhabitants, was decimated with the justification, as an American colonel put it in one of the most widely quoted statements of the war, 'We had to destroy the town to save it.' "[120] The U.S. command conceded that "the enemy" were overwhelmingly NLF, not North Vietnamese; killed and captured outnumbered captured weapons by a factor of five, an indication of who "the enemy" really were. Secretary of Defense McNamara estimated NVA forces at 50,000 to 55,000 at the end of 1967, mostly in northern regions, with some 10,000 troops placed in Viet Cong combat units; the total roughly matches third-country forces, mostly Korean mercenaries, mobilized by the United States as part of its invasion of South Vietnam, and barely 10 percent of the U.S. forces of over half a million men, even excluding the massive forces engaged in the attack against Vietnam and Laos from the sea and from U.S. sanctuaries from Thailand to the Philippines and Guam, employing means of destruction that dwarfed all else in Indochina.[121]

As noted earlier, the Tet offensive not only reduced Washington to gloomy despair and convinced U.S. elites that there was no realistic hope of a military victory in Vietnam at a cost acceptable to the United States, but also changed the character of media reporting and commentary, which mirrored the changes in elite opinion. On the ground, American correspondents were able to witness the war at first hand, gaining a view rather different from the sanitized and edited version presented under the control of the American military command. Media commentary at home reflected elite opinion in recognizing that the optimistic forecasts that had been relayed from Washington with little skepticism were inaccurate, and that a long and bitter war lay ahead.

But on-the-scene reporting and domestic commentary never veered from the framework of the state propaganda system. In reporting the fighting in Ben Tre and My Tho in the Delta, for example, the press observed that American infantry participated while the towns were blasted by American bombers, helicopter gunships, navy patrol boats, and artillery to root out the Viet Cong—that is, the South Vietnamese guerrillas who "were probably living with the people," according to an American officer quoted by Bernard Weinraub. Nonetheless, the news reports speak of the perceived need to "blast the city" with jets and helicopter gunships, particularly the poorer and most crowded sections, "to save other sections of the city and the lives of thousands of people . . ." (Lee Lescaze)—people whose lives were threatened not by the southern NLF guerrillas living among them but by the U.S. forces "defending" them from the NLF. Because of Tet, Weinraub explains, "the protection of Ben Tre was limited," and it was necessary to bring in troops from the U.S. Ninth Infantry Division by helicopter, and to carry out "bombing raids and fire by helicopter gunships and artillery" to "protect" Ben Tre, which "has long been a stronghold of the Vietcong" and is "sometimes considered a Vietcong rest and recreation area," while surrounding hamlets "thought to be controlled by the Vietcong have been razed by allied bombing and artillery attacks and fire from armed helicopters." In Ben Tre itself, "the market place is rubble and near the gutted homes nearby women in shawls sit in the noon heat and mourn with loud groans," while "My Tho still smells of death," with half the homes destroyed—thanks to the effective "protection" the population received from their American defenders.[122]

Throughout, it is taken for granted that the forces armed, trained, and supplied by the only foreign element in the delta are "the South Vietnamese," not the South Vietnamese guerrillas living among the population in their "Vietcong strongholds," from whom the United States is "protecting" the population by ferocious bombardment of civilian areas.

Recall that we are now evaluating the remaining component of the Freedom House thesis: that the media were suppressing the American victory in their antiestablishment zeal. In fact, they were reporting the story accurately in a narrow sense, but completely within the framework of the government propaganda system—never questioned, in a shameful display of media servility. We may imagine what the reaction would be to a comparable performance on the part of the Nazi or Soviet press. Braestrup's final comment that "a free society deserves better" of its media (I, 728) is accurate enough, although not quite in the sense intended in the Freedom House study.

As throughout the war, the standpoint of the media continued to reflect the perceptions and attitudes of the American military; for example, an American official who observed: "What the Vietcong did was occupy the hamlets we pacified just for the purpose of having the allies move in and bomb them. By their presence, the hamlets were destroyed."[123] The same *New York Times* report from Binh Dinh Province—the "showcase" province for pacification—indicates this had been going on, unreported, well before the Tet offensive: "The enemy moves in December—which several military men called a 'softening up' for the offensive—resulted in a wave of allied air strikes on villages. Hundreds of homes were destroyed."

The U.S. military "resistance"—to borrow the Freedom House terminology—took the same form elsewhere. Robert Shaplen reported from the scene that in Saigon,

> A dozen separate areas, comprising perhaps sixty or seventy blocks, had been totally burned out. These were almost all residential areas. . . . Most of the damage was the result of rocket attacks by American armed helicopters or other planes, though some of it had been caused by artillery or ground fighting. . . . A modern ten-million-dollar textile plant, containing forty thousand spindles, was entirely destroyed by bombs because it was suspected of being a Vietcong hideout.[124]

Le Monde correspondent Jean-Claude Pomonti observed that

> in the popular suburbs, the Front [NLF] has proven that the only way to eliminate its control is through systematic destruction. To dislodge it, the air force had to level many residential areas. Fleeing the bombardments, tens of thousands of refugees have poured into the center of the city.[125]

Charles Mohr, whom Freedom House singles out for "perhaps the consistently best reporting from Vietnam," reported that "in towns such as Hué, Vinhlong, Bentre and Mytho appalling destruction was wrought when encircled allied forces took the decision to destroy the attacking Vietcong forces by destroying the places they had occupied." He quotes an American official in Saigon as stating: "The Government won the recent battles, but it is important to consider how they won. At first the Vietcong had won and held everything in some towns except the American military compound and a South Vietnamese position."[126] By "the Government," he means the reader to understand the GVN, who "won" thanks to U.S. firepower and troops.

As in this example, the U.S. government claim that the Tet offensive was a military defeat for the Communists was widely reported, although the U.S. government official's perception of an initial Viet Cong victory goes well beyond the typical media accounts in the crime of "pessimism." "Journalists generally accepted the official claim that Tet was a military defeat for the North Vietnamese and NLF," Daniel Hallin concludes in his review of the press and television; for example, Walter Cronkite, who said at once over CBS—on February 14—that "first, and simplest, the Vietcong suffered a military defeat."[127] Clear and forthright.

These facts do not comport well with what remains of the Freedom House thesis: the charge that until late February, the media portrayed the enemy's defeat as "a defeat for the allies" in "clamourous shouts," only conceding from late February in a "whisper" that this was not quite accurate, television being the worst offender, with Walter Cronkite the arch-criminal.[128] It was this gross incompetence or malevolence that illustrates most dramatically the "mindless readiness . . . to believe the worst of the government or of authority in general." In the real world, the facts were quite the opposite, and the last remnants of the Freedom House thesis thus disappear, apart from the charge, to be evaluated in the appendix, that the reporting was technically incompetent.

Some would contend that the issue of "how they won," which concerned the American official cited earlier, is as important as "who won" in evaluating the significance of the Tet offensive. This idea never penetrated the minds of Braestrup or his Freedom House associates, however, at the time or in their study. Consider political scientist Milton Sacks, a specialist on Vietnam and a GVN adviser, thanked for "providing historical perspective" for the Freedom House Study (I, xxiii). In February 1968, he wrote, with no further comment:

> In conventional terms, it now seems clear that the Communists have suffered a military defeat in their Tet offensive. They have expended the lives of thousands of their soldiers without securing a single province or district town of significance.[129]

U.S. officials, in contrast, were impressed with the fact that the NLF and NVA occupied vast areas previously thought to be "controlled," wreaked havoc with the pacification program, and were dislodged only by a further and still more violent U.S. attack on the civil society of South Vietnam. It was feared that it might not be an easy task to convince the populace that the Communists were to blame for the slaughter and destruction by U.S. forces. The problem, as reported from Hué by Marc Riboud of *Le Monde* in April, was that the population appeared to compare ARVN behavior unfavorably with that of the NVA or NLF, while the deepest bitterness and resentment was directed against the Americans, whose "blind and systematic bombardment" had turned Hué into "an assassinated city"; this reaction may have also been in part a residue of the deep bitterness and resentment left by the U.S.-backed ARVN conquest of Hué a few months earlier.[130] An IVS worker quoted in *Newsweek* said: "As difficult as this may be to believe, not a single Vietnamese I have met in Saigon or in the Delta blames the Viet Cong for the events of the past two weeks," and in its last issue of the Tet period, *Newsweek* reported from Hué, with the same surprise at this inexplicable reaction, that

> Curiously, moreover, few of [the population] point an accusing finger at the North Vietnamese. "When the NVA were here," said one student, "they were polite and well-disciplined, totally different from the government troops, the Americans, or even the Vietcong."

"The hope is that the Vietnamese people will blame the communists rather than the Americans for whatever damage is being done," Don Webster reported from Hué on February 12 in the midst of the reconquest of the city by the U.S. Marines. Two days earlier, John Lengel of AP wrote that

> It is still impossible to gauge the breadth of the damage. . . . But few seasoned observers see the devastation of Hue backfiring on the communists. They see as the greatest hope a massive and instant program of restoration underlined by a careful psychological warfare program pinning the blame on the communists.[131]

Braestrup places the word "devastation" in italics as an illustration of the unfairness and anti-American bias of the media; comment seems superfluous.

While the U.S. media rarely strayed from the framework of the state propaganda system, others were unconstrained by these limits: for example, the *Le Monde* correspondents cited; or British photo-journalist Philip Jones Griffiths, who concluded from his observations on the scene that the thousands of civilian victims of the reconquest of Hué "were killed by the most hysterical use of American firepower ever seen," and then designated "as the victims of a Communist massacre."[132]

To comprehend fully the nature of the Freedom House charges, we may imagine how the inquiry urged by John Roche might proceed. Who else is implicated in the terrible misdeeds that Freedom House perceives? General Westmoreland and the U.S. command in Saigon must surely be placed on the docket because of their estimates of early VC successes (see appendix 3 for further examples), along with William Bundy, assistant secretary of state for Far Eastern affairs, given his extreme pessimism. He thought that the Tet offensive was "shattering to the South, especially in the area of pacification," concluding for a time that "the South Vietnamese were through," "they've had it"—where "South Vietnamese" excludes the South Vietnamese defending their country from a U.S. invasion, as usual. These conclusions, which do conform to the Freedom House parody of the media, were based not on the press but on "reports from people in the field out in Vietnam," so presumably they too are implicated (I, 625). Similarly, Lyndon Johnson was guilty, since he seemed "to some degree 'psychologically defeated' by the threat to Khe Sanh and the onslaught on the cities of Vietnam," so Braestrup concludes (I, 626, 630). The same is true of Johnson's civilian advisers, given the "air of gloom" among them and the "Battle of Bull Run" mood, and the author of the official U.S. government military-historical summary, cited earlier; and Dean Acheson and other "Wise Men" who urged a shift of course because of the same "undue pessimism" for which the media are condemned by Freedom House. Also Ambassador Ellsworth Bunker, who reported that the offensive had "disrupted the pacification effort for the time being," and the pacification adviser who reported that in his "showcase" area, "pacification does not exist" (II, 184–86).

Further candidates for investigation appear in the *Pentagon Papers*—for example, General Wheeler, who summarized the situation in the following terms to the president on February 27, just as Walter Cronkite was speculating about "stalemate," arousing Freedom House ire:

> The enemy is operating with relative freedom in the countryside, probably recruiting heavily and no doubt infiltrating NVA units and personnel. His recovery is likely to be rapid; his supplies are adequate; and he is trying to maintain the momentum of his winter-spring offensive. . . . ARVN is now in a defensive posture around towns and cities and there is concern about how well they will bear up under sustained pressure. The initial attack nearly succeeded in a dozen places, and defeat in these places was only averted by the timely reaction of US forces. In short, it was a very near thing. There is no doubt that the RD Program [pacification] has suffered a severe set back. . . . To a large extent the VC now control the countryside. . . . MACV estimates that US forces will be required in a number of places to assist and encourage the Vietnamese Army to leave the cities and towns and reenter the country. This is especially true in the Delta.

The media reports that Braestrup derides were rarely as "pessimistic" as the chairman of the Joint Chiefs of Staff, whose summary of the situation led the president to order "the initiation of a complete and searching reassessment of the entire U.S. strategy and commitment in South Vietnam," the *Pentagon Papers* analyst reports.[133]

The CIA must also be investigated for contributing to the decline of "free institutions" by its pessimism. A CIA paper of March 1, presumably uninfluenced by Walter Cronkite, expressed grave doubts about the GVN and ARVN and predicted that they might cease "effective functioning in parts of the country," so that "virtually the entire burden of the war would fall on US forces." Like Cronkite a few days earlier, they expected "no better than a standoff" in the coming ten months. Pentagon systems analysis concluded that the offensive "appears to have killed the [pacification] program once and for all," drawing the conclusion that Braestrup falsely attributes to the media (see appendix 3), and estimated that "our control of the countryside and the defense of the urban areas is now at pre–August 1965 levels." It was because of this serious situation—not perceived American successes, as Braestrup intimates—that they recommended what was later to be called "Vietnamization."

The civilian analysts in the Pentagon must be charged not only with undue pessimism, but also with some of the other crimes of the press. For example, they referred to the famous statement that we are destroying South Vietnam in order to save it; citation of this statement is the target of much Braestrup scorn. We must also include Colonel Herbert Schandler, on whom Braestrup relies for his account of the

Wheeler-Westmoreland request for additional troops. He was, Braestrup says, the anonymous author of the *Pentagon Papers* section on this material, and here he described as "a startlingly accurate account" a *New York Times* article by Neil Sheehan and Hedrick Smith which, Braestrup claims, was a major example of "distorted and incomplete" reporting (I, 581, 613). The authors of the "Epilogue" to the *Pentagon Papers* must also be included in the indictment, given their pessimistic post-Tet assessment of "the price for military victory" and the "illusory" nature of claimed progress.

The category of people who were *not* threatening "free institutions" by the standards of Freedom House is small indeed, a fact that some may find suggestive.

It is significant that the major criticism of the media in the Freedom House study is that they were too "pessimistic." Strikingly absent is the obvious standard of comparison: the internal reports from the field and analysis by intelligence and official Washington—which were, if anything, even more pessimistic. The logic of the Freedom House brief against the media is highly revealing. In their view, the media in a free society must not only accept without question the principles of the state doctrinal system, as the media did throughout (a fact that Freedom House never addresses, and apparently cannot perceive), but must do so with a degree of enthusiasm and optimism that exceeds that of U.S. intelligence, the military command, Johnson's "Wise Men," and other leading figures in the military, political, and corporate world who draw their information from a full range of government sources. It is an interesting conception of a "free society."

We might ask how the Freedom House conception of a free press in a free society would be applied by Soviet commissars, let us say, to the case of the mass circulation weekly *Ogonyok*, which published a series of long articles that presented a "bleak picture" of the war in Afghanistan, depicting it "in stark terms," speaking of "poor morale and desertion" among Afghan units and "tough fighting between elite Soviet troops and Afghan guerrillas," and implying that "large areas of Afghanistan are under guerrilla control." The articles also give "a broad hint that drug use is common among Russian troops in Afghanistan," and they include extracts from a helicopter pilot's journal describing "the sight and smell of colleagues' charred bodies" and implying that "helicopter losses are high" after the receipt of sophisticated Western weaponry by the guerrillas, terrorists who finance themselves by producing drugs for the international market (charges verified by Western observers, incidentally). But it would be inhumane for the USSR simply to withdraw without guarantees for the population, because "a Soviet withdrawal would lead to nationwide internecine warfare," as Afghans who are quoted anticipate. The article does not simply mimic standard U.S. media fare, as these excerpts indicate. Thus it describes an attack on Soviet villages by Afghan guerrillas; one can imagine the U.S. reaction had there been a Viet Cong attack on villages in Texas. But by Freedom House standards, it is plain that the editors merit severe censure for their "adversarial stance," "pessimism," and "volatile styles," "always with the dark possibility that, if the managers do not themselves take action, then outsiders [in the government] will seek to apply remedies of their own."[134] And, in fact, in January 1988, General Dimitri T. Yakov, the Soviet defense minister, applied Freedom House and Braestrup principles to the "adversarial" Soviet press, sharply criticizing articles in *Ogonyok* and *Literaturnaya Gazeta* for reporting on the Afghan war in ways that undermined public confidence in the Soviet army and played into the hands of the West.[135]

In the light of the evidence presented in the Freedom House study, and of much that is ignored, the following conclusions seem reasonable. During the Tet offensive and its aftermath, media performance was creditable, sometimes very highly so, in a narrow sense. More broadly, this reporting was highly deceptive in that it was framed within the unchallenged and unrecognized doctrines of the state propaganda system, which impose a severe distortion. Media reports compare favorably in accuracy with those available to official Washington at the highest level from internal sources, although they were regularly less alarmist, perhaps because the media tended to give credence to official statements and were unaware of the internal assessments. The reports from the scene led media commentators to draw approximately the same conclusions as Johnson's high-level advisers. The manner in which the media covered the events had little effect on public opinion, except perhaps to enhance its aggressiveness and, of course, to instill ever more deeply the basic and unexamined tenets of the propaganda system.

As we shall see in appendix 3, a closer examination establishes these conclusions still more firmly, while demonstrating further the utter incompetence—to use the kindest term—of the Freedom House study that has been so influential in the subsequent period.

We have now addressed the argument presented by critics of the media for its alleged "adversarial stance" on their own chosen grounds, the grounds that they select as the strongest for their case. The propaganda model is once again confirmed, thus meeting the most severe test that can be posed. The model is also vindicated by the manner in which Freedom House fulfills its function as a flak machine, attempting to bully the media into a still more thoroughgoing conformity with the propaganda requirements of state policy by methods that are a travesty of honest journalism (let alone scholarship)—all, of course, in the interest of "freedom."

5.5.3. The Paris Peace Agreements

The Tet offensive convinced large sectors of elite opinion that the costs of the U.S. effort were too high. Lyndon Johnson stepped down. In what was termed by the government a "bombing halt," and reported as such, the bombers were shifted from North Vietnamese targets to Laos, where the defenseless rural society of scattered villages in the North was demolished, and later Cambodia, where the same was true on an even more horrendous scale. U.S. forces undertook the violent and destructive post-Tet accelerated pacification campaign in the South, and bombing was intensified to *"step up refugee programs deliberately aimed at depriving the VC of a recruiting base,"* in accordance with the advice of pacification director Robert Komer in April 1967.[136] The Phoenix program was established to destroy the "infrastructure" of the NLF by terror. The burden of ground fighting was shifted to Vietnamese forces supplied and directed by the United States, and U.S. conscripts were withdrawn, a more typical pattern for colonial wars that essentially duplicated the earlier French effort to reconquer Indochina. And the United States finally agreed to pursue the path of a negotiated settlement, although still not relinquishing the aim of preventing the unification of Vietnam and retaining Indochina, apart from North Vietnam, within the U.S. global system.

This was not the maximal goal the United States had pursued; thus in the late 1950s the U.S. government still hoped for unification of Vietnam under anti-Communist leadership, and the U.S. client regime always regarded itself as the government of all of Vietnam (GVN = Government of Vietnam), and so declared in the first and unamendable article of its constitution. But by the late 1960s, if not before, control over all Indochina apart from North Vietnam was regarded as the maximum goal attainable. As we have seen, opportunities for a peaceful diplomatic settlement had long existed, but they had never been pursued because they were regarded as inconsistent with the essential goal: preservation of an "independent" South Vietnam that would be a U.S. client state.

By October 1972, the negotiators in Paris had reached the essential terms of an agreement: the 9-Point Plan. President Nixon, however, objected to the terms of the agreement, and the Thieu government in

Saigon was completely opposed to them. Nixon's hope was to delay further negotiations until after the November presidential elections, when he would have more leverage.[137] The delay would also permit a vast shipment of arms to the GVN, something that would surely be prohibited by the agreements.

In an effort to pressure Nixon to sign the agreements, the DRV made the terms public on October 26 in a radio broadcast. In a Washington press conference, Kissinger stated that the Radio Hanoi broadcast gave "on the whole a very fair account," then offering the following paraphrase: "As was pointed out by Radio Hanoi, the existing authorities with respect to both internal and external politics would remain in office" in the South. Thus Kissinger sought to insinuate that according to the accurate account on Radio Hanoi, the GVN ("the existing authorities") would remain "in office" as the government of the South, and would somehow deal with the other "party," whose status remained mysterious. But "what was pointed out by Radio Hanoi"—correctly, as Kissinger conceded—was something quite different, namely, that "the two present administrations in South Vietnam will remain in existence with their respective domestic and external functions," these being the GVN and the PRG (based upon the NLF). Having reached agreement, these two parties were then to move toward reunification, to be "carried out step by step through peaceful means," with no external—meaning U.S.—interference.

The differences are crucial. From its earliest days, the war was fought over the question of whether "the South Vietnamese people shall decide themselves the political future of South Vietnam," as the October 9-Point Plan explicitly stipulated must be the case, or whether the United States would enforce the rule of its client regime, the GVN, as the sole legitimate government in the South, in accordance with Kissinger's version of the terms to which he had theoretically agreed, a version that plainly departed radically from the text.[138]

Kissinger's announcement that "peace is at hand," designed with the upcoming U.S. presidential elections in mind, was also blatant deception. As his distortion of the essential terms of the agreement clearly revealed, the United States was backing away from the settlement and refusing to implement it. Nixon later explained that "We had to use [Kissinger's press conference] to undercut the North Vietnamese propaganda maneuver [namely, making public the terms of the agreement] and to make sure that our version of the agreement was the one that had great public impact."[139] This result was substantially achieved; the media characteristically accepted Kissinger's version with no recognition that it was diametrically opposed to the terms of the 9-Point Plan, though the facts were plain to anyone who troubled to look at the readily available public record.

The United States then proceeded with a vast shipment of arms to the GVN while demanding substantial changes in the October agreements. Hanoi, in contrast, publicly insisted that the October agreements be signed. The media adopted the version of events relayed regularly by Kissinger, depicting him as caught between two irrational adversaries, Hanoi and Saigon. The Christmas bombings of Hanoi and Haiphong followed, causing great damage and also the loss of several dozen B-52s (the exact numbers are contested, but the losses clearly shocked the Pentagon), as well as a highly adverse world reaction, although the media continued to relay the Washington interpretation of what had happened. Thus Stanley Karnow wrote that "evidently" the primary aim of "Nixon's bombings of Hanoi" was "to compel the North Vietnamese to return to negotiations," a curious version of the readily available facts.[140] After the military and political failures of the Christmas bombings, the U.S. government then signed the January peace agreements, which were virtually identical to the terms it had rejected the preceding October—and, still more significant, were hardly different in essentials from the NLF proposals of the early 1960s, which caused such dismay in Washington and compelled the U.S. government to escalate the war so as to prevent a political settlement, thus virtually destroying Indochina, with millions of casualties and three countries utterly devastated—a fact considered of little moment in the West.

The charade that took place in October was reenacted in January. As the agreements were announced on January 24, the White House made an official statement, and Kissinger had a lengthy press conference in which he explained clearly that the United States was planning to reject every essential provision of the accords the administration had been compelled to sign, presenting a version that explicitly violated them at every crucial point. In yet another astonishing demonstration of servility, the media accepted the Kissinger–White House version unquestioningly, thus guaranteeing that the Vietnamese enemy would appear to be violating the agreements if it adhered to them.

Recall that all of this took place during the period when the media had allegedly reached their peak level of militant opposition to state authority. Let us now briefly inspect this remarkable record.

The Paris Agreements committed "the United States and all other countries [to] respect the independence, sovereignty, unity and territorial integrity of Vietnam as recognized by the 1954 Geneva Agreements on Vietnam" (article 1). Pending reunification of Vietnam, which is to "be carried out step by step through peaceful means . . . and without foreign interference," the "military demarcation line" at the 17th parallel is to be regarded as "only provisional and not a political or territorial boundary" (article 15). In the South, there are two parallel and equivalent "South Vietnamese parties," the GVN and the PRG. This is the central element of the agreements, which proceed to specify in detail the responsibilities and commitments of the two "South Vietnamese parties." These are to achieve national reconciliation through peaceful means, under conditions of full democratic freedoms, while "Foreign countries shall not impose any political tendency or personality on the South Vietnamese people" and "the United States will not continue its military involvement or intervene in the internal affairs of South Vietnam" (articles 9c, 4). "The two South Vietnamese parties undertake to respect the cease-fire and maintain peace in South Vietnam, settle all matters of contention through negotiations, and avoid all armed conflict" (article 10). Furthermore, "the two South Vietnamese parties" will proceed to "Achieve national reconciliation and concord, end hatred and enmity, prohibit all acts of reprisal and discrimination against individuals or organizations that have collaborated with one side or the other," and, in general, "ensure the democratic liberties of the people," which are outlined, along with procedures to ensure the reconcilation undertaken by "the two South Vietnamese parties" (articles 11, 12). The agreements committed "the two South Vietnamese parties" not to "accept the introduction of troops, military advisers, and military personnel including technical military personnel, armaments, munitions, and war material into South Vietnam" and called for a "total withdrawal" of all such personnel within sixty days, while "the two South Vietnamese parties" will settle "The question of Vietnamese armed forces in South Vietnam . . . without foreign interference" (articles 5, 7, 13).

In his January 24 press conference, Kissinger made it clear that the United States maintained the right to provide "civilian technicians serving in certain of the military branches," and as its forces were withdrawn after the signing of the agreements, the United States proceeded to keep or introduce 7,200 "contract civilians" to "handle maintenance, logistics, and training jobs formerly performed by the U.S. military," many of them "retired military men," under the supervision of a U.S. major-general.[141] The provisions concerning technical personnel were thus at once nullified, along with the U.S. pledge to refrain from any intervention "in the internal affairs of South Vietnam."

In a speech of January 23, Nixon announced that the GVN would be recognized as the "sole legitimate government in South Vietnam," nullifying articles 9c and 4 as well as the basic principle of the agreements: that the two parallel and equivalent "South Vietnamese parties" are to proceed toward a settlement with no U.S. interference or effort to impose any "political tendency" on the people of South Vietnam. In its "summary of basic elements of the Vietnam agreements" on January 24, the White House announced that "the government of the Republic of (South) Vietnam continues in existence, recognized by the United States, its constitutional structure and leadership intact and unchanged"—the reason for the parentheses being that this "constitutional structure" identifies the GVN as the government of all Vietnam. This "constitutional structure" also outlawed the second of the two parallel and equivalent parties, along with "pro-communist neutralism" and any form of expression "aimed at spreading Communist policies, slogans and instructions"; and the GVN announced at once that such "illegal" actions would be suppressed by force, while President Thieu stated that "this is solely a ceasefire agreement, no more no less."[142] With these declarations, the United States and its client regime thus nullified the central principle of the Paris Agreements, and flatly rejected the provisions for "the two South Vietnamese parties" to achieve "national reconciliation and concord" by peaceful means without forceful measures or repression.

In short, the United States announced at once, clearly and without equivocation, that it intended to disregard every essential provision of the scrap of paper it was compelled to sign in Paris.

Kissinger attempted to obfuscate the matter in his January 24 press conference, reprinted in full in the *New York Times.*[143] He claimed, falsely, that "we have achieved substantial changes" from the October 9-Point Plan, thus implicitly offering a justification for the Christmas bombings. He stated that "what the civil war has been all about" is "who is the legitimate ruler of South Vietnam" and "is there such a thing as a South Vietnam even temporarily until unification," claiming that the United States had achieved its objectives on these points by virtue of the "specific references to the sovereignty of South Vietnam" and "the right of the South Vietnamese people to self-determination"; and he claimed that the United States had also achieved its goal with regard to the status of the demarcation line.

All of this was blatant deception. The wording of the agreements reflected the DRV-PRG position in all the respects Kissinger mentioned, while Kissinger's insinuation that the agreements permitted the United States to recognize the GVN as "the legitimate ruler of South Vietnam" is in explicit contradiction to the agreements he had just signed, as is his attempt to create the impression that the "civil war" is "between North and South Vietnam." The core provision of the Paris Agreements establishes the GVN and the PRG as "the two South

Vietnamese parties," parallel and equivalent, to move toward unification with the North, abrogating the provisional demarcation line, which has no political status. Kissinger was attempting to confuse "sovereignty *of* South Vietnam" with "sovereignty *within* South Vietnam"; the latter is what the war "was all about" from the outset, and the agreements simply reiterated the position of "the enemy" that this was a matter to be settled by the two South Vietnamese parties without external interference, as in the October 9-Point Plan.[144]

Just as in October, the purpose of this obfuscation was, in Nixon's words, "to make sure that our version of the agreement was the one that had great public impact." And again it succeeded. The media—without exception, to our knowledge—accepted the Kissinger–White House version as expressing the contents of the agreements, enabling them to interpret the PRG-DRV insistence on the actual terms of the Paris Agreements as an effort to disrupt them. Thus Joseph Kraft, a liberal dove on these issues, wrote that "Much of the blame goes to the Communists" for the subsequent breakdown of the cease-fire, because "Hanoi has never abandoned the objective of unifying all of Vietnam"; that is, Hanoi has never abandoned its objective of living up to the terms of the Geneva Accords of 1954, now explicitly reiterated in the Paris Agreements of January 1973.[145] As a dove, he also added that "just as much of the blame goes to President Thieu"—but none, of course, can be assigned to Washington. He cites Communist military actions in the South and dispatch of equipment as the major reason for the breakdown of the cease-fire, citing no evidence; as we shall see, the facts reveal quite a different reason.

At the liberal extreme of U.S. opinion, Tom Wicker wrote that

> American policy, which never accepted the Geneva agreement, came to insist, instead, that South Vietnam was a legally constituted nation being subverted and invaded by another power; and that view is implied even in the documents that finally produced the cease-fire.[146]

Wicker adopts Kissinger's version, which is in explicit contradiction to the actual documents; these simply reiterate the long-held position of the NLF and Hanoi with regard to the status of South Vietnam.

In the *New Republic,* Stanley Karnow wrote that "the Vietcong considers [the PRG] to be a parallel administration," failing to observe that it is not only "the Vietcong," but also *the Paris Agreements just signed by the United States government* that assign to the PRG a status exactly parallel to that of the GVN.[147] In *Newsweek,* Stewart Alsop proclaimed that if the "marvelously elaborate" Nixon-Kissinger settlement "survives more or less intact, we will have won the war"—which would be true, under the Nixon-Kissinger interpretation, although under the evidently irrelevant terms of the Paris Agreements, the United States had abandoned its war aims and accepted the basic proposals of the Vietnamese enemy. *Newsweek* went on to explain in the same issue that Hanoi has now

> accepted the provision that north and south are divided by a sacrosanct demarcation line, thus tacitly acknowledging the legitimacy of the Saigon regime. . . . Equally vital to the Nixon Administration was specific mention of the "sovereignty" of the Saigon government, and on this point, too, the U.S. had its way. Hanoi finally conceded that, in Kissinger's words, "there is an entity called South Vietnam." In one important sense, the dispute over that question was what the war in Vietnam was all about.[148]

Again, utterly and transparently false in every respect, as a comparison with the text just quoted immediately demonstrates, although in accord with Kissinger's deceptive version of the agreements, taken as sacrosanct by the loyal media.

An honest and independent press would have announced the January agreements with headlines reading: "U.S. Announces Intention to Violate the Agreements Signed in Paris." An informed press would have observed further that the Paris Agreements incorporate the principles rejected by the United States at Geneva twenty years earlier, as well as the essential principles of the NLF program of the early 1960s, which were similar to those advocated by Vietnamese quite generally and constituted the crucial fact that impelled the United States to escalate the war so as to block a political settlement among Vietnamese. The actual press simply adopted Washington's version of the agreements, never mentioning that this version contradicted them in every essential respect and thus guaranteed that the war would go on—as it did. Once again, the contribution of the media was to help implement further violence and suffering by adopting Washington's version of events—in this case, in the face of the fact that this version was, transparently, in flat contradiction to the documents readily at hand. One would have to search assiduously to discover a more blatant example of media subservience to state power.

The aftermath was predictable, predicted in the "alternative press," and similar to earlier occasions when the same factors were operative. As after Geneva 1954, the Communists, who had won a political victory (on paper), attempted to pursue "political struggle," while the United States and its GVN client at once turned to military force to overturn the terms of the Paris Agreements. These facts were reported by the more serious journalists on the scene in Vietnam, notably Daniel Southerland, who observed from his extensive investigations that "the Saigon government has been guilty in by far the greatest number of cases of launching offensive operations into territory held by the other side," assuming "that it has the right, despite the cease-fire," to take back territory which it lost in 1972," and giving many examples, as did others.[149] The U.S. government informed Congress cheerily that "the GVN has fared well during the post–cease-fire maneuvering," adding "770 hamlets to the list of those over which it has dominant control" after the agreements—and in violation of them, a fact that passed without notice. The GVN thus added one million people to the areas of its control, while expending sixteen times as much ammunition as the enemy and using the newly provided U.S. equipment, as intended, for massive military operations, including extensive bombardment of PRG areas to prevent refugees from returning to them as provided by the agreements.[150] The media either blamed the Communists, or sometimes the GVN as well, but not the United States, which had announced at once its intention to disrupt the agreements and now publicly expressed its pleasure in the military actions that successfully achieved this objective.

When the North Vietnamese finally responded to U.S.-GVN violence, the GVN quickly collapsed, leading to outrage in the U.S. government and media—which still persists—over this dramatic demonstration of Communist iniquity, which proves that their intentions all along were to destroy the free and independent government of South Vietnam and to reduce its people to Communist tyranny, thus further entrenching the principle that "Communists cannot be trusted."

This useful lesson, firmly established by media complicity in transparent government deceit, has, not surprisingly, been applied in subsequent efforts by the U.S. government to gain its ends by violence. One dramatic example was featured in the media in August 1987, when the Central American presidents confounded Washington strategy by adopting a political settlement that undermined the familiar U.S. reliance on force to compensate for its political weakness. As part of its immediate efforts to sabotage this agreement, the State Department called the Latin American ambassadors to Washington, where they were presented with "a copy of the 1973 Paris peace agreement that was negotiated to end the U.S. involvement in the Vietnam War," the *Wall Street Journal* reported, adding that "the agreement was subsequently ignored by North Vietnam." The *Journal* explained that this unfortunate "Vietnam experience," which proved that agreements with Communists are not worth the paper they are printed on, is one factor in administration "skepticism" about the Central American agreement. Copies of the 1973 Paris Agreements were distributed to the envoys "as a case study of how an agreement with ambiguous provisions could be exploited and even ignored by a Communist government," Neil Lewis reported in the lead story in the *New York Times*, adding: "In violation of the 1973 accord, North Vietnam overran South Vietnam and united the two parts of Vietnam under its banner in 1975."[151] The utility of a carefully crafted historical record, designed by the loyal media to serve the needs of state power, is revealed here with much clarity.

Surveying these events, we reach essentially the same conclusions as before, although once again the performance of the media—at the peak period of their alleged "independence" and "adversarial stance"—goes well beyond the predictions of the propaganda model, exceeding the expected norm of obedience to the state authorities and reaching the level that one finds in totalitarian states. As before, the servility of the media made a significant contribution to ensuring that the slaughter in Indochina would continue and that the U.S. government would be able to exploit its "Vietnam experience," as filtered through the media, for later exercises in international terrorism. The remarkable performance of the media also laid the basis for the postwar interpretation of "what the war was all about" and why the United States failed to attain its ends, a matter to which we turn in the next section.

5.6. THE VIETNAM WAR IN RETROSPECT

In April 1975, the war came to an end, and the thirty-year conflict entered a new phase. Indochina faced the near-insoluble problems of reconstruction in a land that had been reduced to ruin by foreign armies after a century of colonial oppression. In the United States too, elite groups faced a problem of reconstruction, but of a different kind. The problem in the United States was the reconstruction of ideology, the taming of the domestic population that had lost its faith in the nobility of intent and the inspiring benevolence of the elites who determine U.S. policy. It was necessary to overcome what Norman Podhoretz, echoing Goebbels, calls "the sickly inhibitions against the use of military force," the dread "Vietnam syndrome," finally cured by the stirring triumph of U.S. arms in Grenada, so Podhoretz hoped.[152] This was part of a larger problem, the "crisis of democracy" perceived by Western elites as the normally passive general population threatened to participate in the political system, challenging established privilege and power.[153] A further task was to prevent recovery in the societies ravaged by the American assault, so that the partial victory already achieved by their destruction could be sustained.

As we have seen, through the mid-sixties, the media loyally fulfilled their function of service to state violence, and there was no significant popular opposition to the U.S. attack on Indochina. True, in 1964, the population voted 2 to 1 in favor of the "peace candidate," who was assuring them that we want no wider war while laying the groundwork for the rapid escalation planned for the postelection period, a noteworthy illustration of the character of electoral politics in a society lacking genuine opposition parties and a critical and independent press. Nevertheless, the enthusiasm of the ideological institutions for the rapid escalation of U.S. efforts to "defend South Vietnam" from "internal aggression" helped keep the public in line as the U.S. invading army rose to over half-a-million men on the ground and appeared to be attaining some success in "grinding the enemy down by sheer weight and mass," although at "horrendous cost," in the words of pacification chief Robert ("Blowtorch") Komer, later to become a high-ranking official of the Human Rights Administration.[154]

By 1967, the popular mood was shifting, and the public was beginning to defy the hawk-dove consensus of elites for whom the issues were limited to tactics and expedience, a matter of much government concern. Defense Secretary McNamara warned the president, in secret, in May 1967 that expansion of the American war might "polarize opinion to the extent that 'doves' in the US will get out of hand—massive refusals to serve, or to fight, or to cooperate, or worse?"[155] At the time of the Tet offensive, the Joint Chiefs of Staff were concerned with "our capacity to meet the possibility of widespread civil disorder in the months ahead"; in considering further troop deployments, they took care to ensure that "sufficient forces are still available for civil disorder control," including "National Guard forces deployed under State or Federal control" and U.S. Army troops. The Pentagon warned further that a request for more troops might lead to "increased defiance of the draft and growing unrest in the cities," running the risk of "provoking a domestic crisis of unprecedented proportions." Earlier, the Pentagon feared that escalation of the land war beyond South Vietnam might lead to massive civil disobedience, particularly in view of opposition to the war among young people, the underprivileged, women, and segments of the intelligentsia. "The sight of thousands of peaceful demonstrators being confronted by troops in battle gear" during "the massive anti-war demonstration" and "massive march on the Pentagon" in October 1967 was particularly disturbing, the *Pentagon Papers* analyst observed.[156] The gradual withdrawal of the increasingly demoralized U.S. military forces led to a diminution of visible protest by the early 1970s, but the "Vietnam syndrome" was never cured. As late as 1982, 72 percent of the public (but far fewer "opinion makers" and, to judge by other evidence cited earlier, virtually none of the "American intellectual elite") regarded the Vietnam War as "more than a mistake; it was fundamentally wrong and immoral," a disparity between the public and its "leaders" that persists as of 1986.[157]

The primary task facing the ideological institutions in the postwar period was to convince the errant public that the war was "less a moral crime than the thunderously stupid military blunder of throwing half a million ground troops into an unwinnable war," as the respected *New York Times* war correspondent Homer Bigart explained, while chastising Gloria Emerson for her unwillingness to adopt this properly moderate view.[158] The "purpose of the war" must be perceived as "preventing North Vietnam from subjugating South Vietnam" (John Midgley), "the real enemy, of course, [being] North Vietnam, supplied and sustained by the Soviet Union and China" (Drew Middleton)[159]—all in defiance of the plain facts. The primary issue was the cost to the United States in its noble endeavor; thus Robert Nisbet describes the "intellectual pleasure" he derived from "a truly distinguished work of history" with a chapter covering the 1960s, "with emphasis on the Vietnam War and its devastating impact upon Americans," obviously the only victims worthy of concern.[160] To persuade elite opinion was never much of a problem, since these were the reigning conceptions throughout, and clearly privilege, along with media access, accrues to those who follow this path. But the public has nevertheless remained corrupted.

An ancillary task has been to keep the devastation that the United States left as its legacy in Indochina hidden from public view. Indeed, one finds only scattered reference to this not entirely trivial matter in the U.S. media—a remarkable achievement, given the agency of destruction and its scale. Keeping just to Vietnam, the death toll may have passed three million. In an article entitled "Studies Show Vietnam Raids Failed," Charles Mohr observes that the CIA estimated deaths from bombing of the North at well over 30,000 a year by 1967, "heavily weighted with civilians."[161] Crop-destruction programs from 1961 had a devastating impact, including aerial destruction by chemicals, ground operations to destroy orchards and dikes, and land clearing by giant tractors (Rome plows) that "obliterated agricultural lands, often including extensive systems of paddy dikes, and entire rural residential areas and farming hamlets," leaving the soil "bare, gray and lifeless," in the words of an official report cited by Arthur Westing, who compares the operations to the "less efficient" destruction of Carthage during the Punic Wars. "The combined ecological, economic, and social consequences of the wartime defoliation operations have been vast and will take several generations to reverse"; in the "empty landscapes" of South Vietnam, recovery will be long delayed, if possible at all, and there is no way to estimate the human effects of the chemical poison dioxin at levels "300 to 400% greater than the average levels obtaining among exposed groups in North America."[162]

In the South, 9,000 out of 15,000 hamlets were damaged or destroyed, along with some twenty-five million acres of farmland and twelve million acres of forest. One-and-a-half million cattle were killed, and the war left a million widows and some 800,000 orphans. In the North, all six industrial cities were damaged (three razed to the ground) along with twenty-eight of thirty provincial towns (twelve completely destroyed), ninety-six of 116 district towns, and 4,000 of some 5,800 communes. Four hundred thousand cattle were killed and over a million acres of farmland were damaged. Much of the land is a moonscape, where people live on the edge of famine, with rice rations lower than those in Bangladesh. Reviewing the environmental effects, the Swedish peace-research institute SIPRI concludes that "the ecological debilitation from such attack is likely to be of long duration." The respected Swiss-based environmental group IUCN (International Union for Conservation of Nature and Natural Resources) concluded that the ecology is not only refusing to heal but is worsening, so that a "catastrophe" may result unless billions of dollars are spent to "reconstruct" the land that has been destroyed, a "monumental" task that could be addressed only if the United States were to offer substantial reparations, a possibility that cannot be considered in a cultural climate of abysmal ignorance, chauvinism, and the self-righteous pursuit of self-interest. Destruction of forests has increased the frequency of floods and droughts and aggravated the impact of typhoons, and war damage to dikes (some of which, in the South, were completely destroyed by U.S. bombardment) and other agricultural systems has yet to be repaired. The report notes that "humanitarian and conservationist groups, particularly in the United States, have encountered official resistance and red tape when requesting their governments' authorization to send assistance to Vietnam"—naturally enough, since the

United States remains committed to ensure that its achievements are not threatened by recovery of the countries it destroyed.[163]

There is little hint of any of this, or of the similar Carthaginian devastation in Laos and Cambodia, in mainstream U.S. media coverage. Rather, with remarkable uniformity and self-righteousness, the problems of reconstruction, hampered further by the natural catastrophes and continuing war to which the United States has made what contribution it can, are attributed solely to Communist brutality and ineptitude. The sole remaining interest in postwar Vietnam in the U.S. media has been the recovery of remains of U.S. personnel presumed to be killed in action, the Vietnamese preoccupation with other matters serving as further proof of their moral insensitivity.

In one of his sermons on human rights, President Carter explained that we owe Vietnam no debt and have no responsibility to render it any assistance because "the destruction was mutual,"[164] a statement that elicited no comment, to our knowledge, apart from our own—a fact that speaks volumes about the prevailing cultural climate. Some feel that there may once have been a debt but that it has been amply repaid. Under the headline "The Debt to the Indochinese Is Becoming a Fiscal Drain," Bernard Gwertzman quotes a State Department official who "said he believed the United States has now paid its moral debt for its involvement on the losing side in Indochina." The remark, which also passed without comment, is illuminating: we owe no debt for mass slaughter and for leaving three countries in ruins, no debt to the millions of maimed and orphaned, to the peasants who still die today from exploding ordnance left from the U.S. assault. Rather, our moral debt results only from the fact that we did not win. By this logic, if the Russians win in Afghanistan, they will have no moral debt at all. Proceeding further, how have we paid our moral debt for failing to win? By resettling Vietnamese refugees fleeing the lands we ravaged, "one of the largest, most dramatic humanitarian efforts in history" according to Roger Winter, director of the U.S. Committee for Refugees. But "despite the pride," Gwertzman continues, "some voices in the Reagan Administration and in Congress are once again asking whether the war debt has now been paid. . . ."[165]

The media are not satisfied with "mutual destruction" that effaces all responsibility for some of the major war crimes of the modern era. Rather, the perpetrator of the crimes must be seen as the injured party. We find headlines reading: "Vietnam, Trying to Be Nicer, Still Has a Long Way to Go." "It's about time the Vietnamese demonstrated some good will," said Charles Printz, of Human Rights Advocates International, referring to negotiations about the Amerasian children who constitute a tiny fraction of the victims of U.S. aggression in Indochina. Barbara Crossette adds that the Vietnamese have also not been sufficiently forthcoming on the matter of remains of American soldiers, although their behavior may be improving: "There has been progress, albeit slow, on the missing Americans." The unresolved problem of the war is what they did to us. Since we were simply defending ourselves from "internal aggression" in Vietnam, it surely makes sense to consider ourselves the victims of the Vietnamese.

In a derisive account of Vietnamese "laments" over the failure of the United States to improve relations with them, Barbara Crossette reports their "continuing exaggeration of Vietnam's importance to Americans" under the headline: "For Vietnamese, Realism Is in Short Supply." The Vietnamese do not comprehend their "irrelevance," she explains with proper imperial contempt. U.S. interest in Vietnam, she continues, is limited to the natural American outrage over Hanoi's invasion of Cambodia (to overthrow our current ally Pol Pot), and its failure to be sufficiently forthcoming "on the issue of American servicemen missing since the end of the war." She cites a Pentagon statement noting that Vietnam "has agreed to return the remains of 20 more servicemen" and expressing the hope that the Communists will proceed "to resolve this long-standing humanitarian issue." She quotes an "Asian official" as saying that "We all know they have the bones somewhere. . . . If Hanoi's leaders are serious about building their country, the Vietnamese will have to deal fairly with the United States." When a Vietnamese official suggested that the U.S. send food aid to regions where starving villagers are being asked to spend their time and energy searching for the remains of American pilots killed while destroying their country, State Department spokeswoman Phyllis Oakley reacted with great anger: "We are outraged at any suggestion of linking food assistance with the return of remains," she declaimed. So profound is the U.S. commitment to humanitarian imperatives and moral values that it cannot permit these lofty ideals to be tainted by associating them with such trivial concerns and indecent requests.[166] It is difficult to know how to react to a cultural climate in which such words can be spoken, evoking no reaction.

According to standard state and media doctrine, South Vietnam (i.e., the client regime that we established) lost the war to North Vietnam—the official enemy, since the U.S. attack against the South cannot be conceded. "North Vietnam, not the Vietcong, was always the enemy," John Corry proclaims in reporting the basic message of an NBC white paper on the war,[167] a stance that is conventional in the mainstream. Corry is indignant that anyone should question this higher truth. As proof of the absurdity of such "liberal mythology," he cites the battle of Ia Drang Valley in November 1965:

> It was clear then that North Vietnam was in the war. Nonetheless, liberal mythology insisted that the war was being waged only by the Vietcong, mostly righteous peasants.

Corry presents no example of liberals who described the Viet Cong as "righteous peasants," there being none, and no example of anyone who denied that North Vietnamese troops had entered the South by November 1965, since, again, there were none. Furthermore, opponents of the war at that time and for several years after included few representatives of mainstream liberalism. Corry's argument for North Vietnamese aggression, however, is as impressive as any that have been presented.

The NBC white paper was one of a rash of retrospectives on the tenth anniversary of the war's end, devoted to "The War that Went Wrong, The Lessons It Taught."[168] These retrospective assessments provide considerable insight into the prevailing intellectual culture. Their most striking feature is what is missing: the American wars in Indochina. It is a classic example of Hamlet without the Prince of Denmark. Apart from a few scattered sentences, the rare allusions to the war in these lengthy presentations—as in postwar commentary rather generally, including cinema and literature as well as the media—are devoted to the suffering of the American invaders. The *Wall Street Journal,* for example, refers to "the $180 million in chemical companies' compensation to Agent Orange victims"—U.S. soldiers, not the South Vietnamese victims whose suffering was and remains vastly greater.[169] It is difficult to exaggerate the significance of these startling facts.

There is an occasional glimpse of reality. *Time* opens its inquiry by recalling the trauma of the American soldiers, facing an enemy that

> dissolved by day into the villages, into the other Vietnamese. They maddened the Americans with the mystery of who they were—the unseen man who shot from the tree line, or laid a wire across the trail with a Claymore mine at the other end, the mama-san who did the wash, the child concealing a grenade.

No doubt one could find similar complaints in the Nazi press about the Balkans.

The meaning of these facts is almost never perceived. *Time* goes so far as to claim that the "subversion" was "orchestrated" by Moscow, so that the United States had to send troops to "defend" South Vietnam, echoing the fantasies concocted in scholarship—for example, by Walt Rostow, who maintains that in his effort "to gain the balance of power in Eurasia," Stalin turned "to the East, to back Mao and to enflame the North Korean and Indochinese Communists."[170]

Throughout the war, elite groups remained loyal to the cause, apart from expressing qualms about the bombing of North Vietnam, which was regarded as problematic since it might lead to a broader conflict, drawing in China and the USSR, from which the United States might not be immune. This was the "toughest" question, according to the McNamara memo cited earlier, and the only serious question among "respectable" critics of the war. The massacre of innocents is a problem only among emotional or irresponsible types, or among the "aging adolescents on college faculties who found it rejuvenating to play 'revolution.' "[171] Decent and respectable people remain silent and obedient, devoting themselves to personal gain, concerned only that we too might ultimately face unacceptable threat—a stance not without historical precedent. In contrast to the war protestors, two commentators explain, "decent, patriotic Americans demanded—and in the person of Ronald Reagan have apparently achieved—a return to pride and patriotism, a reaffirmation of the values and virtues that had been trampled upon by the Vietnam-spawned counterculture"[172]—most crucially, the virtues of marching in parades chanting praises for their leaders as they conduct their necessary chores, as in Indochina and El Salvador.

The extent of this servility is revealed throughout the tenth-anniversary retrospectives, not only by the omission of the war itself but also by the interpretation provided. The *New York Times* writes sardonically of the "ignorance" of the American people, only 60 percent of whom are aware that the United States "sided with South Vietnam"—as Nazi Germany sided with France, as the USSR now sides with Afghanistan. Given that we were engaged in "a defense of freedom" in South Vietnam (Charles Krauthammer), it must be that the critics of this noble if flawed enterprise sided with Hanoi, and that is indeed what standard doctrine maintains; the fact that opposition to American aggression in South Vietnam, or even against the North, entails no such support, just as opposition to Soviet aggression entails no support for either the feudalist forces of the Afghan resistance or Pakistan or the United States, is an elementary point that inevitably escapes the mind of the well-indoctrinated intellectual. The *Times* retrospective alleges that North Vietnam was "portrayed by some American intellectuals as the repository of moral rectitude." No examples are given, nor is evidence presented to support these charges, and the actual record is, as always, scrupulously ignored. Critics of the peace movement are quoted expounding on its "moral failure of terrifying proportions," and several "former peace activists who had leaped across the ideological divide" and now "are taking their stand with conservative Christians" of the Reaganite variety are quoted at length. But those who are allegedly guilty of these "terrifying" crimes are given no opportunity to explain the basis for their opposition to U.S. aggression and massacre. Nor are they permitted to assign to their proper place in history those who condemn the "moral failure" of opposing U.S. aggression or those who praise themselves for their occasional twitters of protest when the cost to us became too great. We read that the opponents of the war "brandished moral principles and brushed aside complexity" but nothing of what they had to say—as was the case throughout the war.[173] A current pretense is that principled critics of the war had access to the mainstream media during these years. In fact, they were almost entirely excluded, and now we are regaled with accounts of their alleged crimes but are almost never permitted to hear their actual words, exactly as one would expect in a properly functioning system of indoctrination with the task of preserving privilege and authority from critical analysis.

The *Times* informs us that Vietnam "now stands exposed as the Prussia of Southeast Asia," because since 1975 they have "unleashed a series of pitiless attacks against their neighbors," referring to the Vietnamese invasion that overthrew the Pol Pot regime (after two years of border attacks from Cambodia), the regime that we now support despite pretenses to the contrary. Although the *Times* is outraged at the Prussian-style aggression that overthrew our current Khmer Rouge ally, and at the Vietnamese insistence that a political settlement must exclude Pol Pot, the reader of its pages will find little factual material about any of these matters. There are, incidentally, countries that have "unleashed a series of pitiless attacks against their neighbors" in these years—for example, Israel, with its invasions of Lebanon in 1978 and 1982—but as an American client state, Israel inherits the right of aggression, so it does not merit the bitter criticism Vietnam deserves for overthrowing Pol Pot; and in any event, Israel's invasion of Lebanon was a "liberation," as the *Times* explained at the time, always carefully excluding Lebanese opinion on the matter as obviously irrelevant.[174]

The *Times* recognizes that the United States did suffer "shame" during its Indochina wars: "the shame of defeat." Victory, we are to assume, would not have been shameful, and the record of aggression and atrocities generally supported by the *Times* evokes no shame. Rather, the United States thought it was "resisting" Communists "when it intervened in Indochina"; how we "resist" the natives defending their homes from our attack, the *Times* does not explain.

That the United States lost the war in Indochina is "an inescapable fact" *(Wall Street Journal)*, repeated without question throughout the retrospectives and in American commentary generally. The truth is more complex, although to see why, it is necessary to escape the confines of the propaganda system and to investigate the rich documentary record that lays out the planning and motives for the American wars in Indochina over thirty years. This record shows that a rather different conclusion is in order, an important fact to understand.

The United States did not achieve its maximal goals in Indochina, but it did gain a partial victory. Despite talk by Eisenhower and others about Vietnamese raw materials, the primary U.S. concern was not Indochina but rather the "domino effect," the demonstration effect of independent development that might cause "the rot to spread" to Thailand and beyond, perhaps ultimately drawing Japan into a "New Order" from which the United States would be excluded.[175] This threat was averted as the United States proceeded to teach the lesson that a " 'war of liberation' . . . is costly, dangerous and doomed to failure" (Kennedy adviser General Maxwell Taylor, testifying to Congress).[176] The countries of Indochina will be lucky to survive; they will not endanger global order by social and economic success in a framework that denies the West the freedom to exploit, infecting regions beyond, as had been feared. It might parenthetically be noted that although this interpretation of the American aggression is supported by substantial evidence,[177] there is no hint of its existence in the popular histories or the retrospectives, for such ideas do not conform to the required image of aggrieved benevolence. Again, we see here the operation of the Orwellian principle that ignorance is strength.

While proceeding to extirpate the "rot" of successful independent development in Indochina, the United States moved forcefully to buttress the second line of defense. In 1965, the United States backed a military coup in Indonesia (the most important "domino," short of Japan), while American liberals and Freedom House lauded the "dramatic changes" that took place there—the most dramatic being the massacre of hundreds of thousands of landless peasants and the destruction of the only mass-based political party—as a proof that we were right to defend South Vietnam by demolishing it, thus encouraging the Indonesian generals to prevent any rot from spreading there. In 1972, the United States backed the overthrow of Philippine democracy, thus averting the threat of national capitalism there with a terror-and-torture state on the preferred Latin American model. A move toward democracy in Thailand in 1973 evoked some concern, prompting a reduction in economic aid and increase in military aid in preparation for the military coup that took place with U.S. support in 1976. Thailand has had a particularly important role in the U.S. regional system since 1954, when the National Security Council laid out a plan for subversion and eventual aggression throughout Southeast Asia, in response to the Geneva Accords, with Thailand serving as its "focal point" and, subsequently, as a major base for the U.S. attacks on Vietnam and Laos.[178] In his personal *Times* retrospective, *Pentagon Papers* director Leslie Gelb observes that ten years after the war ended, "the position of the United States in Asia is stronger" than at any time since World War II, despite "the defeat of South Vietnam," quoting "policy analysts" from government and scholarship who observe that "Thailand and Indonesia . . . were able to get themselves together politically, economically and militarily to beat down Communist insurgencies," in the manner just indicated, as were the Philippines and South Korea, also graced with a U.S.-backed military coup in 1972.[179] The business press had drawn the same conclusions years earlier, during the latter stages of the war.[180]

In short, the United States won a regional victory, and even a substantial local victory in Indochina, left in ruins. The U.S. victory was particularly significant within South Vietnam, where the peasant-based revolutionary forces were decimated and the rural society was demolished. "One hard-core revolutionary district just outside Saigon, Cu Chi," Paul Quinn-Judge observes, "sent 16,000 men and women to fight for the National Liberation Front. Some 9,900 did not return." Much the same was true throughout the South. "The deaths left a major political gap for the new regime," he adds. "The south was stripped of the trained, disciplined and presumably committed young cadres who would have formed the backbone of the present administration. In many areas the losses were near complete. . . . And the casualties put further strains on the state's limited financial and organisation capacities."[181] The U.S. victory over the overwhelmingly rural society of South Vietnam, always the primary enemy, laid the basis for the takeover by North Vietnam (as anticipated years earlier in the much-derided peace-movement literature),[182] allowing American hypocrites to "prove" that this predictable consequence of the war they supported shows that it was a just "defense of South Vietnam" against northern aggressors. In the cities, swollen with millions of refugees, the lucky and the more corrupt survived on an American dole at a level that had no relation to the now-demolished productive capacity of the country, leaving another near-insoluble problem that can conveniently be blamed on the Communists. The revolutionary forces had gained victory in many rural areas by the time of the outright U.S. invasion, largely through their appeal to the peasantry, as documented in the more serious scholarly work from sources in or close to the U.S. government ("The Early Stages," p. 186). But "many of the conclusions [of this work] have been invalidated by the events after Tet," *New York Times* Asia correspondent Fox Butterfield observes, a coy reference to the fact that this political success was overturned by the U.S. outburst of savagery in the post-Tet mass murder operations.[183]

That the United States suffered a "defeat" in Indochina is a natural perception on the part of those of limitless ambition, who understand "defeat" to mean the achievement only of major goals, while certain minor ones remain beyond our grasp. The perception of an unqualified U.S. "defeat" in the media retrospectives and similar commentary is understandable in part in these terms, in part in terms of the alleged goal of "defending freedom" developed in official propaganda and relayed by the ideological institutions.

Postwar U.S. policy has been designed to ensure that the victory is maintained by maximizing suffering and oppression in Indochina, which then evokes further gloating here. Since "the destruction is mutual," as is readily demonstrated by a stroll through New York, Boston, Vinh, Quang Ngai Province, and the Plain of Jars, we are entitled to deny reparations, aid, and trade, and to block development funds. The extent of U.S. sadism is noteworthy, as is the (null) reaction to it. In 1977, when India tried to send a hundred buffalo to Vietnam to replenish the herds destroyed by U.S. violence, the United States threatened to cancel "food-for-peace" aid, while the press featured photographs of peasants in Cambodia pulling plows as proof of Communist barbarity; the photographs in this case were probable fabrications of Thai intelligence, but authentic ones could, no doubt, have been obtained throughout Indochina. The Carter administration even denied rice to Laos (despite a cynical pretense to the contrary), where the agricultural system was destroyed by U.S. terror bombing. Oxfam America was not permitted to send ten solar pumps to Cambodia for irrigation in 1983; in 1981, the U.S. government sought to block a shipment of school supplies and educational kits to Cambodia by the Mennonite Church.[184]

A tiny report in the *Christian Science Monitor* observes that the United States is blocking international shipments of food to Vietnam during a postwar famine, using the food weapon "to punish Vietnam for its occupation of Cambodia," according to diplomatic sources. Two days later, *Times* correspondent Henry Kamm concluded his tour of duty as chief Asian diplomatic correspondent with a long article in which he comments "sadly" on the "considerably reduced quality of life" in Indochina, where in Vietnam "even working animals are rare," for unexplained reasons, in contrast to "the continuing rise, however uneven in many aspects, of the standard of living" elsewhere in the region. In thirty-five paragraphs, he manages to produce not one word on the effects of the U.S. war or the postwar policy of "bleeding Vietnam," as the *Far Eastern Economic Review* accurately terms it.[185]

The major television retrospective on the war was the award-winning thirteen-part PBS "Television History" of 1983, produced with the cooperation of British and French television, followed by a "Vietnam Op/Ed" in 1985 that included the Accuracy in Media critique and discussion of the two documentaries by a group tilted heavily toward the hawks.[186] The controversy had well-defined bounds. At one extreme, there were those who defended the PBS series as fair and accurate; at the other, critics who claimed that it presented "a war of the good nationalists, represented by Ho Chi Minh, versus the evil imperialist Americans who are trying to quash, sit on, the legitimate aspirations of the South Vietnamese people" (AIM chairman Reed Irvine). The moderator, "the man in the middle," concluded the discussion by stressing the importance of allowing "conflicting views about the Vietnam war to be presented at a time when the nation as a whole is finally allowing itself a close look at the only war we have ever lost." We will not review the AIM critique[187] or the "debate," which reiterates many of the charges we have already discussed (for example, Irvine's sole example of how "the enemy was able to use our free, uncontrolled media to achieve their own objectives," namely, via the media's portrayal of the Tet offensive "as a defeat for our side, even though it was actually a very outstanding military victory"). More to the point here are the contents of the PBS series itself, and the fact that it sets the bounds on critical analysis of the "failed crusade" undertaken for motives that were "noble," although "illusory," as the PBS companion volume describes the U.S. effort "to defend South Vietnam's independence."[188]

With regard to the American war, the PBS series makes a conscious effort to be balanced, to present all sides, to take no side. The French, in contrast, are treated far more harshly, as brutal colonialists, with no pretense of balance. Peter Biskind comments:

> Whereas the narrator referred to Ho Chi Minh and his followers as "rebels," "nationalists," or "the Vietnamese resistance," as long as they were fighting the French, once the Americans arrive they are invariably "Communists" or just "the enemy." Whereas Bao Dai is the "playboy emperor picked by the French," Nguyen Cao

> Ky and Nguyen Van Thieu are simply the "government." Whereas French troops just released from Japanese prison camps go "on a rampage, arresting and attacking Vietnamese," American troops engage in the was-it-or-wasn't-it massacre at Thuy Bo.

The effort to maintain balance is illustrated, for example, in the narrator's concluding words to episode 4, covering Johnson's escalation of the war in 1964–65 and the first appearance of North Vietnamese units in the South in mid-1965. After presenting Lyndon Johnson and other U.S. government spokesmen, the narrator states:

> Johnson called it invasion. Hanoi called it liberation. In the fall of 1965, three North Vietnamese regiments massed in the Central Highlands. Nearly two years had passed since Johnson renewed the U.S. commitment to defend South Vietnam. Nearly two years had passed since Ho Chi Minh renewed his commitment to liberate the South. Now their two armies braced for battle. . . . For the first time, in the Battle of the Ia Drang Valley, Americans fought the North Vietnamese—face to face. For the first time, B-52s supported troops in the field. And for the first time, to Americans, Vietnam meant a major new war.

Here we have "balance," but of a special kind. One may believe, with Johnson, that North Vietnam is invading the South, or, with Ho, that North Vietnam is fighting to liberate the South. We may not believe, however, that the United States is invading South Vietnam, which, we learn two episodes later, it had been bombing since 1961. Rather, we must assume, as a given fact not subject to debate, that the U.S. commitment was "to defend South Vietnam."

To evaluate this effort at "balance," we may observe that during the preceding summer (1965), five months after the United States began the regular bombing of North Vietnam, the Pentagon estimated that the 60,000 U.S. troops then deployed faced an enemy combat force of 48,500, 97 percent of them South Vietnamese guerrillas ("Viet Cong"). A few months after the Ia Drang Valley battle, in March 1966, the Pentagon reported 13,100 North Vietnamese forces in the South, along with 225,000 Viet Cong, facing 216,400 U.S. troops and 23,000 third-country troops (mostly South Korean), in addition to 690,000 ARVN troops.[189] Considering these facts, and the earlier history, it would seem possible to imagine a point of view that departs from the framework established here, one that is, furthermore, plainly accurate: the United States was stepping up its attack against South Vietnam. But that goes beyond "balance," which is construed similarly throughout, thus consigning the series to the familiar system of state propaganda on the most crucial and essential point. A position critical of foreign aggression (that is, the U.S. aggression that was plainly the central element of the war) is excluded as unthinkable, although it may be conceded that "To the Communists in Hanoi, America's presence in the South was yet another act of foreign aggression" (episode 4). The NLF in the South is granted no opinion on the matter, and the episode ends with a ringing declaration by LBJ.[190]

It is not that the facts are entirely hidden. Thus episode 5 ("America Takes Charge") opens with a description by a GI of how "the ARVN and the VC are the same people, the same race, the same culture, and yet one side seems to be chicken and the other side seems to fight in the face of overwhelming disadvantages" in what is clearly "their country." A U.S. major discusses the problem in Binh Dinh Province, which "had never been really in friendly hands" *since 1946* but rather "under VC control" throughout, compelling the United States to resort to "awesome fire power" that turns heavy jungle into a "moonscape." But the plain truth that such facts entail cannot be expressed, or perceived.

Balance is also preserved in an "account from both sides" of what happened in the village of Thuy Bo, in January 1967, where British producer Martin Smith had been shown the site of what villagers claimed to be a My Lai–style massacre, one of many they alleged, with a hundred women and children killed. Fox Butterfield reports that in contrast to the "balanced" picture actually presented by PBS, the British participants in the series argued that "the Marine attack on [Thuy Bo] should be labeled a war crime." This failure to maintain "balance" was in keeping with what a filmmaker involved in the project termed their "more moralistic stance, anxious to accentuate the aspects of the war that were immoral at the expense of looking at it afresh," which would apparently exclude the "more moralistic stance."[191] In this episode, the marines tell their story of an assault on a VC-defended village and then the villagers (given thirty-five lines of the transcript, to ninety for the marines) tell their conflicting version of a marine massacre of wounded and captured civilians. The sequence ends with a marine describing what took place as a "normal procedure," with "burning them hootches down and digging them Vietnamese people out of holes [with grenades and rifle fire] and scattering animals, pigs and chickens around like we normally do," especially after three days in the field under brutal conditions.

The account continues in the same vein. We hear that "American aircraft dropped six times more bombs on South Vietnam than on the Communist North," and that "most of the enemy troops were native southerners" (episode 8). But no conclusion is suggested, except that the purpose of the U.S. bombing of Vietnam, distributed in this curious manner and at "twice the tonnage dropped on Germany and Japan in World War II," was to try "to stop North Vietnam from sending soldiers and supplies to the South." Nevertheless, 140,000 made it through 1967 according to the U.S. government (episode 7), about half the number of South Korean mercenaries and a small fraction of the Americans who were destroying South Vietnam.

The Phoenix program of political assassination is justified at length by its director, William Colby, who denies that it was what it was, and, for balance, some comments are added by critics in the military and by a civilian aide worker, describing apparent random killing and torture. The post-Tet military operations are passed over in total silence. After Nixon's election in 1968, when these wholesale U.S. massacres began in full force, "the war continued," we learn: "The weapons were Vietcong rockets, the victims were Danang civilians" killed by the Viet Cong and North Vietnamese.

After the breakdown of negotiations in October 1972, "The North was again intransigent," we learn—namely, in demanding that the agreements be signed, a fact ignored; and "In South Vietnam, too, the agreement was still unacceptable," the familiar evasion of U.S. responsibility (see "The Paris Peace Agreements, p. 228). The terms of the January 1973 agreement are given, but with no indication that the U.S. government announced at once its intent to disregard them, as it did. Rather, we hear that "to the North Vietnamese and Vietcong, the struggle had not ended," because "Vietnam was still divided." The facts are quite different, as we have seen. They are indeed more accurately stated, although briefly, two episodes later (episode 12), although the U.S. role is suppressed except by implication: "America was still committed to South Vietnam," the narrator says, without noting that this commitment to the GVN, identified with South Vietnam by the U.S. government and by PBS, is in explicit violation of the agreements signed in Paris.

"Whatever their views of the war," the narrator adds, "most Americans now believed that the cost had been too great," particularly the cost of American lives; "They believed that no more Americans should die for Vietnam." The only other Americans are those who thought it proper that "more Americans should die for Vietnam." Americans were dying for Vietnam in the same sense in which Russian boys are dying for Afghanistan, but those who could perceive this fact, and who opposed the war not merely because the cost was too great but because aggression is wrong, are excluded from the category of Americans.

As in the media retrospectives, the antiwar movement is given short shrift. A few activists are quoted, but permitted to discuss only questions of tactics. Even Eugene McCarthy, plainly the favored antiwar figure in this presentation, says nothing except that "I think the case is rather clear about what's wrong about our involvement"—which is fair enough, since the media's favorite dove had never been a serious critic of the war and was to disappear quickly from the scene after failing to gain political power, thus demonstrating again where his commitments lay. James Fallows is permitted to describe "the spirit of the times": "to look for the painless way out, namely, a physical deferment." In the real world, this was a position that hardly defined "the spirit of the times," although it is a facet of this "spirit" that is far more acceptable to mainstream opinion than the principled and courageous resistance of many thousands of young people, an intolerable phenomenon and therefore erased from the record. As Peter Biskind observes, for all the attempt at "balance," and "despite the preference of [the PBS series] for doves over hawks, it is the right, not the left, that has set this film's political agenda," in conformity to elite opinion.

Biskind concludes his review of the PBS series by stating: "The truth is that the war was a crime, not a tragedy. The tragedy is that this film lacks the conviction to say so." The same may be said about the retrospective commentary generally. The war was a "tragic error," but not "fundamentally wrong and immoral" (as the overwhelming majority of the American people continue to believe), and surely not criminal aggression—the judgment that would be reached at once on similar evidence if the responsible agent were not the United States, or an ally or client.

Our point is not that the retrospectives fail to draw what seem to us, as to much of the population, the obvious conclusions; the more significant and instructive point is that principled objection to the war as "fundamentally wrong and immoral," or as outright criminal aggression—a war crime—is *inexpressible.* It is not part of the spectrum of discussion. The background for such a principled critique cannot be developed in the media, and the conclusions cannot be drawn. It is not present even to be refuted. Rather, the idea is unthinkable.

All of this again reveals with great clarity how foreign to the mobilized media is a conception of the media as a free system of information and discussion, independent of state authority and elite interests.

6

The Indochina Wars (II): Laos and Cambodia

THE GENEVA ACCORDS OF 1954 PROVIDED FOR A POLITICAL SETtlement in Laos and Cambodia. Both countries, however, were drawn into the U.S. attack on Indochina, with devastating consequences. In both cases, the media made a noteworthy contribution to this outcome.

6.1. LAOS

In Laos, as in Vietnam, the United States undertook to prevent a political settlement, as described frankly in congressional hearings by Ambassador Graham Parsons, who stated that "I struggled for 16 months to prevent a coalition." A U.S. military mission was established under civilian cover in violation of the Geneva Accords, headed by a general in civilian guise, and U.S. aid flowed in an effort to establish U.S. control. A measure of its scale and purposes is given by the fact that Laos was "the only country in the world where the United States supports the military budget 100 percent."[1]

Nevertheless, a coalition government was established in 1958 after the only elections worthy of the name in the history of Laos. Despite extensive U.S. efforts, they were won handily by the left. Nine of the thirteen candidates of the Pathet Lao guerrillas won seats in the national assembly, along with four candidates of the left-leaning neutralists ("fellow travelers," as they were called by Ambassador Parsons). Thus "Communists or fellow travelers" won thirteen of the twenty-one seats contested. The largest vote went to the leader of the Pathet Lao, Prince Souphanouvong, who was elected chairman of the national assembly.

U.S. pressures—including, crucially, the withdrawal of aid—quickly led to the overthrow of the government in a coup by a "pro-Western neutralist" who pledged his allegiance to "the free world" and declared his intention to disband the political party of the Pathet Lao (Neo Lao Hak Sat, or NLHS), scrapping the agreements that had successfully established the coalition. He was overthrown in turn by the CIA favorite, the ultra-right-wing General Phoumi Nosavan. After U.S. clients won the 1960 elections, rigged so crudely that even the most pro-U.S. observers were appalled, civil war broke out, with the USSR and China backing a coalition extending over virtually the entire political spectrum apart from the extreme right, which was backed by the United States. The U.S. government assessment was that "By the spring of 1961 the NLHS appeared to be in a position to take over the entire country," primarily because of its control of the countryside, where it had "diligently built up an organization covering most of the country's ten thousand villages," as noted ruefully by the bitterly anti-Communist Australian journalist Denis Warner.[2] The problem was the familiar one: the United States and its clients were militarily strong but politically weak.

Recognizing that its policies were in a shambles, the United States agreed to take part in a new Geneva conference, which proposed a new settiement in 1962. This too quickly broke down, and the civil war resumed with a different line-up and with increasing intervention by the United States and its allies, and by North Vietnam, in the context of the expanding war in Vietnam. U.S. clandestine military operations began in 1961, and the regular U.S. bombing began in early 1964: Operation Barrel Roll, directed against northern Laos, was initiated in December 1964, several months before the regular bombing of North Vietnam. The bombing of northern Laos was intensified in 1966, reaching extraordinary levels from 1968 with the "bombing halt" in North

Vietnam—in reality, a bombing redistribution, the planes being shifted to the destruction of Laos.[3]

Media coverage of Laos during the earlier period was sometimes extensive—over three times as great as of Vietnam in the *New York Times* in 1961, the *Pentagon Papers* analyst observes. But its contents were often absurd. For example, the aid cut-off that was the essential factor in the U.S. subversion of the elected government of Laos in 1958 "was never even reported in the national press," which barely mentioned the events, and then with misleading commentary reflecting Washington deceit.[4] Bernard Fall gave a detailed and derisive exposure of some of the more ludicrous incidents, including inflammatory fabrications that helped create major crises and led to deeper U.S. involvement in Thailand and Indochina. Joseph Alsop's fevered reports of largely invented Communist military actions were particularly noteworthy.[5]

As the Vietnam War escalated, Laos became "only the wart on the hog of Vietnam," as Dean Rusk put it, a "sideshow war," in Walter Haney's phrase, as Cambodia was to be later on. Media coverage declined as the "sideshow war" escalated. There were, in fact, three distinct U.S. wars: the bombing of the Ho Chi Minh trail in the South; the bombing of the peasant society of northern Laos, which the U.S. government conceded was unrelated to the war in South Vietnam; and the "clandestine war" between a CIA-run mercenary force based on mountain tribesmen and the Pathet Lao, backed by North Vietnam apparently at about the level of the Thai and other mercenaries introduced by the United States. The bombing of southern Laos was reported; the clandestine war and the bombing of northern Laos were not, apart from tales about North Vietnamese aggression, often fanciful and subjected to no critical analysis.[6]

In July 1968, the Southeast Asia correspondent of *Le Monde*, Jacques Decornoy, published lengthy eyewitness reports of the bombing of northern Laos, which had become ". . . a world without noise, for the surrounding villages have disappeared, the inhabitants themselves living hidden in the mountains . . . it is dangerous to lean out at any time of the night or day" because of the ceaseless bombardment that leads to "the scientific destruction of the areas held by the enemy." He describes "the motionless ruins and deserted houses" of the capital of Sam Neua district, first bombed by the U.S. Air Force in February 1965. Much of this "population center" had been "razed to the ground" by bombing, and as he arrived he observed the smoking ruins from recent raids with phosphorus bombs, the "enormous craters" everywhere in the town, the churches and houses "demolished," the remnants of U.S.

fragmentation bombs dropped to maximize civilian casualties. From this town to a distance of thirty kilometers, "no house in the villages and hamlets had been spared. Bridges had been destroyed, fields up to the rivers were holed with bomb craters."[7] After Decornoy's reports, there could be no doubt that the U.S. Air Force was directing murderous attacks against the civilian society of northern Laos. These reports of terrible destruction were repeatedly brought to the attention of the media, but ignored or, more accurately, suppressed. Later described as "secret bombings" in an "executive war," the U.S. attack was indeed "secret," not simply because of government duplicity as charged but because of press complicity.

Not only did the media fail to publish the information about the attack against a defenseless civilian society or seek to investigate further for themselves, but they proceeded to provide exculpatory accounts that they knew to be inaccurate, on the rare occasions when the bombing was mentioned at all. As the bombing of Laos began to be reported in 1969, the claim was that it was targeted against North Vietnamese infiltration routes to South Vietnam (the "Ho Chi Minh trail"), and, later, that U.S. planes were providing tactical support to government forces fighting North Vietnamese aggressors, a far cry from what Decornoy had witnessed and reported, and a much more tolerable version of the unacceptable facts.[8]

Keeping just to the *New York Times,* through 1968 there was no mention of the bombing apart from tiny items reporting Pathet Lao complaints (Dec. 22, 31, 1968). On May 18, 1969, the *Times* reported U.S. bombing in Laos, alleging that it was "directed against routes, including the so-called Ho Chi Minh Trail, over which the North Vietnamese send men and supplies to infiltrate South Vietnam." A June 14 report states that "American planes bomb targets all over Laos, especially along the Ho Chi Minh Trail in an effort to harass the Pathet Lao, the Communist-led rebel movement in Laos, and to stop the flow of enemy supplies to South Vietnam." Charles Mohr reported on July 16 that U.S. bombing "is directed against infiltration routes from North Vietnam that pass through Laos en route to the South." There is a July 28 reference to "200 American bombing sorties a day over northeastern Laos," directed against North Vietnamese forces, and Hedrick Smith adds from Washington on August 2 that the United States "has been bombing North Vietnamese concentrations" in Laos. T. D. Allman reported bombing sorties "in tactical support" of government forces fighting the North Vietnamese and "harassing attacks against Communist positions all over northeast Laos" on August 25, the latter providing the first glimpse of something beyond the approved version. Further reports of U.S. air power in tactical support and "to cut North Vietnamese supply routes" appear on September 7, followed by Allman's report of successes of a government offensive with forces "stiffened by Thai soldiers," supported by "the most intense American bombing ever seen in Laos" (Sept. 18). Then followed reports from Washington and Vientiane (Sept. 19, 20, 23, 24, 30) confirming that the U.S. Air Force was providing tactical support for government combat missions in addition to bombing North Vietnamese infiltration routes, including a September 23 Agence-France-Presse dispatch reporting "bombing of Pathet Lao areas by United States aircraft," thus implying that the bombing went well beyond infiltration routes and combat operations, common knowledge in Paris and Vientiane but yet to be reported here.

In short, the terror bombing of northern Laos, although known, remained off the agenda, and reporting in general was slight and highly misleading, to say the least. Elterman observes that the war in Laos and Cambodia was virtually "invisible" in the media through 1969, apart from the leftist *National Guardian,* which gave substantial coverage to what was in fact happening.[9]

On October 1, 1969, the *New York Times* finally ran an account by T. D. Allman, whose valuable reporting throughout the war appeared primarily overseas, concluding that "the rebel economy and social fabric" were "the main United States targets now," and that the American bombardment had driven the population to caves and tunnels during the daylight hours, making it difficult for the Pathet Lao "to fight a 'people's war' with fewer and fewer people." Control of territory was now of lesser importance, he wrote, "with United States bombers able to destroy, almost at will, any given town, bridge, road or concentration of enemy soldiers or civilians."[10]

This confirmation of what had long been known in restricted peace-movement circles, and consciously suppressed in the mainstream press, passed without particular notice. The CIA clandestine army had swept through the Plain of Jars in the preceding months, evacuating all remaining civilians to areas near Vientiane, where they and their harrowing stories were largely ignored by the well-represented media, although available elsewhere.[11]

Walter Haney, a Lao-speaking American who compiled a detailed collection of refugee interviews that was described as "serious and carefully prepared" by U.S. Ambassador to Laos William Sullivan, quotes remarks by a UN official in Laos as "the most concise account of the bombing":

> By 1968 the intensity of the bombings was such that no organized life was possible in the villages. The villages moved to the outskirts and then deeper and deeper into the forest as the bombing reached its peak in 1969 when jet planes came daily and destroyed all stationary structures. Nothing was left standing. The villagers lived in trenches and holes or in caves. They only farmed at night. [Each] of the informants, without any exception, had his village completely destroyed. In the last phase, bombings were aimed at the systematic destruction of the [material] basis of the civilian society.[12]

A staff study by a Kennedy subcommittee concluded that a main purpose of the U.S. bombardment was "to destroy the physical and social infrastructure" in areas held by the Pathet Lao, a conclusion well supported by the factual record.[13]

There were also eyewitness reports of the destruction of northern Laos by Western reporters, but published overseas. T. D. Allman flew over the Plain of Jars in late 1971, reporting that "it is empty and ravaged" by the napalm and B-52 saturation bombing being "used in an attempt to extinguish all human life in the target area"; "All vegetation has been destroyed and the craters, literally, are countless" and often impossible to distinguish among the "endless patches of churned earth, repeatedly bombed." At the same time, the *Washington Post* published the statement of Air Force Secretary Robert Seamans, who reported from northern Laos that "I have seen no evidence of indiscriminate bombing"; it is the North Vietnamese who are "rough," and the people are not "against the United States—just the opposite." The Lao-speaking Australian reporter John Everingham traveled in 1970 "through dying village after dying village" of the Hmong tribesmen who had been "naive enough to trust the CIA" and were now being offered "a one-way 'copter ride to death' " in the CIA clandestine army, in the remains of a country where bombing had "turned more than half the total area of Laos to a land of charred ruins where people fear the sky" so that "nothing be left standing or alive for the communists to inherit." No U.S. journal, apart from the tiny pacifist press, was interested enough to run his story, although later the media were to bewail the plight of the miserable remnants of the Hmong, put on display as "victims of Communism." In 1970, the *Bangkok World* (Oct. 7) published an AP report on U.S. bombing that was "wiping out" towns, and by 1972 such reports sometimes appeared in the U.S. press.[14] Later, Nayan Chanda visited the Plain of Jars, reporting overseas that from the air it "resembles a lunar landscape, pockmarked as it is with bomb craters that are a stark testimony to the years of war that denuded the area of people and buildings" during "six years of 'secret' bombing" by U.S. aircraft, while "at ground level, the signs of death and destruction are even more ubiquitous," including the provincial capital, "completely razed," as had been reported earlier by refugees who were ignored. Following the practice of American volunteers during the war, American relief workers with long experience in Laos attempted to bring information about postwar Laos to the media—with little effect—and inform us privately that their accounts were seriously distorted by *New York Times* reporters "by the device of omission and taking the negative side of balanced statements we made" and similar means.[15]

The U.S. government officially denied all of this, continuing the deception even after the facts were exposed and known in some detail to those concerned enough to learn them. Many regarded the U.S. war in Laos as "a success" (Senators Jacob Javits and Stuart Symington), or even *"A spectacular success"* (a former CIA officer in Laos, Thomas McCoy).[16]

In scale and care, the extensive analysis of refugee reports by a few young American volunteers in Laos compares very favorably to the subsequent studies of refugees from Cambodia that received massive publicity in the West after the Khmer Rouge takeover, and the story was both gruesome and highly pertinent to ongoing U.S. operations. But there was little interest, and published materials, which appeared primarily outside of the mainstream, were virtually ignored and quickly forgotten; the agency of terror was inappropriate for the needs of the doctrinal system. Media failure to report the facts when they were readily available, in 1968, and to investigate further when they were undeniable, by late 1969, contributed to the successful deception of the public, and to the continuing destruction.

When the war ended, ABC News commentator Harry Reasoner expressed his hope that Laos and its "gentle folk" could return to peaceful ways after "the clowning of the CIA and the vicious invasion of the North Vietnamese."[17] The "clowning of the CIA" included the destruction of "the rebel economy and social fabric" in northern Laos, with unknown numbers killed in areas that may never recover, and the decimation of the Hmong who were enlisted in the CIA cause and then abandoned when no longer useful. Nothing remotely comparable may be attributed to "the vicious invasion of the North Vietnamese"—which did, however, include such atrocities as killing twelve U.S. Air Force men in March 1968 at a U.S. radar base near the North Vietnamese border used to direct the bombing of North Vietnam and operations in North Vietnam by U.S.-led mercenaries.[18]

The *New York Times* reviewed the war in Laos at the war's end, concluding that 350,000 people had been killed, over a tenth of the population, with another tenth uprooted in this "fratricidal strife that was increased to tragic proportions by warring outsiders." The "fratricidal strife" might well have been terminated by the 1958 coalition government had it not been for "outsiders," with the United States playing a decisive role throughout, a role completely ignored in this purported historical analysis apart from a few misleading comments. At this late date, the *Times* continued to pretend that the U.S. bombing was directed against North Vietnamese supply trails—nothing else is mentioned. The crucial events of the actual history also disappear, or are grossly misrepresented. Subsequent reporting also regularly obliterated the U.S. role in creating the devastation and postwar "problems" attributed to the Communists alone, a shameful evasion in the light of the undisputed historical facts.[19]

Once again, the media record, less than glorious, is well explained throughout by the propaganda model.

6.2. CAMBODIA

6.2.1. "The decade of the genocide"

Few countries have suffered more bitterly than did Cambodia during the 1970s. The "decade of the genocide," as the period is termed by the Finnish Inquiry Commission that attempted to assess what had taken place,[20] consisted of three phases—now extending the time scale to the present, which bears a heavy imprint of these terrible years:

> Phase I: From 1969 through April 1975, U.S. bombing at a historically unprecedented level and a civil war sustained by the United States left the country in utter ruins. Though Congress legislated an end to the bombing in August 1973, U.S. government participation in the ongoing slaughter continued until the Khmer Rouge victory in April 1975.[21]
>
> Phase II: From April 1975 through 1978 Cambodia was subjected to the murderous rule of the Khmer Rouge (Democratic Kampuchea, DK), overthrown by the Vietnamese invasion of Cambodia in December 1978.

Phase III: Vietnam installed the Heng Samrin regime in power in Cambodia, but the Democratic Kampuchea (DK) coalition, based primarily on the Khmer Rouge, maintained international recognition apart from the Soviet bloc. Reconstructed with the aid of China and the United States on the Thai-Cambodia border and in Thai bases, the Khmer Rouge guerrillas, the only effective DK military force, continue to carry out activities in Cambodia of a sort called "terrorist" when a friendly government is the target.

We turn now to the travail of Cambodia during these grim years, and the way it has been depicted, first with some preliminary observations and then in further detail, phase by phase.

6.2.2. Problems of scale and responsibility

The three phases of the "decade of the genocide" have fared quite differently in the media and general culture, and in a way that conforms well to the expectations of a propaganda model. Phase I, for which the United States bore primary responsibility, was little investigated at the time, or since, and has never been described with anything like the condemnatory terms applied to phase II. The vast number of Cambodians killed, injured, and traumatized in this period were, in our conceptualization of chapter 2, "unworthy" victims.

Phase II, the Pol Pot era, is the "holocaust" that was widely compared to the worst atrocities of Hitler and Stalin, virtually from the outset, with massive publicity and outrage at the suffering of these "worthy" victims.

Phase III renewed the status of the people of Cambodia as worthy victims, suffering under Vietnamese rule. The Vietnamese being official enemies of the United States, they quickly became the villains of the piece, responsible for unspeakable conditions within Cambodia and guilty of unprovoked aggression. Meanwhile, the United States backed its ally China as it conducted a punitive invasion of Vietnam in February 1979 and reconstructed the defeated Pol Pot forces.

In the early stages of phase III, it was alleged "that the Vietnamese are now conducting a subtle 'genocide' in Cambodia," a charge tacitly endorsed in a CIA demographic study, which estimated a population drop of 700,000 during "the first year of the Heng Samrin rule."[22] This new "holocaust" was constructed on the basis of serious misinterpretation of available evidence, as was demonstrated by Michael Vickery in a response to William Shawcross's warnings of "the end of Cambodia,"[23] but not before it had left its mark on popular perceptions, and many distortions and, indeed, contradictions persist. In his *Quality of Mercy,* Shawcross agrees that, as Vickery had concluded, there was no large-scale famine of the character initially reported,[24] but he later wrote that the Heng Samrin regime "was responsible for creating many of the conditions that caused the famine" in Cambodia. These conflicting accounts were noted by Australian Cambodia scholar Ben Kiernan, who suggested a partial explanation: "There *was* a threat of famine, as the Heng Samrin government proclaimed in mid-1979. But it was offset by the small but crucial December–January harvest, which Shawcross hardly mentions, *and* by the massive international aid program, which he regularly denigrates."[25]

The eagerness to uncover Vietnamese villainy in "ending Cambodia," the easy reliance on sources known to be unreliable,[26] and the subsequent evasions after the accusations dissolve are readily explained by U.S. (indeed, general Western-bloc) hostility to Vietnam, which led the United States to align itself quietly with Pol Pot and to transform its alleged concern over Cambodians to the victims of the Vietnamese occupation.

Phase III also had a domestic U.S. aspect that is highly relevant to our concerns. In an intriguing exercise, characteristic of system-supportive propaganda campaigns, it was charged that the horrors of phase II were passed over in "silence" at the time. This alleged fact, developed in William Shawcross's influential book *Quality of Mercy,* elicited much commentary on "Holocaust and Modern Conscience," the subtitle of Shawcross's book, and on the failure of civilized people to react appropriately to ongoing atrocities. In "Phase III at home" (p. 288), we will turn to the merits of this charge with regard to phase II. As for phase I of "the decade of the genocide," the charge of silence is distinctly applicable, but it was never raised, then or now, nor is phase I designated a period of "holocaust" or "genocide" in mainstream literature. Phase I elicited no calls for international intervention or trials for crimes against humanity, and it has since been largely expunged from the record. In retrospect, the harshest critics within the mainstream attribute "the destruction of Cambodian society" during phase I to "years of warfare" and "careless policies of the White House," nothing more.[27] The issue of U.S. bombing of Cambodia did arise during the Watergate hearings, but the primary concern there was the failure to notify Congress.

Michael Vickery suggests an "interesting comparison which an investigative journalist might make" if truly concerned about the problems of the region—namely, between Cambodia, during phase III, and Thailand, "where there has been no war, foreign invasion, carpet bombing, nor revolution, and where foreign investment is massive and the sympathy of the most advanced western powers is enjoyed," but where conditions in the peasant society were so terrible that "since 1980 substantial foreign 'refugee' aid near the border has been given to 'Affected Thai Villagers,' whose health and living standard, much to the shock of foreign aid personnel, were found to be little better than the condition of Cambodian refugees."[28] No such comparison was undertaken, nor was there even a flicker of concern over simultaneous reports, buried in appropriate obscurity, about the tens of thousands of children, many under ten years old, working as "virtual slaves" in Thai factories resembling concentration camps,[29] nor over the normal conditions of peasant life in the region, now exposed to the visitors flocking to the border camps to witness the consequences of Communist terror and express their compassion for its victims.

The actual scale of the slaughter and destruction during the two authentic phases of large-scale killings during the "decade of the genocide" (phases I and II) would be difficult to estimate at best, and the problems have been compounded by a virtual orgy of falsification serving political ends that are all too obvious.[30] The Finnish Inquiry Commission estimates that about 600,000 people in a population of over seven million died during phase I, while two million people became refugees.[31] For the second phase, they give 75,000 to 150,000 as a "realistic estimate" for outright executions, and a figure of roughly one million dead from killings, hunger, disease, and overwork. Vickery's analysis is the most careful attempt to sort out the confused facts to date. He accepts as plausible a "war loss" of over 500,000 for the first phase, calculated from the CIA estimates but lower than their conclusions (see note 31), and about 750,000 "deaths in excess of normal and due to the special conditions of DK," with perhaps 200,000 to 300,000 executed and a total population decline for this period of about 400,000.[32]

These estimates, the most careful currently available in print to our knowledge, suggest that the toll under phase II of "the genocide" is somewhat greater than that under phase I, although not radically different in scale. But before accepting these figures at face value we must bear in mind that part of the death toll under phase II must be attributed to the conditions left by the U.S. war. As the war ended, deaths from starvation in Phnom Penh alone were running at about 100,000 a year, and the U.S. airlift that kept the population alive was immediately terminated. Sources close to the U.S. government predicted a million deaths in Cambodia if U.S. aid were to cease. A Western doctor working in Phnom Penh in 1974–75 reported that

> This generation is going to be a lost generation of children. Malnutrition is going to affect their numbers and their mental capacities. So, as well as knocking off a generation of young men, the war is knocking off a generation of children.

The U.S. embassy estimated that available rice in Phnom Penh would suffice for at most a few weeks. The final U.S. AID report observed that the country faced famine in 1975, with 75 percent of its draft animals destroyed by the war, and that rice planting for the next harvest, eight months hence, would have to be done "by the hard labor of seriously malnourished people." The report predicted "widespread starvation" and "Slave labor and starvation rations for half the nation's people" for the coming year, and "general deprivation and suffering . . . over the next two or three years before Cambodia can get back to rice self-sufficiency."[33]

There is also the matter of the effect of the U.S. bombing on the Khmer Rouge and the peasant society that provided their social base, a factor noted by all serious analysts. Cambodia specialist Milton Osborne concludes that Communist terror was "surely a reaction to the terrible bombing of Communist-held regions" by the U.S. Air Force. Another Cambodia scholar, David Chandler, comments that the bombing turned "thousands of young Cambodians into participants in an anti-American crusade," as it "destroyed a good deal of the fabric of prewar Cambodian society and provided the CPK [Khmer Rouge] with the psychological ingredients of a violent, vengeful, and unrelenting social revolution," a "class warfare between the 'base people,' who had been bombed, and the 'new people' who had taken refuge from the bombing and thus had taken sides, in CPK thinking, with the United States." "French intransigence had turned nationalists into Communists," Philip Windsor observes, while "American ruthlessness now turned Communists into totalitarian fanatics."[34] One may debate the weight that should be assigned to this factor in determining Khmer Rouge policies, embittering the peasant society of "base people," and impelling them to force those they perceived as collaborators in their destruction to endure the lives of poor peasants or worse. But that it was a factor can hardly be doubted.

Assessing these various elements, it seems fair to describe the responsibility of the United States and Pol Pot for atrocities during "the decade of the genocide" as being roughly in the same range.

Little is known about phase I of "the genocide." There was little interest in ascertaining the facts, at the time or since. The Finnish Inquiry Commission Report devotes three cursory pages to the topic, because the information available is so meager. The second phase has been far more intensively studied, and by now substantial evidence is available about what took place. David Chandler and Ben Kiernan observe that as a result of the intense interest in phase II, "we know a great deal more about the texture of daily life in Democratic Kampuchea, supposedly a 'hermit' regime, than we do about the ostensibly open regimes of the Khmer Republic (1970–1975) or the Sihanouk era (1954–1970) which preceded it."[35] Despite this already large imbalance in knowledge, the Cambodia Documentation Center in New York City concentrates on phase II of the genocide. The dramatic difference in the information available for the two phases, and the focus of the ongoing research effort, are readily explicable in terms of a propaganda model.

Outside of marginal Maoist circles, there was virtually no doubt from early on that the Khmer Rouge regime under the emerging leader Pol Pot was responsible for gruesome atrocities. But there were differing assessments of the scale and character of these crimes.

State Department Cambodia specialists were skeptical of the allegations that had received wide publicity by 1977—rightly, so subsequent inquiry revealed. The *Far Eastern Economic Review* based its January 1979 conclusion that the population had actually risen during the Pol Pot period on CIA sources, and its very knowledgeable correspondent Nayan Chanda, discussing the background for the Vietnamese invasion, reported that "some observers are convinced that had the Cambodian regime got a year's reprieve, its internal and international image would have been improved enough to make any Vietnamese drive difficult if not impossible."[36]

Differing assessments persisted even after the abundant evidence provided by the flow of refugees to Thailand in 1979 and visits to Cambodia, which also provided the first significant information about the years 1977–78. At one extreme, Pol Pot continued to be described as having forged new patterns of genocide comparable to the worst excesses of Hitler and Stalin. At the other extreme, we have the postwar evaluation by U.S. government specialist Douglas Pike, now head of the University of California Indochina Archives, the "independent-minded" scholar lauded by Freedom House and the exemplar of the new, nonideological scholarship much admired by the *New York Times*. Pike described Pol Pot in November 1979 as the "charismatic" leader of a "bloody but successful peasant revolution with a substantial residue of popular support," under which "on a statistical basis, most of them [peasants] . . . did not experience much in the way of brutality."[37] The 1980 CIA demographic study assigns the Pol Pot–era executions to the period ending in January 1977, and for 1977–78 merely says that "living conditions most likely did not vary during these two years from the conditions during 1976," although as was known when the CIA study was undertaken, these later years were the worst, by far, in the context of internal purges and the escalating conflict with Vietnam at a time when the United States was beginning its "tilt" toward China and Pol Pot. The CIA concludes that among the "old people," the "rural population" who were "the foundation for the new Khmer Rouge revolutionary society," there was a slight increase in population through the DK period. A still more muted assessment is provided by the close U.S. ally Deng Xiaoping, who emerged as "party strongman" in China in December 1978 and soon implemented his plan to "punish Vietnam," and who remained the main supporter of Pol Pot. He bitterly opposed attempts to remove the Khmer Rouge from their leading role in the DK coalition in 1984, stating in a rage that "I do not understand why some people want to remove Pol Pot. It is true that he made some mistakes in the past but now he is leading the fight against the Vietnamese aggressors."[38] Deng has been backed in this stance by the Reagan administration (see "Phase III in Indochina," p. 285).[38]

In addition to such real examples of less harsh interpretations of the Pol Pot period, there are also mythical ones to which we return.

6.2.3. The "not-so-gentle" land: some relevant history

Part of the illusory story constructed about Cambodia during the 1970s and since is that this "gentle land" with its "smiling people" had known little suffering before the country was drawn into the Indochina war and then subjected to Pol Pot "autogenocide." The reality is different. Behind the famous "Khmer smile," as Prince Sihanouk's French adviser Charles Meyer observed, lies ample bitterness and violence.[39] Vickery observes that earlier chronicles "are filled with references to public executions, ambushes, torture, village-burnings and forced emigration," with the destruction of villages and landscapes, torture, and killing a matter of course, and few institutional restraints on terror. The peasantry of inner Cambodia, largely unknown to Western scholarship or to the urban population, appear to have lived under conditions of extreme violence and hatred for the oppressors from outside the village.

During the French war of reconquest in the late 1940s, up to "perhaps one million rural inhabitants . . . were forcibly 'regrouped.' " The huge flow of refugees to Phnom Penh during phase I of the "decade of the genocide" was not the first massive dislocation in recent history, Vickery continues, adding that it is, furthermore, "a strange kind of history" that regards the displacement of people fleeing from U.S. bombs and savage fighting "as somehow less abhorrent or more 'normal' than the reverse movement of 1975," the forcible evacuation when the peasant army of the Khmer Rouge conquered the city. Leaders of the anti-French resistance after World War II describe horrifying atrocities conducted with obvious pleasure as a "normal" part of "Khmer mores." In the same years, government forces led by Lon Nol, who was to head the U.S.-backed client government in the early 1970s, carried out wholesale massacres in villages as the French withdrew, including such "individual tests of strength" as "grasping infants by the legs and pulling them apart," actions that "had probably not been forgotten by the men of that area who survived to become the Khmer Rouge troops" whose later atrocities in this "gentle land" aroused such outrage in the West. "Thus for the rural 80–90 percent of the Cambodian people," Vickery concludes, "arbitrary justice, sudden violent death, political oppression, exploitative use of religion and anti-religious reaction, both violent and quiescent, were common facts of life long before the war and revolution of the 1970s." These conditions elicited no interest in the West. "The creations of Pol Pot-ism were all there in embryo," Vickery continues, to be "directed first of all at the urban population" after a war which was in large measure "a war between town and countryside in which the town's battle was increasingly for the sole purpose of preserving its privileges while the rural areas suffered."[40]

It is superfluous to observe that the United States deployed its ample means of violence in defense of urban privilege. But, in fact, these tasks were only of secondary importance. For the United States, the destruction of rural Cambodia was ancillary to the goal of maintaining in power the client regime in South Vietnam.

Contrary to the arrangements in Laos and Vietnam, the Geneva Accords afforded no recognition to the anti-French resistance in Cambodia, a source of much bitterness. The country was ruled by Prince Sihanouk until March 1970, when he was overthrown in a coup supported by the United States.[41] Throughout this period, Sihanouk attempted a difficult balancing act both internally and externally. Within Cambodia, he repressed the left and peasant uprisings and attempted to hold off the right, although power largely remained in the hands of right-wing urban elites throughout. Externally, he tried to preserve a measure of neutrality against the background of the expanding Indochina war, which, he expected, would end in a Communist victory.[42]

Sihanouk's neutralist efforts were unappreciated by the United States and its allies. Diem's troops attacked border regions from 1957, and there were also Thai provocations. A coup attempt in 1959, probably backed by the CIA, as generally assumed in Cambodia, was foiled; this should be seen in the context of general U.S. subversion in the region in the post-Geneva period, including a CIA-backed coup and invasion aimed at overthrowing Sukarno in Indonesia in 1958, subversion of the elected government of Laos in the same year, and the efforts to destroy the anti-French resistance within South Vietnam and to consolidate the Diem dictatorship while undermining the political arrangements at Geneva. By 1963, CIA-backed Khmer Serei forces frequently attacked Cambodia from South Vietnamese and Thai bases at a time when the United States was intensifying its clandestine operations in Laos and maneuvering, with increasing violence, to block a political settlement in South Vietnam. By 1966, the Khmer Serei "declared war on Cambodia and claimed responsibility for incursions across the border."[43]

Attacks by U.S. and Saigon army forces against border posts and villages in Cambodia intensified from the early 1960s, causing hundreds of casualties a year. Later, Vietnamese peasants and guerrillas fled for refuge to border areas in Cambodia, particularly after the murderous U.S. military operations in South Vietnam in early 1967, giving rise to cynical charges from Washington, echoed in the media, about Communist encroachment into neutral Cambodia. By the time of the 1970 coup that overthrew Sihanouk, Vietnamese were scattered along border areas to a maximum depth of about twenty-five kilometers, according to most sources. The first evidence of Vietnamese encampments in Cambodia was discovered in late 1967, close to the unmarked border. While there was much outrage in the United States about "North Vietnamese aggression," the internal view in Washington was considerably more nuanced. From the *Pentagon Papers* we learn that as late as May 1967—well after the U.S. operations that caused cross-border flight—high Pentagon officials believed that Cambodia was "becoming more and more important as a supply base—now of food and medicines, perhaps ammunition later." A year earlier, an American study team investigated specific charges by the U.S. government on the scene and found them without substance although they did come across the site of a recent U.S. helicopter-gunship attack on a Cambodian village (one of many, according to the local population), first denied by the U.S. government, then conceded, since American eyewitnesses (including CBS-TV) were present—the usual pattern.

The Cambodian government reported many such incidents. Thus Cambodia complained to the United Nations that on February 24, 1967, "a large number of armed forces elements consisting of Americans, South Vietnamese and South Koreans entered Cambodian territory and fired heavily on the Khmer village of Chrak Kranh . . . [which] was then invaded and burnt by the United States–South Vietnamese troops" who occupied the village until March 3. By April 1969, rubber plantations were subjected to defoliation by air attack. In January 1970, an official Cambodian government White Paper reported thousands of such incidents with many deaths, giving pictures, dates, and other details, and also noting that not a single Viet Cong body had ever been found after U.S.-Saigon bombardments or ground attacks.

Virtually none of this was ever reported in the United States—even the official White Paper—although the information was readily available in official documents and reputable foreign sources, and in easily ignored peace-movement literature.[44] The agency of violence was once again the wrong one.

The occasional media reaction to these incursions was instructive. On March 25, 1964, *New York Times* correspondent Max Frankel, now executive editor, reported a Saigon army (ARVN) attack on the Cambodian village of Chantrea with armored cars and bombers, leaving many villagers killed and wounded. The ARVN forces were accompanied by U.S. advisers, including a U.S. army pilot "dragged from the wreckage" of an observer plane "shot down in the action." Diplomats on the scene confirmed that "at least one troop-carrying helicopter had landed at Chantrea with three Americans on board." Frankel was outraged—at Cambodia, which had the gall to demand reparations, leaving Washington "alarmed and saddened, but confused." The headline reads: "Stomping on U.S. Toes: Cambodia Typical of Many Small Nations Putting Strain on a Policy of Patience." Cambodia has "borrowed a leaf from Fidel Castro's book," Frankel stormed, by requesting compensation for this U.S. atrocity: "It is open season again for the weaker nations to stomp on the toes of big ones. . . . Leading the pack in big-power baiting these days is one of the smallest of nations, the Southeast Asian kingdom of Cambodia" with its "clever, headstrong, erratic leader," whom Washington finds "lacking some of the talent and temperament for the job," although "the Administration's instinct has been to try to save a wayward young nation's independence in spite of itself and, at times, despite its own leaders." Washington is also alarmed by "Cambodia's current effort to force the United States into a major conference that would embarrass its Thai and Vietnamese friends," Frankel continues, an effort that will "be resisted"—referring to a conference that would settle border questions and guarantee Cambodia's neutrality at a time when the United States was desperately seeking to undermine international efforts to neutralize South Vietnam, Laos, and Cambodia so as to avert the major war toward which the United States was driving because of its political weakness in Indochina.

This classic of colonialist paternalism reflects quite accurately the general mood of the day—as does the refusal to report such trivial matters as the regular U.S.-ARVN attacks on Cambodia, which have largely passed from history in the United States, apart from the dissident literature.

6.2.4. Phase I: The U.S. destruction of Cambodia

On March 18, 1969, the notorious "secret bombings" began. One week later, on March 26, the Cambodian government publicly condemned the bombing and strafing of "the Cambodian population living in the border regions . . . almost daily by U.S. aircraft," with increasing killing and destruction, alleging that these attacks were directed against "peaceful Cambodian farmers" and demanding that "these criminal attacks must immediately and definitively stop. . . ." Prince Sihanouk called a press conference on March 28 in which he emphatically denied reports circulating in the United States that he "would not oppose U.S. bombings of communist targets within my frontiers." "Unarmed and innocent people have been victims of U.S. bombs," including "the latest bombing, the victims of which were Khmer peasants, women and children in particular." He then issued an appeal to the international press: "I appeal to you to publicize abroad this very clear stand of Cambodia—that is, I will in any case oppose all bombings on Cambodian territory under whatever pretext."[45]

It will come as no surprise that his appeal went unanswered. Furthermore, this material has been suppressed up to the present time, apart from the dissident literature.[46] The standard position within the mainstream, adopted by defenders of the bombing and critics as well, is that "Sihanouk did not protest" (William Shawcross). When the "secret bombings" became public knowledge in 1973, it was claimed that Sihanouk had privately authorized bombing of Vietnamese bases near the border areas. True or false, that is irrelevant to the suppression of Sihanouk's impassioned appeals, which referred to the bombing of *Khmer peasants.* Furthermore, as we observed in earlier discussion, "while commentators and media analysts may draw whatever conclusions they please from the conflicting evidence available, this does not entitle them to suppress what is, by any standards, crucial evidence, in this case, Sihanouk's attempt to arouse international protest over the U.S. bombing of the civilian society."[47]

Reviewing this period in his *Cambodia Year Zero,* François Ponchaud remarks that Sihanouk called the U.S. bombings of "Vietcong bases" a "scandal and a crime over Radio Phnom Penh, but nobody was deceived." Ponchaud and his readers, however, are deceived: Sihanouk publicly denounced the bombing and other attacks on *Khmer peasants,* and not only over Radio Phnom Penh but in quite public documents and appeals to the international press. In his *Sideshow,* Shawcross says only that Cambodia "continued to denounce" American air and artillery attacks through 1969, but "made no public protest that specifically mentioned B-52 attacks" (p. 94)—true, but irrelevant for the reasons repeated in the last paragraph.[48]

In May 1969, William Beecher reported B-52 raids on "Vietcong and North Vietnamese supply dumps and base camps in Cambodia," citing U.S. sources. Beecher stated that "Cambodia has not made any protest," disregarding Sihanouk's appeals and his protest against the murder of "Khmer peasants, women and children in particular," not Vietnamese military bases. Beecher also commented that "in the past, American and South Vietnamese forces had occasionally fired across the border and even called in fighters or helicopter gunships to counter fire they received from enemy units there," ignoring the somewhat more important fact that U.S. aircraft and U.S.–ARVN–South Korean forces had been attacking Cambodian villages, according to the "friendly" government of Cambodia. The headline for his article states falsely: "Raids in Cambodia by U.S. Unprotested." Beecher's article caused consternation in Washington, setting off the first stage of what later became the Watergate scandal. As we have commented elsewhere, "It is remarkable that Beecher's unique though quite inadequate account is now held up as evidence that the press maintained its honor throughout this period, despite the crimes of Richard Nixon."[49]

Once again, the U.S. escalation of the war against Cambodia in 1969 coincided with similar efforts in Laos and Vietnam. The general reaction was similar throughout, and remains so. The post-Tet accelerated pacification campaign, which thoroughly demolished the civilian base of the NLF, was regarded as so uninteresting that it is passed over in virtual silence in the popular retrospectives. As for the wars in Laos and Cambodia, Elterman comments, after reviewing the major media coverage, that apart from the "alternative press," they were virtually "invisible" in the press in 1969 when they were expanding to new heights as the U.S. Air Force was shifted from North Vietnam to Laos and Cambodia after the "bombing halt."[50]

In March 1970, Cambodia was drawn irrevocably into the carnage sweeping Indochina. On March 18, Sihanouk was overthrown in "an upper-class coup, not a revolution," carried out for "interests of domestic and political expedience," and with at least "indirect U.S. support," if not more.[51] Two days later, ARVN ground and air operations began in Svay Rieng Province, at the Vietnamese border, continuing through April and leading to the U.S.-ARVN invasion on April 29, conducted with an extreme brutality sometimes vividly depicted in the media, which were particularly appalled by the behavior of the ARVN forces. Much of the enormous civilian toll, however, resulted from air power, including U.S. bombing strikes that leveled or severely damaged towns and villages.[52] One effect of the invasion was to drive the Vietnamese forces away from the border and deeper into Cambodia, where they began to support the growing peasant resistance against the coup leaders. A second effect, as described by U.S. correspondent Richard Dudman, who witnessed these events at first hand after his capture by the Cambodian resistance, was that "the bombing and shooting was radicalizing the people of rural Cambodia and was turning the countryside into a massive, dedicated, and effective revolutionary base."[53] Cambodia was now plunged into civil war, with increasing savagery on both sides.

U.S. bombing continued at a high level after the withdrawal of U.S. forces from Cambodia. By late 1971, an investigating team of the General Accounting Office concluded that U.S. and Saigon army bombing is "a very significant cause of refugees and civilian casualties," estimating that almost a third of the seven-million population may be refugees. U.S. intelligence reported that "what the villagers feared most was the possibility of indiscriminate artillery and air strikes," and refugee reports and other sources confirm that these were the major cause of civilian casualties and the flight of refugees.[54]

Information about what was happening in the peasant society of Cambodia in the early 1970s was limited but not unavailable. There were, first of all, many refugees with stories to tell, although the media were not interested. There was also an eyewitness account by French Southeast Asia specialist Serge Thion, who spent two weeks in regions controlled by the Cambodian guerrillas. His reports were offered to the *Washington Post,* but rejected.[55] They were of no more interest than the reports of life under the bombing in Laos, or similar questions regarding Vietnam throughout the war and in the retrospectives.

As in Laos, the escalating war remained largely "invisible" in the media. Surveying a five-month period in early 1972 in the national press, Elterman found that "In terms of war casualties, the focus in *The New York Times* and *Time* was on military-related deaths and almost always only those that occurred in Vietnam, ignoring also the civilian deaths and refugees in that country too. . . . During the winter and spring of 1972, the war in Cambodia and Laos was ignored more than usually with most of the Indo-China news coverage given to the North Vietnamese offensive into South Vietnam and the United States bombing of Hanoi and Haiphong. . . . *Time,* in fact, had more coverage on civilian casualties in Northern Ireland during the first half of 1972 than it did on the Indo-China War."[56]

Meanwhile, Cambodia was being systematically demolished, and the Khmer Rouge, hitherto a marginal element, were becoming a significant force with substantial peasant support in inner Cambodia, increasingly victimized by U.S. terror. As for the U.S.-backed Lon Nol regime, Michael Vickery points out that their "client mentality" and subsequent "dependency led them to acquiesce in, or even encourage, the devastation of their own country by one of the worst aggressive onslaughts in modern warfare, and therefore to appear as traitors to a victorious peasant army which had broken with old patron-client relationships and had been self-consciously organized and indoctrinated for individual, group, and national self-reliance."[57]

In early 1973, U.S. bombing increased to a scale that might truly merit the term "genocidal" used by the Finnish Inquiry Commission. In the five-month period after the signing of the Paris peace accords, the bombing matched the level of the preceding three years,[58] and it was to continue at that level until Congress forced a halt in August—although bombing and shelling of the countryside by armies of the U.S.-backed regime were to continue on a substantial scale, with U.S. guidance and supply, until the war's end. Over a million refugees fled to Phnom Penh, which became a horror chamber while the countryside was laid waste, including B-52 bombing targeted "on the most heavily populated areas of Cambodia," where U.S. Air Force maps showed "thousands of square miles of densely populated, fertile areas . . .

marked black from the inundation"—"the careless policies of the White House" criticized by William Shawcross.[59] At just this time, Khmer Rouge programs became extremely harsh, so available studies indicate, including a refugee study by Kenneth Quinn, of the National Security Council staff, who never considers a possible causal connection, however, between the harshening of policy and the sharp increase in the program of saturation bombing. Timothy Carney, the second of the three major U.S. government specialists on Cambodia (Quinn, Carney, Charles Twining), also notes that "sometime in 1973 the party apparently decided to accelerate its program to alter Khmer society," for no suggested reason.[60]

6.2.5. Phase I in the media

During this period, there was extensive media coverage of Cambodia, and there was no dearth of evidence on what was taking place in the regions subjected to U.S. Air Force atrocities. It was not necessary to undertake a difficult expedition to the Thai-Cambodia border to find refugees who would tell what they knew, but the victims of phase I of "the decade of the genocide" who were huddled in the slums of Phnom Penh or other towns and villages to which they fled were of no more interest than those in the miserable camps on the outskirts of Vientiane—unless they had tales of terror by the Cambodian insurgents to recount (the Vietnamese long having faded into the background).[61] No books or articles were written by Father Ponchaud, who lived among the peasants and sympathized deeply with their plight, so he informed us when the time came to expose atrocities of the Khmer Rouge. The same was true of many others who were later to express their heartfelt concerns for Cambodians suffering under Khmer Rouge terror, but who did not seek to investigate and publicize the plight of the rural population during phase I of the genocide, when such efforts might have had a crucial impact on the policies that were destroying Cambodia, a fact that might merit some thought.

The standard U.S. media picture of phase I is something like this. "Until the turning point in 1973, . . . on the surface, Cambodians smiled and were full of pleasantries,"[62] but afterwards the mood of "Cambodians" became one of "apathy" and "resignation" because "impoverished farmers, refugees and soldiers" (most of whom were press-ganged into service from among the poor and refugee communities) felt that their "leaders seem powerless to defend them against human and natural adversities."[63] There is a "spirit of doom" as the government is "teetering on the wreckage of the democratic republic it set out to create" with the coup that overthrew Sihanouk.[64] The Americans try, but with little success, to "give the Cambodians some sense of confidence in their leadership," but, nevertheless, "Cambodian morale has been sliding steadily for a long time." However, "Rather than any sense of urgency here [in Phnom Penh], there is the grand fatalism that is so much a part of Cambodia's Hindu-influenced Buddhism,"[65] although it somehow does not seem to affect "the enemy," whose "determination" in the face of the awesome firepower unleashed against them "baffles" the Americans. But there is still "a feeling that the Americans will save the Cambodians at the last minute because they cannot save themselves." "Almost every conversation with a Cambodian now is the same," namely, fear that the "demoralized army will collapse" when the American bombing terminates on August 15. The impending bombing cutoff is "painful" to the "Cambodians" because of "the recent steady successes of enemy troops" against overwhelming odds. In his final summary report from Phnom Penh as the U.S. bombing ended, Sydney Schanberg raised "the key unanswered question: How have the insurgents—without any planes of their own, and without the extensive artillery support the Government troops have, with only small arms and mobile weapons . . .—been able not just to match the Government forces, which are more than twice their size, but to push the Government forces back and sustain the offensive for six months without any significant lull?" "Since the insurgents are not superhuman, there must be other explanations for their success." Perhaps they are so "determined and capable" because they "are less fatalistic than the Khmers on this side" and "believe they can change their environment" (U.S. embassy official). In this regard, "the enemy" are quite different from "the Cambodian villager," who "usually has no politics" and "is not interested in taking sides, only to be left alone to farm and fish and feed his family and once in a while to celebrate on a Buddhist holiday."[66]

The civil war, then, pits "the Cambodians" against "the enemy," Cambodian peasants who were surely not full of pleasantries during the pre-1973 U.S. bombings. "The Cambodians," fatalistic and resigned, either want to be left alone ("the Cambodian villager") or hope that the United States will save them and their government, striving for democracy ("the Cambodians" generally). The enemy struggle on successfully against overwhelming odds, baffling the Americans—exactly as Americans building "democracy" have been baffled by the same problem in South Vietnam, Central America, and many other places. Since these are the conclusions drawn from "almost every conversation with a Cambodian," they are surely realistic, at least as long as we understand that "Cambodians" are those Cambodians who are not "the enemy" of the objective press, just as "South Vietnamese" were South Vietnamese collaborating with the U.S. aggressors.

The framework is the usual one, although perhaps a shade more egregious in the light of what might have been passing through the minds of those Cambodians who were not "Cambodians" during phase I of the genocide.

About that topic, we learn very little from the media. The refugees flooding Phnom Penh and other areas where U.S. reporters traveled were virtually ignored. To gain a measure of this remarkable fact, let us review the reports during these months in the *New York Times*, most of them by its Pulitzer Prize–winning correspondent Sydney Schanberg, who, more than any other U.S. reporter, came to be regarded as the conscience of the media with regard to Cambodia.

Schanberg arrived in Phnom Penh in May 1973, at the height of the intensified bombing, which continued until the mid-August halt. During this period, the *Times* published twenty-seven of his reports from Cambodia, many of them long and detailed, along with a column in which he expressed his contempt for the "so-called international press corps" who spend their time "interviewing each other" in the Hotel Le Phnom.[67]

From the outset, Schanberg reports "refugees pouring into the city," but there are no interviews with refugees who relate the circumstances of life under the bombs. We hear a "well to do Cambodian woman" who tells us that "The bombing is terrible"; she is "not frightened, just annoyed—because it wakes my baby up every night in the middle of the night, and I have to get up" (May 3). But those villagers who want to be left alone are not granted the opportunity to relay their accounts of somewhat more serious concerns, apart from a few scattered phrases, and there is not a word to suggest that refugees might have had any attitude, apart from fear, with regard to those "determined" fighters who "believe they can change their environment," although plainly they had a solid base in the peasant society that was being torn to shreds by saturation bombing. As in Laos a few years earlier, the refugees simply had the wrong tale to tell, and the kinds of stories that readily flow if one is sufficiently interested to inquire are lacking here.

Running through the columns seriatim for relevant material, number 5 (May 11) quotes a Western European diplomat who says that "American men in American planes are bombing the hell out of this place," and notes that the U.S. aircraft "do not always receive accurate answers" about civilians in the targeted areas "from the Cambodian commanders" who direct the jet fighter-bombers. The Cambodians, then, are to blame for the civilian casualties that must result, although "no reliable figures are available" and refugees are not asked to supplement with their personal knowledge. The next two columns (May 24, 27) are the only ones concerned directly with the effect of the bombing in the countryside. The first reports "extensive" destruction from bombing that has wiped out "a whole series of villages" along the main highway, with often not even a piece of a house left standing for miles, while "a few people wander forlornly through the rubble, stunned by what has happened, skirting the craters, picking at the debris." A group of villagers from Svay Rieng Province, abutting Vietnam, report the destruction of seven villages, with many killed. "The frightened villagers uprooted by the bombing have a great deal to say," Schanberg comments, but we do not read it here. Rather, he explains that "There is no doubt that the Seventh Air Force is making a marked effort to avoid civilian casualties—at least outside the eastern third of the country, which is solidly held by the enemy"; and if there are casualties it is the fault of Cambodian military officials who request air strikes with "almost no concern about civilian lives or property." The second column informs us that "the refugees frequently tell about the bombing," which has destroyed villages and "terrified all the rest of the villagers," a Western diplomat reports. But the refugees are granted only two phrases, an "incongruously polite" request that "I would be very glad if the Government would stop sending the planes to bomb," and a plea from a monk to ask the United States and other governments: "Don't destroy everything in Cambodia."

We hear no more from the refugees until column 15 (July 26), a graphic account of "a terror attack on the civilian population"—by Communist forces who shelled the outskirts of Phnom Penh. A weeping child describes how her little brother's hand was cut off, and the bloodstained road and doorsteps testify to Communist barbarity, as distinct from the operations of the scrupulous American command. Column 19 (Aug. 5) tells of thousands of new refugees "fleeing from enemy assaults," and column 21 (Aug. 7) describes Cambodian soldiers looting a recaptured village that "looked as if struck by a storm with a tongue of fire," with many houses "smashed in by shells," but no word from the victims, who had fled. Then follow three columns (Aug. 7, 9, 12) describing in extensive detail the bombing of the village of Neak Luong—in error—killing many government soldiers and their families. This is the sole example of American bombing that was shown in the film *The Killing Fields*, the only depiction there of phase I of the genocide, a memory that is acceptable since it was plainly an error.

We located eighteen additional reports datelined Cambodia, from

March 25 through August 18.[68] One quotes a villager who says "The bombers may kill some Communists but they kill everyone else, too" (Browne, April 11), but we found no other examples of reactions by the victims, although there is a picture of a Cambodian soldier weeping for his wife and ten children killed in the bombing of Neak Luong by error (Aug. 10).

In forty-five columns, then, there are three in which victims of U.S. bombing are granted a few phrases to describe what is happening in Cambodia. Not a single column seeks to explore the reactions of the refugees not far from the Hotel Le Phnom, or in Battambang, or in the far more miserable refugee camps in the countryside nearby; or to attempt to develop some sense of what must have been happening under the frenzied bombing of these months. Recall that in Phnom Penh alone there were almost 1.5 million refugees who had fled from the countryside, some, surely, who must have had some information to relate about phase I of the genocide at its peak. The reader could no doubt ascertain that terrible things were happening in the Cambodian countryside, but what they were remains obscure, and the Americans are explicitly exonerated, apart from the error of bombing the wrong village.

The story remained much the same as phase I of the genocide continued. The horrors in Phnom Penh itself were sometimes vividly described, primarily abroad,[69] but there was little effort to determine what was happening in the areas held by the enemy of the U.S. government—hence the enemy of the U.S. press; virtually the entire country as "the Cambodians" were confined to urban centers swelled by a huge flood of refugees who remain as hidden from view as those in the teeming slums of Saigon or the camps around Vientiane.

Western correspondents evacuated from Phnom Penh after the Khmer Rouge victory were able to obtain a fleeting picture of what had taken place in the countryside. British correspondent Jon Swain summarizes his impressions as follows:

> The United States has much to answer for here, not only in terms of human lives and massive material destruction; the rigidity and nastiness of the un-Cambodian like fellows in black who run this country now, or what is left of it, are as much a product of this wholesale American bombing which has hardened and honed their minds as they are a product of Marx and Mao. . . . [The mass evacuation of the cities] does not constitute a deliberate campaign of terror, rather it points to poor organisation, lack of vision and the brutalisation of a people by a long and savage war. . . . The

> war damage here [in the countryside], as everywhere else we saw, is total. Not a bridge is standing, hardly a house. I am told most villagers have spent the war years living semi-permanently underground in earth bunkers to escape the bombing. . . . The entire countryside has been churned up by American B-52 bomb craters, whole towns and villages razed. So far I have not seen one intact pagoda.[70]

The conditions are much like those reported in 1970 by refugees from the Plain of Jars, in Laos; in both cases, these accounts were almost entirely excluded from the mainstream media.

So ended phase I of the genocide. In later years, those who had transmitted narrowly selected fragments of this tale of horror expressed their bitterness that Cambodia had been "forgotten." On the tenth anniversary of the Khmer Rouge takeover, Sydney Schanberg wrote two columns in the *New York Times* entitled "Cambodia Forgotten." The first highlights the phrase: "Superpowers care as little today about Cambodians as in 1970," the second dismisses Richard Nixon's 1985 claim that there was no "indiscriminate terror bombing" but only "highly accurate" strikes "against enemy military targets." Schanberg comments that "Anyone who visited the refugee camps in Cambodia and talked to the civilian survivors of the bombing learned quickly about the substantial casualties." He recalls that "the Khmer Rouge were a meaningless force when the war was brought to Cambodia in 1970. . . . In order to flourish and grow, they needed a war to feed on. And the superpowers—including this country, with the Nixon incursion of 1970 and the massive bombing that followed—provided that war and that nurturing material." He does not, however, inform us about which superpower, apart from "this country," invaded Cambodia and subjected it to massive bombing. With comparable even-handedness we might deplore the contribution of the superpowers, including the USSR, to the destruction of Afghanistan, or the attitude of the great powers, including Nazi Germany, toward the victims of the death camps, whom Schanberg brings up in a later column the same month entitled "Memory is the Answer." He also does not comment on what the reader of his columns might have learned about life in the Cambodian countryside from his reporting during the peak period of the bombing.[71]

Others too stress that "memory is the answer." Commenting on the award-winning film *The Killing Fields,* Samuel Freedman writes that "While Holocaust survivors have helped perpetuate the memory of Nazi infamy, the Cambodian genocide is already being forgotten," referring to phase II of the genocide, phase I having passed into oblivion with no concern.[72] The *New York Times* reminds us that "Cambodia remains perhaps the most pitiful victim of the Indochina wars," as it is caught between the forces of Pol Pot and Hanoi, which used Pol Pot attacks against Vietnamese villages as "a long-sought pretext to invade" and now exploits "Pol Pot's Khmer Rouge army of 30,000 inside Cambodia" (in fact, mostly inside Thailand) as "the pretext for remaining in Cambodia." "Unimaginable slaughter, invasion, brutal occupation have followed famine and pestilence," all attributable to the Communists, although the suffering has been "aggravated by the cynicism of big powers," not further differentiated. As for the United States, "When Vietcong guerrillas used a neutral Cambodia as a sanctuary, it was pounded by American bombs and drawn into a war it hoped to avoid," but that is all. In a later comment, the editors concede that "murderous aerial bombing followed by brutal revolution, famine and civil war" brought Cambodia to ruin, but of all of this, "what cannot be sponged away are the Khmer Rouge's butcheries" and the actions of Hanoi, which has "subjugated and impoverished" Cambodia: phases II and III of "the decade of the genocide."[73]

"Memory is the answer," but only when focused on proper targets, far from home.

6.2.6. The Pol Pot era

Phase II of "the decade of the genocide" began with the Khmer Rouge takeover in April 1975. Within a few weeks, the Khmer Rouge were accused in the national press of "barbarous cruelty" and "genocidal policies" comparable to the "Soviet extermination of the Kulaks or with the Gulag Archipelago."[74] This was at a time when the death toll was perhaps in the thousands; the half million or more killed during phase I of the genocide never merited such comment, nor were these assessments of the first days of phase II (or later ones, quite generally) accompanied by reflection on the consequences of the American war that were anticipated by U.S. officials and relief workers on the scene, reviewed earlier, or by any recognition of a possible causal link between the horrors of phase II and the American war against the rural society during phase I.

We will not document here the flood of rage and anger directed against the Khmer Rouge from the outset and the evidence on which it was based, having done so elsewhere in detail.[75] Several facts documented there bear emphasis: (1) the outrage, which was instant and overwhelming, peaked in early 1977 and, until the overthrow of Pol Pot, was based almost exclusively on evidence through 1977, primarily 1975–76;[76] (2) apart from a few knowledgeable journalists, the State Department's Cambodia experts, and probably the majority of the small group of Cambodia scholars—that is, most of those with a basis for judgment—the most extreme accusations were adopted and proclaimed with a great show of indignation over Communist atrocities, the integrity of which can be measured by comparison to the reaction to phase I of the genocide and U.S. responsibility for it; (3) these skeptical assessments, almost entirely suppressed in the media, proved fairly accurate for the period in question; (4) the evidence that provided the crucial basis for the denunciations of Communist genocide was of a kind that would have been dismissed with derision had something of the sort been offered with regard to phase I of the genocide or other U.S. atrocities, including faked interviews and photographs and fabricated statements attributed to Khmer Rouge officials, constantly repeated even after they had been conceded to be frauds; fabricated casualty estimates based on misquoted studies that became unquestionable doctrine even after they were publicly withdrawn as inventions; and highly selective refugee reports that ignored much refugee testimony, including detailed studies by Cambodia scholars, that could not be exploited for what soon became a propaganda campaign at a level of deceit of astonishing proportions.[77]

As we also noted from the first paragraph of our earlier review of this material, to which we will simply refer here for specifics, "there is no difficulty in documenting major atrocities and oppression, primarily from the reports of refugees"; there is little doubt that "the record of atrocities in Cambodia is substantial and often gruesome" and represents "a fearful toll"; "when the facts are in, it may turn out that the more extreme condemnations were in fact correct," although if so, "it will in no way alter the conclusions we have reached on the central question addressed here: how the available facts were selected, modified, or sometimes invented to create a certain image offered to the general population. The answer to this question seems clear, and it is unaffected by whatever may yet be discovered about Cambodia in the future." As we repeatedly stressed, in this chapter of a two-volume study on U.S. policy and ideology, our concern remained the United States, not Indochina; our purpose was not to "establish the facts with regard to postwar Indochina" on the basis of the evidence available, but rather to examine the constructions developed on the basis of this evidence, to analyze the way this evidence was refracted "through the prism of Western ideology, a very different task."[78] The conclusions drawn there remain valid. To our knowledge, no error or even misleading statement or omission has been found.[79]

This review of an impressive propaganda exercise aroused great outrage—not at all surprisingly: the response within Soviet domains is similar, as are the reasons, when dissidents expose propaganda fabrications with regard to the United States, Israel, and other official enemies. Indignant commentators depicted us as "apologists for Khmer Rouge crimes"[80]—in a study that denounced Khmer Rouge atrocities (a fact always suppressed) and then proceeded to demonstrate the remarkable character of Western propaganda, our topic throughout the two-volume study in which this chapter appeared. There was also a new wave of falsification, often unanswerable when journals refused to permit response. We will not review these further propaganda exercises here, but merely note that they provide an intriguing expression of what, in other contexts, is described as the totalitarian mentality: it is not enough to denounce official enemies; it is also necessary to guard with vigilance the right to lie in the service of power. The reaction to our challenge to this sacred right again fits neatly within the expectations of a propaganda model, standing alongside the Freedom House attack on the media for failure to serve state policy with sufficient vigor and optimism.

By early 1977, denunciations of the Khmer Rouge for having caused unprecedented "murder in a gentle land" and "autogenocide" extended from mass circulation journals such as *Reader's Digest* (with tens of millions of readers) and *TV Guide* (circulation nineteen million), to the *New York Review of Books* and the media generally, in addition to a best-selling book by John Barron and Anthony Paul based on their *Reader's Digest* article and the widely misquoted study by François Ponchaud mentioned earlier. Similar material continued to flow in abundance in the press and newsweeklies, the *New York Times Magazine,* and elsewhere. Evidence about the 1977–78 period became available primarily after the Vietnamese expulsion of the Khmer Rouge regime, which brought phase II of the genocide to a close, eliciting new outrage over the alleged "genocide" brought about by the "Prussians of Asia."

The picture created by this chorus of denunciation, from the first days of Democratic Kampuchea (DK) in 1975, is described sardonically by Michael Vickery as "the standard total view" (STV). According to the STV, prior to the Khmer Rouge victory in April 1975, Cambodia had been a "gentle land" (Barron and Paul) of "gentle if emotional people" who "wanted only to live in peace in their lush kingdom" (Jack Anderson), a land in which hunger was "almost unknown" (Henry

Kamm). But in 1975, the "formerly fun-loving, easy-going Cambodians" were subjected to the "harsh regime" of the Khmer Rouge, who ordered that all those not under their rule before the victory can be "disposed of" because they are "no longer required," even if only one million Khmers remain (Donald Wise, citing several of the frequently quoted Khmer Rouge statements that were conceded to be fabrications).[81]

According to the STV, during the pre-1977 period on which the conclusions were based, the Khmer Rouge leadership was engaged in a policy of systematic extermination and destruction of all organized social and cultural life apart from the Gulag run by the "nine men at the top," Paris-trained Communists, without local variation and with no cause other than inexplicable sadism and Marxist-Leninist dogma. By early 1977, it was alleged that they had "boasted" of having slaughtered some two million people (Jean Lacouture in the *New York Review*). This figure remained the standard even after Lacouture withdrew it a few weeks later, acknowledging that he had misread his source (Ponchaud) and that the actual figure might be in the thousands, but adding that he saw little significance to a difference between thousands killed and a "boast" of two million killed. This position expresses with some clarity the general attitude toward fact during this period and since, as does his further statement that it is hardly important to determine "exactly which person uttered an inhuman phrase"—the case in question had to do with inhuman phrases he attributed to Khmer Rouge officials but which turned out to be mistranslations of phrases that had been fabricated outright by his source (Ponchaud) or that had appeared not in a Cambodian journal, as he asserted, but in a Thai journal mistranslated by Ponchaud that expressed virtually the opposite of what was claimed. The two-million figure was later upgraded to three million or more, often citing Vietnamese wartime propaganda. The examples are quite typical.

Not everyone joined in the chorus. The most striking exceptions were those who had the best access to information from Cambodia, notably, the State Department Cambodia specialists. Their view, based on what evidence was then available (primarily from northwestern Cambodia), was that deaths from all causes might have been in the "tens if not hundreds of thousands," largely from disease, malnutrition, and "brutal, rapid change," not "mass genocide." These tentative conclusions were almost entirely ignored by the media—we found one important exception in our review—because they were simply not useful for the purpose at the time, just as refugee testimony that did not conform to the STV was ignored. Overseas, journalists who had special knowledge of Indochina also gave rather nuanced accounts, notably, Nayan Chanda.[82]

In his detailed, region-by-region study, Vickery shows that the STV was a picture with little merit, and that the few skeptics had been essentially accurate for the period in question, although in 1977–78, something approaching the STV came to be correct in the context of brutal inter-party purges and the expanding war with Vietnam. He also makes the obvious logical point that "the evidence for 1977–78," which only became available after the Vietnamese conquest in 1979, "does not retrospectively justify the STV," which reigned on the basis of evidence from the 1975–76 period; "and the Vietnamese adoption of some of the worst Western propaganda stories as support for their case in 1979 does not prove that those stories were valid."[83] Recent work indicates that the worst massacres, including those that left the mass graves and horrifying heaps of skulls found by journalists who entered Cambodia after the Vietnamese conquest, were in the eastern zone bordering Vietnam in mid- to late 1978.[84]

The nature of the Western agony over Cambodia during phase II of the genocide, as a sociocultural phenomenon, becomes clarified further when we compare it to the reaction to comparable and simultaneous atrocities in Timor. There, as in phase I of the Cambodia genocide, the United States bore primary responsibility and could have acted to reduce or terminate the atrocities. In contrast, in Cambodia under DK rule, where the blame could be placed on the official enemy, nothing at all could be done, a point that was stressed by government experts when George McGovern called for international intervention in August 1978, eliciting much media ridicule.[85] Neither McGovern nor anyone else recommended such intervention against the United States during phase I of the genocide, or against Indonesia and the United States during the Timor atrocities, to which the United States (and, to a much lesser extent, other powers) lent material and diplomatic support, just as there has been no call for intervention as the armies of El Salvador and Guatemala proceeded to slaughter their own populations with enthusiastic U.S. support in the early 1980s.

The comparison between Timor and phase II in Cambodia was particularly striking, and was occasionally noted after the fact. The excuses now produced for this refusal to report what was happening in Timor, or to protest these atrocities or act to stop them, are instructive in the present context. Thus, William Shawcross rejects the obvious interpretation of the comparative response to Timor and Cambodia in favor of a "more structurally serious explanation": "a comparative lack of sources" and lack of access to refugees.[86] Lisbon is a two-hour flight from London, and even Australia is not notably harder to reach than the Thai-Cambodia border, but the many Timorese refugees in Lisbon and Australia were ignored by the media, which preferred "facts" offered by the State Department and Indonesian generals. Similarly, the media ignored readily available refugee studies from sources at least as credible as those used as the basis for the ideologically serviceable outrage over the Khmer Rouge, and disregarded highly credible witnesses who reached New York and Washington along with additional evidence from church sources and others. The coverage of Timor actually declined sharply as massacres increased with mounting U.S. support. The real and "structurally serious" reason for this difference in scope and character of coverage is not difficult to discern (see chapter 1), although not very comfortable for Western opinion, and becomes still more obvious when a broader range of cases is considered that illustrate the same conclusions.[87]

6.2.7. Phase III in Indochina: Cambodia and the bleeding of Vietnam

As we write in 1987, Western moralists remain silent as their governments provide the means for Indonesia to continue its campaign of terror and repression in Timor. Meanwhile, the United States backs the DK coalition, largely based on the Khmer Rouge, because of its "continuity" with the Pol Pot regime, so the State Department informed Congress in 1982. The reason for this differential reaction to the Fretilin guerrillas resisting Indonesian aggression in Timor, and the Khmer Rouge guerrillas attacking Cambodia from Thai bases, is also explained by the State Department: the Khmer Rouge–based coalition is "unquestionably" more representative of the people of Cambodia than Fretilin is of the Timorese.[88] There is, therefore, no need to puzzle over the apparent inconsistency during the late 1970s in U.S. attitudes toward Pol Pot and the Indonesian generals: the former, the object of hatred and contempt for the massacres in Cambodia under his rule during phase II; the latter, our friends whom we cheerfully supplied and supported as they conducted comparable massacres in Timor at the same time. This apparent inconsistency, which briefly troubled even the editors of the *Wall Street Journal* in the early 1980s,[89] is now happily resolved: we support *both* the Khmer Rouge and the Indonesian generals.

The current U.S. support for the Khmer Rouge merits little attention in the media, just as little notice is given to the Vietnamese position: a political settlement among Cambodians excluding Khmer Rouge leaders Pol Pot and his close associate Ieng Sary.[90] As noted earlier, U.S. aid to the Khmer Rouge is reported by congressional sources to be extensive. Furthermore, the Reagan administration, following "Chinese rather than Southeast Asian inclinations," has refused to back the efforts of its Southeast Asian allies "to dilute the strength of China's ally, the deposed Pol Pot regime, by giving greater weight to non-Communist guerrillas and political groupings."[91] Nayan Chanda reported in 1984 that the United States had "more than doubled its financial assistance to the resistance forces," mainly through funds earmarked for humanitarian assistance that permit U.S. allies to divert funds to arms purchases, a familiar ploy.[92] While it is claimed that the funds are limited to the (generally ineffectual) non-Communist resistance, this is a shallow pretense. "Both Sihanouk's army and Son Sann's KPNLF," the two components of the non-Communist resistance, "are completely discounted in Phnom Penh," James Pringle reports from Phnom Penh in the *Far Eastern Economic Review.* " 'All they do is sit drinking coca-cola on the border,' said one well-informed Soviet bloc diplomat." From the Thai border areas, Barbara Crossette reports that "Trucks loaded with men and boys, 150 or 200 at a time, pull away from settlements controlled by Pol Pot's Khmer Rouge and rumble into Cambodia," where the supplies are carried "into the Cambodian interior to stockpile supplies for the Khmer Rouge," in the expectation that they will be able to prevail by military force and terror once the Vietnamese withdraw as demanded by the United States. A spokesman for the Sihanoukist National Army in Bangkok comments that "The main problem we now have is how to get the Vietnamese to pull out without bringing back the Khmer Rouge," the probable consequence of U.S. policy. Former Assistant Secretary of State Richard Holbrooke comments that the U.S. aid "will end up going to Pol Pot and his people," a fact noted also by several journalists. Sydney Schanberg's Cambodian associate Dith Pran, whose story of suffering under DK terror was the basis for the widely publicized film *The Killing Fields* and much media commentary, found somewhat greater difficulty in reaching the public with his view that "Giving U.S. weapons [to the Khmer resistance] is like putting gasoline on a fire," and is the last thing Cambodia needs. David Hawk alleges that "it is common knowledge that Reagan-administration political officers and defence attachés from the US Embassy in Bangkok have visited Khmer Rouge enclaves."[93]

The reasons for supporting the Thai-based DK coalition go beyond their "continuity" with the Khmer Rouge regime. A more fundamental reason was outlined by our ally Deng Xiaoping in 1979: "It is wise to force the Vietnamese to stay in Kampuchea because that way they will suffer more and more and will not be able to extend their hand to Thailand, Malaysia, and Singapore."[94] This motive of "bleeding Vietnam" to ensure that it does not recover from its victimization at the hands of the West has additional advantages. By acting in such a way as to enhance suffering and repression in Indochina, we demonstrate retrospectively the "benevolence" of our "noble crusade" of earlier years.

As we discussed earlier, the Cambodians were "worthy victims" when they were being terrorized by the Khmer Rouge under phase II of the genocide, and they achieved this status once again after the Vietnamese invasion brought phase II of the genocide to an end, although with a change in the cast of characters, as the United States joined China in support of the Khmer Rouge. After early efforts to charge the Vietnamese with "genocide," the condemnation of the official enemy shifted to the terrible acts of "the Prussians of Asia," who have "subjugated and impoverished" Cambodia since overthrowing Pol Pot, according to the editors of the *New York Times.* Recall that of all the horrors of the past years, including the atrocities of phase I, "what cannot be sponged away" are "the Khmer Rouge's butcheries"—evidently of lesser moment in Washington now that the Pol Pot forces qualify as resistance forces under the Reagan doctrine.

One would be hard put to find any serious observers of the current Cambodian scene who believe that the Vietnamese have reduced Cambodia to a level below that of the DK period, as these comments imply. Rather, among people who are concerned about the people of Cambodia for themselves and not merely because of their value for propaganda exercises, few would question that "it is clear that life for the people is far better now than under Democratic Kampuchea,"[95] and some Cambodia specialists have suggested that the current regime compares favorably with any of its predecessors. Consistent opponents of aggression would have a moral basis for condemning the Vietnamese invasion, despite the rapidly escalating atrocities of 1977–78 and the murderous raids against Vietnam by Cambodian forces under Pol Pot's rule.[96] It is a little difficult to take this argument seriously, however, when it is put forth by people who condemn the West for not having undertaken more vigorous actions to "rescue" the Cambodians from Pol Pot—a "rescue" that would have been no less self-serving in intent than the Vietnamese invasion, as history makes clear. And we need not tarry over the argument when it is offered by those who tolerate or applaud murderous aggression when it suits their ends: the Indonesian invasion of Timor, the "liberation" of Lebanon by Israeli forces in 1982 (as the *Times* editors called it), or the "defense of South Vietnam," to mention a few obvious cases.

6.2.8. Phase III at home: the great silence and the hidden potency of the left

Turning to the home front, phase III illustrates the expectations of a propaganda model in yet a different way. The truth about the response to the Pol Pot atrocities in the media and "the culture" in general, and the dramatic contrast to comparable examples where the United States bears primary responsibility, is not pleasant to contemplate. Since the facts are too overwhelming to refute, it is a better strategy simply to dispatch them to the memory hole. This task having been achieved with the customary alacrity, we may now observe with wonder that "The West awoke to the suffering of Kampuchea in autumn, 1979" (William Shawcross), and then go on to ruminate about the curious inability of the West, always consumed with self-flagellation, to perceive the atrocities of its enemies.[97] And so matters have proceeded in the latest phase of the sad tale of Cambodia.

"There was silence in the mid-1970s during the mass murders by the Khmer Rouge" (Floyd Abrams), and "The atrocity stories coming out of Cambodia after 1975 quite simply were not believed" (David Hawk)—at a time when accusations of genocide of the Hitler-Stalin variety were resounding from the *New York Times* and *Washington Post* to the *Reader's Digest* and *TV Guide* to the *New York Review of Books,* and the mass media extensively. "The West woke up to the horror of what had happened only after the Vietnamese invasion" *(Economist),* and "hardly anyone outside, on Left or Right, had noticed [the horrors of the Pol Pot regime] at the time they were actually going on (1975–1978)" (Conor Cruise O'Brien)—that is, at the time when Jimmy Carter branded Pol Pot "the world's worst violator of human rights," and a British Foreign Office report condemned the regime for the death of "many hundreds of thousands of people."[98] One might imagine that such outlandish claims could not pass without a raised eyebrow at least, but that is to underestimate the ability of the ideological institutions to rally to a worthy cause: in this case, the cause of suppressing the truth about the Western response to "the decade of the genocide" and other atrocities.

That there was "silence" over Pol Pot atrocities was also an insistent claim right at the peak of the bitter outrage over Pol Pot genocide. *Time* magazine published a major article by David Aikman on July 31, 1978, claiming that the Khmer Rouge "experiment in genocide" was being ignored, and adding a new twist that was also taken up with enthusiasm in the subsequent reconstruction of history: "there are intellectuals in the West so committed to the twin Molochs of our day—'liberation' and 'revolution'—that they can actually defend what has happened in Cambodia"; "some political theorists have defended it, as George Bernard Shaw and other Western intellectuals defended the brutal social engineering in the Soviet Union during the 1930s." No one was mentioned, for the simple reason that no one could be found to fit the bill, although *Time* did vainly attempt to elicit positive statements about the Pol Pot regime from antiwar activists to buttress this useful thesis.

Each of these themes—the "silence" of the West, the defense of Pol Pot by Western intellectuals—is unequivocally refuted by massive evidence that is well known, although ignored, by the mobilized intellectual culture. But this level of misrepresentation in the service of a noble cause still does not suffice. The two themes were combined by William Shawcross in an inspired agitprop achievement that carried the farce a step further.[99] This new contribution evoked much enthusiasm; several of the comments just cited are from reviews of his book, or are obviously inspired by it.

In his study of "Cambodia, Holocaust and Modern Conscience," Shawcross muses on the relative "silence" of the West in the face of Khmer Rouge atrocities. The facts are radically different, but the idea that the West ignores Communist atrocities while agonizing over its own is far more appealing to the Western conscience. Shawcross then proceeds to adopt Aikman's second thesis, applying it in an ingenious way to explain the mechanism that lies behind this unwillingness of the West to face up to Communist atrocities, so notable a feature of Western life. The silence over phase II of the genocide, he argues, resulted from "the skepticism (to use a mild term) displayed by the Western left toward the stories coming out of Democratic Kampuchea. That skepticism was most fervently and frequently expressed by Noam Chomsky . . ., [who] asserted that from the moment of the Khmer Rouge victory in 1975 the Western press colluded with Western and anti-Communist Asian governments, notably Thailand, to produce a 'vast and unprecedented' campaign of propaganda against the Khmer Rouge."[100]

To buttress this claim, Shawcross provides what purports to be a quote—but without citing an identifiable source, for two good reasons. First, the quote does not exist,[101] although even his version undermines his basic claim, with its reference to "the grim reality" of Cambodia under Khmer Rouge rule. Second, the source of the manufactured quote is a work published in November 1979, almost a year after the fall of the Pol Pot regime. To cite the date would have raised the question of how this "fervent and frequent" expression of skepticism could have intimidated governments and the media from 1975 through 1978. Furthermore, we made it crystal clear that the record of atrocities was "gruesome," perhaps even at the level of the most outlandish fabrications.

Note that Shawcross could have cited real examples of "skepticism"; for example, the skepticism of State Department analysts at the height of the furor over Cambodia, or the retrospective comments of Douglas Pike and others cited earlier (pp. 265–66), or the comments of journalists during phase II who were willing to conclude only that refugee accounts "suggest that the Khmer Rouge is finding it hard to govern the country except by coercion" and "even suggest that terror is being employed as a system of government," noting that refugees "did not appear to be in a sorry condition" and that if the Khmer Rouge are perpetrating an "atrocity," as claimed, then "the atrocity did not begin in April [1975]—it simply entered its sixth year" (William Shawcross).[102] But the truth plainly would not have served the purposes of this exercise.[103]

Perhaps there was some other example of this "fervent and frequent" expression of skepticism that silenced the West. Shawcross is wise to avoid examples, because as he knows well, his primary source, Ponchaud, went out of his way to praise Chomsky for "the responsible attitude and precision of thought" shown in what he had written on Cambodia, referring to our 1977 review of his book cited earlier and unpublished correspondence he had seen, which exhausts anything relevant that appears during the DK period.[104] So Shawcross would have us believe that a single 1977 article in *The Nation* silenced the West, an article in which, furthermore, we praised the book written by his primary source, Ponchaud, as "serious and worth reading," with its "grisly account of what refugees have reported to him about the barbarity of their treatment at the hands of the Khmer Rouge," and stated that we are in no position to draw any conclusion about the actual extent of the atrocities, in conformity to State Department specialists and other informed sources at the time.

To be clear, in our one article, to which Ponchaud alludes, we did express some "skepticism," not only about claims that had already been withdrawn as fabrications but also about others that remained to be assessed. Thus in reviewing Ponchaud, we expressed skepticism about his estimate of casualties caused by American bombing, which appeared to us excessive and possibly based on misinterpretation of figures he cited; and we raised questions about some of the quotes attributed to the Khmer Rouge on which he (and later others) crucially relied, but which he had presented in very different forms on different occasions—and which he later conceded to have no basis whatsoever.[105] It is noteworthy that our skepticism about charges against the United States, although based merely on suspicion, has elicited no comment, while our skepticism about charges against the Khmer Rouge, which was based on textual evidence and, as it later turned out, was much understated, has aroused great fury in what Vickery describes as "incompetent, even dishonest" and "often scurrilous" commentary.[106] The differential reaction is easily explained. It is taken for granted that U.S. actions must be recounted with scrupulous care and in nuanced manner, so our insistence on this is simply what is to be expected, meriting no comment. (We agree.) In contrast, the acts of official enemies merit no such scruples, and it is an unforgivable crime to question propaganda exercises undertaken in the service of power.

Notice that even had the "skepticism" of "the Western left" to which Shawcross alludes existed to any significant degree, the idea that this could have the consequences he describes, coming from people systematically barred from the media and mainstream discussion, is a construction of such audacity that one must admire its creator. Shawcross argues further that this alleged "left-wing skepticism" not only silenced Western media and governments but also prevented any meaningful Western response to Khmer Rouge atrocities. This thesis is too ludicrous to merit comment, and we can assess Shawcross's seriousness in advancing it by turning to his own proposals at the time as to what could be done, recalling that he had easy access to the mainstream media throughout. We find not a word suggesting what might be done[107]—for the simple reason that neither he nor anyone else could think of anything useful. The situation was, of course, quite different during phase I of the genocide, or with regard to Timor during phase II and since, and in innumerable other cases where Shawcross's charge would indeed be valid. We learn a good deal about "holocaust and the modern conscience" by observing this exercise and the reaction it elicited.

Shawcross attributes this "left-wing skepticism," which had such awesome consequences because of the influence of the left on Western institutions, in part to Vietnamese propaganda. Vietnam's "spokesmen had undercut the refugee stories about Khmer Rouge conduct," he writes, "thus adding to disbelief in them, particularly on the Western left,"[108] which naturally takes its cues from Hanoi and closely parrots its doctrines, according to approved dogma—although it is interesting that Shawcross also insinuates that the influence of Hanoi extended beyond its acolytes. And why not? If we have reached the point of claiming that the Western left silenced the media and governments, why not proceed to maintain that even outside these dangerous circles, Vietnamese propaganda is a powerful force in shaping opinion? Naturally Shawcross does not make even a pretense of providing any evidence for what he knows perfectly well to be the sheerest fantasy, from beginning to end.

We may place this outlandish explanation of the "silence" of the West alongside the similar claims that State Department Communists lost China, that the media are threatening the foundations of democracy with their "adversarial stance," etc. The reaction, however, was not ridicule, but rather great enthusiasm. To cite just one typical example, David Hawk observes that Shawcross "attributes the world's indifference" to "the influence of antiwar academics and activists on the American left who obfuscated Khmer Rouge behavior, denigrated the post-1975 refugee reports and denounced the journalists who got those stories."[109] He accepts this thesis as valid but cites no evidence either for the "indifference" to the atrocities, which were being denounced worldwide as genocidal, or for the alleged behavior of the American left, nor does he explain the mechanisms whereby this behavior, had it existed, could have controlled the mainstream media, or even marginally influenced them. Convenient mythologies require neither evidence nor logic. Nor do they require any attention to Hawk's own performance at the time, as an Amnesty International official and specialist on Southeast Asia. The AI Annual Report for 1977 noted that the number of alleged executions in Cambodia was "fewer than during the preceding year," and while it summarizes a number of reports of executions and disappearances, its account is restrained. The 1978 Annual Report, while stronger in its allegations of violence, pointed out that refugee reports, on which it was necessary to rely heavily, "are often imprecise or conflicting," thus leaving AI and Hawk in the Shawcross-Hawk category of those who "denigrated the post-1975 refugee reports." It is so easy to moralize in retrospect.

Shawcross develops his thesis further in interesting ways.[110] To show that Western commentators refused to recognize that "the Khmer Rouge was a Marxist-Leninist government," he states that British journalist John Pilger "constantly compared" the Khmer Rouge with the Nazis, suppressing the fact that he explicitly compared their actions with "Stalin's terror," as Pilger noted in a response to one of the many reviews that repeated Shawcross's inventions.[111] Shawcross claims further that the present authors "were to believe for years" that "the refugees were unreliable, that the CIA was cooking up a bloodbath to say, 'We told you so.' " He cites our one article (*The Nation*, 1977), in which there is no hint of any such thesis, as there is none elsewhere. In that article we were clear and explicit, as also subsequently, that refugee reports left no doubt that the record of Khmer Rouge atrocities was "substantial and often gruesome," and that "in the case of Cambodia, there is no difficulty in documenting major atrocities and oppression, primarily from the reports of refugees."[112] To support his contention with regard to our alleged denial of the reliability of refugees, Shawcross cites our comment on the need to exercise care in analyzing refugee reports, carefully suppressing the fact that we are quoting Ponchaud, his primary source, and that the comment he cites is a familiar truism. His reference to the CIA cooking up a bloodbath is pure fantasy, although we might add that by the time he wrote, although after our book appeared, Michael Vickery did present evidence that the Barron-Paul *Reader's Digest* account was in part a CIA disinformation effort.[113] Shawcross states further his view, "contrary to Chomsky and Herman," that the U.S. government was "remarkably inactive" in anti–Khmer Rouge propaganda. We proposed no U.S. government role whatsoever in orchestrating the deceit we documented, by William Shawcross and others, and in fact endorsed State Department reports as the most plausible then available. And so on, throughout.

But Shawcross and others who are deeply offended by our challenge to the right to lie in the service of one's favored state understand very well that charges against dissident opinion require no evidence and that ideologically useful accusations will stand merely on the basis of endless repetition, however ludicrous they may be—even the claim that the American left silenced the entire West during the Pol Pot period.

Shawcross's charges against other enemies follow the same pattern—another factor, presumably, in the appeal of his message. Thus in pursuit of his fashionable quest to attribute primary responsibility for the continuing tragedy of Cambodia to Vietnam, not to those who were responsible for phase I of the genocide with their "careless" policies and who are now supporting Pol Pot, Shawcross rationalizes the current support for Pol Pot as a natural response to Vietnamese actions. Given Hanoi's invasion of Cambodia and subsequent conduct, he explains, China and the ASEAN countries of Southeast Asia (not to speak of their "Western partners") were bound "to seek to apply all possible forms of pressure upon Hanoi" to renounce its intentions, and "the Vietnamese could have predicted that such pressures would include support for the Khmer Rouge." Thus the Vietnamese are to blame if China and the United States support Pol Pot, along with such dedicated advocates of human rights and the strict reliance on peaceful means as Indonesia and Thailand. Such analysis is, however, not extended to the Vietnamese, who are always carrying out cold-blooded strategies in a world without threats from China or the United States, threats that might allow us to "predict" (and thus implicitly exonerate) these strategies. According to Shawcross, "Vietnam's conduct since its invasion of Cambodia rarely suggested that it wished to see a compromise in which the Khmer Rouge were removed as a viable force in Cambodia—which was what the ASEAN countries and their Western partners insisted was their aim." "It is impossible to predict whether any such suggestion [from Hanoi] would have been accepted by the Chinese or the ASEAN countries, but the point is that it was never made," Shawcross asserts without qualification.[114] Hanoi has repeatedly offered to withdraw in favor of an indigenous regime, the only condition being the exclusion of the top Khmer Rouge leadership. Whether these offers were serious or not, we do not know, as they have been dismissed by the Deng-Reagan alliance and, with more vacillation, the ASEAN countries. These rejections, in favor of continued support for Pol Pot, have not been featured in the media, which would hardly surprise a rational observer. But these facts are hardly supportive of Shawcross's analysis, to say the least.

In a further effort to cast the blame on the approved enemy, Shawcross asserts that the Vietnamese "placed more confidence in the torturers than in their victims, that many of those people were actually being promoted by the new order into positions of new authority over them." As his sole evidence, he cites a story, told twice in his book, about an old woman he met in Cambodia "who described with great passion how the Khmer Rouge murderer of her son was living, unpunished, in the neighboring village." He repeated the same story in the *New York Review of Books,* eliciting a letter from Ben Kiernan, who accompanied him when this alleged incident took place (and was his interpreter). Kiernan cited the tape of the woman's statement, which reveals that she had simply said that the murderer had "run away" to a neighboring "district," suggesting, as Kiernan notes, that he feared punishment, but not that he had been "promoted" to "new authority." Confronted with this evidence, Shawcross maintained his position while retreating to the claim that some officials he met "seemed rather unpleasant," which suffices to prove the point, according to his logic.[115] These examples are quite typical.[116]

6.2.9. Summary

Summarizing, prior to "the decade of the genocide," media treatment of Cambodia was as predicted by the propaganda model, and the same is true, quite dramatically, during the two phases of this terrible period and since. During phase I, refugee testimony was considered uninteresting, and little is known today apart from the fact that there was obviously vast slaughter and destruction; this phase does not enter the record as a "holocaust" or exercise in "genocide," and the source is forgotten. During phase II, the myth of the "gentle land" was extended through 1975, and the U.S. role and responsibility for what then took place was also quite commonly effaced, although some did not sink to this level of vulgarity. Refugee testimony was eagerly sought, although only if it lent support to the STV, and evaluations by State Department specialists and other knowledgeable commentators that gave a more nuanced (and in retrospect, essentially accurate) picture were dismissed as lacking utility. There was massive outrage, reaching its peak in early 1977 when the death toll was still well below that of phase I, with a record of deception that is highly illuminating.[117] As something like the STV came to be realized in 1977–78, its horrors were downplayed in official government circles, and subsequent U.S. support for Pol Pot arouses little notice.

Phase III proceeded along a dual course. In a fanciful reconstruction that maintains the level of integrity shown throughout, it is alleged that "left-wing skepticism" so dominated Western opinion and governments that there was "silence" throughout the DK period; the wide acceptance of this thesis, despite the quality of the evidence provided and its manifest absurdity, counts as yet another example of how readily the most implausible contentions can become doctrine, as long as they are serviceable. In Indochina, a new phase of Western concern about the victimization of Cambodia began, with outrage now directed not against Pol Pot but against the new oppressors who overthrew him. The United States took a leading role in orchestrating the new concern, which combined Chinese and U.S. interest in "bleeding Vietnam" with a renewed exhibition of the Western conscience, properly bounded to exclude phase I and its long-term effects, and bypassing the U.S. role in support of Pol Pot—in part via its Chinese allies, who have been admirably frank in explaining their stand. This carefully channeled benevolence succeeded in the goal of keeping the Pol Pot forces active and injuring Vietnam and also, incidentally, the suffering people of Cambodia who are the objects of our profound concern. The relief effort in 1979–80 did succeed in aiding Cambodians in distress, but it has also sustained the Pol Pot forces and thereby impeded Cambodia's recovery and, perhaps, its independence, although about this we can only speculate.

Putting aside the undoubtedly sincere reactions of many people who were exposed to evidence of properly selected atrocities that passed through the media filter, the only rational conclusion from this illuminating record is that the West was consumed with horror over Khmer Rouge atrocities during phase II not because of a sudden passion for the fate of the suffering people of Cambodia—as the record during phase I, and elsewhere, makes sufficiently clear—but because the Khmer Rouge had a useful role to play: namely, to permit a retrospective justification for earlier French and American crimes in Indochina, and to facilitate the reconstruction of Western ideology after the Vietnam trauma, so as to overcome the dread "Vietnam syndrome" and prepare the ground for a "resurgent America" pursuing its historical vocation of defending freedom and justice. The actual facts were, and remain, of little interest, for the same reason.

7

Conclusions

DEFENDING THE MEDIA AGAINST THE CHARGE THAT THEY HAVE become too independent and too powerful for the public good, Anthony Lewis of the *New York Times* writes that

> The press is protected [by the First Amendment] not for its own sake but to enable a free political system to operate. In the end, the concern is not for the reporter or the editor but for the citizen-critic of government.

What is at stake when we speak about freedom of the press "is the freedom to perform a function on behalf of the polity."[1] Lewis cites Supreme Court Justice Powell, who observed: "no individual can obtain for himself the information needed for the intelligent discharge of his political responsibilities. . . . By enabling the public to assert meaningful control over the political process, the press performs a crucial function in effecting the societal purpose of the First Amendment." Therefore, as Judge Gurfein ruled in supporting the right of the *New York Times* to publish the *Pentagon Papers* after the government had failed to show any threat of a breach of security but only the possibility of embarrassment: "a cantankerous press, an obstinate press, a ubiquitous press must be suffered by those in authority in order to preserve the even greater values of freedom of expression and the right of the people to know."

We do not accept the view that freedom of expression must be defended in instrumental terms, by virtue of its contribution to some higher good; rather, it is a value in itself. But that apart, these ringing declarations express valid aspirations, and beyond that, they surely express the self-image of the American media. Our concern in this book has been to inquire into the relation between this image and the reality. In contrast to the standard conception of the media as cantankerous, obstinate, and ubiquitous in their search for truth and their independence of authority, we have spelled out and applied a propaganda model that indeed sees the media as serving a "societal purpose," but not that of enabling the public to assert meaningful control over the political process by providing them with the information needed for the intelligent discharge of political responsibilities. On the contrary, a propaganda model suggests that the "societal purpose" of the media is to inculcate and defend the economic, social, and political agenda of privileged groups that dominate the domestic society and the state. The media serve this purpose in many ways: through selection of topics, distribution of concerns, framing of issues, filtering of information, emphasis and tone, and by keeping debate within the bounds of acceptable premises. We have sought to show that the expectations of this model are realized, and often considerably surpassed, in the actual practice of the media in a range of crucial cases. We quite agree with Chief Justice Hughes, whom Lewis also cites, on "the primary need of a vigilant and courageous press" if democratic processes are to function in a meaningful way. But the evidence we have reviewed indicates that this need is not met or even weakly approximated in actual practice.

It is frequently asserted that the media were not always as independent, vigilant, and defiant of authority as they allegedly are today; rather, the experiences of the past generation are held to have taught the media to exercise "the power to root about in our national life, exposing what they deem right for exposure," without regard to external pressures or the dictates of authority (Lewis). It is this period, then, that poses a challenge to a propaganda model, and we have therefore taken it as the focus of our inquiry. Many of the examples we discuss are from the past decade, when the liberal media were allegedly in confrontation with a "conservative" administration that they would have been expected to oppose vigorously. In a further effort to ensure that we are not selecting exceptional cases, we have cast the net widely. We have selected for close examination cases that pose the most severe challenge to our model, namely, those put forth by critics as demonstrating that the media have gone too far in their exuberant independence and challenge to authority, so far that they must be curbed if democracy is to survive: for example, the coverage of the Tet offensive, the prime illustration of alleged excesses of the media offered in the 1970s and 1980s. Even these cases demonstrate the subordination of the media to the requirements of the state propaganda system. At the peak of alleged media independence, as the Vietnam War entered its final period and the media were threatening Nixon's presidency, the subordination to these demands never flagged, as illustrated by the media coverage of the Paris peace treaty of 1973, one of the most flagrant examples of media misrepresentation based on an uncritical reiteration of official claims and adherence to the political agenda of the state.

We may illustrate the point in yet another case, chosen by those who defend the standard version of the media as their strongest ground: the Watergate affair. To many critics of the media, this incident illustrates their irresponsible excesses; to those who proudly defend the media, it illustrates their independence of higher authority and commitment to the values of professional journalism. What, then, are the lessons of Watergate?

The major scandal of Watergate as portrayed in the mainstream press was that the Nixon administration sent a collection of petty criminals to break into the Democratic party headquarters, for reasons that remain obscure. The Democratic party represents powerful domestic interests, solidly based in the business community. Nixon's actions were therefore a scandal. The Socialist Workers party, a legal political party, represents no powerful interests. Therefore, there was no scandal when it was revealed, just as passions over Watergate reached their zenith, that the FBI had been disrupting its activities by illegal break-ins and other measures for a decade, a violation of democratic principle far more extensive and serious than anything charged during the Watergate hearings. What is more, these actions of the national political police were only one element of government programs extending over many administrations to deter independent political action, stir up violence in the ghettos, and undermine the popular movements that were beginning to engage sectors of the generally marginalized public in the arena of decision-making.[2] These covert and illegal programs were revealed in court cases and elsewhere during the Watergate period, but they never entered the congressional proceedings and received only limited media attention. Even the complicity of the FBI in the police assassination of a Black Panther organizer in Chicago was not a scandal, in marked contrast to Nixon's "enemies list," which identified powerful people who were denigrated in private but suffered no consequences. As we have noted, the U.S. role in initiating and carrying out the first phase of "the decade of the genocide" in Cambodia entered the Watergate proceedings only marginally: not because hundreds of thousands of Cambodians were slaughtered in the course of a major war crime, but because Congress was not properly notified, so that its privileges were infringed, and even this was considered too slight an infraction to enter the final charges. What was true of Congress was also true of the media and their investigative reporting that "helped force a President from office" (Lewis) in what is held to be a most remarkable display of media independence, or arrogance, depending on one's point of view.

History has been kind enough to contrive for us a "controlled experiment" to determine just what was at stake during the Watergate period, when the confrontational stance of the media reached its peak. The answer is clear and precise: powerful groups are capable of defending themselves, not surprisingly; and by media standards, it is a scandal when their position and rights are threatened. By contrast, as long as illegalities and violations of democratic substance are confined to marginal groups or distant victims of U.S. military attack, or result in a diffused cost imposed on the general population, media opposition is muted or absent altogether.[3] This is why Nixon could go so far, lulled into a false sense of security precisely because the watchdog only barked when he began to threaten the privileged.

Exactly the same lessons were taught by the Iran-contra scandals and the media reaction to them.[4] It was a scandal when the Reagan administration was found to have violated congressional prerogatives during the Iran-contra affair, but not when it dismissed with contempt the judgment of the International Court of Justice that the United States was engaged in the "unlawful use of force" and violation of treaties—that is, violation of the supreme law of the land and customary international law—in its attack against Nicaragua. The sponsorship and support of state terror that cost some 200,000 lives in Central America in the preceding decade was not the subject of congressional inquiries or media concern. These actions were conducted in accord with an elite consensus, and they received steady media support, as we have seen in reviewing the fate of worthy and unworthy victims and the treatment of elections in client and errant states.[5]

In the case of the Vietnam War as well, as we showed in chapter 5, even those who condemn the media for their alleged adversarial stance acknowledge that they were almost universally supportive of U.S. policy until *after* large numbers of U.S. troops had been engaged in the "intervention" in South Vietnam, heavy casualties had been taken, huge dollar sums had been spent, and elite protest had surfaced on grounds of threats to elite interests. Only then did elements of the media undertake qualified reassessments of the "cost-benefit" trade-off. But during the period of growing involvement that eventually made extrication difficult, the watchdog actually encouraged the burglar to make himself at home in a distant land, and to bomb and destroy it with abandon.

In short, the very examples offered in praise of the media for their independence, or criticism of their excessive zeal, illustrate exactly the opposite. Contrary to the usual image of an "adversary press" boldly attacking a pitiful executive giant, the media's lack of interest, investigative zeal, and basic news reporting on the accumulating illegalities of the executive branch have regularly permitted and even *encouraged* ever larger violations of law, whose ultimate exposure when elite interests were threatened is offered as a demonstration of media service "on behalf of the polity." These observations reinforce the conclusions that we have documented throughout.

The existing level of media subordination to state authority is often deemed unsatisfactory by critics. We have discussed several examples. Thus, Freedom House and others who are concerned to protect state authority from an intrusive public condemn the media for lack of sufficient enthusiasm in supporting official crusades, and even the limited challenge to established authority during the Vietnam War and the Watergate period aroused concerns over the excessive power of the media. Quite commonly, the slight opening occasionally granted to dissent is considered far too dangerous to permit. This perception sometimes even takes the form of a paranoid vision of left-wing power that sweeps all in its path: for example, the plea of Claire Sterling and others who dominated media coverage of the Bulgarian Connection that they could barely be heard above the din of Soviet propaganda. A still more striking case is the Aikman-Shawcross fantasy, eagerly echoed by many others, about the "silencing" of the international media and governments by the left during the Pol Pot era. In reality, there was a huge chorus of protest over Khmer Rouge atrocities, which reached an extraordinary level of fabrication and deceit. The significance of these facts, and of the pretense of left-imposed "silence," is highlighted by the contrast with the real silence over comparable atrocities in Timor at the same time, and the evasions and suppressions during the first phase of "the decade of the genocide," to mention two cases where the United States was the responsible agent and protest could have been effective in diminishing or terminating large-scale atrocities.

A propaganda model provides a ready explanation for this quite typical dichotomous treatment. Atrocities by the Khmer Rouge could be attributed to the Communist enemy and valuable propaganda points could be scored, although nothing useful could be done, or was even proposed, for the Cambodian victims. The image of Communist monsters would also be useful for subsequent U.S. participation in terror and violence, as in its crusades in Central America shortly after. In El Salvador, the United States backed the murderous junta in its struggle against what was depicted as "the Pol Pot left," while Jeane Kirkpatrick mused darkly about the threat to El Salvador of "well-armed guerrillas whose fanaticism and violence remind some observers of Pol Pot"—shortly after the archbishop had denounced her junta friends for conducting a "war of extermination and genocide against a defenseless civilian population."[6] Some are more circumspect—for example, William Buckley, who observes that "the Sandinistas have given their people genocide" and are clearly heading in the direction of Pol Pot, although they have not quite reached that level yet.[7] The utility of the show of outrage over Pol Pot atrocities is evident from the way the fate of these worthy victims was immediately exploited to justify U.S. organization of atrocities that, in fact, do merit comparison to Pol Pot.

Atrocities in East Timor, however, have no such utilitarian function; quite the opposite. These atrocities were carried out by our Indonesian client, so that the United States could readily have acted to reduce or terminate them. But attention to the Indonesian invasion would have embarrassed a loyal ally and quickly disclosed the crucial role of the United States in providing military aid and diplomatic support for aggression and slaughter. Plainly, news about East Timor would not have been useful, and would, in fact, have discomfited important domestic power groups. The mass media—and the intellectual community generally—therefore channeled their benevolent impulses elsewhere: to Cambodia, not Timor.

As we have stressed throughout this book, the U.S. media do not function in the manner of the propaganda system of a totalitarian state. Rather, they permit—indeed, encourage—spirited debate, criticism, and dissent, as long as these remain faithfully within the system of presuppositions and principles that constitute an elite consensus, a system so powerful as to be internalized largely without awareness. No one instructed the media to focus on Cambodia and ignore East Timor.

They gravitated naturally to the Khmer Rouge and discussed them freely[8]—just as they naturally suppressed information on Indonesian atrocities in East Timor and U.S. responsibility for the aggression and massacres. In the process, the media provided neither facts nor analyses that would have enabled the public to understand the issues or the bases of government policies toward Cambodia and Timor, and they thereby assured that the public could not exert any meaningful influence on the decisions that were made. This is quite typical of the *actual* "societal purpose" of the media on matters that are of significance for established power; not "enabling the public to assert meaningful control over the political process," but rather averting any such danger. In these cases, as in numerous others, the public was managed and mobilized from above, by means of the media's highly selective messages and evasions. As noted by media analyst W. Lance Bennett,

> The public is exposed to powerful persuasive messages from above and is unable to communicate meaningfully through the media in response to these messages. . . . Leaders have usurped enormous amounts of political power and reduced popular control over the political system by using the media to generate support, compliance, and just plain confusion among the public.[9]

More significantly for our particular concerns here, the media typically provide their own independent contribution even without being "used," in the manner and for the reasons that we have discussed. Another media analyst, Ben Bagdikian, observes that the institutional bias of the private mass media "does not merely protect the corporate system. It robs the public of a chance to understand the real world."[10] That conclusion is well supported by the evidence we have reviewed.

A propaganda model has a certain initial plausibility on guided free-market assumptions that are not particularly controversial. In essence, the private media are major corporations selling a product (readers and audiences) to other businesses (advertisers). The national media typically target and serve elite opinion, groups that, on the one hand, provide an optimal "profile" for advertising purposes, and, on the other, play a role in decision-making in the private and public spheres. The national media would be failing to meet their elite audience's needs if they did not present a tolerably realistic portrayal of the world. But their "societal purpose" also requires that the media's interpretation of the world reflect the interests and concerns of the sellers, the buyers, and the governmental and private institutions dominated by these groups.

A propaganda model also helps us to understand how media personnel adapt, and are adapted, to systemic demands. Given the imperatives of corporate organization and the workings of the various filters, conformity to the needs and interests of privileged sectors is essential to success. In the media, as in other major institutions, those who do not display the requisite values and perspectives will be regarded as "irresponsible," "ideological," or otherwise aberrant, and will tend to fall by the wayside. While there may be a small number of exceptions, the pattern is pervasive, and expected. Those who adapt, perhaps quite honestly, will then be free to express themselves with little managerial control, and they will be able to assert, accurately, that they perceive no pressures to conform. The media are indeed free—for those who adopt the principles required for their "societal purpose." There may be some who are simply corrupt, and who serve as "errand boys" for state and other authority, but this is not the norm.[11] We know from personal experience that many journalists are quite aware of the way the system operates, and utilize the occasional openings it affords to provide information and analysis that departs in some measure from the elite consensus, carefully shaping it so as to accommodate to required norms in a general way. But this degree of insight is surely not common. Rather, the norm is a belief that freedom prevails, which is true for those who have internalized the required values and perspectives.

These matters are of some importance. We can readily understand why Guatemalan reporters do not report the atrocities of the 1980s; some fifty corpses dramatically illustrate the costs of deviance from authority on the part of independent journalists. To explain why American reporters avoid such topics, and even go so far as to describe Guatemala as a model for Nicaragua (see p. 115), requires further explanation, and the same is true in innumerable other similar cases, some of which we have analyzed in detail. A propaganda model provides a basis for understanding this pervasive phenomenon.

No simple model will suffice, however, to account for every detail of such a complex matter as the working of the national mass media. A propaganda model, we believe, captures essential features of the process, but it leaves many nuances and secondary effects unanalyzed. There are other factors that should be recognized. Some of these conflict with the "societal purpose" of the media as described by the propaganda model; some support it. In the former category, the humanity and professional integrity of journalists often leads them in directions that are unacceptable in the ideological institutions, and one should not underestimate the psychological burden of suppressing obvious truths and maintaining the required doctrines of benevolence (possibly gone awry), inexplicable error, good intentions, injured innocence, and so on, in the face of overwhelming evidence incompatible with these patriotic premises. The resulting tensions sometimes find limited expression, but more often they are suppressed either consciously or unconsciously, with the help of belief systems that permit the pursuit of narrow interest, whatever the facts.

In the category of supportive factors, we find, first of all, elemental patriotism, the overwhelming wish to think well of ourselves, our institutions, and our leaders. We see ourselves as basically good and decent in personal life, so it must be that our institutions function in accordance with the same benevolent intent, an argument that is often persuasive even though it is a transparent *non sequitur.* The patriotic premise is reinforced by the belief that "we the people" rule, a central principle of the system of indoctrination from early childhood, but also one with little merit, as an analysis of the social and political system will quickly reveal. There are also real advantages in conformity beyond the rewards and privilege that it yields. If one chooses to denounce Qaddafi, or the Sandinistas, or the PLO, or the Soviet Union, no credible evidence is required. The same is true if one repeats conventional doctrines about our own society and its behavior—say, that the U.S. government is dedicated to our traditional noble commitment to democracy and human rights. But a critical analysis of American institutions, the way they function domestically and their international operations, must meet far higher standards; in fact, standards are often imposed that can barely be met in the natural sciences. One has to work hard, to produce evidence that is credible, to construct serious arguments, to present extensive documentation—all tasks that are superfluous as long as one remains within the presuppositional framework of the doctrinal consensus. It is small wonder that few are willing to undertake the effort, quite apart from the rewards that accrue to conformity and the costs of honest dissidence.

There are other considerations that tend to induce obedience. A journalist or commentator who does not want to have to work too hard can survive, even gain respectability, by publishing information (official or leaks) from standard sources;[12] these opportunities may well be denied to those who are not content to relay the constructions of state propaganda as fact. The technical structure of the media virtually compels adherence to conventional thoughts; nothing else can be expressed between two commercials, or in seven hundred words, without the appearance of absurdity that is difficult to avoid when one is challenging familiar doctrine with no opportunity to develop facts or argument. In this respect, the U.S. media are rather different from those in most other industrial democracies, and the consequences are noticeable in the narrowness of articulated opinion and analysis. The critic must also be prepared to face a defamation apparatus against which there is little recourse, an inhibiting factor that is not insubstantial. Many such factors exist, related to the essential structural features brought to light by a propaganda model but nevertheless worthy of detailed examination in themselves. The result is a powerful system of induced conformity to the needs of privilege and power.

In sum, the mass media of the United States are effective and powerful ideological institutions that carry out a system-supportive propaganda function by reliance on market forces, internalized assumptions, and self-censorship, and without significant overt coercion. This propaganda system has become even more efficient in recent decades with the rise of the national television networks, greater mass-media concentration, right-wing pressures on public radio and television, and the growth in scope and sophistication of public relations and news management.

This system is not all-powerful, however. Government and elite domination of the media have not succeeded in overcoming the Vietnam syndrome and public hostility to direct U.S. involvement in the destabilization and overthrow of foreign governments. A massive Reagan-era disinformation and propaganda effort, reflecting in large measure an elite consensus, did succeed in its major aims of mobilizing support for the U.S. terror states (the "fledgling democracies"), while demonizing the Sandinistas and eliminating from Congress and the mass media all controversy beyond tactical debate over the means that should be employed to return Nicaragua to the "Central American mode" and "contain" its "aggressiveness" in attempting to defend itself from a murderous and destructive U.S. assault on all fronts. But it failed to win public support even for proxy army warfare against Nicaragua, and as the costs to the U.S. mounted, and the proxy war accompanied by embargo and other pressures succeeded in restoring the "Central American mode" of misery and suffering in Nicaragua and aborting the highly successful reforms and prospects for development of the early years after the overthrow of Washington's ally Somoza, elite opinion too shifted—quite dramatically, in fact—toward resort to other, more cost-effective means to attain shared ends.[13] The partial failures of the very well organized and extensive state propaganda effort, and the simultaneous rise of an active grass-roots oppositional movement with very limited media access, was crucial in making an outright U.S. invasion of Nicaragua unfeasible and driving the state underground, to illegal clandestine operations that could be better concealed from the domestic population—with, in fact, considerable media complicity.[14]

Furthermore, while there have been important structural changes centralizing and strengthening the propaganda system, there have been counterforces at work with a potential for broader access. The rise of cable and satellite communications, while initially captured and dominated by commercial interests, has weakened the power of the network oligopoly and retains a potential for enhanced local-group access. There are already some 3,000 public-access channels in use in the United States, offering 20,000 hours of locally produced programs per week, and there are even national producers and distributors of programs for access channels through satellites (e.g., Deep-Dish Television), as well as hundreds of local suppliers, although all of them must struggle for funding. Grass-roots and public-interest organizations need to recognize and try to avail themselves of these media (and organizational) opportunities.[15] Local nonprofit radio and television stations also provide an opportunity for direct media access that has been underutilized in the United States. In France, many local groups have their own radio stations. In a notable case, the progressive cooperative Longo Mai, in Upper Provence, has its own 24-hour-a-day Radio Zinzine, which has become an important community institution that has helped inform and activate many previously isolated farmers. The potential value of noncommercial radio can be perceived in sections of the country where stations such as Pacifica Radio offer a view of the world, depth of coverage, and scope of discussion and debate that is generally excluded from the major media. Public radio and television, despite having suffered serious damage during the Reagan years, also represent an alternative media channel whose resuscitation and improvement should be of serious concern to those interested in contesting the propaganda system.[16] The steady commercialization of the publicly owned air waves should be vigorously opposed. In the long run, a democratic political order requires far wider control of and access to the media. Serious discussion of how this can be done, and the incorporation of fundamental media reform into political programs, should be high on progressive agendas.[17]

The organization and self-education of groups in the community and workplace, and their networking and activism, continue to be the fundamental elements in steps toward the democratization of our social life and any meaningful social change. Only to the extent that such developments succeed can we hope to see media that are free and independent.

Appendix 1

THE U.S. OFFICIAL OBSERVERS IN GUATEMALA, JULY 1–2, 1984

For the July 1, 1984, elections in Guatemala, the Reagan administration sent an observer team, headed by Republican Congressman Ralph Regula, that also included Congressmen Jack Hightower (Democrat, Texas) and Mickey Edwards (Republican, Oklahoma); Secretaries of State Jack Brier, of Kansas, and Ed Simcox, of Indiana; Father Kenneth Baker, editor of *Homiletic and Pastoral Review,* New York City; John Carbaugh, a Washington attorney; Jesse Friedman, of the American Institute of Free Labor Development; Tom Kahn, of the AFL-CIO; Max Singer, of the Potomac Organization; and Howard Penniman, the election specialist of the American Enterprise Institute.[1] This group, in Guatemala for a very brief stay, was transported around the country to "observe" on election day by helicopter, and made a brief statement and held a press conference on July 2. That statement and the press conference proceedings were released by the U.S. embassy in Guatemala City on July 18, 1984, and form the basis for the discussion below.

Although Guatemala had been assailed by human-rights organizations for years for political murder on a vast scale and record-breaking numbers of "disappeared," the words "murder" and "disappeared" do not appear in the remarks of any of the ten observers who spoke at the press conference. Other words or phrases never uttered were: "National Security Doctrine," "Law of Illicit Association," "state terrorism," "death squad," "massacre," "torture," "forced relocations," "civil-defense patrols," "freedom of the press," or "voting requirement." None of the observers doubted the authenticity of "positive" responses by Guatemalan peasants to questions by non-Spanish-speaking foreigners flown in by helicopter in a country subject to military occupation. All of the observers felt quite capable of assessing the true feelings of the Guatemalan people on the basis of long lines, facial expressions, and a handful of responses to visitors under official protection. There was no dissent among the observers from the conclusion that the election was fair, inspiring, a testimonial to the eagerness of the Guatemalan people to participate and express their patriotic sentiments, and a first step toward democracy. No demonstration-election cliché was omitted—history was blacked out, and no basic condition of a free election was examined by the observers.

Let us sample a few of the clichés offered by these Guatemalan election observers:

1. *People full of hope—very positive start.* This was a "dynamic beginning, . . . a first step," according to delegation head Ralph Regula. Father Kenneth Baker found a "great sense of hope for the future . . . the spirit of hopefulness." Jack Brier also observed "a spirit of hopefulness about the future, but not necessarily confidence in whatever actions may come about as a result of the elections." (This is a very nuanced distinction that Brier was able to make on the basis of translated brief answers by a few voters.) Tom Kahn claimed that "many of the workers whom we spoke to on the voting lines told us that they had great hope, that this was a first step." Kahn was asked during the press conference whether he had visited any of the embattled Coca-Cola workers. He hadn't. Neither Kahn nor his AIFLD colleague, Jesse Friedman, mentioned the enormous decline in union membership or the decimation of union leadership by murder.

2. *Long lines, patient voters.* The observers were deeply impressed with "the way the people patiently waited" to vote (Regula). Howard Penniman noted "the extraordinary patience of the people voting." Ed Simcox pointed out that the voters "did go out, they formed lines very early in the morning, they waited in some instances two, three, four hours to go up and vote." According to Congressman Hightower, "The thing that impressed us instantly was the long lines." Tom Kahn was impressed with the "calm and order which prevailed around the voting tables."

Long lines and patient voters are quite compatible with voting by a terrorized population desiring mainly to survive. The official observers, who never once mention the record of spectacular state terror in Guatemala, merely *postulate* that voters who get in line and wait patiently do so for reasons that are benign.

3. *The patriotic imperative.* The main theme of this observer team is that the voters are eager to vote as good patriots, loyal to the militarized terrorist state that Ronald Reagan and the State Department find acceptable. Max Singer says that "I did sense that Guatemalans feel that voting is important to them." (This is correct, but Singer was not contemplating the possibility that its importance to them might lie in fear and a desire to avoid retribution by the omnipresent army.) Regula said that the people were patiently waiting "for an opportunity to share in the process of choosing the constituent assembly." According to Simcox, "They know that this was the patriotic thing to do, that this was important for their country." Tom Kahn found that the people he talked to in voting lines "expressed a great sense of national pride."

4. *Absence of any sign of coercion.* Father Kenneth Baker stated that "there seemed to be a general atmosphere of no intimidation." Baker didn't say how he sensed this atmosphere, and whether it was assuredly reliable in a foreign country observed for a day under military guard. Baker referred to the bishops having urged people to vote, but he failed to note their extended observations suggesting that a meaningful election couldn't be held in an environment of disappearances, terror, and catastrophic socioeconomic conditions. Jack Brier saw "absolutely no violence. I saw no evidence of direct military involvement." A problem that Brier doesn't discuss is that if pacification is thorough, no violence or substantial military presence will be necessary to confirm military choices. There is absolutely no violence or evidence of direct military involvement in elections in the Soviet Union. Brier plays dumb, pretending that violence on election day is really relevant, and ignoring the long-term violence that strips away institutional protections and produces a terrorized population.[2] Congressman Mickey Edwards did find a military presence in Guatemala, but it was not "oppressive": "We did not find anything to indicate that the people in those areas were under any pressure or intimidation." How hard Edwards looked must remain in doubt.[3]

5. *Amazing turnout.* Jack Brier referred to the "surprisingly large turnout," and Ed Simcox found the 60–70 percent turnout "really an incredibly positive statistic." Even the U.S. embassy noted that voting in Guatemala is compulsory (although it tried to discount this by citing a Guatemalan official who said that the law was only rarely enforced). The official observers, however, never mentioned this small matter of a legal requirement, or the need to get an ID card stamped, let alone the army warnings and the background of mass killings and disappearances.

6. *Human rights improving.* Congressman Mickey Edwards found that "by all objective observations, the human-rights record in this country has improved tremendously over the last two or three years." He does not say what objective observations he is referring to. Max Singer also found that "the human-rights record is improving in Guatemala, as near as I can tell," partly because the guerrilla movement has weakened, and that movement has been a serious threat to the human rights of the Guatemalan people. Singer was asked in the press conference how he determined this improvement. His answer was "From the statements of people living in the countryside."

7. *Reason for the blank and spoiled votes.* Some 26 percent of the ballots cast in the Guatemalan election, far exceeding the total for any party, were blank or spoiled. This would seem to compromise the notion that the Guatemalan people had gotten into long lines out of patriotic enthusiasm. Howard Penniman explained, however, that this was a result of illiteracy. Other possibilities are unmentioned. Why the illiteracy rates were so high thirty years after the United States saved Guatemala for freedom is also not discussed.

8. ***The case for further aid.*** The observers showed their objectivity, and the labor representatives Kahn and Friedman demonstrated their commitment to liberal principles, by acknowledging that this election was only a "first step," and that a full-fledged democracy such as that just established in El Salvador (Regula) was still to come. Some of the observers would sanction additional aid immediately, Mickey Edwards urging that the Guatemalan army would benefit from being "exposed to American values and to American training."[4] The others were more noncommittal, but agreed that the election was fair, meaningful, and deserving of U.S. recognition and support.

In sum, this was a caricature of observation, but a fairly typical performance of U.S. "official observers." The report of this group was cited by Stephen Kinzer in the *New York Times* and elsewhere in the U.S. press as a serious source of information on the Guatemalan election. The official report of the Latin American Studies Association on the Nicaraguan election, written by specialists in the region after an intensive eight-day investigation, Kinzer and his mass-media colleagues never mentioned.

Appendix 2

TAGLIABUE'S FINALE ON THE BULGARIAN CONNECTION:

A Case Study in Bias

To show in another way the propagandistic quality of the mass media's coverage of the Bulgarian Connection, we will examine in detail the article by John Tagliabue, "Verdict on Papal Plot, But No Answer," published in the *New York Times* on March 31, 1986. This piece, which provides a final wrap-up that enters "history" as the mature judgment of the veteran *Times* newsman assigned to the Rome trial, is a model illustration of the systematic bias that we believe characterized mass-media reporting of the Bulgarian Connection, with only minor exceptions. A close examination shows how Tagliabue incorporates all of the elements of the Sterling-Henze-Kalb (SHK) model of the connection, selects facts in accordance with the requirements of that model, and bypasses conflicting facts and interpretations.[1]

The Framing of the Issue: The Case Still "Unresolved"

The court dismissal of the case against the Bulgarians in Rome confronted the *Times* with a problem of framing. The *Times* had presented the case as plausible for years, and now had to confront the rejection of the case in a court decision. The solution was to latch on to the peculiar feature of the Italian judicial system whereby a party found not guilty can be declared positively innocent or not guilty for reason of lack of evidence. Thus, as the title of Tagliabue's article suggests, there was a verdict, but "no answer," and Tagliabue's first paragraph focuses on the "unresolved" nature of the case. It would have been possible to stress the fact that the Bulgarians were found *not guilty* for lack of evidence, and to emphasize that Western law requires positive proof of guilt. But the *Times* was not about to acknowledge defeat after five years of finding the Bulgarians guilty.

Tagliabue also downplays the court decision by making it an unsurprising event. "Few people were surprised by the verdict," states Tagliabue. But the failure to find the Bulgarians guilty should have been quite surprising, given the earlier assurances by Sterling and associates that the Bulgarians were clearly behind the plot, and that, as Paul Henze stated, the "evidence" has "steadily accumulated to the point where little real doubt is now possible."[2]

An alternative frame would have been as follows: After a three-year investigation and lengthy trial, backed by the resources of the Italian state, and despite the powerful interests in Italy and the West with a stake in finding the Bulgarians guilty, the prosecution still failed to persuade an Italian jury of Bulgarian guilt. These vested interests and their propaganda vehicles were given a bone to chew on, however, in the form of a decision to dismiss the charge for "lack of evidence," rather than complete exoneration. This then allowed the propaganda agencies to frame the case in the Tagliabue manner.

Protection of the Italian Judicial Process

Throughout the history of the case, the U.S. mass media blacked out evidence of the compromised quality of the Italian institutions involved in pursuing the connection. Investigating Judge Martella was always treated as a model of probity, and conflicting facts were ignored.[3] Operating in this tradition, Tagliabue wastes space on a gratuitous and irrelevant accolade to Martella (which is also given a subheading for emphasis). His statement that "Few people stood up to assail the magistrate" is absurd, as the trial witnesses were asked to give concrete evidence on the facts of the case; they were not in a position to assail the pretrial investigating magistrate, and any such attempts would have been impermissible in the courtroom. Only the Bulgarian defense was well qualified and able to assail Martella, and they did so, in effective statements on March 4–8, 1986, that were unreported in the *Times* and the rest of the mass media. Tagliabue points out that although the trial was supposed merely to verify the findings of the preliminary investigation, in fact the prosecution did a great deal of new investigative work. This suggests that the trial court may have found Martella's investigation sadly lacking, but Tagliabue never addresses the point.

Agca's Desertion of the Case

An important part of the apologetic framework is the claim that Agca, who had presented an allegedly coherent version of a connection up to the trial, suddenly did an about face and refused to testify altogether. Tagliabue devotes several paragraphs to this theme, eventually suggesting that Agca's increasingly erratic behavior "may have been designed to torpedo the efforts of the court." He suggests that the prosecutor couldn't overcome this difficulty, so that the loss of the case is lodged in Agca's behavior rather than in any inherent deficiencies in the prosecution's case.

In reality, Agca's claims emerged very slowly and contradictorily, with dozens of retractions that, taken together, are best explained by coaching, outside information, and guesses by Agca as to what Martella and the press would like to hear. There is no reason to believe that Agca ever offered or settled upon a coherent version of a Bulgarian connection. On the contrary, it appears that his version changed continually, and that the final result in Martella's report was Martella's own arbitrary synthesis.[4]

The claim that Agca became more erratic during the trial is also not based on evidence. Agca's persistently erratic behavior was obscured by the secrecy of his earlier testimony, but it is clear from the Martella report that he was already claiming to be Jesus and displaying other symptoms of irrationality. Furthermore, Tagliabue's statement that Agca refused to cooperate during the trial is false—Agca periodically withdrew from the proceedings when his testimony became too incoherent, but he always returned to the stand, and he answered a vast number of questions. One hypothesis that Tagliabue never entertains is that if Agca's claims were based on coaching and/or imagination, in an open court he would be vulnerable and quickly pushed to the wall.

Tagliabue also never asks this further question: Even if Agca had clammed up (which was not true), given the extensive Martella investigation and report, why would the court not be able to follow the already established leads to a successful outcome? Why was not a single witness produced to confirm Agca's allegations of numerous meetings and trips with Bulgarians in Rome? Why was the car allegedly rented by the Bulgarians never found? Where is the money supposedly given to Agca? Tagliabue fails to address these questions.

"Partial Confirmation" of Agca's Tale

Tagliabue describes some alleged partial confirmations of Agca's claims. The first is that "Mr. Ozbey said the Bulgarians had indeed wanted to use Mr. Agca to shoot the Pope, but did not trust him." But this is not a partial confirmation if the net result was that the Bulgarians failed to hire Agca. Furthermore, another reporter present when Ozbey testified in Rome claims that Ozbey did *not* tell the court that the Bulgarians "wanted to use" Agca. According to Wolfgang Achtner, of ABC-TV News, in Rome, the only thing Ozbey said was that the Bulgarians "listened with interest, but behaved with indifference" (the translation by the Turkish interpreter in court), or "listened with interest but didn't take it seriously" (Achtner's own translation). In short, it would appear that Tagliabue has doctored the evidence.

The other "partial confirmation" is that "Catli hinted at obscure secret service contacts with West German intelligence, and of payments for unspecified purposes to Turks involved in the investigations." This vague statement does not even mention the plot against the pope and is partial confirmation of nothing. The most important Catli evidence bearing on this point was his description of the attempt by the West German police to bribe Agca's supposed co-conspirator Oral Celik to come to West Germany and confirm Agca's claims. This supports the coaching hypothesis: accordingly, Tagliabue blacks it out. The only other testimony by Catli mentioning the secret services involved Gray Wolves leader Ali Batman, who told Catli he had heard from the German secret police that at a meeting in Romania, the Warsaw Pact powers had decided to kill the pope. This was apparently a leak of the forged SISMI document of May 19, 1981, which had made this claim. Thus the hearsay recounting of the substance of a forgery is Tagliabue's "partial confirmation" of Agca's claims of a plot.

We should also note that while he cites these alleged "partial confirmations," nowhere does Tagliabue list the contentions of Agca that remained unconfirmed.

The Soviet-Bulgarian Motive

Two of Tagliabue's thirty-two paragraphs were devoted to expounding the Soviet motive in allegedly sponsoring Agca's assassination attempt: "to crack religiously inspired resistance to Communist rule in Poland." Tagliabue here follows a long-standing *Times* tradition of absolutely refusing to allow a counterargument to be voiced on this issue. Even if they covered their tracks well, a Soviet-inspired murder of the pope would have been blamed on the Soviets, solidified Polish hostility, and had enormously damaging effects on Soviet relations with Western Europe. Thus it would have been risky without any offsetting benefits.[5]

Who gained and who lost from the plot? Were there any possible Western motives that might bear on the case? Tagliabue follows the SHK line in failing to raise these questions. But once Agca was imprisoned in Italy, cold warriors of the West had much to gain and little to lose by manipulating Agca to pin the assassination attempt on the East. Tagliabue mentions that the charges of a Bulgarian Connection surfaced "at the nadir" of U.S.-Soviet relations. While he notes how this added to the credibility of the plot in the West, he never hints at the possibility that its serviceability to the new Cold War might *explain* Agca's belated confession.

Agca's Stay in Bulgaria

This has always been critical in the Sterling-*Times* scenarios, and Tagliabue drags it in. It is given further emphasis with the heading "Spent 2 Months in Bulgaria." Tagliabue does not mention that Agca stopped in eleven other countries. He fails to note here, and the *Times* suppressed throughout, Catli's testimony in Rome that the Gray Wolves liked to go through Bulgaria to reach Western Europe because the heavy Turkish traffic made it easy to hide. Tagliabue fails to mention that bringing Agca for a long stay in Sofia would have been a violation of the rule of plausible deniability. Even more so would be using Bulgarians to help Agca in Rome. Tagliabue does not discuss the question of plausible deniability. He also fails to note that if Agca had stayed in Sofia for a while, this would allow a prima facie case to be made by a Western propagandist that the East was behind the shooting, and could provide the basic materials for working Agca over for the desired confession.

Bulgarian Involvement in Turkey

Tagliabue asserts that the Bulgarians were "purportedly" supporting both the extreme left and right in Turkey "to promote instability" in a conflict "that pitted violent leftist terrorists against their counterparts on the right." This is a Sterling myth, with Tagliabue hiding behind "purportedly" to allow him to pass off myth as purported evidence. The equating of left and right in the Turkish violence of the 1970s is false: the great majority of violent attacks were launched by the Gray Wolves, under the protection of the police and military. Tagliabue also fails to discuss the fact that the extreme right actually participated in the government in 1977 and had extensive links to the army and intelligence services. The claim of Bulgarian support for both the right and left has never been supported by evidence. Tagliabue never mentions that the United States had more than "purported" links with the Turkish army, the secret services, and the Fascist Nationalist Action party, and that the terrorist events of the late 1970s eventually served U.S. interests well.

Key Question: How Agca Knew So Much

The "key question" for Tagliabue is "how Agca knew what he knew and when he knew it." This is an important issue, but there are others that he might have raised if he had worked outside the SHK format. Why did it take Agca so long to name Bulgarians? Was he subject to any coercion or offered any positive inducements to make him talk. Why did he have to make major retractions? Is it not suspicious that when Agca finally talked, he said just what his interrogators wanted him to say? How are we to evaluate a judicial process where the witness (Agca) was in regular contact with outside sources of information, and where he could lie and retract evidence without penalty?

"Even the Attorneys for the Bulgarians...."

In assessing how Agca knew so much, Tagliabue allocates only one paragraph to the possibility that Agca was coached. On the other hand, he goes to great pains to stress that Agca knew an awful lot—telephone numbers, personal habits, nicknames. Tagliabue gives as the "simplest explanation" of Agca's knowledge that he had access to books, newspapers, magazines, and other materials from the outside. Interestingly, he fails to mention the numerous prison contacts between Agca and secret service, Mafia, and Vatican agents and emissaries. Agca even wrote a letter to the Vatican complaining of the pressure from its representative in prison (also linked to the Mafia), a fact long blacked out by the *Times.* These visits would point to the ease with which Agca could have been fed information while in prison. Tagliabue will not admit facts that get into this dangerous territory.

A major question is how Agca knew details about Antonov's apartment *when he later admitted to Martella that he had never been there.* The Bulgarians and Antonov's defense went to great pains to prove that the information Agca provided about Antonov's apartment had never been divulged in the media before Agca enumerated the details. This implied coaching, as did a mistake in identification where Agca described a characteristic of Antonov's apartment that fitted other apartments in the building, but not Antonov's. Tagliabue says that "Even the attorneys for the Bulgarians acknowledge" that Agca named things not available through reading the papers, as if they were conceding a point, not making a devastating case for coaching. Newspaper work couldn't be more dishonest than this.

"The More Sinister View"

In a single, late paragraph devoted to the possibility of coaching, Tagliabue merely asserts it as a claim, without providing a single supportive point of evidence, although there are many.[6] He uses a double propagandist's put-down—ironically designating the coaching hypothesis as "the more sinister view," and stating that it is "espoused by critics of the case on the political left, including Soviet bloc governments." Even Tagliabue, in his earlier news reports, had mentioned Mafia official Giovanni Pandico's statement in Italy outlining a scenario of coaching at which he claimed to be present, but Tagliabue doesn't even cite this or any other documents or facts that lend support to the coaching hypothesis. He sticks to the ingredients that fit the SHK format—good Martella, Agca the betrayer of the case, the Soviet motive, Agca's visit to Bulgaria, and his knowledge of details. All other materials are designated "sinister" or blacked out to enhance the credibility of the party line.

Agca Helped the Bulgarians

Tagliabue closes his article with a quote from Agca's attorney that the Bulgarians "should be thankful" to Agca. This reiterates one of Tagliabue's preferred themes—that Agca deliberately blew the case. This is derived from Sterling's theory that Agca's vacillations were really "signals" to the Bulgarians, alternately threatening and rewarding them, but aiming at getting them to help him out of jail. In his earlier articles Tagliabue followed this line, and it is implicit in this summing-up article, although it is a wholly unproven Sterling gimmick.[7] What was Agca bargaining for in the trial? Did he expect the Bulgarians to spring him? To admit their own involvement in the case by arranging a deal for his release? And if he was sabotaging the case in order to win favor with the Bulgarians, and since the Bulgarians obviously refused to respond, why did he not finally decide to do them injury? Tagliabue never addresses these points.

In sum, this is a model case of propaganda under the guise of "news" or "news analysis." In this instance there are a number of lies, but these are less important than the other systematic distortions. Tagliabue and the *Times* frame the issue in terms of probable Bulgarian guilt and the factors that caused the case to be lost—exclusive of those suggesting that there was no case to begin with. They refuse to discuss the failure to obtain confirmation of any factual claims of meetings or deals with Bulgarians. They fail to discuss—or even to mention—problems of plausible deniability. They reiterate the elements of the preferred SHK model without noting the illogic or the incompatible facts. They ignore evidence that would support the coaching model. They use invidious language only for the disfavored line of argument and spokespersons, manipulating words and bending evidence to the desired end. This article should be perfect for classroom use in courses on propaganda, media bias, and related subjects.

Appendix 3

BRAESTRUP'S *BIG STORY*:

Some "Freedom House Exclusives"

In "The Tet offensive" (p. 211), we considered the example that has regularly been put forth to substantiate the charge that the media adopt an "adversarial stance" with regard to established power—coverage of the Tet offensive—and the Freedom House study on which this charge is based. As we saw, in this case too the behavior of the media conforms to the expectations of the propaganda model, and the major theses advanced in the Freedom House study are refuted even by their own evidence. What remains of their charge is the possibility that media coverage of the Tet offensive was technically incompetent, although subordinated to elite requirements. Turning to a closer examination of this charge, we find that the shoe is on the other foot: when "Freedom House exclusives" are corrected, the performance of the media appears quite creditable, while the incompetence of the Freedom House study is seen to transcend even the level already demonstrated. That this study has been taken seriously, and permitted to set much of the agenda for subsequent discussion, is a most intriguing fact.

According to Freedom House, television commentary and *Newsweek* are the worst offenders in this "extreme case" of journalistic incompetence, so let us begin by reviewing some of their sins. One example to which Braestrup reverts several times is Walter Cronkite's "much publicized half-hour CBS 'special' on the war" on February 27 (*Big Story,* I, 158). According to Braestrup, Cronkite's "assessment" here is "that U.S. troops would have to garrison the countryside" (I, 645). In his foreword, Leonard Sussman properly observes that "We do not expect the reader to accept on faith our various analyses or judgments," and so "the complete texts of many of the reports discussed" are presented, primarily in volume II (I, x). Following his advice, we turn to volume II, where we find the complete text of Cronkite's "special" (180ff.). There is not even a remote hint of the "assessment" that Braestrup attributes to him.

In this important "special," Braestrup claims, "In effect, Cronkite seemed to say, the ruins, the refugees, the disruption of pacification that came at Tet added up to a defeat for the allies that would force President Johnson to the negotiating table" (I, 158). Cronkite says nothing of the kind. He reports that "there are doubts about the measure of success or setback," noting accurately that "the experts do not agree on the objectives or on the amount of success the communists had in achieving them." They "failed" in many of their aims, but in a third phase the enemy might "recoup there what he lost in the first two phases." In what he calls a "speculative, personal, subjective" judgment, Cronkite states that he is "not sure . . . who won and who lost," or to what extent. He concludes that the United States is probably "mired in stalemate," and that historians may conclude that the Tet battle was "a draw"; "To suggest we are on the edge of defeat is to yield to unreasonable pessimism." He does not say that Johnson will be "forced" to the negotiating table by a "defeat," but rather that if indeed there is a "stalemate," then "the only rational way out then will be to negotiate, not as victors, but as an honorable people who lived up to their pledge to defend democracy, and did the best they could." Note the typical reiteration of government propaganda concerning American aims, unsullied by the factual record—enormous in scale, by this time—of U.S. government efforts to undermine democracy and to destroy all popular forces—the NLF, the Buddhist "third force," etc.—in South Vietnam, on the assumption, openly admitted, that the forces placed in power by U.S. violence could not survive political competition. Recall also that in these comments that Freedom House derides, Cronkite reaches essentially the same conclusion as did the chairman of the Joint Chiefs of Staff, General Wheeler, in his summary to the president on the same day as Cronkite's broadcast, and the president's advisers a month later.

We may note also that two weeks earlier, Cronkite had "assessed" the impact of the Communist offensive, on the basis of U.S. and Vietnamese sources, reporting that "first, and simplest, the Vietcong suffered a military defeat" (I, 158). Similarly, on an NBC-TV special of March 10 that Braestrup repeatedly condemns, Howard Tuckner stated that "Militarily the allies won" (I, 159), as did others repeatedly.

Cronkite's "special" is exhibit A in the Freedom House indictment. The example is typical of the relation between their conclusions and the evidence they cite.

Braestrup refers to a television comment by Robert Schakne on February 28 for which he gives the following paraphrase: "In short, the United States would now have to take over the whole war, including the permanently damaged pacification program, because of Saigon's failures" (I, 562–63). Braestrup claims further that Schackne attributed "this argument" to Robert Komer. This he calls "a CBS exclusive," his standard term of derision. In fact, "this argument" is yet another "Freedom House exclusive." What Schackne said, according to Braestrup, is that it was "likely" that Komer was in Washington with General Wheeler to ask for more troops "to help get the Vietnam pacification program back on the road." The preceding day, Wheeler had requested that the troop level be raised from 525,000 to 731,756, one primary concern being that "There is no doubt that the RD Program [pacification] has suffered a severe set back," that "To a large extent the VC now control the countryside," and that "US forces will be required in a number of places to assist and encourage the Vietnamese Army to leave the cities and towns and reenter the country."[1] While Braestrup's version of Schackne's "argument" has little resemblance to the actual words he attributes to Schackne, these words were, if anything, understated.

Braestrup then goes on to claim that Cronkite "used the same argument almost verbatim, but with an even stronger conclusion" in a February 28 radio broadcast. There is no hint in the actual broadcast of Braestrup's "argument." The closest Cronkite came to this "argument" is his statement that *"presumably, Ambassador Komer told a sad tale to President Johnson"* (Braestrup's emphasis). Cronkite then repeated accurately the basic facts presented by Komer in a briefing four days earlier. He concluded that "it seems likely that today Ambassador Komer asked President Johnson for more American troops so that we can permanently occupy the hamlets and fulfill the promise of security [*sic*] to their residents, a promise the Vietnamese alone apparently cannot honor," the NLF not being Vietnamese, as usual. Apart from the tacit assumption of the propaganda system that the villagers yearn for the fulfillment of this "promise of security" from the NLF, Cronkite's speculation that U.S. troops would have to fulfill a promise that ARVN *alone* apparently could not honor hardly seems unreasonable, three days after General Westmoreland had stated that "additional U.S. forces would probably be required" (II, 159), and that with them "we could more effectively deny the enemy his objectives"; four days after Komer had described the Tet offensive as a "considerable setback" to pacification; a day after Cronkite had presented a television interview with Captain Donald Jones, deputy pacification adviser for the district regarded as "the bowl of pacification," who said that "for most of the District, pacification does not exist," and travel there is impossible (CBS-TV "special" of February 27, cited above); and one day after General Wheeler had asked for a huge troop increase justified in part by the need to overcome the fact that "To a large extent the VC now control the countryside."

Television and radio are not alone in being subjected to "Freedom House exclusives." Here are a few examples.

Exuding contempt and derision, the study informs us that "no one" except for George McArthur (AP) and Don Oberdorfer (Knight) "reported . . . on what happened to Hue's civilians under Vietcong rule" (I, 299). Again demonstrating his considerable gift for self-refutation, Braestrup cites reports on Vietcong executions, kidnappings, burial of executed civilians in mass graves, etc., in Hué under Viet Cong rule by *Newsweek*, UPI, *Washington Post*, William Ryan, Reuters, *New York Times*, *Time*, *London Times*, and the NBC "Today" show (I, 277, 281–84, 472). On page 283, Braestrup writes that "The television networks, as far as our records show, made no mention of the executions at all"; on page 472, he refutes this claim, noting that on February 28, in an "aftermath film report from Hue . . . at battle's end," the NBC "Today" show "hinted at the Hue massacre with this statement: 'Hundreds of government workers were killed and thrown into temporary graves.' " A rather broad "hint," it would seem. The example is typical of the Freedom House style of handling evidence.

In this connection, we should observe that the numerous stories on the Hué massacre cited by Braestrup in self-refutation referred to the official allegations that 300 to 400 government officials were killed in Hué, a considerable massacre but "only one-tenth of the civilian toll in the fighting," so that "it did not seem like a major story," Gareth Porter comments; he adds that "What made the 'Hue massacre' a major story was the publicizing by U.S. embassy propagandist Douglas Pike, who wrote a pamphlet on the subject in late 1969 at the request of the American ambassador to Saigon, Ellsworth Bunker." Pike's account was given wide coverage when it appeared and has become the basis for the standard versions since, despite the dubious source: "given the fact that Pike was relying on the Saigon political warfare department for most of his data, which was otherwise unverified, one might have asked for more skepticism and reserve from the press," Porter observes—rather plausibly, it would seem. Porter adds that the documents made available by the U.S. mission in 1971 "contradicted Pike on every major point." According to former CIA analyst Frank Snepp, "The whole idea of a bloodbath was conjured out of thin air," and the stories were planted in the press by American officials "to generate sympathy for the South Vietnamese abroad"—in short, the "careful psychological warfare program pinning the blame on the communists" urged by "seasoned observers," as John Lengel of AP reported from Hué.[2]

Presenting no evidence or argument, Braestrup accepts Pike's analysis and the U.S. government position as correct. In a footnote, he remarks that "Pike's account was challenged by D. Gareth Porter, a Cornell University graduate student, admirer of the National Liberation Front, and, briefly, a Saigon resident," but dismisses this as part of "a minor point of political contention" (I, 285–86). He describes Pike, in contrast, as "the independent-minded USIA specialist on the Vietcong" (I, 196),[3] and makes no reference to the detailed analysis of Pike's allegations that had been presented by Porter, one of the few American scholars concerned with Vietnam. Similarly, Leonard Sussman takes it as obvious, without argument, that the government position must be correct, and that "the war's largest systematic execution of civilians" is the responsibility of the Viet Cong—thus excluding the systematic slaughter of thousands of civilians in Hué by U.S. firepower, possibly including many of those attributed to the Viet Cong massacre.[4] Also unmentioned here is the curious timing of the exposures that have since become the standard version of the Hué massacre, a few days after the belated exposure of the My Lai massacre in late November 1969, when

> Army officers in Saigon made available "newly found" captured Viet Cong documents showing that Communist troops killed nearly 2,900 Vietnamese during the Hue offensive in February, 1968. Officers said the documents went unnoticed in U.S. military files for nineteen months until a correspondent's questions about Hue brought them to light. "I know it sounds incredible, but that's the truth," one official said.[5]

We will not attempt to explore in this review what is not so much as attempted in the Freedom House study, but merely note, once again, that we have here not a work of scholarship but rather a government propaganda tract.

Max Frankel commented in the *New York Times* (Feb. 11, 1968) that pressures at home and in Vietnam "are thought to have raised once again the temptation of further military escalation" (I, 584, italicized by Braestrup for emphasis as an example of raising "straw men"). Frankel was quite accurate in this measured statement. As Braestrup points out, "Wheeler and Westmoreland agreed that it was also a good time to urge a bolder Vietnam strategy, with more troops to gain quicker results: i.e., forays into Laos, Cambodia, and possibly that part of North Vietnam just above the DMZ." Why then the "straw man" charge? Because, Braestrup objects, escalation "was hardly a *tempting* prospect for Johnson" (his emphasis), hardly Frankel's point. Braestrup claims further that Frankel, in this article, suggested "that escalation—notably a reserve call-up—was probable" (I, 586). Frankel's article does not appear in the accompanying volume of documents; turning to it, we discover that Braestrup's claim is another Freedom House exclusive, suggested nowhere in Frankel's article, which is noteworthy only for its standard reiteration of government propaganda about the goal of bringing "security" to "the people of South Vietnam"—by B-52 bombing of villages, the exploits of Task Force Barker at and around My Lai at just that time as part of the general ravaging of Quang Ngai Province, etc.

After television, *Newsweek* is the worst offender. Let us therefore inquire further into its misdeeds. In what Braestrup describes as "*Newsweek*'s major statement on the Thieu-Ky regime," a March 18 feature entitled "Vietnam: A Reappraisal," the journal commented accurately in an editorial entitled "The Political Morass" that "land reform, a vital element in any effort to win the loyalty of the peasantry, has not been tackled seriously" (I, 534–36), a truism familiar to everyone from the American high command to officials in Washington. Braestrup comments: "It is difficult, once again, to fathom *Newsweek*'s logic. Surely, neither *Newsweek* nor the Vietnamese peasant expected the regime to tackle land reform seriously in the aftermath of Tet." It is perfectly obvious that in this "reappraisal," *Newsweek* is referring to the general picture, not specifically to the post-Tet period of one month.

According to Braestrup, "*Newsweek*, throughout the February–March 1968 period, was to refer, in passing, to the 'wily' Giap, 'tough' North Vietnamese regulars, 'ominous' enemy activity, and in general, to a foe without setbacks or flaws" (I, 229). Turning to the facts, on March 11, *Newsweek* presented an analysis in which it reported that the Communists "were still plagued by the confusion that is characteristic of all military operations." The report (II, 216f.) goes on to describe "inexplicable" failure to blow up a crucial bridge, failure to use main forces adequately to maintain momentum, misassessment of popular moods and U.S.-ARVN tactics, inadequate preparation of troops, etc., concluding that "the communists did not achieve most of their objectives." The following week's article on Khe Sanh reports a marine view that "Charlie missed his golden opportunity" by bad tactics. *Newsweek*'s picture of "a foe without setbacks or flaws" is another Freedom House exclusive.

What of the other sins? As for the reference to the "wily" Giap, compare *Newsweek* with what Braestrup regards as the outstanding analysis by Douglas Pike, who describes Giap as a "master tactician," "one of the best tactical commanders of the 20th century," etc. (I, 196f.). On the "toughness" of the North Vietnamese and their "ominous" activity, see the regular reports of the U.S. military command, and an extensive literature by Vietnam veterans.

Braestrup claims that "one searches in vain through most of the media descriptions of the foe, even well into March 1968, for indications that the enemy's planning, tactics, execution, zeal, and weaponry were less than flawless"; "there were few hints in *Times* analyses or battlefield reporting that the foe was anything but shrewd, tenacious, ascetic, infallible and menacing, and in this case the paper had plenty of company" (I, 186, 216). Apart from "flawless" and "infallible," further Freedom House exclusives, the adjectives can be taken from the military reports and seem unexceptionable. The claim that the media regarded the enemy as infallible is defended through pages 186 to 231, along with typical Freedom House self-refutation: example after example to the contrary is cited, in addition to those just mentioned. The media reported that the VC "undoubtedly" alienated the population, as they caused "indiscriminate slaughter" and "totally misjudged the mood of the South Vietnamese." They may be suffering "a severe manpower problem" and "hurting badly."[6] They "failed to achieve their main objectives." Captured VC got lost in Saigon and were falsely told that they would be welcomed. (This appears under Braestrup's heading "Television: in praise of the VC.") They did not "get—or heed" important information. And so on. All in all, hardly the picture of an "infallible" and "flawless" enemy.

Note also the Freedom House assumption that a free press, militantly guarding its objectivity, should not only consider those who are resisting the U.S. attack as "the enemy," "the foe," etc., but must also refrain from accurately describing "the enemy" as tough, resolute, and courageous. To play its proper role in a free society by Freedom House standards, the media should never veer a moment from the kind of service to the state demanded and secured by force in totalitarian states, so it appears.

The impact of the Freedom House study comes from the impression of massive documentation and the huge resources that were employed to obtain and analyze it. Case by case, the examples collapse on inspection. Here are a few more examples, far from exhaustive.[7]

On pacification, "TV and radio commentators went far beyond the available information to imply the dramatic worst." Three examples are cited to prove the point (I, 565). Howard Tuckner, of NBC-TV, reported from New York the views of "U.S. intelligence officials" and "Some U.S. officials in Vietnam"—correctly, as Braestrup concedes in a footnote, adding that these were the views of "CIA in *Washington*" and "Disheartened junior CORDS officials in Vietnam." By Freedom House standards, it is improper to cite such sources accurately. The second example is a CBS radio report criticized only for being "depressed"—as were pacification officials on the ground. The third example is from an NBC-TV "special," in which Dean Brelis says that we don't know what is happening in the rural areas but "can only imagine," and that "the cities are no longer secure; perhaps they never were."[8] Hardly remarkable, and far from the fevered conclusion drawn in Braestrup's paraphrase.

Examples of what Braestrup calls "straw man journalism" abound in his own presentation. Thus he faults the media for claiming that the pacification program had been destroyed, whereas his own conclusion is that "pacification, although hit hard, was not 'dead' . . . it was a mixed picture, but clearly neither a military nor a psychological 'disaster' " (I, 716). The media regularly reported that pacification was hit hard, not dead, as his own evidence clearly shows—in contrast to the Pentagon, which took a more pessimistic view, as we shall see directly. Braestrup's "straw man journalism" may impress careless readers skimming the text for dramatic conclusions, but it presents no evidence and amounts to no argument.

Braestrup refers sarcastically to "insights into Vietnamese psychology," as when Morley Safer, watching marines burning down huts in Cam Ne, concluded that a peasant whose home was destroyed would find it hard to believe "that we are on his side" (I, 43). How does Safer know? Perhaps the peasant enjoyed watching the flames. Not all such "psychoanalyzing" is derided, however, as when General Westmoreland explains that "the people in the cities are largely indignant at the Vietcong for violating the sanctity of the Tet period and for their tactics which brought about damage to the cities" (II, 164), or when he expounds on the peasant "state of mind" (I, 78). Note that Safer is not criticized for accepting the tacit assumption that the press is an agency of the invading army ("*we* are on his side").

Braestrup states that "the embassy fight became the *whole* Tet offensive on TV and in the newspapers during that offensive's second day" (his emphasis; I, 126); this illustration of the incompetence of the media is thoroughly refuted by his story index. He also claims that the media exaggerated VC success in the early confusion by claiming that the embassy had been entered—failing, however, to compare these accounts with the reports by military police that they were taking fire from inside the embassy, or the message log of the 716th MP Battalion, which reads: "General Westmoreland calls; orders first priority effort to *recapture* U.S. Embassy" (I, 92; our emphasis). It is intriguing to read Braestrup's outrage over quite accurate press reporting of what was said by Westmoreland, military police involved in the fight, and others, and in particular over the fact that the press did not simply rely on Westmoreland's later account (his apparent belief that the embassy had been "captured" goes beyond any reporter's error that Braestrup cites). A careful reading shows that media reports were surprisingly accurate, given the confusion of the moment, although one cannot fault Braestrup's profound conclusion that "first reports are always partly wrong," which will come as a startling insight to the working journalist.

Repeatedly, the study claims that the media were "vengeful" or bent on "retribution" in reacting skeptically to government claims. An alternative possibility is that this reaction reflected a newfound realism. Braestrup agrees, for example, that "Westmoreland was wrong in publicly underestimating (in November [1967]) the enemy" (I, 69), and cites many other false and misleading optimistic statements, among them Robert Komer's prediction of "steady progress in pacification" a week before the Tet offensive (I, 72; Braestrup's paraphrase). In fact, part of the shock of the Tet offensive resulted from the faith of the media in previous government assessments, undermined by the Tet offensive, as the U.S. military and official Washington were well aware.

Furthermore, General Westmoreland's accounts were hardly persuasive during the offensive. Thus he claimed that "all 11 of the Vietnamese division commanders . . . commanded their units effectively," whereas, as a journalist learned, one "had gone into a state of shock during the Tet attacks" (I, 454–55). Or consider Westmoreland's claim that allegations about inaccuracy and inflation of body counts were "one of the great distortions of the war" by the media—there were at most "relatively small inaccuracies" (II, 163). His own generals had a rather different view. In his study of the opinions of the generals, General Douglas Kinnard reports that 61 percent of those responding describe the body count as "often inflated," and only 26 percent "within reason accurate." The responses include: "a fake—totally worthless," "often blatant lies," "a blot on the honor of the Army," and "grossly exaggerated by many units primarily because of the incredible interest shown by people like McNamara and Westmoreland." Perhaps journalists had some reason for skepticism, apart from "vengefulness."[9]

To demonstrate the absurd extent of press efforts to find shock value, Braestrup cites a story in *Time* on enemy tunneling at Khe Sanh, *"as occurred around Dienbienphu"* (I, 435; his emphasis), in general ridiculing the analogy—but forgetting to ridicule the remark by Marine Commander General Cushman, who said that "He is digging trenches and doing other tricks of the trade which he learned to do at Dienbienphu" (I, 403).

"All Vietnam, it appeared on film at home, was in flames or being battered into ruins, and all Vietnamese civilians were homeless refugees," Braestrup alleges (I, 234), in typically fanciful rhetoric, adding that "there were virtually no films shown or photographs published during this period of *undamaged* portions of Saigon, Hue, or other cities" (his emphasis). This shows that coverage was unbalanced, supportive of the enemy. One wonders how many films and photographs of peaceful English villages or Hawaiian towns appeared on the days that Coventry and Pearl Harbor were bombed, to balance the picture.

Braestrup seeks the causes for the "exoneration of the Vietcong" for "killing noncombatants or causing the exodus of refugees" (I, 234), overlooking the fact that before seeking the cause of *x* it is necessary to show that *x* is true. In this case, it is not. The accounts he cites regularly blame the Viet Cong for civilian suffering and emphasize Viet Cong atrocities. In fact, he himself points out that "both *Time* and *Newsweek* put the onus on the Vietcong" in Saigon (I, 246)—as elsewhere. *Newsweek* titled an article "The VC's Week of Terror" (Feb. 12) and described VC terror squads executing civilians in Saigon (I, 490). Typically, the media blamed the Viet Cong for having "brought bullets and bombs into the very midst of heavily populated areas, causing indiscriminate slaughter of civilians caught in the cross fire and making homeless twice over the refugees who had fled to the cities for safety . . ." (*Time,* [I, 246]), adopting the position of U.S. government propaganda that the enemy is to blame if the United States kills and destroys, and failing to add that the refugees had fled to the cities for safety from massive U.S. violence and that such refugee generation was explicit policy.[10] In the *New York Times,* Charles Mohr wrote that "In one sense the Vietcong have been responsible for civilian deaths by launching the urban attacks," citing American officials who are "sure that the population will be bitter about the guerrillas because of their 'callous disregard for human life' " (I, 243). Meanwhile, AP, the *Washington Post,* NBC, and others reported Viet Cong causing destruction, using civilians as shields, preventing civilians from fleeing attack, murdering civilians, etc., often on the basis of flimsy evidence that would elicit much Freedom House derision if used to support accounts of American atrocities. In a typical misrepresentation, Braestrup claims that NBC-TV "attributed Saigon's losses *solely* to an allied military decision to 'kill or maim some of the people' to protect the rest" (our emphasis), citing Howard Tuckner's statement that there was a decision "that in order to protect most of the . . . people, they had to kill or maim some of the people"—a statement that is quite different from the paraphrase and is noteworthy only for its standard reference to "protecting" the victims (I, 249).

In general, far from "exonerating the Vietcong," the media bent over backwards to blame them for the casualties and destruction caused by the U.S. forces who were "protecting" and "defending" South Vietnam and its population, according to unquestioned dogma. While the reporting was generally accurate in a narrow sense, the framework and the general picture presented are outlandish, and conform closely to the demands of the state propaganda system. It is, once again, highly revealing that Freedom House regards such service to the state as unremarkable—indeed, insufficient, by its standards.

The more general summaries in the Freedom House study leave the evidence presented far behind. Thus the ruins and destruction "were presented as symbolic evidence of a stunning 'defeat' (variously implied or defined) for allied forces" (I, 621). "The Americans, by their heavy use of firepower in a few cities, were implicitly depicted as callously destroying all Vietnam . . ., while the Vietcong's indiscriminate use of their own firepower, as well as the Hue killings, were largely overlooked" (I, 286). The dominant themes in the media "added up to a portrait of defeat for the allies" (I, 705). "At Tet, the press shouted that the patient was dying" (I, 714). And so on.

We have already cited enough to show how much merit there is in these characterizations. Furthermore, as already indicated, the media reports generally conformed to those of the U.S. military, although they were often less extreme in suggesting enemy success, as we have seen. Braestrup is not unaware of this. He writes, for example, that "MACV spokesmen in Saigon themselves contributed in February to a general journalistic perception that no logistics, organizational, or manpower limitations inhibited the NVA's capacity, even after the 'first wave,' to strike anywhere at will ('No place was safe any more')" (I, 190). Furthermore, "most eyewitness combat reporting, rare and restricted as it was, showed up better in February than the MACV communiqués or the communiqué rewrites in Saigon" (I, 334). In fact, the military briefings cited are closely similar to media commentary in basic content, e.g., Brigadier General John Chaisson, February 3, who described "a real battle," "a very successful offensive in its initial phases," "surprisingly well coordinated," "surprisingly intensive," conducted with "a surprising amount of audacity"—for example, in Hué, where "the VC had the town," etc. Naturally the media varied more widely in content and style, but characterizations of the sort cited above must simply be dismissed as hysteria, even apart from the numerous misrepresentations and sheer fabrications.

If this is one of the great achievements of contemporary scholarship, as John Roche claims, then scholarship is in a bad way indeed.

Notes

Preface

1. We use the term "special interests" in its commonsense meaning, not in the Orwellian usage of the Reagan era, where it designates workers, farmers, women, youth, blacks, the aged and infirm, the unemployed—in short, the population at large. Only one group did not merit this appellation: corporations, and their owners and managers. They are not "special interests," they represent the "national interest." This terminology represents the reality of domination and the operational usage of "national interest" for the two major political parties. For a similar view, with evidence of the relevance of this usage to both major political parties, see Thomas Ferguson and Joel Rogers, *Right Turn: The Decline of the Democrats and the Future of American Politics* (New York: Hill and Wang, 1986), pp. 37–39 and passim.
2. Herbert Gans, for example, states that "The beliefs that actually make it into the news are *professional* values that are intrinsic to national journalism and that journalists learn on the job. . . . The rules of news judgment call for ignoring story implications . . ." ("Are U.S. Journalists Dangerously Liberal?" *Columbia Journalism Review* [Nov.–Dec. 1985], pp. 32–33). In his book *Deciding What's News* (New York: Vintage, 1980), Gans contends that media report-

ers are by and large "objective," but within a framework of beliefs in a set of "enduring values" that include "ethnocentrism" and "responsible capitalism," among others. We would submit that if reporters for *Pravda* were found to operate within the constraints of belief in the essential justice of the Soviet state and "responsible communism," this would be found to make any further discussion of "objectivity" pointless. Furthermore, as we shall document below, Gans greatly understates the extent to which media reporters work within a limiting framework of assumptions.

3. Neoconservative critiques of the mass media commonly portray them as bastions of liberal, antiestablishment attacks on the system. They ignore the fact that the mass media are large business corporations controlled by very wealthy individuals or other corporations, and that the members of what the neoconservatives describe as the "liberal culture" of the media are hired employees. They also disregard the fact that the members of this liberal culture generally accept the basic premises of the system and differ with other members of the establishment largely on the tactics appropriate to achieving common ends. The neoconservatives are simply not prepared to allow deviations from their own views. In our analysis in chapter 1, we describe them as playing the important role of "enforcers," attempting to browbeat the media into excluding from a hearing even the limited dissent now tolerated. For an analysis of the neoconservative view of the media, see Edward S. Herman and Frank Brodhead, "Ledeen on the Media," in *The Rise and Fall of the Bulgarian Connection* (New York: Sheridan Square Publications, 1986), pp. 166–70; George Gerbner, "Television: The Mainstreaming of America," in *Business and the Media,* Conference Report, Yankelovich, Skelly and White, November 19, 1981; Gans, "Are U.S. Journalists Dangerously Liberal?"

4. See Walter Lippmann, *Public Opinion* (1921; reprint, London: Allen & Unwin, 1932); Harold Lasswell, "Propaganda," in *Encyclopedia of the Social Sciences* (New York: Macmillan, 1933); Edward Bernays, *Propaganda* (New York: H. Liveright, 1928); M. J. Crozier, S. P. Huntington, and J. Watanuki, *The Crisis of Democracy: Report on the Governability of Democracies to the Trilateral Commission* (New York: New York University Press, 1975). For further discussion, see Noam Chomsky, *Towards a New Cold War* (New York: Pantheon, 1982), chapter 1. and references cited, particularly, Alex Carey, "Reshaping the Truth: Pragmatists and Propagandists in America," *Meanjin Quarterly* (Australia), vol. 35, no. 4 (1976).

5. *Public Opinion,* p. 248. Lippmann did not find this objectionable, as "the common interests very largely elude public opinion entirely, and can be managed only by a specialized class whose personal interests reach beyond the locality" (p. 310). He was distressed that the incorrigible bias of the press might mislead the "specialized class" as well as the public. The problem, therefore, was how to get adequate information to the decision-making elites (pp. 31–32). This, he believed, might be accomplished by development of a body of independent experts who could give the leadership unbiased advice. Lippmann raised no question about possible personal or class interests of the "specialized class" or the "experts" on whom they might choose to rely, on their ability, or their right, to articulate "the common interest."

6. For example, Claire Sterling and the experts of the Georgetown Center for Strategic and International Studies—Walter Laqueur, Michael Ledeen, and

Robert Kupperman—have been established as the authorities on terrorism by the mass media; on the Sterling and Paul Henze role in working up the Bulgarian Connection in the plot against the pope, see chapter 4. In the case of Latin America, the media have been compelled to avoid the usual resort to the academic profession for expression of approved opinion, as the profession largely rejects the framework of state propaganda in this instance. It has therefore been necessary to create a new cadre of "experts" (Robert Leiken, Ronald Radosh, Mark Falcoff, Susan Kaufman Purcell, etc.) to whom they can turn to satisfy doctrinal needs. See Noam Chomsky, *The Culture of Terrorism* (Boston: South End Press, 1988), for examples. On the process of creating experts to meet system demands, see our chapter 1 under "Sourcing Mass-Media News."

7. Like other terms of political discourse, the word "democracy" has a technical Orwellian sense when used in rhetorical flights, or in regular "news reporting," to refer to U.S. efforts to establish "democracy." The term refers to systems in which control over resources and the means of violence ensures the rule of elements that will serve the needs of U.S. power. Thus the terror states of El Salvador and Guatemala are "democratic," as is Honduras under the rule of the military and oligarchy, and the collection of wealthy businessmen, bankers, etc., organized by the United States as a front for the Somocista-led mercenary army created by the United States is entitled "the democratic resistance." See further, chapter 3.

8. In the eighty-five opinion columns on Nicaragua that appeared in the *New York Times* and the *Washington Post* in the first three months of 1986, during the "national debate" preceding the congressional votes on contra aid, not a single one mentioned this elementary fact. For a detailed review, see Noam Chomsky, "Introduction," in Morris Morley and James Petras, *The Reagan Administration and Nicaragua,* Monograph 1 (New York: Institute for Media Analysis, 1987).

9. Only two phrases in the eighty-five opinion columns cited in the previous footnote mentioned that the Nicaraguan government had carried out reforms; none of them compared Nicaragua with El Salvador and Guatemala on this important question.

10. See Dianna Melrose, *Nicaragua: The Threat of a Good Example?* (Oxford: Oxfam, 1985); see also chapters 3, 5, and 7, below.

11. In an article highly critical of the Reagan "peace plan" for Nicaragua in August 1987, Tom Wicker says, "Whatever his doctrine, the United States has no historic or God-given right to bring democracy to other nations; nor does such a purpose justify the overthrow of governments it does not like" ("That Dog Won't Hunt," *New York Times,* Aug. 6, 1987). Wicker does not contest the claim that Reagan seeks democracy in Nicaragua; it is just that his means are dubious and his plan won't work. We should note that Wicker is at the outer limits of expressible dissident opinion in the U.S. mass media. See further, chapter 3. For additional references and discussion, see Chomsky, *Culture of Terrorism.*

12. For example, in response to the Guatemala peace accords of August 1987, the United States immediately escalated the supply flights required to keep its forces in Nicaragua in the field to the phenomenal level of two to three per day. The purpose was to undermine the accords by intensifying the fighting,

and to prevent Nicaragua from relaxing its guard so that it could be accused of failing to comply with the accords. These U.S. initiatives were by far the most serious violations of the accords, but they were virtually unmentioned in the media. For a detailed review, see Noam Chomsky, "Is Peace at Hand?" *Z* magazine (January 1988).

13. Jacques Ellul, *Propaganda* (New York: Knopf, 1965), pp. 58–59.

14. A careful reader of the Soviet press could learn facts about the war in Afghanistan that controvert the government line—see chapter 5, pp. 226–27—but these inconvenient facts would not be considered in the West to demonstrate the objectivity of the Soviet press and the adequacy of its coverage of this issue.

Chapter 1: A Propaganda Model

1. See note 4 of the preface.

2. Media representatives claim that what the government says is "newsworthy" in its own right. If, however, the government's assertions are transmitted without context or evaluation, and without regard to the government's possible manipulative intent, the media have set themselves up to be "managed." Their objectivity is "nominal," not substantive.

In early October 1986, memos were leaked to the press indicating that the Reagan administration had carried out a deliberate campaign of disinformation to influence events in Libya. The mass media, which had passed along this material without question, expressed a great deal of righteous indignation that they had been misled. To compound the absurdity, five years earlier the press had reported a CIA-run "disinformation program designed to embarrass Qaddafi and his government," along with terrorist operations to overthrow Quaddafi and perhaps assassinate him (*Newsweek*, Aug. 3, 1981; P. Edward Haley, *Qaddafi and the United States since 1969* [New York: Praeger, 1984], p. 272). But no lessons were learned. In fact, the mass media are gulled on an almost daily basis, but rarely have to suffer the indignity of government *documents* revealing their gullibility. With regard to Libya, the media have fallen into line for each propaganda ploy, from the 1981 "hit squads" through the Berlin discotheque bombing, swallowing each implausible claim, failing to admit error in retrospect, and apparently unable to learn from successive entrapment—which suggests willing error. See Noam Chomsky, *Pirates & Emperors* (New York: Claremont, 1986), chapter 3. As we show throughout the present book, a series of lies by the government, successively exposed, never seems to arouse skepticism in the media regarding the next government claim.

3. For a description of the government's strategy of deflecting attention away from the Nicaraguan election by the fabricated MIG story, and the media's service in this government program, see chapter 3, under "The MIG Crisis Staged during the Nicaraguan Election Week."

4. James Curran and Jean Seaton, *Power Without Responsibility: The Press and Broadcasting in Britain,* 2d ed. (London: Methuen, 1985), p. 24.

5. Quoted in ibid., p. 23.

6. Ibid., p. 34.

7. Ibid., pp. 38–39.
8. Alfred McClung Lee, *The Daily Newspaper in America* (New York: Macmillan, 1937), pp. 166, 173.
9. Earl Vance, "Freedom of the Press for Whom," *Virginia Quarterly Review* (Summer 1945), quoted in *Survival of a Free, Competitive Press: The Small Newspaper: Democracy's Grass Roots,* Report of the Chairman, Senate Small Business Committee, 80th Cong., 1st session, 1947, p. 54.
10. Note that we are speaking of media with substantial outreach—mass media. It has always been possible to start small-circulation journals and to produce mimeographed or photocopied news letters sent around to a tiny audience. But even small journals in the United States today typically survive only by virtue of contributions from wealthy financial angels.
11. In 1987, the Times-Mirror Company, for example, owned newspapers in Los Angeles, Baltimore, Denver, and Hartford, Connecticut, had book publishing and magazine subsidiaries, and owned cable systems and seven television stations.
12. Ben Bagdikian, *The Media Monopoly,* 2nd ed. (Boston: Beacon Press, 1987), p. xvi.
13. David L. Paletz and Robert M. Entman, *Media . Power . Politics* (New York: Free Press, 1981), p. 7; Stephen Hess, *The Government/Press Connection: Press Officers and Their Offices* (Washington: Brookings, 1984), pp. 99–100.
14. The four major Western wire services—Associated Press, United Press International, Reuters, and Agence-France-Presse—account for some 80 percent of the international news circulating in the world today. AP is owned by member newspapers; UPI is privately owned; Reuters was owned mainly by the British media until it went public in 1984, but control was retained by the original owners by giving lesser voting rights to the new stockholders; Agence-France-Presse is heavily subsidized by the French government. As is pointed out by Jonathan Fenby, the wire services "exist to serve markets," and their prime concern, accordingly, "is with the rich media markets of the United States, Western Europe, and Japan, and increasingly with the business community. . . ." They compete fiercely, but AP and UPI "are really U.S. enterprises that operate on an international scale. . . . Without their domestic base, the AP and UPI could not operate as international agencies. With it, they must be American organizations, subject to American pressures and requirements" (*The International News Services* [New York: Schocken, 1986], pp. 7, 9, 73–74). See also Anthony Smith, *The Geopolitics of Information: How Western Culture Dominates the World* (New York: Oxford University Press, 1980), chapter 3.
15. The fourteenth annual Roper survey, "Public Attitudes toward Television and Other Media in a Time of Change" (May 1985), indicates that in 1984, 64 percent of the sample mentioned television as the place "where you usually get most of your news about what's going on in the world today . . ." (p. 3). It has often been noted that the television networks themselves depend heavily on the prestige newspapers, wire services, and government for their choices of news. Their autonomy as newsmakers can be easily exaggerated.
16. The members of the very top tier qualify by audience outreach, importance as setters of news standards, and asset and profit totals. The last half dozen or so in our twenty-four involve a certain amount of arbitrariness of choice, although audience size is still our primary criterion. McGraw-Hill is included

because of its joint strength in trade books and magazines of political content and outreach.

17. As noted in table 1-1, note 7, Storer came under the temporary control of the securities firm Kohlberg Kravis Roberts & Co. in 1985. As its ultimate fate was unclear at the time of writing, and as financial data were no longer available after 1984, we have kept Storer on the table and list it here, despite its uncertain status.

18. John Kluge, having taken the Metromedia system private in a leveraged buyout in 1984 worth $1.1 billion, sold off various parts of this system in 1985–86 for $5.5 billion, at a personal profit of some $3 billion (Gary Hector, "Are Shareholders Cheated by LBOs?" *Fortune*, Jan. 17, 1987, p. 100). Station KDLA-TV, in Los Angeles, which had been bought by a management-outsider group in a leveraged buyout in 1983 for $245 million, was sold to the Tribune Company for $510 million two years later (Richard Stevenson, "Tribune in TV Deal for $510 Million," *New York Times*, May 7, 1985). See also "The Media Magnates: Why Huge Fortunes Roll Off the Presses," *Fortune*, October 12, 1987.

19. A split among the the heirs of James E. Scripps eventually resulted in the sale of the *Detroit Evening News*. According to one news article, "Daniel Marentette, a Scripps family member and a self described 'angry shareholder,' says family members want a better return on their money. 'We get better yields investing in a New York checking account,' says Mr. Marentette, who sells race horses" (Damon Darlin, "Takeover Rumors Hit Detroit News Parent," *Wall Street Journal*, July 18, 1985). The Bingham family division on these matters led to the sale of the *Louisville Courier-Journal*; the New Haven papers of the Jackson family were sold after years of squabbling, and "the sale price [of the New Haven papers], $185 million, has only served to publicize the potential value of family holdings of family newspapers elsewhere" (Geraldine Fabrikant, "Newspaper Properties, Hotter Than Ever," *New York Times*, Aug. 17, 1986).

20. The Reagan administration strengthened the control of existing holders of television-station licenses by increasing their term from three to five years, and its FCC made renewals essentially automatic. The FCC also greatly facilitated speculation and trading in television properties by a rule change reducing the required holding period before sale of a newly acquired property from three years to one year.

The Reagan era FCC and Department of Justice also refused to challenge mergers and takeover bids that would significantly increase the concentration of power (GE-RCA) or media concentration (Capital Cities–ABC). Furthermore, beginning April 2, 1985, media owners could own as many as twelve television stations, as long as their total audience didn't exceed 25 percent of the nation's television households; and they could also hold twelve AM and twelve FM stations, as the 1953 "7-7-7 rule" was replaced with a "12-12-12 rule." See Herbert H. Howard, "Group and Cross-Media Ownership of Television Stations: 1985" (Washington: National Association of Broadcasters, 1985).

21. This was justified by Reagan-era FCC chairman Mark Fowler on the grounds that market options are opening up and that the public should be free to choose. Criticized by Fred Friendly for doing away with the law's public-

interest standard, Fowler replied that Friendly "distrusts the ability of the viewing public to make decisions on its own through the marketplace mechanism. I do not" (Jeanne Saddler, "Clear Channel: Broadcast Takeovers Meet Less FCC Static, and Critics Are Upset," *Wall Street Journal*, June 11, 1985). Among other problems, Fowler ignores the fact that true freedom of choice involves the ability to select options that may not be offered by an oligopoly selling audiences to advertisers.

22. CBS increased its debt by about $1 billion in 1985 to finance the purchase of 21 percent of its own stock, in order to fend off a takeover attempt by Ted Turner. The *Wall Street Journal* noted that "With debt now standing at 60% of capital, it needs to keep advertising revenue up to repay borrowings and interest" (Peter Barnes, "CBS Profit Hinges on Better TV Ratings," June 6, 1986). With the slowed-up growth of advertising revenues, CBS embarked on an employment cutback of as many as six hundred broadcast division employees, the most extensive for CBS since the loss of cigarette advertising in 1971 (Peter Barnes, "CBS Will Cut up to 600 Posts in Broadcasting," *Wall Street Journal*, July 1, 1986). In June 1986, Time, Inc., embarked on a program to buy back as much as 10 million shares, or 16 percent of its common stock, at an expected cost of some $900 million, again to reduce the threat of a hostile takeover (Laura Landro, "Time Will Buy as Much as 16% of Its Common," *Wall Street Journal*, June 20, 1986).

23. In response to the Jesse Helms and Turner threats to CBS, Laurence Tisch, of Loews Corporation, was encouraged to increase his holdings in CBS stock, already at 11.7 percent. In August 1986, the Loews interest was raised to 24.9 percent, and Tisch obtained a position of virtual control. In combination with William Paley, who owned 8.1 percent of the shares, the chief executive officer of CBS was removed and Tisch took over that role himself, on a temporary basis (Peter Barnes, "Loews Increases Its Stake in CBS to Almost 25%," *Wall Street Journal*, Aug. 12, 1986).

24. The number would be eight if we included the estate of Lila Wallace, who died in 1984, leaving the controlling stock interest in *Reader's Digest* to the care of trustees.

25. As we noted in the preface, the neoconservatives speak regularly of "liberal" domination of the media, assuming or pretending that the underlings call the shots, not the people who own or control the media. These data, showing the wealth position of media owners, are understandably something they prefer to ignore. Sometimes, however, the neoconservatives go "populist," and—while financed by Mobil Oil Corporation and Richard Mellon Scaife—pretend to be speaking for the "masses" in opposition to a monied elite dominating the media. For further discussion, see Edward S. Herman's review of *The Spirit of Democratic Capitalism*, "Michael Novak's Promised Land: Unfettered Corporate Capitalism," *Monthly Review* (October 1983), and the works cited in the preface, note 3.

26. Similar results are found in Peter Dreier, "The Position of the Press in the U.S. Power Structure," *Social Problems* (February 1982), pp. 298–310.

27. Benjamin Compaine et al., *Anatomy of the Communications Industry: Who Owns the Media?* (White Plains, N.Y.: Knowledge Industry Publications, 1982), p. 463.

28. Ibid., pp. 458–60.

29. See Edward S. Herman, *Corporate Control, Corporate Power* (New York: Cambridge University Press, 1981), pp. 26–54.
30. For the interests of fifteen major newspaper companies in other media fields, and a checklist of other fields entered by leading firms in a variety of media industries, see Compaine, *Anatomy of the Communications Industry,* tables 2.19 and 8.1, pp. 11 and 452–53.
31. The merger had been sanctioned by the FCC but was stymied by intervention of the Department of Justice. See "A broken engagement for ITT and ABC," *Business Week,* January 6, 1967.
32. Ibid.
33. On the enormous and effective lobbying operations of GE, see Thomas B. Edsall, "Bringing Good Things to GE: Firm's Political Savvy Scores in Washington," *Washington Post,* April 13, 1985.
34. The widely quoted joke by A. J. Liebling—that if you don't like what your newspaper says you are perfectly free to start or buy one of your own—stressed the impotence of the individual. In a favorable political climate such as that provided by the Reagan administration, however, a giant corporation not liking media performance *can* buy its own, as exemplified by GE.
35. Allan Sloan, "Understanding Murdoch—The Numbers Aren't What Really Matters," *Forbes,* March 10, 1986, pp. 114ff.
36. On the Nixon-Agnew campaign to bully the media by publicity attacks and threats, see Marilyn Lashner, *The Chilling Effect in TV News* (New York: Praeger, 1984). Lashner concluded that the Nixon White House's attempt to quiet the media "succeeded handily, at least as far as television is concerned . . ." (p. 167). See also Fred Powledge, *The Engineering of Restraint: The Nixon Administration and the Press* (Washington: Public Affairs Press, 1971), and William E. Porter, *Assault on the Media: The Nixon Years* (Ann Arbor: University of Michigan Press, 1976).
37. Of the 290 directors in his sample of large newspapers, 36 had high-level positions—past or present—in the federal government (Dreier, "The Position of the Press," p. 303).
38. One study showed that of sixty-five FCC commissioners and high-level staff personnel who left the FCC between 1945 and 1970, twelve had come out of the private-communications sector before their FCC service, and thirty-four went into private-firm service after leaving the commission (Roger Noll et al., *Economic Aspects of Television Regulation* [Washington: Brookings, 1973], p. 123).
39. "The symbiotic growth of American television and global enterprise has made them so interrelated that they cannot be thought of as separate. They are essentially the same phenomenon. Preceded far and wide by military advisers, lobbyists, equipment salesmen, advertising specialists, merchandising experts, and telefilm salesmen as advance agents, the enterprise penetrates much of the non-socialist world. Television is simply its most visible portion" (Erik Barnouw, *The Sponsor* [New York: Oxford University Press, 1978], p. 158). For a broader picture, see Herbert I. Schiller, *Communication and Cultural Domination* (White Plains, N.Y.: International Arts and Sciences Press, 1976), especially chapters 3–4.
40. Is it not possible that if the populace "demands" program content greatly disliked by the owners, competition and the quest for profits will cause them

to offer such programming? There is some truth in this, and it, along with the limited autonomy of media personnel, may help explain the "surprises" that crop up occasionally in the mass media. One limit to the force of public demand, however, is that the millions of customers have no means of registering their demand for products that are not offered to them. A further problem is that the owners' class interests are reinforced by a variety of other filters that we discuss below.

41. Quoted in Curran and Seaton, *Power Without Responsibility,* p. 31.

42. Ibid., p. 41.

43. ". . . producers presenting patrons [advertisers] with the greatest opportunities to make a profit through their publics will receive support while those that cannot compete on this score will not survive" (Joseph Turow, *Media Industries: The Production of News and Entertainment* [New York: Longman, 1984], p. 52).

44. Noncommercial television is also at a huge disadvantage for the same reason, and will require a public subsidy to be able to compete. Because public television does not have the built-in constraints of ownership by the wealthy, and the need to appease advertisers, it poses a threat to a narrow elite control of mass communications. This is why conservatives struggle to keep public television on a short leash, with annual funding decisions, and funding at a low level (see Barnouw, *The Sponsor,* pp. 179–82). Another option pursued in the Carter-Reagan era has been to force it into the commercial nexus by sharp defunding.

45. Bagdikian, *Media Monopoly,* pp. 118–26. " 'The dominant paper ultimately thrives,' Gannett Chairman Allen H. Neuharth says. 'The weaker paper ultimately dies' " (Joseph B. White, "Knight-Ridder's No-Lose Plan Backfires," *Wall Street Journal,* Jan. 4, 1988).

46. Quoted in Curran and Seaton, *Power Without Responsibility,* p. 43.

47. "Advertising and the Press," in James Curran, ed., *The British Press: A Manifesto* (London: Macmillan, 1978), pp. 252–55.

48. Ibid., p. 254.

49. *1984 CBS Annual Report,* p. 13. This is a further refinement in the measurement of "efficiency" in "delivering an audience." In the magazine business, the standard measure is CPM, or "costs per thousand," to an advertiser to reach buyers through a full-page, black-and-white ad. Recent developments, like CBS's CAP, have been in the direction of identifying the special characteristics of the audience delivered. In selling itself to advertisers, the *Soap Opera Digest* says: "But you probably want to know about our first milestone: today *Soap Opera Digest* delivers more women in the 18–49 category at the lowest CPM than any other women's magazine" (quoted in Turow, *Media Industries,* p. 55).

50. William Evan, *Organization Theory* (New York: Wiley, 1976), p. 123.

51. Turow asserts that "The continual interaction of producers and primary patrons plays a dominant part in setting the general boundary conditions for day-to-day production activity" (*Media Industries,* p. 51).

52. Quoted in Todd Gitlin, *Inside Prime Time* (New York: Pantheon, 1983), p. 253.

53. Pat Aufderheide, "What Makes Public TV Public?" *The Progressive* (January 1988).

54. "Castor oil or Camelot?" December 5, 1987. For further materials on such

interventions, see Harry Hammitt, "Advertising Pressures on Media," Freedom of Information Center Report no. 367 (School of Journalism, University of Missouri at Columbia, February 1977). See also James Aronson, *Deadline for the Media* (New York: Bobbs-Merrill, 1972), pp. 261–63.

55. According to Procter & Gamble's instructions to their ad agency, "There will be no material on any of our programs which could in any way further the concept of business as cold, ruthless, and lacking in all sentiment or spiritual motivation." The manager of corporate communications for General Electric has said: "We insist on a program environment that reinforces our corporate messages" (quoted in Bagdikian, *Media Monopoly,* p. 160). We may recall that GE now owns NBC-TV.

56. Barnouw, *The Sponsor,* p. 135.

57. Advertisers may also be offended by attacks on themselves or their products. On the tendency of the media to avoid criticism of advertised products even when very important to consumer welfare [e.g., the effects of smoking], see Bagdikian, *Media Monopoly,* pp. 168–73.

58. This is hard to prove statistically, given the poor data made available by the FCC over the years. The long-term trend in advertising time/programming time is dramatically revealed by the fact that in 1929 the National Association of Broadcasting adopted as a standard of commercial practice on radio the following: "Commercial announcements . . . shall not be broadcast between 7 and 11 P.M." William Paley testified before the Senate Commerce Committee in 1930 that only 22 percent of CBS's time was allocated to commercially sponsored programs, with the other 78 percent sustaining; and he noted that advertising took up only "seven-tenths of 1 percent of all our time" (quoted in *Public Service Responsibility of Broadcast Licensees,* FCC [Washington: GPO, Mar. 7, 1946], p. 42). Frank Wolf states in reference to public-affairs programming: "That such programs were even shown at all on commercial television may have been the result of FCC regulation" (*Television Programming for News and Public Affairs* [New York: Praeger, 1972], p. 138; see also pp. 99–139).

59. Barnouw, *The Sponsor,* p. 134.

60. For Alcoa's post–antitrust-suit sponsorship of Edward R. Murrow, and ITT's post–early-1970s-scandals sponsorship of "The Big Blue Marble," see Barnouw, *The Sponsor,* ibid., pp. 51–52, 84–86. Barnouw shows that network news coverage of ITT was sharply constrained during the period of ITT program sponsorship.

61. Barnouw, *The Sponsor,* p. 150.

62. Mark Fishman, *Manufacturing the News* (Austin: University of Texas Press, 1980), p. 143.

63. Ibid., pp. 144–45.

64. Gaye Tuchman, "Objectivity as Strategic Ritual: An Examination of Newsmen's Notions of Objectivity," *American Journal of Sociology* 77, no. 2 (1972), pp. 662–64.

65. United States Air Force, "Fact Sheet: The United States Air Force Information Program" (March 1979); "News Releases: 600,000 in a Year," *Air Force Times,* April 28, 1980.

66. J. W. Fulbright, *The Pentagon Propaganda Machine* (New York: H. Liveright, 1970), p. 88.

67. Ibid., p. 90.

68. An Associated Press report on "Newspapers Mustered as Air Force Defends B1B," published in the *Washington Post,* April 3, 1987, indicates that the U.S. Air Force had 277 newspapers in 1987, as compared with 140 in 1979.
69. "DOD Kills 205 Periodicals; Still Publishes 1,203 Others," *Armed Forces Journal International* (August 1982), p. 16.
70. Its nine regional offices also had some public-information operations, but personnel and funding are not readily allocable to this function. They are smaller than the central office aggregate.

The AFSC aggregate public-information budget is about the same size as the contract given by the State Department to International Business Communications (IBC) for lobbying on behalf of the contras ($419,000). This was only one of twenty-five contracts investigated by the GAO that "the Latin American Public Diplomacy office awarded to individuals for research and papers on Central America, said a GAO official involved in the investigation" (Rita Beamish, "Pro-contra Contracts are Probed," *Philadelphia Inquirer,* July 22, 1987, p. 4A).
71. The NCC's news services are concentrated in the Office of Information, but it has some dispersed staff in communications functions elsewhere in the organization that produce a few newsletters, magazines, and some videotapes and filmstrips.
72. In 1980, Mobil Oil had a public-relations budget of $21 million and a public-relations staff of seventy-three. Between 1976 and 1981 it produced at least a dozen televised special reports on such issues as gasoline prices, with a hired television journalist interviewing Mobil executives and other experts, that are shown frequently on television, often without indication of Mobil sponsorship. See A. Kent MacDougall, *Ninety Seconds To Tell It All* (Homewood, Ill.: Dow Jones–Irwin, 1981), pp. 117–20.
73. John S. Saloma III, *Ominous Politics: The New Conservative Labyrinth* (New York: Hill & Wang, 1984), p. 79.
74. MacDougall, *Ninety Seconds,* pp. 116–17.
75. Thomas B. Edsall, *The New Politics of Inequality* (New York: Norton, 1984), p. 110.
76. Peggy Dardenne, "Corporate Advertising," *Public Relations Journal* (November 1982), p. 36.
77. S. Prakash Sethi, *Handbook of Advocacy Advertising: Strategies and Applications* (Cambridge, Mass.: Ballinger, 1987), p. 22. See also Edsall, *New Politics,* chapter 3, "The Politicization of the Business Community"; and Saloma, *Ominous Politics,* chapter 6, "The Corporations: Making Our Voices Heard."
78. The April 14, 1986, U.S. bombing of Libya was the first military action timed to preempt attention on 7 P.M. prime-time television news. See Chomsky, *Pirates & Emperors,* p. 147.
79. For the masterful way the Reagan administration used these to manipulate the press, see "Standups," *The New Yorker,* December 2, 1985, pp. 81ff.
80. Fishman, *Manufacturing the News,* p. 153.
81. See note 70.
82. On January 16, 1986, the American Friends Service Committee issued a news release, based on extended Freedom of Information Act inquiries, which showed that there had been 381 navy nuclear-weapons accidents and "incidents" in the period 1965–77, a figure far higher than that previously claimed.

The mass media did not cover this hot story directly but through the filter of the navy's reply, which downplayed the significance of the new findings and eliminated or relegated to the background the AFSC's full range of facts and interpretation of the meaning of what they had uncovered. A typical heading: "Navy Lists Nuclear Mishaps: None of 630 Imperilled Public, Service Says," *Washington Post,* January 16, 1986.

83. The Harvard professor in charge of the program, Harvey Mansfield, stated that the invitation to White had been a mistake anyway, as he "is a representative of the far left," whereas the forum was intended to involve a debate "between liberals and conservatives" (*Harvard Crimson,* May 14, 1986).

84. See Edward S. Herman and Frank Brodhead, *The Rise and Fall of the Bulgarian Connection* (New York: Sheridan Square Publications, 1986), pp. 123–24.

85. Mark Hertsgaard, "How Reagan Seduced Us: Inside the President's Propaganda Factory," *Village Voice,* September 18, 1984; see also "Standups," cited in note 79 above.

86. Stephen L. Vaughn, *Holding Fast the Inner Lines* (Chapel Hill: University of North Carolina Press, 1980), p. 194.

87. Bruce Owen and Ronald Braeutigam, *The Regulation Game: Strategic Use of the Administrative Process* (Cambridge, Mass.: Ballinger, 1978), p. 7.

88. See Edward S. Herman, "The Institutionalization of Bias in Economics," *Media, Culture and Society* (July 1982), pp. 275–91.

89. Henry Kissinger, *American Foreign Policy* (New York: Norton, 1969), p. 28.

90. Quoted in Alex Carey, "Managing Public Opinion: The Corporate Offensive" (University of New South Wales, 1986, mimeographed), p. 32.

91. Ibid., pp. 46–47, quoting Feulner papers given in 1978 and 1985.

92. For a good discussion of many of these organizations and their purpose, funding, networking, and outreach programs, see Saloma, *Ominous Politics,* chapters 4, 6, and 9.

93. See Herman and Brodhead, *Bulgarian Connection,* p. 259; Fred Landis, "Georgetown's Ivory Tower for Old Spooks," *Inquiry,* September 30, 1979, pp. 7–9.

94. The CSIS's expert on terrorism, Robert Kupperman, was probably the most widely used participant on radio and television talk shows on terrorism in the last several years.

95. On Sterling's qualifications as an expert, see Herman and Brodhead, *Bulgarian Connection,* pp. 125–46; on Shevchenko, see Edward J. Epstein, "The Invention of Arkady Shevchenko, Supermole: The Spy Who Came In to Be Sold," *New Republic,* July 15–22, 1985.

96. See David Caute, *The Great Fear: The Anti-Communist Purge under Truman and Eisenhower* (New York: Simon & Schuster, 1978), pp. 114–38, who stresses the importance of the *lying* informer. This McCarthyite pathology was replicated in Robert Leiken's 1982 book on "Soviet hegemonism"—the standard Maoist phrase—which conjures up a Soviet strategy of taking over the Western Hemisphere by means of Cuba and the Sandinistas, and guerrilla movements elsewhere (Leiken, *Soviet Strategy in Latin America* [New York: Praeger, 1982]).

97. Then and now, former dissidents are portrayed as especially valuable experts for the seeming authenticity they can bring to the mistakes of their

former associates. The fact that their claims are often fraudulent is not a problem because the mass media refuse to point this out. Thus Jean Lacouture lent credence to his criticisms of the Khmer Rouge by claiming to have been a former sympathizer—not only a falsehood, as he was pro-Sihanouk, but an absurdity, as nothing had been known about the Khmer Rouge. David Horowitz added to his value as a born-again patriot by claiming that along with protesters against the Vietnam War generally, he came "to acquire a new appreciation for foreign tyrants like Kim Il Sung of North Korea" (Peter Collier and David Horowitz, "Confessions of Two New-Left Radicals: Why We Voted for Reagan," *Washington Post National Weekly Edition,* April 8, 1985). Robert Leiken became more potent as a critic of the Sandinistas as an alleged former peace-movement activist and early supporter of the Sandinistas. Each of these claims was a fabrication, but this fact went unmentioned in the mass media. On Leiken's claims, and the "special force" his anti-Sandinista writings gained by his alleged conversion from "fan of the Sandinistas," see Michael Massing, "Contra Aides," *Mother Jones* (October 1987). While dismissing this pretense, Massing credits Leiken's claim that he "was active in the antiwar movement," but that is highly misleading. Activists in the Boston area, where he claims to have been an antiwar organizer, recall no participation by Leiken until about 1970—at which time McGeorge Bundy could also have been described as an activist leader.

98. See above, note 55.

99. See "The Business Campaign Against 'Trial by TV,' " *Business Week,* June 22, 1980, pp. 77–79; William H. Miller, "Fighting TV Hatchet Jobs," *Industry Week,* January 12, 1981, pp. 61–64.

100. See Walter Schneir and Miriam Schneir, "Beyond Westmoreland: The Right's Attack on the Press," *The Nation,* March 30, 1985.

101. An ad widely distributed by United Technologies Corporation, titled "Crooks and Clowns on TV," is based on the Media Institute's study entitled *Crooks, Conmen and Clowns: Businessmen in TV Entertainment,* which contends that businessmen are treated badly in television entertainment programs.

102. John Corry, *TV News and the Dominant Culture* (Washington: Media Institute), 1986.

103. See S. Robert Lichter, Stanley Rothman, and Linda Lichter, *The Media Elite* (Bethesda, Md.: Adler & Adler, 1986). For a good discussion of the Lichters' new center, see Alexander Cockburn, "Ashes and Diamonds," *In These Times,* July 8–21, 1987.

104. Louis Wolf, "Accuracy in Media Rewrites News and History," *Covert Action Information Bulletin* (Spring 1984), pp. 26–29.

105. AIM's impact is hard to gauge, but it must be recognized as only a part of a larger corporate–right-wing campaign of attack. It has common funding sources with such components of the conservative labyrinth as AEI, Hoover, the Institute for Contemporary Studies, and others (see Saloma, *Ominous Politics,* esp. chapters 2, 3, and 6), and has its own special role to play. AIM's head, Reed Irvine, is a frequent participant in television talk shows, and his letters to the editor and commentary are regularly published in the mass media. The media feel obligated to provide careful responses to his detailed attacks on their news and documentaries, and the Corporation for Public Broadcasting even helped fund his group's reply to the PBS series on Vietnam. His ability

to get the publisher of the *New York Times* to meet with him personally once a year—a first objective of any lobbyist—is impressive testimony to influence. On his contribution to the departure of Raymond Bonner from the *Times*, see Wolf, "Accuracy in Media Rewrites News and History," pp. 32–33.
106. For an analysis of the bias of the Freedom House observers, see Edward S. Herman and Frank Brodhead, *Demonstration Elections: U.S.-Staged Elections in the Dominican Republic, Vietnam, and El Salvador* (Boston: South End Press, 1984), appendix 1, "Freedom House Observers in Zimbabwe Rhodesia and El Salvador."
107. R. Bruce McColm, "El Salvador: Peaceful Revolution or Armed Struggle?" *Perspectives on Freedom* 1 (New York: Freedom House, 1982); James Nelson Goodsell, "Freedom House Labels US Reports on Salvador Biased," *Christian Science Monitor*, February 3, 1982.
108. For a discussion of Ledeen's views on the media, see Herman and Brodhead, *Bulgarian Connection*, pp. 166–70.
109. Among the contributors to AIM have been the Reader's Digest Association and the DeWitt Wallace Fund, Walter Annenberg, Sir James Goldsmith (owner of the French *L'Express*), and E. W. Scripps II, board chairman of a newspaper-television-radio system.
110. George Skelton, White House correspondent for the *Los Angeles Times*, noted that in reference to Reagan's errors of fact, "You write the stories once, twice, and you get a lot of mail saying, 'You're picking on the guy, you guys in the press make mistakes too.' And editors respond to that, so after a while the stories don't run anymore. We're intimidated" (quoted in Hertsgaard, "How Reagan Seduced Us").
111. Piero Gleijeses, *The Dominican Crisis* (Baltimore: Johns Hopkins University Press, 1978), pp. 95–99.
112. Jan K. Black, *United States Penetration of Brazil* (Philadelphia: University of Pennsylvania Press, 1977), pp. 39–56.
113. See above, pp. 24–25; below, pp. 157–61.
114. "The Stalinists of Anti-Communism," in Ralph Miliband, John Saville, and Marcel Liebman, *Socialist Register, 1984: The Uses of Anticommunism* (London: Merlin Press, 1984), p. 337.
115. Daix, in 1949, referred to the Stalin concentration camps as "one of the Soviet Union's most glorious achievements," displaying "the complete suppression of man's exploitation of man" (quoted in Miliband et al., *Socialist Register*, p. 337). Kriegel, formerly a hard-line Communist party functionary, was the author of a 1982 book explaining that the KGB organized the Sabra-Shatila massacres, employing German terrorists associated with the PLO and with the tacit cooperation of the CIA, in order to defame Israel as part of the Soviet program of international terrorism. For more on this profound study, and its influence, see Noam Chomsky, *Fateful Triangle* (Boston: South End Press, 1983), pp. 291–92, 374–75.
116. *Socialist Register*, p. 345.
117. Where dissidents are prepared to denounce official enemies, of course, they can pass through the mass-media filtering system, in the manner of the ex-Communist experts described in "Anticommunism as a Control Mechanism" (p. 29).
118. See chapter 2, "Worthy and Unworthy Victims." Of interest in the Turk-

ish case is the Western press's refusal to publicize the Turkish government's attacks on the press, including the U.S. press's own reporters in that country. UPI's reporter Ismet Imset, beaten up by the Turkish police and imprisoned under trumped-up charges, was warned by UPI not to publicize the charges against him, and UPI eventually fired him for criticizing their badly compromised handling of his case. See Chris Christiansen, "Keeping In With The Generals," *New Statesman*, January 4, 1985.

119. We believe that the same dichotomization applies in the domestic sphere. For example, both British and American analysts have noted the periodic intense focus on—and indignation over—"welfare chiselers" by the mass media, and the parallel de-emphasis of and benign attitudes toward the far more important fraud and tax abuses of business and the affluent. There is also a deep-seated reluctance on the part of the mass media to examine the structural causes of inequality and poverty. Peter Golding and Sue Middleton, after an extensive discussion of the long-standing "criminalization of poverty" and incessant attacks on welfare scroungers in Britain, point out that tax evasion, by contrast, is "acceptable, even laudable," in the press, that the tax evader "is not merely a victim but a hero." They note, also, that "The supreme achievement of welfare capitalism" has been to render the causes and condition of poverty almost invisible (*Images of Welfare: Press and Public Attitudes to Poverty* [Oxford: Martin Robertson, 1982], pp. 66–67, 98–100, 186, 193).

In a chapter entitled "The Deserving Rich," A. J. Liebling pointed out that in the United States as well, "The crusade against the destitute is the favorite crusade of the newspaper publisher," and that "There is no concept more generally cherished by publishers than that of the Undeserving Poor" (*The Press* [New York: Ballantine, 1964], pp. 78–79). Liebling went into great detail on various efforts of the media to keep welfare expenses and taxes down "by saying that they [the poor] have concealed assets, or bad character, or both" (p. 79). These strategies not only divert, they also help split the employed working class from the unemployed and marginalized, and make these all exceedingly uncomfortable about participating in a degraded system of scrounging. See Peter Golding and Sue Middleton, "Attitudes to Claimants: A Culture of Contempt," in *Images of Welfare*, pp. 169ff. President Reagan's fabricated anecdotes about welfare chiselers, and his complete silence on the large-scale chiseling of his corporate sponsors, have fitted into a long tradition of cynical and heartless greed.

120. For a full discussion of this dichotomized treatment, see Edward S. Herman, "Gatekeeper versus Propaganda Models: A Critical American Perspective," in Peter Golding, Graham Murdock and Philip Schlesinger, eds., *Communicating Politics* (New York: Holmes & Meier, 1986), pp. 182–94.

121. Editorial, March 1, 1973. The Soviets apparently didn't know that they were shooting down a civilian plane, but this was covered up by U.S. officials, and the false allegation of a knowing destruction of a civilian aircraft provided the basis for extremely harsh criticism of the Soviets for barbaric behavior. The Israelis openly admitted knowing that they were shooting down a civilian plane, but this point was of no interest in the West in this particular case.

122. The *New York Times Index*, for example, has seven full pages of citations to the KAL 007 incident for September 1983 alone.

123. Patriotic orgies, such as the 1984 Olympic Games in Los Angeles, the

space-shuttle flights, and "Liberty Weekend," perform a similar function in "bringing us all together." See Elayne Rapping, *The Looking Glass World of Nonfiction TV* (Boston: South End Press, 1987), chapter 5, "National Rituals."

124. See below, chapter 6.

125. On issues where the elite is seriously divided, there will be dissenting voices allowed in the mass media, and the inflation of claims and suspension of critical judgment will be subject to some constraint. See the discussion of this point in the preface, pp. xii–xiii, and examples in the case studies that follow.

126. The role of the government in these cases cannot be entirely discounted, given the close ties of the *Reader's Digest* to the CIA and the fact that Paul Henze, one of the primary sources and movers in the Bulgarian Connection campaign, was a longtime CIA official. On the CIA–*Reader's Digest* connection, see Epstein, "The Invention of Arkady Shevchenko," pp. 40–41. On Henze, see below, chapter 4. On the strong likelihood that an influential *Reader's Digest* best-seller on Cambodia was in part a CIA disinformation effort, see below chapter 6, p. 293, and sources cited.

127. We provide many illustrations of these points in the chapters that follow. Watergate and, more recently, the late-Reagan-era exposures of Iran-Contragate, which are put forward as counterexamples, are discussed in chapter 7, below.

128. These points apply clearly to the case of the alleged Bulgarian Connection in the plot to assassinate the pope. See below, chapter 4.

129. We have noted elsewhere that the *New York Times* regularly relied upon Indonesian officials in "presenting the facts" about East Timor, which was being invaded by Indonesia, and ignored refugees, church sources, etc. In contrast, refugees, not state officials, were the prime source in the *Times*'s reporting on postwar events in Vietnam and Cambodia (*The Washington Connection and Third World Fascism* [Boston: South End Press, 1979], pp. 151–52, 169–76, 184–87). On attempts to evade the obvious implications, see chapter 6, under "The Pol Pot Era" (pp. 284–85).

130. Thus when the CIA directs Nicaraguan contras to attack such "soft targets" as farming cooperatives, with explicit State Department approval, the media commentators, including doves, either applaud or offer philosophical disquisitions on whether such targets are legitimate, given that they are defended by lightly armed militia. Terrorist attacks on Israeli kibbutzim, also defended by armed settlers, are regarded somewhat differently. For details, see Noam Chomsky, *The Culture of Terrorism* (Boston: South End Press, 1988).

131. The variable use of agendas and frameworks can be seen with great clarity in the treatment of Third World elections supported and opposed by the United States, as described in chapter 3.

132. Classic in their audacity are Michael Ledeen's assertions that: (1) Qaddafi's word is given more credence in the mass media than that of the U.S. government; and (2) "Relatively minor human rights transgressions in a friendly country (especially if ruled by an authoritarian government of the Right) are given far more attention and more intense criticism than far graver sins of countries hostile to us . . ." (*Grave New World* [New York: Oxford University Press, 1985], p. 131; Qaddafi's superior credence is described on pp. 132–33). See chapter 2 of this book for documentation on the reality of mass-media treatment of abuses by clients and enemy states.

Chapter 2: Worthy and Unworthy Victims

1. In a speech of July 19, 1986, Nicaraguan President Daniel Ortega, in answering charges of religious persecution, asserted that of 138 religious persons murdered and 278 kidnapped or disappeared in Central America since 1979 (a figure that includes Lay Delegates of the Word), none had been victimized by the Nicaraguan government. (*Central America News Update,* Aug. 4, 1986). Many had been killed by the contras, however, in an ongoing tradition of Somocista violence. See Andrew Reding, "The Church in Nicaragua," *Monthly Review* (July–August 1987), pp. 34–36. The large majority were murdered by the army and security forces of U.S. client states, or the death squads affiliated with them.
2. In *The Real Terror Network* (Boston: South End Press, 1982), Edward Herman shows that in the years 1976–81, the only massive coverage of the victimization of individuals abroad by the *New York Times* was of Soviet dissidents, most notably Sharansky and Sakharov (pp. 196–99), although there were numerous cases of comparable or far worse treatment within U.S. domains.
3. Computed by dividing the number of articles and CBS News reports (or column inches) devoted to Popieluszko by the number dealing with the one hundred religious victims and multiplying by 100.
4. Anthony Lewis says that the Soviet dissidents "are enough like us so that we identify with them" ("A Craving for Rights," *New York Times,* Jan. 31, 1977), a partially valid point, as the vast majority of victims of U.S. foreign policy are Third World peasants, but invalid in that victims in U.S. client states as much "like us" as Soviet dissidents do not get comparable attention, as shown in the cases mentioned and the reference in note 2.
5. It is not coincidental that the U.S. secretary of state, Alexander Haig, and the U.S. ambassador to the United Nations, Jeane Kirkpatrick, actually *defended* the assassinations of the American women, as described below.
6. Apart from the details by the *New York Times* shown in table 2-2, there were at least four other *Times* articles that repeated such information, and similar detail was given in *Time* and *Newsweek* and on CBS News. To give a sample of one of many in *Time,* an article entitled "Grim Tale: Details of a Martyr's Death" (Nov. 19, 1984), reads as follows: "Church officials who viewed the martyred priest's body reported that he had been savagely beaten. A rope had been tied around his neck, wrists and ankles so that he would strangle himself if he struggled to get free. Three fingers of Popieluszko's left hand were sliced through to the bone, and there were deep gouges on his arms. His lungs contained enough water to indicate that he was still breathing, even if unconscious, when he was tossed, bound hand and foot, into a reservoir." *Time* repeats these details and others with obvious relish at every opportunity. As we will see, *Time* is less lavish in details on unworthy victims.
7. *Time*'s account entitled "Memories of Father Jerzy" (Nov. 12, 1984) has no counterpart in the articles on the deaths of the unworthy victims discussed below.
8. "A Polish General is Tied to Death of Warsaw Priest," November 3, 1984; "Pole in Killing Tells of Hints of Top-Level Backup," January 9, 1985; "Pole

on Trial Names 2 Generals," January 5, 1985; "Second Abductor of Polish Priest Says Order Came 'From the Top,'" January 3, 1985.

9. See chapter 4, below.

10. On May 6, 1986, Laura Pinto, a member of the Salvadoran "Mothers of the Disappeared," was picked up by three armed men, beaten, raped, and left on the street. On May 29 she was again abducted and tortured, and shortly thereafter twelve members of her group were detained by the police. The British *New Statesman* expressed surprise that this kind of terror could take place, given the fact that Laura Pinto had previously traveled to Europe and made Western Europeans aware of her existence (Jane Dibblin, "El Salvador's Death Squads Defy European Opinion," June 13, 1986). Western Europeans did, in fact, protest these abuses. What made this terror feasible, however, was the fact that the power directly involved in El Salvador, the United States, has media well attuned to state policy. The two assaults on Laura Pinto and the detention of the twelve members of the Mothers were totally suppressed by the *New York Times* and its confreres. There was not a word in the quality papers when a member of the "Mothers of the Disappeared" who had herself been a victim of the atrocities of Duarte's security forces was denied entry to the United States in March 1987, to visit several small towns where she had been invited to speak on the occasion of International Women's Day. See Noam Chomsky, *The Culture of Terrorism* (Boston: South End Press, 1988). The attention that the *Times* mentions as a constraint on Polish violence was not available to protect an unworthy victim.

11. For a review of *Times* editorials on El Salvador in the 1980s, exculpating the state terrorists throughout, see Noam Chomsky, "U.S. Polity and Society," in Thomas Walker, ed., *Reagan versus the Sandinistas* (Boulder, Colo.: Westview, 1987), pp. 295–96.

12. The press may also have been constrained by the fact that reporters who dig deeply and provide accounts unfavorable to the military regimes in Latin America may be barred from the country, or even murdered. Western reporters are very rarely physically threatened—let alone murdered—in Poland, the Soviet Union, Cuba, or Nicaragua. They are often threatened and sometimes murdered in El Salvador, Guatemala, and other U.S. clients in Latin America. This irony is not commented upon in the free press, nor are the effects of this potential and actual violence against dissident reporters on the possibilities of honest reporting. This point is discussed further in chapter 3, pp. 97–98.

13. Penny Lernoux, *Cry of the People* (New York: Doubleday, 1980), p. 73.

14. James R. Brockman, *The Word Remains: A Life of Oscar Romero* (Maryknoll, N.Y.: Orbis, 1982), p. 11.

15. We discuss this link later in this section.

16. Carter sent former New York mayor Robert Wagner to persuade the pope to rein in Romero, which the pope then tried to do. See Raymond Bonner, *Weakness and Deceit* (New York: Times Books, 1984), p. 176. The provincial of the Jesuit order in Central America, Father César Jerez, was called to Rome shortly after to explain the Romero letter. Father Jerez, who had fled from Guatemala after the military had threatened his life, was very close to Archbishop Romero. Subsequently he was forced to flee El Salvador as well and is now a refugee in Nicaragua, where he is rector of the Universidad Cen-

troamericana, unable to return to the two "fledgling democracies" except for brief (and dangerous) visits.

17. Quoted in Bonner, *Weakness and Deceit*, p. 172.

18. On September 27, 1981, Alan Riding wrote in the *New York Times* that "under the Carter administration, United States officials said security forces were responsible for 90 percent of the atrocities," not "uncontrollable right-wing bands." In short, not only was Bushnell lying, but the media knew it, and failed to use that information. Riding had an article on March 23, 1980, entitled "El Salvador's Junta Unable to Halt the Killing." On media coverage of El Salvador during 1980, including gross falsification and cover-up of even congressional reports, see Noam Chomsky, *Towards A New Cold War*, pp. 35ff., reprinted in James Peck, ed., *The Chomsky Reader* (New York: Pantheon, 1987).

19. Church estimates were that the government was responsible for some nine hundred civilian deaths in the first three months of 1980, exceeding the total for all of 1979; a report of Amnesty International dated March 21, 1980, contains seven pages of incidents in which security forces, army units, or paramilitary groups under general military control or guidance killed unarmed civilians, usually peasants (quoted in Bonner, *Weakness and Deceit*, p. 172).

20. This is a point that was conceded by Duarte himself, who admitted in an interview with Raymond Bonner that the army ruled El Salvador, but that he hoped to do so *in the future* (see *New York Times*, Mar. 1, 1982).

21. *Weakness and Deceit*, p. 146.

22. See chapter 3, pp. 101–102.

23. One proof of the fact that the paramilitary forces kill under official protection is that, year after year, paramilitary murders never resulted in arrests (see Herman, *Real Terror Network*, pp. 115–19). As for the regular forces, through 1986, "there were no known instances of military officers or soldiers who were criminally punished for human rights abuses against Salvadoran civilians" (*The Reagan Administration's Record on Human Rights in 1986* [New York: The Watch Committees and Lawyers Committee for Human Rights, February 1987], p. 46).

24. Laurie Becklund, "Death Squads: Deadly 'Other War,'" *Los Angeles Times*, December 18, 1983.

25. Michael McClintock, *The American Connection*, vol. 1 (London: Zed, 1985), p. 221.

26. Bonner, *Weakness and Deceit*, p. 162.

27. "United States Network News Coverage of El Salvador: The Law and Order Frame" (manuscript, 1986), pp. 17–18. Andersen provides many illustrations of how the networks continued to label the junta "moderate" throughout 1980, as atrocities mounted to what Archbishop Romero's successor, Bishop Rivera y Damas, described in October 1980 as the armed forces' "war of extermination and genocide against a defenseless civilian population" (Bonner, *Weakness and Deceit*, p. 207).

28. "23 Die in El Salvador As Clashes Continue; 3 Officials Step Down," *New York Times*, March 29, 1980.

29. Quoted in Robert Armstrong and Janet Shenk, *El Salvador: The Face of Revolution* (Boston: South End Press, 1982), p. 146.

30. From White's cable to the State Department, quoted in Bonner, *Weakness and Deceit,* p. 184.
31. This statement is quoted in Armstrong and Shenk, *El Salvador,* p. 152. Others present claim that troops were on the scene, contradicting Duarte, junta, and Treaster assertions to the contrary. Phillip Berryman, who was at the funeral, told the authors that he saw quite clearly two truckloads of troops in the vicinity. Treaster is cagey, though—he speaks only of troops *in the plaza,* not near the plaza, or in the national palace and other buildings.
32. The view expressed in Ambassador White's cables was that the leftists acted to provoke a response by the security forces, a self-destructive tactic not supported by any evidence.
33. Quoted in Brockman, *The Word Remains,* p. 212.
34. See note 18. *Time* magazine did the same kind of misrepresenting as Treaster, but with a little more finesse: "From his pulpit, he regularly condemned the tyranny and terrorism that have torn tiny, impoverished El Salvador apart and brought it to the verge of civil war" (Apr. 7, 1980).
35. "Church in Salvador Now Follows the Middle Path," *New York Times,* March 22, 1981.
36. For a more detailed discussion of Schumacher's manipulation of the archbishop's cautious remarks for an apologetic purpose, see Herman, *Real Terror Network,* pp. 178–79.
37. It is possible that this failure was based on an honest lack of knowledge of the event. Lack of knowledge, however, reflects in part a lack of concern, and a distorting perspective that removes certain questions from the focus of investigation.
38. Actually, this may be true. The killer may have been a contra assassin hired by the Salvadoran security forces.
39. For the numerous *acknowledged* attempts to murder Fidel Castro, and the CIA-organized murder of Patrice Lumumba, see *Alleged Assassination Plots Involving Foreign Leaders,* Senate Select Committee to Study Government Operations, 94th Cong., 1st sess., November 20, 1975, S. Rep. 94-465, pp. 13–180.
40. Graham Hovey, "Salvador Prelate's Death Heightens Fear of War," *New York Times,* March 26, 1980.
41. See Craig Pyes, "Who Killed Archbishop Romero?" *The Nation,* October 13, 1984.
42. Bonner, *Weakness and Deceit,* p. 178.
43. Stephen Kinzer, "Ex-Aide in Salvador Accuses Colleagues on Death Squads," *New York Times,* March 3, 1984.
44. Craig Pyes, "Dirty War in the Name of Freedom," *Albuquerque Journal,* December 18, 1983. In November 1987, Duarte announced new (and rather flimsy) evidence implicating D'Aubuisson, but no one associated with the reigning security forces, in the assassination. The announcement was a transparent effort to maintain his image as a "moderate," holding the middle ground between extremists of right and left. It was carefully timed to coincide with a daring visit to El Salvador by two actual "moderates," FDR leaders Rubén Zamora and Guillermo Ungo, who have lived in exile under threat of assassination in this terror state.

45. Noam Chomsky, *Turning the Tide* (Boston: South End Press, 1985), p. 103.
46. Armstrong and Shenk, *El Salvador,* pp. 160–61.
47. In an article of February 11, 1982, datelined San Salvador, the Mexican paper *El Día* quoted D'Aubuissón telling two European reporters, one a German, that "You Germans are very intelligent; you realized that the Jews were responsible for the spread of communism and you began to kill them." While the U.S. press played up the fabricated claims of Sandinista anti-Semitism, this statement of approval of the Holocaust was not picked up by the elite media.
48. "Peace Is Still a Long Shot in El Salvador," *New York Times,* September 27, 1987, Week in Review.
49. This statement was left out of the edition of the report finally released to the public.
50. Report, p. 8.
51. Ana Carrigan, *Salvador Witness* (New York: Simon & Schuster, 1984), p. 271.
52. *Foreign Assistance Legislation for Fiscal Year 1982,* part 1, Hearings before the House Committee on Foreign Affairs, 97th Cong., 1st sess., March 1981, p. 163. Letter from David E. Simcox, State Department, to William P. Ford, dated April 16, 1981. At the time Haig made his statement, the evidence was quite clear that the women had been raped, and killed by close-range shots from behind. Haig himself never apologized for this insulting lie, nor did he suffer any serious attack for this in the mass media, with the honorable exception of Anthony Lewis. This episode also appears to have had no noticeable effect on Haig's reputation.
53. "We ought to be a little more clear about this than we actually are [*sic*]. They were political activists on behalf of the Frente and somebody who is using violence to oppose the Frente killed these women" (interview in *Tampa Tribune,* Dec. 16, 1980, quoted in Carrigan, *Salvador Witness,* p. 279.) Former ambassador Robert White pointed out that remarks like these by Kirkpatrick, in the context of El Salvador, were "an incitement to murder" (T. D. Allman, *Unmanifest Destiny* [New York: Doubleday, 1984], p. 17).

Jean Donovan asked Ambassador Robert White, "What do you do when even to help the poor, to take care of the orphans, is considered an act of subversion by the government?" (quoted in Allman, p. 3). Helping orphans in the Salvadoran countryside was also regarded as an act of subversion by officials of the Reagan administration.
54. The *New York Times*'s version, shown on table 2-2, gives a succinct and inaccurate version of the use of the underwear.
55. "Statement by Revolutionary Governing Junta," December 8, 1980. The statement also notes that "the Revolutionary Government repudiates and condemns violence and the irrational crimes it generates"!
56. Juan de Onis, December 24. The question does not arise for the *Times* of why the security forces would want to conceal the bodies if they were uninvolved in the murders.
57. We discussed this myth in "Archbishop Oscar Romero" (p. 48).
58. Juan de Onis, "Rightist Terror Stirs Argentina," *New York Times,* August 29, 1976.

59. See below, note 67.
60. John Dinges, "Evidence Indicates Military Planned Missionaries' Deaths," *National Catholic Reporter,* July 17, 1981.
61. Stephen Kinzer, "Ex-Aide in Salvador Accuses Colleagues on Death Squads," March 3, 1984. Note the "soft" headline. An option forgone by the *Times* was a headline like: "Duarte and Defense Minister Casanova Accused of Cover-up of Murder of Four American Women." Santivánez was paid $50,000 to give his evidence, a sum he requested on the ground of the risk he was taking and the probability that he would be income-short in the future as a result of his confession. This payment was given unusual publicity as suggesting a compromising quality to his testimony, and the *New York Times* squelched a second installment of his evidence on this principled ground—which they never apply to Soviet defectors, who are less in need of protection. The revelation that the "leading democrats" who were formed into a civilian front for the contras by the CIA have been receiving over $80,000, tax-free, annually from the CIA for years has never compromised their integrity as media sources. Nicaraguan defector Miranda got $800,000 for his services without being discredited.
62. Excellent accounts were produced by Michael Posner and the Lawyers' Committee for International Human Rights in a series of investigatory reports, dated September 1981, July 20, 1982, and February 1, 1983, which contain detailed and crushing evidence of a completely broken-down judicial process and an official cover-up. Once again, as with the Dinges report, these documents were essentially ignored in the U.S. mass media and their facts and leads suppressed. News coverage of the lawyers' committee documents was negligible. Michael Posner and Scott Greathead did succeed in placing an Op-Ed article in the *Times* on December 6, 1983, entitled "3 Years after Killings, No Justice in Salvador."
63. Both *Time* and *Newsweek* had articles featuring stonewalling in February 1981—*Time*'s article was entitled "Stonewalling" (Feb. 23)—but although the stonewalling continued for years, this was the end of the news magazines' interest in the matter.
64. Lawyers' Committee for International Human Rights, *Update: Justice in El Salvador: A Case Study,* February 1, 1983, p. 17.
65. Bonner, *Weakness and Deceit,* p. 80.
66. Larry Rohter, "Salvador Defense Lawyer Charges Cover-Up in Slaying of U.S. Nuns," *New York Times,* May 6, 1985.
67. In the same month that Hinton was asserting with assurance that the low-level guardsmen were acting on their own, internal State Department memos were stating that "Reading the documents provoked several questions which we think should have occurred to an investigator whose real aim was to determine who committed the crime" (quoted in *Update,* p. 31).
68. Quoted in *Update,* pp. 30–31.
69. On the Tyler investigation, see Bonner, *Weakness and Deceit,* pp. 78–80.
70. Stephen Kinzer, "Ex-Aide in Salvador Accuses Colleagues on Death Squads," *New York Times,* March 3, 1984.
71. Carrigan, *Salvador Witness,* p. 265.
72. See Stephen Schlesinger and Stephen Kinzer, *Bitter Fruit* (New York: Doubleday, 1982), pp. 32–47, 54–63.

73. Virtually all independent observers were of the view that land reform was also highly desirable for both equity and efficiency. See, especially, José M. Aybar de Soto, *Dependency and Intervention: The Case of Guatemala in 1954* (Boulder: Westview, 1978), chapter 6.
74. Ibid. See also Richard H. Immerman, *The CIA in Guatemala* (Austin: University of Texas Press, 1982).
75. See Blanche Wiesen Cook, *The Declassified Eisenhower* (New York: Doubleday, 1981), p. 222.
76. Piero Gleijeses, "Guatemala: Crisis and Response," in Richard B. Fagen and Olga Pellicer, *The Future of Central America: Policy Choices for the U.S. and Mexico* (Stanford, Calif.: Stanford University Press, 1983), p. 188.
77. Ibid., pp. 191–92.
78. Ibid., p. 192.
79. U.S. officials have often pressed for purely formal democratic reforms and reductions in rates of murder, but they have consistently supported and helped organize the *framework* that eroded the democratic reforms and *increased* rates of murder. In Guatemala (and elsewhere), the reasons for the regular backing of antidemocratic institutions have been the fear of the left and the chronic hostility of U.S. officials and businessmen to popular organizations (unions, peasant organizations, mass political parties), for both economic and political reasons. Thus the periodic support for liberal *forms* has been rendered nugatory by the systematic bolstering up of institutions that regularly undermine the *substance* of liberalism. As Lars Schoultz points out, the function of "military authoritarianism," beginning with the U.S.-backed Brazilian coup of 1964 and widely prevalent in Latin America and elsewhere within the U.S. sphere of influence, has been "to destroy permanently a perceived threat to the existing structure of socioeconomic privilege by eliminating the participation of the numerical majority, . . ." (*Human Rights and United States Policy toward Latin America* [Princeton: Princeton University Press, 1981], p. 7). We may let them "participate," however, with elections held after extended periods of military pacification and the dismantling of popular organizations. See chapter 3.
80. See "Counterrevolution and the 'Shakedown States,' " in Noam Chomsky and Edward S. Herman, *The Washington Connection and Third World Fascism* (Boston: South End Press, 1979), pp. 61–66.
81. From 1977, Guatemala turned for aid to Israel, which has provided similar services regularly for the U.S. government. For details, see Bishara Bahbah, *Israel and Latin America: The Military Connection* (New York: St. Martin's, 1986); Benjamin Beit-Hallahmi, *The Israeli Connection* (New York: Pantheon, 1987); and Jane Hunter, *Israeli Foreign Policy* (Boston: South End Press, 1987). On the continued flow of arms from the United States to Guatemala during the Carter years, see Lars Schoultz, "Guatemala," in Martin Diskin, ed., *Trouble in our Backyard* (New York: Pantheon, 1983), pp. 187ff.
82. Piero Gleijeses estimates that "the Guatemalan army has killed close to 100,000" since 1979 ("The Reagan Doctrine and Latin America," *Current History* [December 1986]).
83. See, for example, Amnesty International, *Guatemala: A Government Program of Political Murder* (London: AI, 1981); Parliamentary Human Rights Group, "Bitter and Cruel . . . ," Report of a Mission to Guatemala by the

British Parliamentary Human Rights Group, October 1984; Americas Watch, *Civil Patrols in Guatemala* (New York: AW, 1986).

84. Amnesty International, *Guatemala: Massive Extrajudicial Executions in Rural Areas under the Government of General Efraín Ríos Montt,* October 11, 1982.

85. According to State Department testimony of July 20, 1981, "We need to try a new, constructive policy approach to Guatemala . . ." (quoted in Americas Watch, *Guatemala Revisited: How the Reagan Administration Finds "Improvements" in Human Rights in Guatemala* [New York: AW, 1985], p. 4).

86. Quoted in Americas Watch, *Guatemala Revisited,* p. 5.

87. See Amnesty International, *Guatemala: A Government Program of Political Murder,* p. 8.

88. Americas Watch, *Guatemala Revisited,* p. 6.

89. State Department 1984 Human Rights Country Report, quoted in Americas Watch, *Guatemala Revisited,* p. 15.

90. *Guatemala: A Government Program of Political Murder,* p. 5.

91. While this is true almost without exception for news articles, there were perhaps a dozen Op-Ed columns in the *New York Times* and the *Washington Post,* and some letters, in the period 1980–86, that criticized Guatemalan state terrorism; some of these were harshly critical of U.S. policy.

92. A few of the opinion pieces cited in the previous note did discuss the U.S. role.

93. "Requiem for a Missionary," August 10, 1981.

94. The documents include the following four put out by Amnesty International: *Guatemala: A Government Program of Political Murder,* February 1981; *"Disappearances": A Workbook,* 1981; *Guatemala: Massive Extrajudicial Executions in Rural Areas under the Government of General Efraín Ríos Montt,* October 1982; *"Disappearances" in Guatemala under the Government of General Oscar Humberto Mejía Víctores,* March 1985. We also included six studies by Americas Watch: *Human Rights in Guatemala: No Neutrals Allowed,* November 1982; *Guatemala Revisited: How the Reagan Administration Finds "Improvements" in Human Rights in Guatemala,* September 1985; *Little Hope: Human Rights in Guatemala, January 1984–January 1985,* February 1985; *Guatemala: The Group for Mutual Support,* 1985; *Civil Patrols in Guatemala,* August 1986; *Human Rights in Guatemala during President Cerezo's First Year,* 1987.

95. This letter is reproduced in Americas Watch, *Human Rights in Guatemala: No Neutrals Allowed,* November 1982.

96. For a full discussion of the last of these murders, that of Marianela García Villas, on March 15, 1983, see Edward S. Herman and Frank Brodhead, *Demonstration Elections: U.S.-Staged Elections in the Dominican Republic, Vietnam, and El Salvador* (Boston: South End Press, 1984), pp. x–xi.

97. Quoted in Americas Watch, *Guatemala: The Group for Mutual Support, 1984–1985,* p. 2 (hereafter, AW, *Mutual Support*).

98. Council on Hemispheric Affairs, *News and Analysis,* April 26, 1986, p. 222.

99. McClintock, *American Connection,* vol. 2, p. 83.

100. AW, *Mutual Support,* p. 3.

101. "Bitter and Cruel," British Parliamentary Human Rights Group, October 1984.

102. AW, *Mutual Support*, p. 8.
103. Ibid., p. 7.
104. An open letter of November 15, 1984, quoted in AW, *Mutual Support*, p. 24.
105. AW, *Mutual Support*, pp. 24–25.
106. Ibid., p. 36. This was, of course, a complete fabrication. What Mejía Víctores is referring to is an investigative body that he established, manned entirely by government personnel, including the deputy minister of defense, and that, predictably, gave the government a clean bill of health.
107. Ibid., p. 38.
108. Ibid., p. 41.
109. Two very terse exceptions should be noted: On April 13, an article on the case mentions that Gómez was tortured; and one on April 19 notes that his tongue was cut out. No details whatsoever were provided about the murders of Godoy de Cuevas and her brother and son.
110. As we will see in the next chapter, the new civilian government did nothing to stem the army assault on the civilian population; but as we might also expect, the optimism of the press on the promise of the new civilian administration was not followed up with reports on what actually happened.
111. As we pointed out earlier, the U.S. press entirely ignored the administration's refusal to allow one of the El Salvador "Mothers of the Disappeared" to come to speak in the United States. See note 10, above.
112. This press release was featured in an "Urgent Action" memo of the Guatemala Human Rights Commission/USA, dated October 3, 1986.

Chapter 3: Legitimizing versus Meaningless Third World Elections

1. See Edward S. Herman and Frank Brodhead, *Demonstration Elections: U.S.-Staged Elections in the Dominican Republic, Vietnam, and El Salvador* (Boston: South End Press, 1984), passim.
2. In the case of the Salvadoran elections of 1982 and 1984, the government relied on the media to play down not only this plan, but also the fact that the rebels were driven into rebellion by decades of refusal of the army to allow any democratic option, and that the rebels could not have participated in the election anyway because they would run heavy risks of being murdered—the five leaders of the political opposition in El Salvador were tortured, murdered, and mutilated in San Salvador in November 1980.
3. As we pointed out in chapter 1, the government and other power groups try to monopolize media attention not only by flooding the media with their own propaganda, but also by providing authentic and reliable "experts" to validate this propaganda.
4. For a model illustration of observer bias and foolishness, see appendix 1 on the findings of a U.S. official-observer team at the Guatemalan election of July 1, 1984.
5. "The observer delegation's mission was a simple one: to assess the fairness, honesty and propriety of the voting, the counting of ballots and the reporting

of final results in the Salvadoran elections" (Senator Nancy Kassenbaum, *Report of the U.S. Official Observer Mission to the El Salvador Constituent Assembly Elections of March 28, 1982,* Report to the Senate Foreign Relations Committee, 97th Cong., 2d sess., p. 2. This agenda does not include consideration of any of the basic framework conditions—like free speech and the absence of state terror—that determine in advance whether an election can be meaningful. See the text below.

6. The *New York Times* even allowed the right-wing Freedom House observers to dominate its reports on the election staged by Ian Smith in Rhodesia in 1979 (articles of April 22 and May 11, 1979). Although a brutal civil war raged and the rebel black groups were off the ballot, Freedom House found the election fair. In a rerun held a year later under British government auspices, the black candidate sponsored by Ian Smith who had received 65 percent in the "fair" election got only 8 percent of the vote, whereas the previously excluded black rebels received a commanding majority. Freedom House found the second election doubtful! See Herman and Brodhead, *Demonstration Elections,* appendix 1, "Freedom House Observers in Zimbabwe Rhodesia and El Salvador."

7. Herman and Brodhead, *Demonstration Elections,* pp. 71–72.

8. Philip Taubman, "Shultz Criticizes Nicaragua Delay," *New York Times,* February 6, 1984; *Security and Development Assistance,* Hearings before the Senate Foreign Relations Committee, 98th Cong., 2d sess., February 22, 1984, p. 83.

9. George Orwell, *1984* (New York: Signet, 1950), p. 163.

10. "The Electoral Process in Nicaragua: Domestic and International Influences," Report of the LASA Delegation to Observe the Nicaraguan General Election of November 4, 1984, Latin American Studies Association (Nov. 19, 1984), p. 32 (hereafter, LASA, Report).

11. The U.S. media quite properly condemned in advance the January 1947 elections held in Poland, under Soviet control and with security forces omnipresent in the country, although not killing on anywhere near the scale seen in El Salvador and Guatemala, 1979–87. See Herman and Brodhead, *Demonstration Elections,* pp. 173–80.

12. LASA, Report, p. 5.

13. *Nicaragua: The Threat of a Good Example?* (Oxford: Oxfam, 1986), p. 14. Oxfam's U.S. affiliate also has warm words for the Sandinista effort, stating that

> Among the four countries in the region where Oxfam works [Guatemala, El Salvador, Honduras, and Nicaragua], only in Nicaragua has a substantial effort been made to address inequities in land ownership and to extend health, educational, and agricultural services to poor peasant families. (*Oxfam America Special Report: Central America,* Fall 1985).

14. See below, under "Free speech and assembly" (p. 93) and "Freedom of the press" (p. 97).

15. See Herman and Brodhead, *Demonstration Elections,* pp. 119–20.

16. See Amnesty International, *Guatemala: A Government Program of Political Murder* (London: AI, 1981); Michael McClintock, *The American Connection,* vol. 2 (London: Zed, 1985).

17. UN General Assembly, *Report of the Economic and Social Council: Situation*

of Human Rights in Guatemala, November 13, 1985, p. 15. On Viscount Colville's apologetics, see Americas Watch, *Colville for the Defense: A Critique of the Reports of the U.N. Special Rapporteur for Guatemala* (February 1986).

18. Guatemala Human Rights Commission, "Report for the 39th General Assembly of the United Nations on the Human Rights Situation in Guatemala" (New York, 1984), p. 18 (Hereafter, HRC, Report).

19. Ibid., p. 23.

20. "Bitter and Cruel . . . ," Report of a Mission to Guatemala by the British Parliamentary Human Rights Group, October 1984, p. 21.

21. Bishop Maurice Taylor and Bishop James O'Brien, "Brief Report on Visit to Guatemala," October 27–November 3, 1984, quoted in Americas Watch, *Little Hope: Human Rights in Guatemala, January 1984—1985* (New York: AW, 1985), p. 25.

22. InterAmerican Commission on Human Rights, *Civil and Legal Rights in Guatemala* (1985), p. 156. Development Poles are organizational units established by the army, nominally to foster "development," actually mere convenient units for control and surveillance.

23. International Human Rights Law Group, *The 1985 Guatemalan Elections: Will the Military Relinquish Power?* (Washington: December 1985), p. 56 (hereafter, IHRLG, Report).

24. Ibid., p. 61.

25. LASA, Report, p. 27.

26. Ibid., p. 25.

27. See further, Herman and Brodhead, *Demonstration Elections,* pp. 120–21.

28. "Journalists Killed and Disappeared since 1976," Committee to Protect Journalists (December 1986), pp. 6–8.

29. Council on Hemispheric Affairs and the Newspaper Guild, "A Survey of Press Freedom in Latin America, 1984–85" (Washington: 1985), p. 38.

30. See IHRLG, Report, pp. 59–60.

31. Howard H. Frederick, "Electronic Penetration," in Thomas S. Walker, ed., *Reagan versus the Sandinistas* (Boulder: Westview, 1987), pp. 123ff.

32. For a full account of media conditions, see John Spicer Nichols, "The Media," in Thomas S. Walker, ed., *Nicaragua: The First Five Years* (New York: Praeger, 1985), pp. 183–99.

33. Ibid., pp. 191–92. For comparison of media conditions in Nicaragua with those of the United States in wartime and its leading client state, Israel, see Noam Chomsky, "U.S. Polity and Society: The Lessons of Nicaragua," in Walker, ed., *Reagan versus the Sandinistas.*

34. For a discussion of this decimation process and a tabulation of murders by group, see Herman and Brodhead, *Demonstration Elections,* pp. 121–26.

35. "The Grass Roots Organizations," in Walker, ed., *Nicaragua,* p. 79.

36. Ibid., p. 88.

37. It has often been observed by serious students of American democracy that the relative weakness of intermediate organizations (unions, political clubs, media not under corporate control, etc.) is a severe impediment to meaningful political democracy in the United States—one reason, no doubt, why voter participation is so low and cynicism about its significance so high.

38. Raymond Bonner, *Weakness and Deceit* (New York: Times Books, 1984), pp. 278–79.

39. Herman and Brodhead, *Demonstration Elections,* pp. 122–24.
40. Enrique A. Baloyra, who argues that there was a real choice, says that people voted "primarily because they wanted to make use of this massive action to urge an end to violence and civil war." But Baloyra nowhere discusses Duarte's and D'Aubuisson's views on a negotiated settlement of the war, which allows him to convey the erroneous impression that one of them supported a nonmilitary route to ending the violence and civil war (*El Salvador in Transition* [Chapel Hill: University of North Carolina Press, 1982], p. 175).
41. See Dennis Hans, "Duarte: The Man and the Myth," *Covert Action Information Bulletin* 26 (Summer 1986), pp. 42–47; Noam Chomsky, *Turning the Tide* (Boston: South End Press, 1985), pp. 109ff.
42. *Weakness and Deceit,* p. 205.
43. The top leadership of the Social Democratic party had been murdered in 1980, and its remaining officials fled the country. Only a portion of this exiled leadership returned for the 1985 election.
44. The guerrilla position was that with the army having set up a national control system, military domination had been institutionalized and elections would have no meaning. See "Guerrillas' View of Elections: Army Will Hold Power Despite Polls," *Latin America Weekly Report,* October 25, 1985, p. 11.
45. HRC, Report, p. 7.
46. Americas Watch, *Civil Patrols in Guatemala* (New York: AW, 1986), p. 2.
47. "El Señor Presidente?" An interview of Cerezo by George Black in October 1985, *NACLA Report on the Americas* (November–December 1985), p. 24.
48. "In a meeting several months ago with the ultra-rightist organization Amigos del Pais, which allegedly has strong death squad connections, PDCG deputies to the Constituent Assembly pledged that if the party came to power, they would refrain from agrarian and banking reforms, investigation into human rights abuses by the armed forces, and any interference in the counterinsurgency program" ("Guatemala Votes," *Washington Report on the Hemisphere,* Nov. 27, 1985). Stephen Kinzer also reports on a private meeting between Cerezo and right-wing landowners, in which "he said we all needed each other at this moment . . ." ("When a Landslide Is Not a Mandate," *New York Times,* Dec. 15, 1985).
49. Allen Nairn and Jean-Marie Simon, in their "The Bureaucracy of Death," *New Republic,* (June 30, 1986), describe the "tactical alliance" between Cerezo and the army, which protected them against any accountability for past actions, in exchange for which the army would allow Cerezo to occupy office.
50. See "Cerezo Adapts to Counterinsurgency," *Guatemala,* Guatemala News and Information Bureau (May–June 1986).
51. American Watch, *Human Rights in Guatemala during President Cerezo's First Year,* February 1987. Cerezo argued for not prosecuting the military for old crimes on the ground that everyone wanted to start afresh. But Americas Watch points out that if terrible crimes of the past are exempt from the rule of law, it suggests that Cerezo doesn't have the power to stop further military crimes. "It is a sign that the rule of law has not been established in Guatemala, and that it cannot be established" (p. 4). This point is supported by Cerezo's inaction in the face of a hundred violent deaths a month—many of them political murders by the army—after he assumed office.
52. See Michael Parenti, "Is Nicaragua More Democratic Than the United

States?" *Covert Action Information Bulletin* 26 (Summer 1986), pp. 48–52.
53. Wayne S. Smith, "Lies About Nicaragua," *Foreign Policy* (Summer 1987), p. 93. Smith states that Cruz "now says that he regrets not taking part and that his failure to participate in the 1984 elections was one of his major political mistakes."
54. See LASA, Report, pp. 24–25, 29–31. We discuss this point, and the likelihood that Cruz's withdrawal was part of a public-relations strategy, in our treatment below of the media's handling of the Nicaraguan election.
55. LASA, Report, p. 23.
56. Doherty's statement appears in *U.S. Policy toward El Salvador,* Hearings before the Subcommittee on Inter-American Affairs of the House Committee on Foreign Affairs, 97th Cong., 1st sess., 1981, p. 290; Gomez's statement is in *Presidential Certification of El Salvador,* House Committee on Foreign Affairs, 97th Cong., 2d sess., 1982, vol. 1, p. 330.
57. AW, *Little Hope,* p. 1.
58. IHRLG, Report, p. 4.
59. They were being murdered on a regular basis by U.S.-sponsored terrorists entering Nicaragua from Honduras and Costa Rica, however.
60. Rev. Daniel Long and seven other ecumenical group observers, "March 25, 1984, Elections in El Salvador" (1984, mimeographed), p. 4.
61. Based on conversations with voters, the Long group states that "most people waited these long hours because of their desire to have their *cedula* stamped and their finger inked to avoid fines for not voting and/or possible reprisals from the government and military. . . ." They note that at many places voting officials stamped the *cedulas* of those unable to vote because of crowding just so they could leave (ibid., p. 6).
62. In the July 1, 1984, election for a constituent assembly, null and blank votes exceeded those of any party and were a staggering 26 percent of the total.
63. IHRLG, Report, p. 54.
64. This procedure was put into the rules at the request of several opposition parties (LASA, Report, p. 15).
65. The media generally suppressed the fact that the number of voting booths was sharply restricted in 1982, allegedly for security reasons but making for longer lines.
66. "Media Coverage of El Salvador's Election," *Socialist Review* (April 1983), p. 29.
67. "Salvadorans Jam Polling Stations; Rebels Close Some," *New York Times,* March 29, 1982.
68. See further, Herman and Brodhead, *Demonstration Elections,* pp. 164–67.
69. Warren Hoge did quote García, but only to suggest an open election: "Without any lies, you can see here what it is that the people want . . ." ("Salvadorans Jam Polling Stations," *New York Times,* Mar. 29, 1982).
70. Eleven days before the 1982 election, four Dutch journalists were murdered by the Salvadoran security forces. The foreign press corps was trooped into the morgue to see the bodies, whose ripped genitals were exposed to media view. This episode—described in the 1984 documentary film *In the Name of Democracy*—was suppressed in the U.S. mass media, led to no large outcries and generalizations about the qualities of the Salvadoran government, and may have contributed to the remarkable silence of journalists in El Salvador on the

unfavorable media (as well as other) conditions in the incipient democracy.
71. "Salvador Vote: Uncertainty Remains," April 3, 1982.
72. The *Times* devoted an entire article to the Salvadoran chief of staff's promises that "his troops would provide adequate security for the election of March 25" (1984); Blandon is quoted as saying "I'm giving you the assurance that there will be secure elections for all of the country" (Lydia Chavez, "Salvadoran Promises Safe Election," *New York Times,* Mar. 14, 1984).
73. *Time,* July 16, 1984. "Moderation" is a favorite media word in descriptions of demonstration elections. *Newsweek*'s article of May 7, 1984, on Duarte and the Salvadoran election of May 1984 is entitled "El Salvador: A Miracle of Moderation." For a discussion of some of the ways in which the media use the word "moderate," see Noam Chomsky, *The Culture of Terrorism,* (Boston: South End Press, 1988), chapter 2.8.
74. The Guatemalan extreme right-wing leader, Mario Sandoval Alarcón, often described as the godfather of the death squads in Central America, was present at Reagan's first inauguration, met with his defense and foreign-policy advisers, and claimed that "verbal agreements" were entered into at that time to cut back on criticism of Guatemalan human-rights abuses and to renew military aid. See Marlise Simons, "Guatemala: The Coming Danger," *Foreign Policy* (Summer 1981), p. 101; Scott Anderson and John Lee Anderson, *Inside the League: The Shocking Exposé of How Terrorists, Nazis, and Latin American Death Squads Have Infiltrated the Anti-Communist League* (New York: Dodd, Mead, 1986), p. 175; and Alan Nairn, "Controversial Reagan Campaign Links with Guatemalan Government and Private Sector Leaders," Research Memo for Council on Hemispheric Affairs, October 30, 1980, p. 11.
75. The Polish election of January 1947 was so designated by the U.S. mass media, although Polish state terrorism was much less severe than that of Guatemala in 1984–85. See Herman and Brodhead, *Demonstration Elections,* pp. 173–80.
76. Council on Hemispheric Affairs, *News and Analysis,* February 6, 1987.
77. We may be quite certain that *Time* will not assert that "Much of the killing in Afghanistan is linked to General Zakov's success against the insurgents."
78. For evidence of the complete servility and dishonesty of *Time* in its coverage of the elections in the Dominican Republic and Vietnam in the 1960s, see Herman and Brodhead, *Demonstration Elections,* pp. 45, 46, 51–52, 83–86.
79. A summary of this document was given in Enfoprensa News Agency, "Information on Guatemala," June 22, 1984. This excellent weekly bulletin of news on Guatemala reports a continuing flow of seemingly newsworthy items—regrettably, however, on unworthy victims, and therefore not of interest to the mass media.
80. This statement, dated October 1985, is reproduced in IHRLG, Report.
81. The two stories that follow were discussed in Enfoprensa, "Information on Guatemala."
82. "A New Chance in Guatemala," December 12, 1985. The *Times* never found that the Sandinistas had "honored" a promise in 1984, but then neither did the Reagan administration. Nor did the editorial consider the meaning of the fact that the ruling generals had declared an amnesty—for themselves—before allowing the electoral "project" to proceed.
83. The *Times*'s editorial of December 12, 1985, congratulates Cerezo for

pledging to "take charge without vengeance against the military for its murderous rule." Translated from the propaganda format, this means Cerezo is too weak to promise minimal justice for terrible crimes, which raises serious doubts about whether he has any real power. The newspaper of record makes this exoneration of mass murderers a virtue, and pretends that it is just an act of mercy on Cerezo's part! The *Times* also does not speculate on what would happen to President Cerezo if he chose to wreak "vengeance against the military," or how exactly he might proceed with this mission under conditions of effective military rule.

84. Stephen Schlesinger and Stephen Kinzer, *Bitter Fruit* (New York: Doubleday, 1982).

85. Of course, there was an even deeper hypocrisy in failing to call attention to the administration's devotion to a free election in Nicaragua but not in Chile, Indonesia, Namibia, or South Korea, among many others, and its pretense that the elections in the terror states of El Salvador and Guatemala are free and have anything to do with democracy.

86. The *New York Times* had an article on the numerous observers in Nicaragua, but *before* the election ("Election Draws Many U.S. Observers," Nov. 4, 1984). The thrust of the article was to suggest observer bias favorable to the Sandinistas, a subject the *Times* never addresses in regard to official observers. In later discussion of the elections, the 450 observers, including even the professional society of Latin American scholars, were entirely ignored by the *Times.* An excellent study by Lucinda Broadbent, "Nicaragua's Elections: A Cruz Around the Issues; Comparative Analysis of Media Coverage of the 1984 Elections," as yet unpublished, parallels our findings in detail, based on an analysis of a wide sample, including U.S. network TV and the British as well as U.S. press. Broadbent points out that in her sample, the opposition to the Nicaraguan government is given more than twice the space accorded the government, "an unusual priority for media usually so wedded to 'official sources' in whichever country they find themselves" (p. 77). Broadbent stresses, as we do, the domination of the Reaganite frame, even in Britain and in the liberal press, and the massive distortion of reality that resulted from this biased framing. She notes also that the media *never* addressed the programs of the contesting parties in Nicaragua, which allowed Reaganite clichés about Sandinista intentions and policies to prevail. The media portrayals were "roughly the opposite of what was witnessed by international observers of the election" (p. 99), which is why, in our view, these observers had to be ignored.

87. For further details, see Noam Chomsky, "Introduction," in Morris Morley and James Petras, *The Reagan Administration and Nicaragua,* Institute for Media Analysis, Monograph 1 (New York: 1987), note 32, which also discusses the distortion of the Dutch observers' report by Robert Leiken in the *New York Review of Books,* December 5, 1985. Leiken dismisses the LASA report without comment as pro-Sandinista, i.e., as coming to the wrong conclusions.

88. LASA, Report, p. 2.

89. This was partially true, as the Sandinistas were trying to alter their image. But the same was true in El Salvador, with the added problem that the election was held in an environment of ongoing state terror. *Time* never used the word "theatre" to describe either of the two Salvadoran elections.

90. As in 1982, the FMLN carried out no military operations directed at the

election-day process, and made no threats against Salvadoran voters. But as in 1982, this has no impact on *Time* reporting. The real threats, broadcast to voters in Nicaragua by contra radio, and the several contra killings of poll watchers, were never reported by *Time*.

As we have noted, the stress on superficialities like long lines is part of the propaganda agenda for a demonstration election. So is blacking out the fact that the length of the lines might be a function of the restricted number of voting booths, as was the case in El Salvador. *Time* provides both the emphasis on long lines and the suppression of relevant evidence on why the lines were so long. See Herman and Brodhead, *Demonstration Elections*, pp. 126–27.

91. Cruz was mentioned by Kinzer in eleven, and quoted, usually at some length, in five, of the fourteen articles he wrote on the Nicaraguan election; disruption and harassment are mentioned or featured in seven of the articles.

92. See particularly his "Sandinista Is Favored but Runs Hard" (Oct. 30, 1984), "Going Through the Motions in Nicaragua" (Nov. 4), and "Sandinistas Hold Their First Elections" (Nov. 5).

93. We will see below that *Time* even tries to make out a coercive threat that produced the vote in Nicaragua.

94. See the quotation from Warren Hoge given above, on p. 108.

95. These points were discussed in the LASA report, as we note below, but for Kinzer and the rest of the mass media, they were off the agenda.

96. Note that the exact opposite is true in the United States, reflecting the recognition on the part of the general public in both societies of who stands to gain through the electoral process.

97. The rate was, in fact, far higher than in the 1984 U.S. presidential election, in which just over half the electorate participated.

98. "Sandinistas Hold Their First Election," *New York Times*, November 5, 1984.

99. Duarte is quoted to this effect by Edward Schumacher in the *New York Times*, February 21, 1981.

100. On April 23, 1985, the *Wall Street Journal* revealed that Cruz was on the CIA payroll. Oliver North then took over his financing, hoping that this might divert attention from the fact that Cruz had been funded by the CIA during the period when the U.S. government was trying to discredit the Nicaraguan elections. See Stephen Engelberg, *New York Times*, July 15, 1987.

101. Stephen Kinzer, "Ex-Contra Looks Back Finding Much to Regret," *New York Times*, January 8, 1988. Cruz now expresses the belief that the anti-Sandinista coalition (the Coordinadora) that nominated him "was dominated by people who never intended to go through with an election campaign," and "sought to embarrass the Sandinistas by withdrawing."

102. See note 91, above, and tables 3-2 and 3-3, below.

103. Philip Taubman, "U.S. Role in Nicaragua Vote Disputed," *New York Times*, October 21, 1984. Robert McCartney, in the *Washington Post* of June 30, 1984, stated that "Opposition leaders admitted in interviews that they never seriously considered running in the Nov. 4 election but debated only whether to campaign for two months and then withdraw from the race on grounds that the Sandinistas had stacked the electoral deck against them."

104. Lord Chitnis, a veteran British election observer who attended the Salvadoran election on behalf of the British Parliamentary Human Rights Group,

noted that "First, and crucial to the whole standing of the exercise, was the fact that no politicians to the left of the Christian Democrats [PDC], and not all of them, were free to contest the election. . . . [Exclusion of the FDR made the election] a contest of vague promises and inferences by two candidates who already bore a heavy responsibility for the situation in which El Salvador finds itself today." The 1984 elections in El Salvador, he continued, were held in an "atmosphere of terror and despair, of macabre rumour and grisly reality" (Pratap C. Chitnis, "Observing El Salvador: The 1984 Elections," *Third World Quarterly* [October 1984], pp. 971–73). Chitnis was never cited as a source anywhere in the U.S. mass media.

105. Stephen Kinzer, "Ortega: Can He Be Trusted?" *New York Times Magazine,* January 10, 1988; Kinzer, "Ex-Contra Looks Back" *New York Times,* January 8, 1988. On the realities of the peace accords, and the media contribution to effacing them in serving the government's agenda, see Chomsky, *Culture of Terrorism,* and articles updating the record in *Z* magazine (January 1988, March 1988).

106. There is also an elaborate media pretense that *La Prensa* is the journal that courageously opposed Somoza, and whose editor was a victim of this U.S.-backed gangster. But the media are surely well aware that the relation of the two journals is barely more than that of a shared name. The editor left in 1980, after a conflict with the owners, to form the new journal *El Nuevo Diario,* and was joined by 80 percent of the staff. It is this journal, if any, that can fairly claim to be the descendant of the old *La Prensa* (Council on Hemispheric Affairs, *Washington Report on the Hemisphere,* July 23, 1986).

107. The leading church opponent of the state in El Salvador, Archbishop Oscar Romero, was murdered, and his murderers have never been apprehended. In Nicaragua, the leading church opponent of the state, Cardinal Obando, continues to live and speak out without fear. This difference is never pointed out in the free press.

108. For a more detailed discussion of the *Times*'s articles on these subjects, see Edward S. Herman, " 'Objective' News as Systematic Propaganda: The New York Times on the 1984 Salvadoran and Nicaraguan Elections," *Covert Action Information Bulletin* 21 (Spring, 1984).

109. In a larger framework, too, Nicaragua is playing the dangerous game of trying to defend itself against external attack, resisting the demands of the godfather. The absurdity of the claim that Nicaragua would become a military "threat" to its neighbors with added MIGs, when the Reagan administration has been looking for an excuse to attack Nicaragua and would welcome any such Nicaraguan move as an opportunity to intervene directly, never strikes the U.S. mass media. The possibility that the administration wants to constrain Nicaraguan arms imports to reduce its capacity to defend itself against ongoing aggression against it also never arises for the press. Note that unlike guerrilla forces, the contras can survive only with regular airdrops, reaching the level of thirty to forty a month by mid-1987, and two or three times that amount after August, as the U.S. sought to undermine the Guatemala accords. Hence Nicaragua would have good reason to obtain vintage 1950s jet planes to defend itself from the U.S. proxy army.

110. For an account of the performance of U.S. official and semi-official observers in the Dominican Republic, Vietnam, El Salvador, and Zimbabwe, see

Herman and Brodhead, *Demonstration Elections*. Appendix 1 provides a summary of the views of an official U.S. observer team to Guatemala in July 1984. All of these fully confirm the statement made in the text.
111. LASA, Report, p. 5.

Chapter 4: The KGB-Bulgarian Plot to Kill the Pope

1. Some qualification is required by the fact that the three principal sources hired by and/or relied upon by the private media—Claire Sterling, Paul Henze, and Michael Ledeen—all had long-standing relations with the government, and that various Italian government organizations such as the intelligence agency SISMI played a role in the genesis and propagandizing of the charges, as described in the text below.
2. The limited exceptions to these generalizations will be noted below.
3. See further, Edward S. Herman and Frank Brodhead, *The Rise and Fall of the Bulgarian Connection* (New York: Sheridan Square Publications, 1986), pp. 66–71; also Philip Paull, "International Terrorism: The Propaganda War" (M.A. thesis in international relations, San Francisco State University, June 1982).
4. The reasons why this was important to Begin are discussed in the works cited in the previous footnote.
5. Tying the assassination attempt to the Soviet Union and KGB was especially helpful in discrediting the Soviet leadership in 1982 and early 1983, as Yuri Andropov, who had just succeeded Brezhnev as head of state, was at one time head of the KGB. The Bulgarian, Sergei Antonov, was arrested in Italy within three weeks of Andropov's assuming power.
6. See Herman and Brodhead, *Bulgarian Connection*, pp. 102–3, 206–7.
7. For an analysis of these NBC-TV programs, see Edward S. Herman and Frank Brodhead, "The KGB Plot to Assassinate the Pope: A Case Study in Free World Disinformation," *Covert Action Information Bulletin* 19 (Spring–Summer 1983), pp. 13–24.
8. Both Sterling and Henze asserted this many times, without providing any evidence and without attempting to explain how destabilization would serve Soviet interests, given the likelihood—eventually realized, in fact—that instability and internal disorder in Turkey would bring into power a military regime even more closely aligned with the United States. Sterling and Henze were fortunate that they were never called upon to explain these things to Western audiences.
9. Marvin Kalb expounded this precise sequence, without the benefit of a single piece of evidence beyond the fact that Agca had had a brief stay in Bulgaria—among twelve countries—asserting that "it seems safe to conclude that he had been drawn into the clandestine network of the Bulgarian secret police and, by extension, the KGB—perhaps without his even being aware of their possible plans for him" (transcript of the Sept. 21, 1982, show, pp. 44–45).
10. See how Sterling handles the problem of Agca's gun, in the text below.

11. SHK regularly assume that the Soviet leadership is wild, and regularly engages in "Dr. No"–type plots, and the mass media do not challenge this image. On the conservative reality, see George Kennan, *The Nuclear Delusion: Soviet-American Relations in the Nuclear Age* (New York: Pantheon, 1982); John Lowenhardt, *Decision-Making in Soviet Politics* (New York: St. Martin's, 1981); and Jerry Hough and Merle Fainsod, *How the Soviet Union Is Governed* (Cambridge, Mass.: Harvard University Press, 1979).
12. NBC-TV stressed an alleged note sent by the pope to Brezhnev threatening that in case of a Soviet invasion, the pope would give up his papal crown and return to Poland to lead the Polish resistance. Thus the assassination attempt was to get the pope out of the way to clear the ground for a prospective invasion. This note has never been produced, and the Vatican has denied its authenticity. See page 162. For a further discussion of these issues, see Herman and Brodhead, *Bulgarian Connection,* pp. 14–15, 200.
13. *Papa, Mafya, Agca* (Istanbul: Tekin Yayinevi, 1984), pp. 213–20. Mumcu also wrote a substantial volume on Agca and his record, *Agca Dosyasi* (Ankara: Tekin Yayinevi, 1984).
14. After Agca decided to "confess," he explained to the Italian magistrates that he was a killer for hire by anyone who wanted a reliable "international terrorist." He sounded just as Claire Sterling said he ought to sound. This was taken quite seriously by the Italian judiciary and Western press. See Herman and Brodhead, *Bulgarian Connection,* pp. 113–14.
15. For a full analysis of this theory, see Herman and Brodhead, *Bulgarian Connection,* pp. 138–40.
16. Michael Dobbs, "Child of Turkish Slums . . . ," *Washington Post,* October 14, 1984. Agca's shooting of the pope may have been motivated in part by his quest for notoriety.
17. For a full account of this strategy and the other matters dealt with in this paragraph, see Herman and Brodhead, *Bulgarian Connection,* pp. 71–98.
18. Criminal Court of Rome, *Judgment in the Matter of Francesco Pazienza, et al.,* July 29, 1985, signed by Francesco Amato, president of the court.
19. Diana Johnstone, "Latest Scandal Leads to Reagan Administration," *In These Times,* December 5–11, 1984.
20. Tana de Zulueta and Peter Godwin, "Face to Face with the Colonel Accused of Plotting to Kill the Pope," *Sunday Times,* May 26, 1983, p. 50.
21. "Behind the Scenes of the 'Agca Investigation,' " *Milliyet,* November 1984. This excellent two-part series by *Milliyet*'s correspondent in West Germany describes the Italian investigation then in process as an extremely biased and incompetently managed exercise. Its many inconvenient but highly relevant facts may also have contributed to it being entirely ignored in the Western press.
22. For a discussion of the various suspicious aspects of this photo identification, see Herman and Brodhead, *Bulgarian Connection,* pp. 110–11.
23. De Zulueta and Godwin, "Face to Face with the Colonel . . . ," p. 50. Even during the investigative phase of the case, it was disclosed that Agca's sensational knowledge of the telephone numbers of the Bulgarian embassy in Rome was slightly compromised by the disclosure that he had "inadvertently" been left alone with a copy of the Rome phone directory. For other illustrations, see Herman and Brodhead, *Bulgarian Connection,* pp. 112, 118–19.

24. The first significant departure in the mass media from the SHK model, even though no alternative was offered, did not occur till May 12, 1983, on ABC-TV's "20/20." On the pattern of deviations here and later, see note 26 below.
25. Late in this long article, *Newsweek* does state in passing that "It is difficult to believe that the Soviets would expect the murder of the pope to solve their Polish problem. To some, it seems odd that the Soviets would put their fate in the hands of Bulgarians and Turks, depriving themselves of the control that is so essential to a ticklish intelligence operation." These sentences, unusual in the mass media for raising such questions, sit alone and undeveloped, after a lengthy discourse that accepts the SHK analysis as valid.
26. The *only* programs on national television that challenged the propaganda frame were on ABC: one, and the only program in five years of television coverage that showed the slightest degree of network enterprise, critical capability, and honesty, was a program "To Kill the Pope," aired on "20/20" on May 12, 1983. Subsequently, ABC also had a program in which Sterling debated with Alexander Cockburn, although this was arranged unbeknownst to Sterling, who was enraged at having to have her views contested. (See Herman and Brodhead, *Bulgarian Connection,* pp. 123–24, for the story of this encounter.) Among the newspapers, a propaganda conformity prevailed until the time that prosecutor Albano's report was made public in June 1984, when Michael Dobbs, of the *Washington Post,* began to take a more critical view, along with Don Schanche, of the *Los Angeles Times.* While skeptical of Agca's claims over the next several years, Dobbs remained equally skeptical of the idea that Agca was coached, which he referred to as "the Bulgarian view." Dobbs never seriously explored the coaching hypothesis. See Herman and Brodhead, *Bulgarian Connection,* "The Small Voices of Dissent," pp. 199–202.
27. Martella visited Washington, D.C., in October 1982, during which time he benefited not only from the insights of Arnauld de Borchgrave, but was also given a special viewing of the NBC-TV special on "The Man Who Shot the Pope" (see Herman and Brodhead, *Bulgarian Connection,* pp. 24–27). Ledeen may have had a more direct involvement in the initiation of the case in Italy, a charge made by Francesco Pazienza. See Diana Johnstone, "Bulgarian Connection: Finger-pointing in the Pontiff Plot Labyrinth," *In These Times,* January 29–February 4, 1986.
28. For a statistical tabulation of the extent of this bias, see table 7-1, "Sterling-Henze-Ledeen Dominance of Media Coverage of the Bulgarian Connection, September 1982–May 1985," in Herman and Brodhead, *Bulgarian Connection,* pp. 182–83.
29. Their coercive tactics were effective because their preestablished prominence and drawing power made them important to program organizers, which gave them leverage. This is the basis for "tying agreements," outlawed under section 3 of the Clayton Act.
30. This Sterling theme and the ends sought by these conferees also reflected an elite consensus in the United States; otherwise the mass media would not have accepted her views so readily.
31. See Herman and Brodhead, *Bulgarian Connection,* chapter 6, "The Disinformationists."
32. In a characteristic lie, Sterling says in her *Terror Network* ([New York:

Holt, Rinehart & Winston/Reader's Digest Press, 1984], p. 290) that Sejna got out of Czechoslovakia "a jump ahead of the invading Soviet army," when in fact Sejna defected in the middle of the Czech Spring, long before the Soviet invasion, and in the midst of a corruption scandal in which Sejna was a principal. See Leslie Gelb, "Soviet-Terror Ties Called Outdated," *New York Times,* October 18, 1981. In his book *Veil,* Bob Woodward notes that CIA analysts had at once dismissed Sterling's concoctions as "preposterous," giving some examples, including her reliance on Italian press stories that had been planted in CIA disinformation operations ([New York: Simon & Schuster, 1987], pp. 124–29). For detailed refutation, see Edward S. Herman, *The Real Terror Network* (Boston: South End Press, 1982).

33. Sejna, of course, failed this test by "recognizing" the forged document, which had slipped his mind, and used it in later years for its spectacular disclosures. See Lars-Erik Nelson, "The Deep Terror Plot: A Thickening of Silence," *New York Daily News,* June 24, 1984; Alexander Cockburn, "Beat the Devil," *The Nation,* August 17–24, 1985. Sterling was introduced to this Sejna information windfall by Michael Ledeen. (see Sterling, *Terror Network* p. 34).

34. See also "Why Is the West Covering Up for Agca? An Exclusive Interview with Claire Sterling," *Human Events,* April 21, 1984.

35. This quotation and line of thought was presented by Sterling in her speech given at the Conference on Disinformation, in Paris, December 5, 1984, sponsored by Internationale de la Resistance, a coalition of right-wing resistance/"liberation" organizations and support groups. We quote from page 2 of the copy of her speech distributed by the sponsor organization. The booklet by Andronov to which she attributes such great influence was, to our knowledge, never mentioned in the U.S. mass media except by Sterling and Henze.

36. Even Michael Dobbs failed to deal with the fact that the Bulgarian defense claimed that no publicly available sources—i.e., newspapers, or radio and television programs—had ever had details on Antonov's apartment *before* Agca provided those details to the investigating magistrate. This would seem to imply that Agca got the details by some form of coaching while in prison. Dobbs dismisses coaching as the "Bulgarian view," but never explains what other view could account for Agca's knowledge of places he had never visited.

37. *Panorama,* May 26, 1985, p. 107.

38. Ugur Mumcu's books, cited earlier, are a running commentary on what Mumcu repeatedly and explicitly calls Henze's "lies."

39. "... I believe we are past the point where it serves the interests of any party except the Soviets to adopt the minimalist, legalistic approach which argues that if there is no 'documentary evidence' or some other form of incontrovertible proof that the Government of the U.S.S.R. is behind something, we must assume that it is not" (Paul Henze, "The Long Effort to Destabilize Turkey," *Atlantic Community* [Winter 1981–82], p. 468).

40. Ledeen had three Op-Ed articles in the *New York Times* in the years 1984–87.

41. *New York Times Book Review,* May 19, 1985. For an analysis of Ledeen's neoconservative theory of the media, see Herman and Brodhead, *Bulgarian Connection,* pp. 166–70.

42. For documentation and sources, see Herman and Brodhead, *Bulgarian Connection,* pp. 93–98, 160–61; see also Jonathan Kwitny, "Tale of Intrigue:

Why an Italian Spy Got Closely Involved in the Billygate Affair," *Wall Street Journal*, August 8, 1985.

43. The comprehensiveness of the *Times*'s protection of its disinformation sources was shown amusingly in February 1987 when Charles Babcock, of the *Washington Post*, revealed that Ledeen had very possibly been dismissed from Washington University in St. Louis in 1972 for plagiarism. On the very same day, an article by Stephen Engelberg in the *Times*, on Ledeen, describes Ledeen's history as follows: "After being denied tenure at Washington University in St. Louis in 1972, Mr. Ledeen became. . . . " This was all the news fit to print about a useful asset.

44. "McNeil-Lehrer News Hour," program of May 27, 1985.

45. See our reference earlier to its wholly uncritical presentation in the *Newsweek* article of January 3, 1983.

46. For a discussion of the compromised character of the photo identification of the Bulgarians on November 9, 1982, as well as the general conduct of the case by Investigating Judge Martella, see Herman and Brodhead, *Bulgarian Connection*, chapter 5.

47. On the likelihood that this Antonov photo had been "manufactured" as an instrument of disinformation, see Howard Friel, "The Antonov Photo and the 'Bulgarian Connection,' " *Covert Action Information Bulletin* 21 (Spring–Summer 1984), pp. 20–21.

48. This was treated outstandingly in the ABC "20/20" program of May 12, 1983; and Agca's shifting testimony was also discussed well by Michael Dobbs in the *Washington Post*, beginning in June 1984. These were exceptional, however, as pointed out in note 26 above.

49. Dobbs is an honorable exception, although he remained very cautious in generalizing about Martella's handling of the case, and, as noted, he failed to take seriously the obvious alternative model.

50. Initially, Sterling suggested obliquely that any retracted claims had already been "corroborated"—a falsehood. Later, Sterling followed Italian prosecutor Albano's solution to the problem: that Agca really *was* in Antonov's apartment but was denying it to signal the Bulgarians that they had better break him out of jail.

Chapter 5: The Indochina Wars (I)

1. Among these, the most comprehensive, to our knowledge, are unpublished studies by Howard Elterman: *The State, The Mass Media and Ideological Hegemony: United States Policy Decisions in Indochina, 1945–75—Historical Record, Government Pronouncements and Press Coverage* (Ph.D. diss., New York University, 1978); and *The Circle of Deception: The United States Government, the National Press and the Indochina War, 1954–1984* (ms., n.d.). See also Daniel C. Hallin, *The "Uncensored War": The Media and Vietnam* (New York: Oxford University Press, 1986). The latter is based on a complete coverage of the *New York Times* from 1961 through mid-1965, and an extensive sample of television network news from August 1965 through January 1973. Elterman's work covers

the *New York Times* and the newsweeklies, contrasting their coverage with that of the "alternative press." The most extensive analysis of a particular incident is Peter Braestrup, *Big Story*, 2 vols. (Boulder: Westview, 1977), on the Tet offensive, published in cooperation with Freedom House. For detailed examination of this highly influential study, to which we return in "The Tet Offensive," pp. 211–228, and appendix 3, see Noam Chomsky, "The U.S. Media and the Tet Offensive," *Race & Class* (London) XX, 1 (1978), and an excerpted version in the journalism review *More* (June 1978); also Gareth Porter, "Who Lost Vietnam?" *Inquiry*, February 20, 1978.

2. *Inside Story Special Edition: Vietnam Op/ED*, Press and the Public Project, Inc. (1985), transcript of the AIM critique with discussion; Robert Elegant, cited from *Encounter* by narrator Charlton Heston, on camera. Transcripts of the PBS series *Vietnam: A Television History* are published by WGBH Transcripts (Boston: 1983). See also the "companion book" by the chief correspondent for the PBS series, Stanley Karnow, *Vietnam: A History* (New York: Viking, 1983).

3. Samuel Huntington, in M. P. Crozier, S. J. Huntington, and J. Watanuki, *The Crisis of Democracy: Report on the Governability of Democracies to the Trilateral Commission* (New York: New York University Press, 1975), pp. 98, 102, 106, 113. The final remarks are from the summary of discussion by commission members, appendix I, 4.

4. "Introduction" to Braestrup, *Big Story*, p. xviii; the latter phrase is the title of a 1967 Freedom House pamphlet inspired in part by Vietnam War coverage; see also p. vii.

5. John P. Roche, *Washington Star*, October 26, 1977, commenting on Braestrup's study.

6. John Corry, "Is TV Unpatriotic or Simply Unmindful?" *New York Times*, May 12, 1985. Corry alleges that this is true with regard not only to Vietnam but also to Central America—and, in fact, generally.

7. General Kinnard, now a military historian, was field commander for the 1970 Cambodia invasion. One of the commentators is the French historian Philippe Devillers, elsewhere a critic of the war but appearing here only in endorsement of one element of the AIM critique.

8. In Braestrup, *Big Story*, I, xix.

9. Bernard Fall, "Vietnam Blitz," *New Republic*, October 9, 1965. A French military historian and journalist, Fall was one of the few genuine experts on Vietnam writing in the United States at that time. He was also an extreme hawk, although he turned against the war when he saw that it was simply destroying the country and society of Vietnam.

10. Hallin, *"Uncensored War,"* pp. 192ff.

11. Editorial, *New York Times*, May 7, 1972.

12. "An Irony of History," *Newsweek*, April 28, 1975; final document in William Appleman Williams, Thomas McCormick, Lloyd Gardner, and Walter LaFeber, *America in Vietnam: A Documentary History* (New York: Anchor, 1985).

13. Lewis, *New York Times*, April 21, 24, 1975; December 27, 1979. For these and similar comments by perhaps the most outspoken critic of the war in the mainstream media, see Noam Chomsky, *Towards a New Cold War* (New York: Pantheon, 1982), pp. 28, 144f. and 417n.

14. Karnow, *Vietnam,* pp. 9, 439, 650.
15. John King Fairbank, "Assignment for the '70's," *American Historical Review* 74.3 (February 1969); Irving Howe, *Dissent* (Fall 1979); Stanley Hoffmann, *International Security* (Summer 1981).
16. David Fromkin and James Chace, "What *Are* the Lessons of Vietnam?" in "Vietnam: The Retrospect," *Foreign Affairs* (Spring 1985).
17. McGeorge Bundy, *Foreign Affairs* (January 1967); secret memorandum of February 7, 1965, in *Pentagon Papers,* Senator Gravel edition (Boston: Beacon Press, 1972), III, 309; henceforth *PP.*
18. The notion that the United States seeks American-style democracy in areas of intervention persists in liberal thought despite obvious and durable U.S. satisfaction with regimes such as those of Somoza, Pinochet, or Mobutu, and despite regular intervention to overthrow or bar democratic regimes, as in Guatemala in 1954 and since, among many other examples, some discussed earlier. To postulate otherwise would be to acknowledge something other than benevolent ends. This would be intolerable.
19. For extensive references, see Chomsky, *Towards a New Cold War,* particularly chapter 4.
20. Lawrence Lifschultz, *Far Eastern Economic Review,* January 30, 1981.
21. "Don't Forget Afghanistan," *Economist,* October 25, 1980.
22. See Noam Chomsky, *At War with Asia* (New York: Pantheon, 1970; hereafter, *AWWA*), pp. 213–14, noting also an exception: D. S. Greenway, *Life,* April 3, 1970. See also pp. 214ff. and Chomsky, *For Reasons of State* (New York: Pantheon, 1973; hereafter, *FRS*), 179, for a review of official data readily available to journalists, had they been interested to ascertain the facts. See also Fred Branfman, "Presidential War in Laos," in Nina S. Adams and Alfred W. McCoy, eds., *Laos: War and Revolution* (New York: Harper & Row, 1970).
23. See Hallin, *"Uncensored War,"* pp. 39f., for discussion.
24. Hallin, *"Uncensored War,"* p. 53. In 1962, the USIA announced a contest in Saigon to find a term more effective than "Vietcong" in inspiring "contempt," or "disgust," or "ridicule" among the country's illiterate masses (AP, *New York Times,* June 4, 1962). Apparently, no more effective term of abuse could be devised.
25. E. W. Kenworthy, *New York Times,* May 10, 1961; David Halberstam, *New York Times,* January 20, 1963; *New York Times,* May 13, 1961; cited in Hallin, *"Uncensored War,"* 53–54.
26. "Where Washington Reporting Failed," *Columbia Journalism Review* (Winter 1970–71), cited by James Aronson, "The Media and the Message," in Noam Chomsky and Howard Zinn, eds., *Critical Essays and Index,* vol. 5 of *PP.*
27. *New York Times,* September 28, 1987; our emphasis.
28. State Department, "Policy and Information Statement on Indochina" (July 1947), cited by George C. Herring, *America's Longest War* (New York: Wiley, 1979), p. 8.
29. Department of Defense, *United States–Vietnam Relations, 1945–67* (the U.S. government version of the *Pentagon Papers*), bk. 8, pp. 144–45; Chomsky, *FRS,* pp. 7, 32 (see this book for documentation when not specifically cited below). For general discussion of the war see, inter alia, Herring, *America's Longest War*; Gabriel Kolko, *Anatomy of a War* (New York: Pantheon, 1985),

with particular focus on Vietnamese Communist planning; R. B. Smith, *An International History of the Vietnam War* (New York: St. Martin's, 1983, 1985), the first two volumes of a projected four-volume history, a somewhat mistitled study focusing on "international Communist strategy." For the pre-1965 period, see particularly George M. Kahin, *Intervention: How America Became Involved in Vietnam* (New York: Knopf, 1986). A useful documentary record and commentary appears in Williams et al., *America in Vietnam.*

30. In R. Lindholm, ed., *Vietnam: The First Five Years* (Lansing: Michigan State University Press, 1959), p. 346.

31. Douglas Pike, *Viet Cong* (Cambridge, Mass.: MIT Press, 1966), pp. 91–92, 101. For some samples of Pike's rhetoric in this study, see Appendix 3, note 3, below.

32. Douglas Pike, *War, Peace and the Vietcong* (Cambridge, Mass.: MIT Press, 1969), p. 6; the estimate was common in the U.S. government and by outside specialists. Pike, *Viet Cong,* pp. 110, 362. Henry Cabot Lodge, in *PP,* II, 376.

33. Guenter Lewy, *America in Vietnam* (Oxford: Oxford University Press, 1978). For detailed discussion of this vulgar propaganda exercise disguised as "scholarship," see our review, reprinted in Chomsky, *Towards a New Cold War,* chapter 5. Lewy tacitly concedes the accuracy of this critique by evasion; compare the review with his response to critics, *Washington Quarterly* (Autumn 1979). For further insight into the commitments and intellectual level of a man taken seriously as a scholar, see his discussion of the need for the state to take stern action to protect the public from "lies" by subversives, and to ensure that the public is not deceived by the "hidden agenda" of such groups as Clergy and Laity Concerned, the Coalition for a New Foreign and Military Policy, NACLA, and others who seek to conceal "their espousal of Cuban-style Communism" and who are engaged in "deception" and "subversion." As he correctly notes, and inadvertently reveals in his discussion, "to totalitarianism, an opponent is by definition subversive" (Lewy, "Does America Need a Verfassungsschutzbericht?" *Orbis* [Fall 1987]—a respected journal with a distinguished editorial board).

34. Unpublished memorandum on pacification problems circulated within the military in 1965, a copy of which was given by Vann to Professor Alex Carey, University of New South Wales, Australia.

35. *PP,* II, 304.

36. Interview in *Stern,* reprinted in *New Advocate* (Los Angeles), April 1–15, 1972; Maxwell Taylor, in *PP,* III, 669.

37. U.S. involvement dates back to the export of Diem from the United States to Vietnam in 1954, and his forcible imposition as a "leader" of the southern part of the country, in a context where U.S. officials readily admitted that the great majority of South Vietnamese supported Ho Chi Minh and that Diem lacked an indigenous base of support.

38. We saw in chapter 3 that in El Salvador, too, while it was admitted by the media that the population wanted peace above all else, the elections under U.S. auspices—again, held only after the ground had been cleared by mass killing for reasons that the media never confronted or tried to explain—produced governments dedicated to military victory.

39. Walter LaFeber, in Williams et al., *America in Vietnam,* p. 236, with the text of the resolution.

40. *PP,* 715–16, Stevenson's speech before the UN Security Council, May 21, 1964. See *FRS,* 114f., for documentation on the U.S. concept of "aggression."
41. Bernard Fall, "Vietcong—The Unseen Enemy in Vietnam," *New Society* (London), April 22, 1965, reprinted in Bernard B. Fall and Marcus G. Raskin, eds., *The Viet-Nam Reader* (New York: Vintage, 1965). See note 9.
42. Bernard Fall, *Last Reflections on a War* (New York: Doubleday, 1967).
43. Samuel Huntington, *Foreign Affairs* (July 1968).
44. Paul Quinn-Judge reports that deaths from 1965 on in Vietnam alone may have passed three million (*Far Eastern Economic Review,* Oct. 11, 1984). A standard Western estimate is about 500,000 killed in the U.S.-backed French war. Hundreds of thousands more were killed in South Vietnam before 1965, in Laos, and in Cambodia.
45. According to congressional sources that cite unpublished studies of the Congressional Research Service, which are alleged to give the figure $84.5 million, in fiscal-year 1987 dollars, from FY 1980 through FY 1986. We return to this matter in the next chapter.
46. See Charles Kadushin, *The American Intellectual Elite* (Boston: Little, Brown, 1974). This study was based on lengthy interviews taken in May 1970, after the Cambodia invasion, when public opposition to the war reached its highest peak. Virtually all of those interviewed were "doves," some active in opposition to the war. Virtually none opposed the war on the principled grounds of opposition to aggression (called "ideological grounds" by the author) that all would have adopted had they been asked about the Soviet invasion of Czechoslovakia.
47. *Philadelphia Inquirer,* August 30, 1987.
48. Charles Mohr, quoting a "South Vietnamese official" (*New York Times,* Oct. 24, 1966). One of the authors (Herman) published in 1971 a compilation of quotations, many from Saigon generals and other officials, on the need for time because of their lack of indigenous support, which made political competition intolerable. See "Free Choice or Subjugation," *American Report,* May 7, 1971.
49. Kahin, *Intervention,* pp. 89, 60–61; on the secret record revealed in the *Pentagon Papers,* see *FRS,* pp. 104–5.
50. See *FRS,* pp. 100f.
51. March 13, 1964; Kahin, *Intervention,* pp. 91, 208.
52. Elterman, *Circle of Deception,* reviewing stories from May 1955 through July 1956; Elterman, *State-Media-Ideological Hegemony,* pp. 182f.
53. Susan Welch, "The American Press and Indochina," in Richard L. Merritt, ed., *Communications in International Politics* (Urbana: University of Illinois Press, 1972). Only the isolationist *Chicago Tribune* was opposed to U.S. intervention and challenged administration assumptions, in her sample.
54. Fall, "Vietcong—The Unseen Enemy," cites as credible the figure 66,000 killed between 1957 and 1961. Gabriel Kolko gives the figure of 12,000 killed as a "conservative" estimate for 1955–57, with 40,000 political prisoners, reaching 150,000 by 1961—50,000, according to the government (*Anatomy of a War,* p. 89).
55. "Lösung für Vietnam," *Neues Forum* (August/September 1969); see our *Political Economy of Human Rights* (Boston: South End Press, 1979; hereafter *PEHR*), I, 302, 422.

56. See, among others, U.S. government specialist Douglas Pike, *Viet Cong*, and particularly Jeffrey Race, *War Comes to Long An* (Berkeley: University of California Press, 1972), the major study of the period preceding the outright U.S. invasion, by a U.S. military adviser with extensive access to U.S. and Saigon intelligence as well as direct evidence.
57. "The Situation and Tasks for 1959," from the Race document collection, cited by Gareth Porter, *A Peace Denied: The United States, Vietnam, and the Paris Agreement* (Bloomington: Indiana University Press, 1975), p. 281.
58. Race, *War Comes to Long An*. Essentially the same picture is presented—despairingly—in Pike's 1966 study.
59. *New York Times*, September 15, 1969.
60. Kahin, *Intervention*, p. 208; chapters 8, 9.
61. Kahin, *Intervention*, pp. 183f. William Bundy, January 21, 1970, cited by Kahin, p. 183.
62. Lyndon Johnson, March 20, 1964; Maxwell Taylor, November 27, 1964. See *FRS*, pp. 127f., for documentation and more extensive discussion based on the *Pentagon Papers* record.
63. Kahin, *Intervention*, pp. 238, 241, 245.
64. For references and further discussion, see *FRS*, pp. 110f. See also Wallace J. Thies, *When Governments Collide: Coercion and Diplomacy in the Vietnam Conflict, 1964–68* (Berkeley: University of California Press, 1980).
65. E. W. Kenworthy, *New York Times*, November 17, 1961, reporting President Kennedy's decisions; Kenworthy, *New York Times*, May 10, 1961, reporting Lyndon Johnson's mission to Asia; Hallin, *"Uncensored War"*, pp. 31, 53.
66. Robert Trumbull, February 18, 1962; Hanson Baldwin, September 16, 1962, May 13, 1961; Tom Wicker, February 11, 1965; David Halberstam, January 20, 1963, March 11, 1963; Homer Bigart, April 1, 15, 1962. Hallin, *"Uncensored War,"* pp. 51–56, 84.
67. Kahin, *Intervention*, p. 142.
68. James Reston, *New York Times*, April 25, 1965; Peter Jennings, ABC-TV, March 8, 1966; Jack Perkins, NBC-TV, January 11, 1966; Hallin, *"Uncensored War,"* pp. 89, 91, 229, 137, 140, 141.
69. Kahin, *Intervention*, p. 287.
70. For an extensive collection of press reports, see Seymour Melman, ed., *In the Name of America* (Annandale, Va.: Turnpike Press, 1968). For analysis of the material available at the time, see Edward S. Herman, *Atrocities in Vietnam: Myths and Realities* (Boston: Pilgrim Press, 1970).
71. *New York Times*, May 6, 1972.
72. Takashi Oka, *Christian Science Monitor*, December 4, 1965; Bernard Fall, "Vietnam Blitz," *New Republic*, October 9, 1965.
73. Sidney Hook, "Lord Russell and the War Crimes 'Trial,'" *New Leader*, October 24, 1966.
74. See *AWWA*, pp. 98f.
75. "Truck versus Dam," *Christian Science Monitor*, September 5, 1967.
76. Henry Kamm, *New York Times*, November 15, 1969; *New York Times*, April 6, 1971. See *FRS*, pp. 225f., for more details.
77. E.g., Amando Doronila, "Hanoi Food Output Held Target of U.S. Bombers," AP, *Christian Science Monitor*, September 8, 1967, three days after Joseph Harsch's philosophical reflections just cited.

78. See Kahin, *Intervention*, pp. 338f., 384, 400, on these perceived risks.
79. See *FRS*, pp. 4f., 70ff., for documentation from the official record.
80. Seymour Hersh, *My Lai Four* (New York: Random House, 1970); Hersh, *Cover-up* (New York: Random House, 1972); and Hersh, *New York Times*, June 5, 1972, on My Khe. *FRS*, pp. 251, xx.
81. Henry Kamm, "New Drive Begins in Area of Mylai," *New York Times*, April 1, 1971; Martin Teitel, "Again, the Suffering of Mylai," *New York Times*, June 7, 1972; see above, p. 196.
82. *FRS*, p. 222.
83. Cited in *PEHR* I, 316f., from Buckley's unpublished notes provided to the authors. See pp. 313f. on Operation Speedy Express; and our review of Guenter Lewy, note 33, on his falsification and apologetics for this and other atrocities.
84. "Five years later, My Lai is a no man's town, silent and unsafe," AP, *New York Times*, March 16, 1973; our emphasis.
85. Edward Jay Epstein, "The War in Vietnam: What Happened vs. What We Saw," *TV Guide*, September 29, October 6, October 13, 1973; reprinted in his *Between Fact and Fiction* (New York: Vintage, 1975).
86. The character of the bombing of North Vietnam is denied by apologists—notoriously, the respected "scholar" Guenter Lewy, who proves that it was directed solely at military targets on the grounds that the U.S. government says so, discounting eyewitness reports from a wide range of sources; see our review, cited in note 33, for a few examples.
87. Hallin, *"Uncensored War,"* pp. 110, 161–62; Johnson cited in Herring, *America's Longest War*, p. 204, from Roger Morris, *An Uncertain Greatness.*
88. Ibid., pp. 201–3. On the elections, see Edward S. Herman and Frank Brodhead, *Demonstration Elections: U.S.-Staged Elections in the Dominican Republic, Vietnam, and El Salvador* (Boston: South End Press, 1984), and chapter 3, above.
89. CBS-TV August 23, 1965; our emphasis. Hallin, pp. 118, 130–41.
90. Kevin Buckley; see *PEHR*, I, 313f., for more details on this major war crime. Hallin points out that the delta looked like a wilderness because "it was devastated by B-52 strikes in the late 1960s."
91. Hallin, pp. 172, 143.
92. Ibid., pp. 148–58.
93. Ibid., pp. 209–10.
94. *PP*, II, 668–69, 653. See Pike, *Viet Cong; PP*, II, III; and for detailed discussion, Kahin, *Intervention.*
95. *PP*, III, 150; Kahin, *Intervention*, p. 205.
96. Kahin, *Intervention*, pp. 219f.; Smith, *International History*, II, 280.
97. Smith, *International History*, II, 277, 280; Kahin, *Intervention*, pp. 219f.
98. Hallin, *"Uncensored War,"* pp. 19, 16, 20, 70f.
99. See Elterman, *State-Media-Ideological Hegemony*, pp. 274ff., and *Circle of Deception*, chapter 6, for detailed documentation and analysis.
100. *Time*, cover story, August 14; *Newsweek*, August 17, 24; *U.S. News & World Report*, August 17; cited with discussion by Elterman.
101. Hallin, *"Uncensored War,"* p. 21.
102. *New Statesman*, August 7, 14; *National Guardian*, August 8, 15 (three articles), 22; *I.F. Stone's Weekly*, August 10, 24, September 7; cited with discussion by Elterman, who notes also that the *New Republic* accepted the U.S.

government version with no question, although with some pessimism about the prospects, echoed in *The Nation.*

103. *PP,* III, 107.

104. *PP,* III, 531, 207.

105. James Reston, *New York Times,* February 26, 1965.

106. Braestrup, *Big Story;* see section 1, note 1; hereafter cited with volume and page number only. Don Oberdorfer, *Washington Post Magazine,* January 29, 1978; Oberdorfer is the author of *Tet!* (New York: Doubleday, 1971), praised as a "fine" study (I, xiii). Diamond, *New York Times Book Review,* December 4, 1977; a journalist, he headed the News Study Group in the MIT Political Science department. Roche, see note 5. Mohr, "Hawks and Doves Refight Tet Offensive at Symposium," *New York Times,* February 27, 1978; Smith, "Reading History: The Vietnam War," *History Today* (October 1984).

107. Herring, *America's Longest War,* pp. 200–201.

108. On the record of Freedom House in service to the state and in opposition to democracy, see Herman and Brodhead, *Demonstration Elections,* appendix 1, a small fragment of a record that merits more detailed exposure.

109. For additional evidence and discussion, see the review in *Race & Class* and *More,* from which we will draw extensively, particularly in appendix 3, and Porter's review, both cited in note 1, above.

110. Thies, *When Governments Collide,* p. 201. This analysis, familiar in the scholarly literature, is quite different from Braestrup's conclusions, which, as Porter comments, he attributes to a consensus of historians without a single reference. Porter adds that "few independent historians" would endorse Braestrup's conclusions or his analysis of Communist objectives, quoting CIA analyst Patrick McGarvey and others. See his *A Peace Denied,* pp. 67f., for further discussion of these issues.

111. *New York Times,* February 20, April 4, 1968. On internal U.S. government assessments, see below, and Kolko, *Anatomy of a War,* p. 329. Kolko goes on to describe how these assessments underestimated the success of U.S. terror in decimating the NLF infrastructure in rural areas, and were thus overly "pessimistic." Note that by virtue of these conclusions, Kolko counts as "optimistic" by Freedom House logic, that is, supportive of U.S. goals. In fact, quite the opposite is true, still another illustration of the absurdity of the Freedom House assumptions—or, more accurately, of their blind adherence to the doctrines of state propaganda, reaching to the way in which the issues are initially framed.

112. Herring, *America's Longest War,* p. 189. Hoopes quoted from his *Limits of Intervention* (New York: McKay, 1969), p. 145, by Herring and Thies.

113. *PP,* IV, 548, 558. April USG study cited by Porter, review of *Big Story.* McNamara, Statement before the Senate Armed Services Committee, Jan. 22, 1968 (II, 20).

114. See Kahin, *Intervention,* pp. 386f.

115. Herring, *America's Longest War,* p. 204.

116. Braestrup, *Big Story,* I, 671ff.; Burns W. Roper in *Big Story,* I, chapter 14.

117. For serious interpretations of the basis for the shift of government policy, putting Freedom House fantasies aside, see Herbert Schandler, *The Unmaking of a President* (Princeton: Princeton University Press, 1977); Thies, *When Governments Collide;* Kolko, *Anatomy of a War,* noting particularly the crucial

issue of the perceived economic crisis resulting from the costs of the war.
118. See Kahin, *Intervention,* pp. 421ff., for discussion of these important events.
119. Oberdorfer, *Tet!;* Porter, *A Peace Denied,* p. 66. On this forgotten massacre, and the various attempts to shift attention to the massacre carried out by the retreating NLF forces, see our *PEHR,* I, 345ff., and sources cited, particularly Gareth Porter, "The 1968 'Hué Massacre,' " *Congressional Record,* February 19, 1975, pp. S2189–94," and Porter's review of *Big Story.* Porter notes that Braestrup's estimate of destruction in Hué is far below that of US AID, which estimated in April that 77 percent of Hué's buildings were "seriously damaged" or totally destroyed.
120. Kolko, *Anatomy of a War,* p. 309.
121. *PP,* IV, 539. On third-country forces, introduced well before the first sighting of a battalion of North Vietnamese regulars in the South, see Kahin, *Intervention,* pp. 333f. Korean mercenaries began to arrive in January 1965, while Taiwanese soldiers had reached "several hundred" by mid-1964, in addition to "a considerable number of soldiers seconded from Chiang Kai-shek's army on Taiwan," possibly as early as 1959 but certainly under the Kennedy administration, often disguised as members of the Nung Chinese ethnic minority in Vietnam and employed for sabotage missions in the North as well as fighting in the South. For McNamara's estimate, see his statement before the Senate Armed Services Committee, January 22, 1968; excerpts in *Big Story,* II, 14ff.
122. Bernard Weinraub, *New York Times,* February 8, 1968; Lee Lescaze, *Washington Post,* February 6, 1968; in *Big Story,* II, 116ff.
123. *New York Times,* April 4, 1968. See appendix 3 for similar comments from news reporting.
124. Robert Shaplen, "Letter from Saigon," *The New Yorker,* March 2, 1968. He estimates the NVA component of the forces engaged at 10 percent of some 50,000 to 60,000.
125. Jean-Claude Pomonti, *Le Monde hebdomadaire,* February 4–8, 1968. Pomonti was expelled from the country soon after. The head of the *Newsweek* Saigon bureau had already been expelled.
126. Charles Mohr, *New York Times,* February 14, 1968. On Mohr, see *Big Story,* I, 718.
127. CBS-TV, February 14, 1968, Hallin, *"Uncensored War,"* 171; *Big Story,* I, 158.
128. We return in appendix 3 to the evidence that Braestrup presents, comparing the facts with his rendition of them, including Cronkite's reports.
129. *Boston Globe,* February 24, 1968.
130. See note 118, above.
131. Marc Riboud, *Le Monde,* April 13, 1968; *Newsweek,* February 19 (banned from Saigon), March 30; "CBS-TV Morning News," February 12, 1968, cited in *Big Story,* I, 274; John Lengel, AP, February 10, 1968, cited in *Big Story,* I, 269. Such a psychological warfare program was indeed conducted, although not recognized as such by the media; see note 119 above and Appendix 3.
132. Philip Jones Griffiths, *Vietnam Inc.* (New York: Macmillan, 1971), with pictures of the ongoing fighting. We return to coverage of Hué in appendix 3. See also note 119 above, and sources cited.

133. *PP,* IV, 546f.
134. Paul Quinn-Judge, "Soviet Publication Paints Bleak Picture of War in Afghanistan," *Christian Science Monitor,* Moscow, July 21, 1987. Quotes are Quinn-Judge's paraphrases.
135. Bill Keller, "Soviet Official Says Press Harms Army," *New York Times,* January 21, 1988.
136. *PP,* IV, 441; his emphasis. On Komer's role, as he sees it and as the record shows it, see *FRS,* pp. 84f.
137. See Seymour Hersh, *The Price of Power* (New York: Summit, 1983), pp. 582, 597, citing presidential aide Charles Colson and General Westmoreland.
138. For explicit references on these matters, here and below, see Noam Chomsky, "Indochina and the Fourth Estate," *Social Policy* (September–October 1973), reprinted in *Towards a New Cold War,* expanding an earlier article in *Ramparts* (April 1973). See also Porter, *A Peace Denied;* Kolko, *Anatomy of a War;* and Hersh, *Price of Power.* On the media during the October–January period, see also Elterman, *State-Media-Ideological Hegemony,* p. 347f., documenting overwhelming media conformity to the U.S. government version of the evolving events.
139. Cited by Hersh, *Price of Power,* p. 604.
140. *New Republic,* January 27, 1973. He notes that the Paris Agreements were "nearly the same" as the October agreements that "broke apart two months later," for reasons unexamined.
141. James N. Wallace, *U.S. News & World Report,* February 26, 1973.
142. *Boston Globe,* January 25, 1973, cited by Porter, *A Peace Denied,* 181.
143. January 25, 1973; see *State Department Bulletin,* February 12, 1973, with slight modifications.
144. For a detailed examination, see Chomsky "Indochina and the Fourth Estate."
145. *Boston Globe,* April 2, 1973.
146. *New York Times,* March 1, 1973.
147. *New Republic,* February 17, 1973.
148. *Newsweek*, February 5, 1973.
149. *Christian Science Monitor,* March 30, 1973.
150. For documentation, see our article in *Ramparts* (December 1974); Maynard Parker, *Foreign Affairs* (January 1975); Porter, *A Peace Denied.* See Porter on Pentagon assessments of North Vietnamese military activities and operations, very limited in comparison to the U.S.-GVN offensive in violation of the cease-fire and the agreements generally.
151. Robert Greenberger, *Wall Street Journal,* August 17; Neil Lewis, *New York Times,* August 18, 1987. For further details and the general background, see Noam Chomsky, *The Culture of Terrorism* (Boston: South End Press, 1988), part 2, chapter 7.
152. "Proper Uses of Power," *New York Times,* October 30, 1983. On the ways the task was addressed in the early postwar years, see our *PEHR,* vol. 2, largely devoted to the media and Indochina during the 1975–78 period.
153. See the Trilateral Commission study cited in note 3.
154. *PP,* IV, 420; *Journal of International Affairs* 25.1 (1971).
155. Mark McCain, *Boston Globe,* December 9, 1984; memo of May 19, 1967, released during the Westmoreland-CBS libel trial.

156. Memorandum for the secretary of defense by the Joint Chiefs of Staff, February 12, 1968, in Gareth Porter, ed., *Vietnam: A History in Documents* (New York: Meridian, 1981), pp. 354f.; *PP,* IV, 541, 564, 482, 478, 217, 197.
157. John E. Rielly, *Foreign Policy* (Spring 1983, Spring 1987). Rielly, ed., *American Public Opinion and U.S. Foreign Policy 1987,* Chicago Council on Foreign Relations, p. 33. In the 1986 poll, the percentage of the public that regarded the Vietnam War as "fundamentally wrong and immoral" was 66 percent, as compared with 72 percent in 1978 and 1982. Among "leaders" (including representatives of churches, voluntary organizations, and ethnic organizations), the percentage was 44 percent, as compared with 45 percent in 1982 and 50 percent in 1978. The editor takes this to indicate "some waning of the impact of the Vietnam experience with the passage of time"; and, perhaps, some impact of the propaganda system, as memories fade and people are polled who lack direct experience.
158. *New Republic,* January 22, 1977; see Marilyn Young, "Critical Amnesia," *The Nation,* April 2, 1977, on this and similar reviews of Emerson's *Winners and Losers.*
159. John Midgley, *New York Times Book Review,* June 30, 1985; Drew Middleton, *New York Times,* July 6, 1985.
160. Review of Paul Johnson, *Modern Times,* in *New York Times Book Review,* June 26, 1983, p. 15.
161. *New York Times,* May 28, 1984. A CIA analysis of April 1968 estimated that "80,000 enemy troops," overwhelmingly South Vietnamese, were killed during the Tet offensive. See note 44, above.
162. Arthur Westing, *Bulletin of the Atomic Scientists* (February 1981); Colin Norman, *Science,* March 11, 1983, citing the conclusion of an international conference in Ho Chi Minh City; Jim Rogers, *Indochina Issues,* Center for International Policy (September 1985). On the effects of U.S. chemical and environmental warfare in Vietnam, unprecedented in scale and character, see SIPRI, *Ecological Consequences of the Second Indochina War* (Stockholm: Almqvist & Wiksell, 1976).
163. Ton That Thien, *Pacific Affairs* (Winter 1983–84); Chitra Subramaniam, Pacific News Service, November 15, 1985; both writing from Geneva.
164. News conference, March 24, 1977; *New York Times,* March 25, 1977.
165. Bernard Gwertzman, *New York Times,* March 3, 1985.
166. Barbara Crossette, *New York Times,* November 10, 1985, February 28, 1988; AP, April 7, 1988.
167. John Corry, *New York Times,* April 27, 1985.
168. *Time,* April 15, 1985. The discussion here is in part drawn from Noam Chomsky, "Visions of Righteousness," *Cultural Critique* (Spring 1986).
169. *Wall Street Journal,* April 4, 1985. An exception was *Newsweek* (Apr. 15, 1985), which devoted four pages of its thirty-three-page account to a report by Tony Clifton and Ron Moreau on the effects of the war on the "wounded land." The *New York Times* retrospective includes one Vietnamese, a defector to the West, who devotes a few paragraphs of his five-page denunciation of the enemy to the character of the war, and there are scattered references in other retrospectives.
170. Presidential adviser Walt W. Rostow, formerly a professor at MIT, now a respected commentator on public affairs and economic historian at the

University of Texas, *The View from the Seventh Floor* (New York: Harper & Row, 1964), p. 244. Rostow's account of Mao and North Korea is as fanciful as his remarks on Indochina, as serious scholarship shows.

171. Stuart Creighton Miller, *"Benevolent Assimilation"* (New Haven: Yale University Press, 1982), p. 271.

172. Allan E. Goodman and Seth P. Tillman, *New York Times,* March 24, 1985.

173. *New York Times,* March 31, 1985. Charles Krauthammer, *New Republic,* March 4, 1985.

174. On Lebanese opinion and the scandalous refusal of the media to consider it, and the general context, see Noam Chomsky, *Fateful Triangle* (Boston: South End Press, 1983).

175. It is widely argued that the United States supported France in Indochina out of concern for French participation in the U.S.-run European military system. This appears to be a minor factor at best, and one can also make a case that the reverse was true: that support for France in Europe was motivated by concern that France might "abandon Indochina" (see Geoffrey Warner, "The USA and the Rearmament of West Germany," *International Affairs* [Spring 1985]). This factor also fails to explain U.S. efforts to keep the French in Indochina, and to take up their cause after they withdrew.

176. Cited by Porter, *A Peace Denied,* p. 36, from 1966 congressional hearings.

177. See, inter alia, essays in *PP,* V, by John Dower, Richard DuBoff, and Gabriel Kolko; *FRS,* chapter 1.V; Thomas McCormick, in Williams et al., *America in Vietnam;* Michael Schaller, "Securing the Great Crescent," *Journal of American History* (September 1982).

178. See p. 187, above, and *PEHR,* vol. 1, chapter 4.

179. Gelb, "10 Years After Vietnam, U.S. a Power in Asia," *New York Times,* April 18, 1985, quoting Professor Donald Zagoria.

180. See *FRS,* pp. 48f., citing upbeat analyses from the *Far Eastern Economic Review* in 1972.

181. *Far Eastern Economic Review,* October 11, 1984.

182. See *AWWA,* p. 286.

183. Fox Butterfield, "The New Vietnam Scholarship: Challenging the Old Passions," *New York Times Magazine,* February 13, 1983, referring specifically to Race's study cited earlier, an in-depth analysis of the NLF victory in rural areas prior to the escalation of the U.S. war in 1965, "invalidated" by events that occurred years later, according to Butterfield's interesting logic.

184. See our *PEHR,* II, 84, 166ff., 342; Daniel Southerland, "No Pens and Pencils for Cambodia," *Christian Science Monitor,* December 4, 1981; AP, "U.S. Bars Mennonite School Aid to Cambodia," *New York Times,* December 8, 1981; Joel Charny and John Spragens, *Obstacles to Recovery in Vietnam and Kampuchea: U.S. Embargo of Humanitarian Aid* (Boston: Oxfam America, 1984), citing many examples of "explicit U.S. policy" under the Reagan administration "to prevent even private humanitarian assistance from reaching the people of Kampuchea and Vietnam."

185. Louis Wiznitzer, *Christian Science Monitor,* November 6, 1981; Kamm, "In Mosaic of Southeast Asia, Capitalist Lands Are Thriving," *New York Times,* November 8, 1981.

186. See p. 187 and note 2.

187. For a point-by-point response, demonstrating that the accusations are a

mélange of falsehoods and misrepresentations apart from a few minor points changed in subsequent broadcasts, see the "Content Analysis and Assessment," included in *Inside Story Special Edition: Vietnam Op/Ed*, cited in note 2, above.

188. Karnow, *Vietnam*. For a detailed critique of this highly praised best-seller, see Noam Chomsky, "The Vietnam War in the Age of Orwell," *Race & Class* 4 (1984 [*Boston Review*, January 1984]). See Peter Biskind, "What Price Balance," *Race & Class* 4 (1984 [parts in *The Nation*, December 3, 1983]), on the PBS television history.

189. Kahin, *Intervention*, pp. 307–8.

190. Later, in another context, we hear that "to many peasants, [the U.S. Marines] were yet another threatening foreign force" (episode 6, on "America's Enemy" and their point of view).

191. Biskind, citing a *London Times* account; Butterfield, *New York Times*, October 2, 1983.

Chapter 6: The Indochina Wars (II)

1. Cited by Bernard Fall, *Anatomy of a Crisis* (1961; reprint, New York: Doubleday, 1969), p. 163, from congressional hearings. The reasons were political: the Pentagon was not in favor. See also Walter Haney, "The Pentagon Papers and U.S. Involvement in Laos," in *Pentagon Papers*, Senator Gravel edition (Boston: Beacon Press, 1972; hereafter *PP*), vol. 5.

2. State Department *Background Notes* (March 1969); Denis Warner, *Reporting Southeast Asia* (Sydney: Angus & Robertson, 1966), p. 171.

3. On this period, see, among others, Haney, "U.S. Involvement in Laos"; Noam Chomsky, *At War with Asia* (New York: Pantheon, 1970; hereafter *AWWA*); Nina S. Adams and Alfred W. McCoy, eds., *Laos: War and Revolution* (New York: Harper & Row, 1970); Charles Stevenson, *The End of Nowhere* (Boston: Beacon Press, 1972).

4. Howard Elterman, *The State, the Mass Media and Ideological Hegemony: United States Policy Decisions in Indochina, 1974–75—Historical Record, Government Pronouncements and Press Coverage* (Ph.D. diss., New York University, 1978), p. 198.

5. Fall, *Anatomy of a Crisis*.

6. A request to the (very cooperative) American embassy in Vientiane to obtain their documentation would have quickly revealed to reporters that the claims they were relaying on the basis of embassy briefings had little relation to the facts, as one of us discovered by carrying out the exercise in Vientiane in early 1970. For a detailed review of the available facts concerning foreign (North Vietnamese, Thai, Chinese Nationalist, and U.S.) involvement through the 1960s, and their relation to what the media were reporting, see *AWWA*, pp. 203–36; and Noam Chomsky, *For Reasons of State* (New York: Pantheon, 1973; hereafter *FRS*), pp. 178–79. See also chapter 5, p. 177, and note 22.

7. In Adams and McCoy, *Laos;* excerpts in *AWWA*, pp. 96–97.

8. On attempts by former *Times* Saigon bureau chief A. J. Langguth to explain

away the suppression of the bombing of northern Laos by obscuring the crucial distinction between the bombing of the civilian society of the North and the bombing of the Ho Chi Minh trail in the South (acceptable within the doctrinal system in terms of "defense of South Vietnam against North Vietnamese aggression"), see Noam Chomsky, *Towards a New Cold War* (New York: Pantheon, 1982), p. 402.

9. Elterman, *State-Media-Ideological Hegemony,* pp. 332ff. and appendixes.

10. The report states that "until early this spring, when North Vietnamese troops began a series of advances in northeast Laos," the war had been "limited," U.S. bombing had been aimed at "North Vietnamese supply routes" and "concentrations of enemy troops," and "civilian population centers and farmland were largely spared." Extensive refugee reports were soon to show that this account was inaccurate, as Decornoy's eyewitness reports had done fifteen months earlier.

11. See references cited above, and, shortly after, Fred Branfman, *Voices from the Plain of Jars* (New York: Harper & Row, 1972); and Walter Haney, "A Survey of Civilian Fatalities among Refugees from Xieng Khouang Province, Laos," in *Problems of War Victims in Indochina,* Hearings before the [Kennedy] Subcommittee on Refugees and Escapees, U.S. Senate, May 9, 1972, pt. 2: "Laos and Cambodia," appendix 2. There were some 1970 reports in the media: e.g., Daniel Southerland, *Christian Science Monitor,* March 14; Laurence Stern, *Washington Post,* March 26; Hugh D. S. Greenway, *Life,* April 3; Carl Strock, *New Republic,* May 9; Noam Chomsky, "Laos," *New York Review of Books,* July 23, 1970, with more extensive details (reprinted in *AWWA*).

12. Haney, *PP,* V. See *FRS,* pp. 176f., on Sullivan's misrepresentation of Haney's conclusions.

13. *Refugee And Civilian War Casualty Problems in Indochina,* Staff Report for the [Kennedy] Subcommittee on Refugees and Escapees, U.S. Senate, September 28, 1970.

14. One of the authors participated in a public meeting of media figures in New York, in 1986, at which a well-known television journalist defended media coverage of the bombing of northern Laos on the grounds that there was a report from a refugee camp in 1972. One wonders how much credit would be given to a journal that reported the bombing of Pearl Harbor in 1945.

15. T. D. Allman, *Manchester Guardian Weekly,* January 1; *Far Eastern Economic Review,* January 8, 1972 (hereafter *FEER*); see *FRS,* pp. 173f., for a lengthy excerpt. Robert Seamans, cited by George Wilson, *Washington Post–Boston Globe,* January 17, 1972; see *FRS,* pp. 172f., for this and similar testimony before Congress by Ambassador William Sullivan. John Everingham and subsequent commentary on the Hmong (Meo) tribes, cited in Noam Chomsky and Edward S. Herman, *Political Economy of Human Rights* (Boston: South End Press, 1979; hereafter *PEHR*) II, 119f.; Chanda, *FEER,* December 23, 1977; see *PEHR,* II, 131f., 340, for these and other direct testimonies, far from the mainstream, with a few noteworthy exceptions cited. *Bangkok World,* cited by Haney, "U.S. Involvement in Laos," p. 292, along with a Jack Anderson column in the *Washington Post* (Feb. 19, 1972). On postwar experiences of U.S. relief workers, see *PEHR,* pp. 132f., 340.

16. McCoy's emphasis, in a letter to the *Washington Post;* cited by Haney, "U.S. Involvement in Laos," p. 293.
17. Television commentary reprinted in *Christian Science Monitor,* June 10, 1975.
18. See *AWWA,* pp. 119f., and Haney, "U.S. Involvement in Laos," citing congressional hearings and the *Washington Post,* March 16, 1970.
19. Walter Saxon, *New York Times,* August 24, 1975. See *PEHR,* chapter 5, for further details on this report and general discussion of postwar reporting of Laos.
20. Kimmo Kiljunen, ed., *Kampuchea: Decade of the Genocide,* Report of a government-backed Finnish Inquiry Commission (London: Zed, 1984). See also Kiljunen, "Power Politics and the Tragedy of Kampuchea during the Seventies," *Bulletin of Concerned Asian Scholars* (April–June 1985).
21. See William Shawcross, *Sideshow* (New York: Simon & Schuster, 1979), and Seymour Hersh, *The Price of Power* (New York: Summit, 1983).
22. William Shawcross, "The End of Cambodia?" *New York Review of Books,* January 24, 1980, relying on reports by François Ponchaud, a French priest whose work provided the major source of evidence about Khmer Rouge atrocities in 1975–76: François Ponchaud, *Cambodia: Year Zero* (New York: Holt, Rinehart & Winston, 1978), a revised version of a 1977 French study that became perhaps the most influential unread book in recent political history after a review by Jean Lacouture ("The Bloodiest Revolution," *New York Review of Books,* Mar. 31, 1977); see also his "Cambodia: Corrections," *New York Review of Books,* May 26, 1977, withdrawing the most sensational claims. Our review (*The Nation,* June 25, 1977) was the first, to our knowledge, to attend to the actual text, which appeared in English a year later. See our *PEHR,* II.6, on the record of falsification based on this book, and on Ponchaud's own remarkable record, further analyzed by Michael Vickery in his *Cambodia: 1975–1982* (Boston: South End Press, 1984). CIA Research Paper, *Kampuchea: A Demographic Catastrophe* (Washington: CIA, May 1980). For a critique of this study revealing extensive falsification conditioned by U.S. government priorities—specifically, suppression of the worst Pol Pot atrocities during the later period—see Michael Vickery, "Democratic Kampuchea—CIA to the Rescue," *Bulletin of Concerned Asian Scholars* 14.4 (1982), and his *Cambodia.* The latter is the major study of the Khmer Rouge period, by one of the few authentic Cambodia scholars, widely and favorably reviewed abroad by mainstream Indochina scholars and others but virtually ignored in the United States, as was the Finnish Inquiry Commission report. See Noam Chomsky, "Decade of Genocide in Review," *Inside Asia* (London, February 1985, reprinted in James Peck, ed., *The Chomsky Reader* [New York: Pantheon, 1987]), on several serious studies of the period, including these.
23. Michael Vickery, "Ending Cambodia—Some Revisions," submitted to the *New York Review of Books* in June 1981 but rejected. See his *Cambodia* for more extended discussion. Shawcross himself had had second thoughts by then (see "Kampuchea Revives on Food, Aid, and Capitalism," *The Bulletin* [Australia], March 24, 1981). See his *Quality of Mercy: Cambodia, Holocaust and Modern Conscience* (New York: Simon & Schuster, 1984), for a later version, now recast in ways to which we return.

24. Page 370, blaming Vietnamese deception for the account he had relayed in 1980.
25. Shawcross, *The Nation,* September 21, 1985; Ben Kiernan, letter to *The Nation,* October 3, 1985, unpublished. For evaluation of the international relief efforts, see Vickery, *Cambodia;* Kiljunen, *Kampuchea;* Joel Charny and John Spragens, *Obstacles to Recovery in Vietnam and Kampuchea: U.S. Embargo of Humanitarian Aid* (Boston: Oxfam America, 1984); Shawcross, *Quality of Mercy.*
26. François Ponchaud, on whom Shawcross relied, is a highly dubious source for reasons that have been extensively documented; see note 22. No one with a record of duplicity approaching his would ever be relied on for undocumented charges of any significance if the target were not an official enemy.
27. Shawcross, *Quality of Mercy,* pp. 49–50. He observes that "those years of warfare saw the destruction of Cambodian society and the rise of the Khmer Rouge from its ashes, in good part as a result of White House policies"; "with the forces of nationalism unleashed by the war at their command, the Khmer Rouge became an increasingly formidable army," while in the "massive American bombing campaign" to which the Khmer Rouge were subjected through August 1973, "their casualties are thought to have been huge." The phrase "their casualties" presumably refers to Khmer Rouge military forces; there is no mention of civilian casualties. On the limited scope of Shawcross's "quality of mercy," see "Phase III at home" (p. 288), below.
28. Vickery, *Cambodia,* p. 293.
29. AP, *Boston Globe,* September 24, 1978, citing the Report of the International Labor Organization in Geneva on over fifty million child laborers in the world, with Thailand singled out as one of the worst offenders, thanks to grinding poverty, an effective military government backed by the United States, lack of labor union power, and "wide-open free enterprise." See *PEHR,* II.6, 359, for excerpts and other examples that have elicited even less interest, and *PEHR,* II, xv, on a World Bank description of the situation in Thailand. On the brutal treatment of many of the estimated 10.7 million child laborers in Thailand, see *Human Rights in Thailand Report* 9.1. (January–March 1985) (Coordinating Group for Religion in Society, Bangkok); *Thai Development Newsletter* 3.1 1985 (December 1986) (Bangkok). On the treatment of women in "the brothel of Asia," with its estimated 500,000 prostitutes, masseuses, and bar-waitresses, 20 percent of them under fourteen years of age, drawn to Bangkok (and sometimes sold off to Europe) from the impoverished rural areas through "a huge underground network of brothels and workshops feeding on child flesh and labor," see several articles in *Beyond Stereotypes: Asian Women in Development, Southeast Asia Chronicle* (January 1985).
30. For extensive evidence on this matter, see *PEHR,* II.6, and Vickery, *Cambodia,* extending the story to phase III.
31. Others give higher estimates. Ponchaud gives the figure of 800,000 killed, but, as noted in our 1977 review, he seems to have exaggerated the toll of the U.S. bombing, and as shown in the references of note 22, he is a highly unreliable source. "US Government sources put the figure unofficially at 600,000 to 700,000" (CIA demographic study, which accepts the lower figure).
32. Vickery, *Cambodia,* pp. 184f. Other estimates vary widely. At the low end, the CIA demographic study gives the figure of 50,000 to 100,000 for people

who "may have been executed," and an estimate of deaths from all causes that is meaningless because of misjudgment of postwar population and politically motivated assessments throughout; the *Far Eastern Economic Review* reported a substantial *increase* in the population under DK to 8.2 million, "mostly based on CIA estimates" (*Asia 1979* and *Asia 1980* yearbooks of the *FEER*, the latter reducing the estimate from 8.2 to 4.2 million, the actual figure apparently being in the neighborhood of 6.5 million); in the U.S. government journal *Problems of Communism* (May–June 1981), Australian Indochina specialist Carlyle Thayer suggests a figure of deaths from all causes at 500,000, of which 50,000 to 60,000 were executions. At the high end, estimates range to three million or more, but without any available analysis. As all serious observers emphasize, the range of error is considerable at every point.

33. George Hildebrand and Gareth Porter, *Cambodia: Starvation and Revolution* (New York: Monthly Review Press, 1976), based on U.S. and international aid reports, cited by Vickery, *Cambodia*, p. 79; *FEER* correspondent Nayan Chanda in several articles, cited in *PEHR*, I.6, 229f.; Western doctor is Dr. Penelope Key, of the World Vision Organization, cited by Hildebrand and Porter, along with similar reports from Catholic Relief Services and Red Cross observers; Shawcross, *Sideshow*, pp. 370f. Hildebrand and Porter's book, the only extensive study of the situation at the war's end, was highly praised by Indochina scholar George Kahin but ignored in the media, or vilified. See *PEHR*, II.6, 232f., for a particular egregious example, by William Shawcross in the *New York Review of Books*. When *PEHR*, II.6 was circulating to Cambodia scholars and journalists in manuscript, we received a letter from Shawcross demanding that references to him be eliminated. We responded that we would be glad to consider any specific case that he found wrong or misleading and delayed publication of the book awaiting his response, which never arrived. On his public response, see below.

34. Milton Osborne, *Before Kampuchea* (London: Allen & Unwin, 1980), p. 191; David Chandler, *Pacific Affairs* (Summer 1983); Philip Windsor, *The Listener*, BBC (London), July 11, 1985.

35. David Chandler and Ben Kiernan, eds., *Revolution and Its Aftermath in Kampuchea*, Monograph 25/Yale University Southeast Asia Series (1983), p. 1.

36. See note 32, above; *FEER*, January 19, 1979.

37. Douglas Pike, *St. Louis Post-Dispatch*, November 29, 1979, and *Christian Science Monitor*, December 4, 1979; cited by Vickery, *Cambodia*, p. 65. On the Freedom House and *Times* assessments of Pike's work, see p.p. 324, 326; Fox Butterfield, "The New Vietnam Scholarship," *New York Times Magazine* cover story, February 13, 1983, where Pike is regarded as the exemplar of the "new breed" of dispassionate scholars.

38. Nayan Chanda, *Brother Enemy* (New York: Harcourt Brace Jovanovich, 1986), pp. 329, 394, for a detailed analysis of the maneuverings during this period. See also Grant Evans and Kelvin Rowley, *Red Brotherhood at War* (London: Verso, 1984).

39. *Derrière le sourire khmer* (Paris: Plon, 1971); see *FRS*, chapter 2, section 2.

40. Vickery, *Cambodia*, pp. 7, 17, 5–6, 17, 43; Vickery, "Looking Back at Cambodia," *Westerly* (Australia) (December 1976). See *PEHR*, II.6 for excerpts from the latter study.

41. See *FRS*, pp. 192ff., and sources cited, particularly the fall 1971 studies by T. D. Allman, based on interviews with members of the Cambodian elite.
42. See Elizabeth Becker, *When The War Was Over* (New York: Simon & Schuster, 1987), p. 28, citing a 1963 U.S. embassy cable quoting Sihanouk; Chanda, *Brother Enemy*, pp. 61f. See *AWWA* and *FRS* on contemporary studies of the Sihanouk period that provide more detail.
43. Michael Leifer, "Cambodia," *Asian Survey* (January 1967). Becker, *When the War Was Over*, p. 27, asserts that the CIA was behind the 1959 plot. For sources on these developments here and below, largely French, see *AWWA* and *FRS*. See Peter Dale Scott in *PP*, V, on the regional context of the 1963 escalation.
44. See *AWWA* and *FRS* for references and other examples.
45. *Bombing in Cambodia*, Hearings before the Committee on Armed Services, U.S. Senate, 93d Cong., 1st sess., July / August 1973, pp. 158–60, the primary source on the "secret bombings."
46. See *PEHR*, II.6, 288.
47. *PEHR*, II.6, 380; also 383. Shawcross, *Quality of Mercy*, p. 49, referring solely to B-52 bombings of Vietnamese "sanctuaries" in the border areas, the standard evasion of the issue.
48. See *PEHR*, II.6, 383, where the same point is noted, and its irrelevance discussed. These matters had been specifically brought to Shawcross's attention during the period when he was working on his *Sideshow*, in commentary (which he had requested) on earlier articles of his on the topic in the British press.
49. William Beecher, *New York Times*, May 9, 1969; *PEHR*, II.6, 271, 289, 383.
50. Elterman, *State-Media-Ideological Hegemony*, p. 344. Note that the post-Tet operations were in part reported at the time, although often in the highly distorted framework already discussed. For samples, see *AWWA*. On media coverage of the Laos bombings in 1969, see "Laos" (p. 253).
51. T. D. Allman, *FEER*, April 9, 1970; *Manchester Guardian*, September 18, 1971. See note 41.
52. See *FRS*, p. 194, and sources cited; see *AWWA* on media coverage of the invasion.
53. Richard Dudman, *Forty Days with the Enemy* (New York: H. Liveright, 1971), p. 69.
54. Terence Smith, *New York Times*, December 5, 1971; Iver Peterson, *New York Times*, December 2, 1971. See *FRS*, pp. 188f., for citations from U.S. and primarily French sources. See also Fred Branfman, in *PP*, V.
55. See *FRS*, pp. 190–92, for excerpts from *Le Monde*.
56. Elterman, *State-Media-Ideological Hegemony*, pp. 335f.
57. Vickery, *Cambodia*, p. 15.
58. UPI, *New York Times*, June 22, 1973, citing Pentagon statistics.
59. Shawcross, *Sideshow*, pp. 272, 297; see p. 262, above.
60. See *PEHR*, II.6, 154f., 220f., 365f., for sources, excerpts, and discussion.
61. E.g., Henry Kamm, *New York Times*, March 25, 28, 1973.
62. Becker, *When the War Was Over*, p. 32.
63. Malcolm Browne, "Cambodians' Mood: Apathy, Resignation," *New York Times*, June 29, 1973. On the forceful recruiting from "the poorer classes,

. . . refugees and the unemployed," including the "poor peasants" who have "poured into the capital" after their villages were destroyed, but not the children of the wealthy elites, see Sydney Schanberg, *New York Times*, August 4, 1973.

64. Kamm, *New York Times*, March 25, 1973.

65. See Vickery, *Cambodia*, pp. 9f., on Buddhism, about which "probably more arrant nonsense has been written in the West . . . than about any other aspect of Southeast Asian life," particularly with regard to Cambodia.

66. Schanberg, *New York Times*, May 3, 8, July 19, July 30, August 16, August 12, 1973.

67. August 22, 1973. The material reviewed here is from May 3 to August 16.

68. Mostly Malcolm Browne; also Henry Kamm, wire services, specials. We omit brief reports here, and this record may not be complete.

69. Compare, for example, Jon Swain's horrifying account of the situation in the hospitals in Phnom Penh at the time of the 1975 evacuation with Sydney Schanberg's cursory remark that "many of the wounded were dying for lack of care" (Swain, *Sunday Times* (London), May 11; Schanberg, *New York Times*, May 9, 1975); see *PEHR*, II.6, 370–71, for details.

70. *Sunday Times* (London), May 11, 1975. See *PEHR*, II.6, 249f., for longer excerpts.

71. Schanberg, *New York Times*, April 6, 8, 23, 1985.

72. *New York Times*, October 28, 1984.

73. Editorials, *New York Times*, April 11, 1985; April 7, September 9, 1985. Others do note "America's role in the tragic destruction of Cambodian civilization," which "renders suspect any belated show of concern for Cambodian sovereignty" (Editorial, *Boston Globe*, April 12, 1985).

74. Editorial, *New York Times*, July 9, 1975; also Jack Anderson, *Washington Post*, June 4, 1975.

75. See *PEHR*, II.6.

76. Our review cited in the preceding footnote was therefore limited to materials based on this earlier period, all that was available at the time we wrote.

77. See *PEHR*, II.6, VI; Vickery, *Cambodia*.

78. *PEHR*, II.6, 135–36, 290, 293, 140, 299.

79. In the only scholarly assessment, Vickery concludes that "very little of [the discussion in *PEHR*, II.6] requires revision in the light of new information available since it appeared." He also comments on the "scurrilous," "incompetent," and "dishonest criticism of Chomsky and Herman which has characterized media treatment of their work," noting falsifications by William Shawcross, among others (*Cambodia*, pp. 308, 310).

80. Guenter Lewy, *Commentary* (November 1984), a typical example of a substantial literature. To our knowledge, Lewy, like other infuriated critics, did not condemn the Khmer Rouge in print as harshly, or as early, as we did. Recall that Lewy has experience with these matters, given his record as an apologist for war crimes, which reaches levels rarely seen. See chapter 5, notes 33, 86.

81. John Barron and Anthony Paul, *Murder in a Gentle Land* (New York: Reader's Digest Press, 1977). Anderson, *Washington Post*, October 1, 1978. Kamm, *New York Times Magazine*, November 19, 1978, including fabricated photographs; see *PEHR*, II.6, 202, 253; and 367, 372, on the scholarly literature

describing a country where "the population is ever on the edge of starvation" in earlier years and completely lacking an economy by 1975. Wise, *FEER,* September 23, 1977. See *PEHR,* II.6, for further examples and details, here and below; and Vickery, *Cambodia,* for additional evidence.

82. See our citations from his writings in the *Far Eastern Economic Review* (Hong Kong) and *Le Monde diplomatique* (Paris), in *PEHR,* II.

83. *Cambodia,* p. 48. See also the review of his book by British Indochina scholar R. B. Smith, emphasizing the same point (*Asian Affairs* [February 1985]).

84. *Cambodia,* chapter 3. Also essays by Vickery and Ben Kiernan in Chandler and Kiernan, *Revolution and Its Aftermath;* and Ben Kiernan, *Cambodia: The Eastern Zone Massacres,* Center for the Study of Human Rights, Documentation Series, no.1 [c. 1986], (New York: Columbia University).

85. *PEHR,* II.6, 138–39, 152–53, 156–57, 163.

86. Shawcross, in Chandler and Kiernan, *Revolution and Its Aftermath.*

87. See *PEHR,* and Edward S. Herman, *The Real Terror Network* (Boston: South End Press, 1982), for extensive discussion. See particularly chapter 2, above.

88. John Holdridge (State Department), Hearing before the Subcommittee on Asian and Pacific Affairs of the Committee on Foreign Affairs, House of Representatives, 97th Cong., 2d sess., September 14, 1982, p. 71.

89. For discussion of their qualms, and how they resolved them, and similar concerns elsewhere, see Chomsky, *Towards a New Cold War,* chapter 13.

90. Nayan Chanda, *FEER,* November 1, 1984; November 7, 1985, with minor modifications, their general position from early on in phase III.

91. Henry Kamm, *New York Times,* November 8, 1981. See chapter 5, note 45 above, on the reported level of U.S. support for the Khmer Rouge.

92. *FEER,* August 16, 1984. Essentially the same story appeared in the *Washington Post,* July 8, 1985, with no acknowledgment of their source, as the *FEER* commented editorially with some annoyance on August 8, 1985.

93. Pringle, *FEER,* February 25, 1988; Crossette, New York Times, April 1, 1988. Holbrooke, quoted in *Indochina Issues* (June 1985). See also Robert Manning, *South* (September 1984), and Elizabeth Becker, "U.S. Backs Mass Murderer," *Washington Post,* May 22, 1983, on U.S. pressures to force the non-Communist resistance "into an ignominious coalition with Pol Pot." Dith Pran, quoted by Jack Colhoun, *Guardian* (New York), June 5, 1985. Hawk, letter, *FEER,* August 2, 1984, with a picture of Alexander Haig "meeting, drink in hand, a smiling Ieng Sary" (Khmer Rouge foreign minister) in New York.

94. Chanda, *Brother Enemy,* p. 379.

95. Chanthou Boua, "Observations of the Heng Samrin Government," in Chandler and Kiernan, *Revolution and Its Aftermath.*

96. Our own expressed view at the time was that "the Vietnamese invasion can be explained, but it cannot be justified" (*PEHR,* II, preface, xix). With the information that has since appeared about the Pol Pot terror in 1977–78 and the border attacks against Vietnam, that judgment might have to be qualified, even in terms of a rather restrictive interpretation of the right of self-defense under international law.

97. *London Guardian,* October 26, 1984.

98. Abrams, letter, *New York Times,* January 8, 1985; also Abrams and Diane

Orentlicher, *Washington Post Weekly,* September 9, 1985. Hawk, *New Republic,* November 15, 1982; *Economist,* October 13, 1984; O'Brien, *London Observer,* September 30, 1984.

99. *Quality of Mercy*; *Washington Post,* September 2, 1984; his article in Chandler and Kiernan, *Revolution and Its Aftermath.*

100. *Quality of Mercy,* pp. 55; *Washington Post,* September 2, 1984.

101. It is concocted from a series of phrases that appear in various places in the introduction to volume I of *PEHR,* pp. 19–20, with crucial omissions—not noted—that would at once demonstrate the absurdity of the argument he presents.

102. Cited by Vickery, *Cambodia,* pp. 58f., in a discussion of Shawcross's subsequent effort "to efface his earlier good judgment and claim to have been a purveyor of a sensationalist STV, when he clearly was not."

103. Shawcross may indeed have had other motives; see note 33.

104. See author's preface, American edition of Ponchaud's *Cambodia: Year Zero.* On Ponchaud's remarkable deception concerning this matter, see *PEHR,* II.6, 278f.

105. For a record based on further inquiry, see *PEHR,* II.6, 253–84.

106. See note 79 above.

107. To be precise, we have found one suggestion, although well after the event. In *The Times Higher Education Supplement,* December 6, 1981, along with a series of falsifications of our position of the sort discussed here, Shawcross states that given our "political influence," we could have played an important part in mobilizing world opinion to bring pressure on China to call off Khmer Rouge atrocities—as he was no doubt desperately trying to do, but failing, because of his lack of outreach comparable to ours. Comment should be superfluous. Evidently the editors of the journal so believed, refusing publication of a response, despite our awesome "political influence." It seems doubtful that Shawcross would have published such childish absurdities had he not been assured that no response would be permitted.

108. *Quality of Mercy,* p. 357.

109. Review of *Quality of Mercy, Washington Post Weekly,* July 30, 1984, Book World.

110. See his essay in Chandler and Kiernan, *Revolution and Its Aftermath,* his only attempt to provide evidence for his widely heralded claims.

111. *New Statesman,* November 2, 1984. On the question of whether DK was "Marxist-Leninist"—whatever that is supposed to mean, exactly—see Vickery, *Cambodia.*

112. The opening pages of our chapter on Cambodia in *PEHR,* II, 135–36. For some of our comments in the article in question, see p. 290, above.

113. See references of note 22.

114. *Quality of Mercy,* p. 357.

115. Ibid., pp. 358–59; *New York Review of Books,* September 27, 1984. We emphasize that the correctness of his accusation is not at issue here, but, rather, the evidence he uses to support it.

116. For many earlier cases, see *PEHR,* II.6, and Vickery, *Cambodia.*

117. And, significantly, comparable and ongoing atrocities for which the United States bore primary responsibility were suppressed (and still largely are), with shameful apologetics when the facts could no longer be denied.

Chapter 7: Conclusions

1. Lewis, "Freedom of the Press—Anthony Lewis Distinguishes Between Britain and America," *London Review of Books,* November 26, 1987. Lewis is presenting his interpretation of the views of James Madison and Justice Brennan (in the case of *The New York Times v. Sullivan* that Lewis describes as the "greatest legal victory [of the press] in modern times"), with his endorsement.
2. See, among others, N. Blackstock, ed., *COINTELPRO* (New York: Vintage, 1976); Frank J. Donner, *The Age of Surveillance: The Aims and Methods of America's Political Intelligence System* (New York: Knopf, 1980); Robert J. Goldstein, *Political Repression in America* (Cambridge: Schenkman, 1978); Morton H. Halperin et al., *The Lawless State* (New York: Penguin, 1976); Christy Macy and Susan Kaplan, eds., *Documents* (New York: Penguin, 1980).
3. The diffused-cost cases would include the multi-billion-dollar outlays borne by the taxpayers for CIA covert operations and the subsidization of client regimes, the overhead costs of empire and the arms race, the enormous ripoffs by the military-industrial complex in providing unneeded weapons at inflated prices, and the payoffs to campaign contributors in the form of favorable tax legislation and other benefits (e.g., the huge tax bonanzas given business following Reagan's election in 1981, and the increase in milk prices given by Nixon in 1971 immediately after substantial gifts were given by the milk lobby to the Republican party).
4. In fact, the scandals and illegalities detailed by the Tower Commission and congressional inquiries were largely known long before these establishment "revelations," but were suppressible; see Noam Chomsky, *The Culture of Terrorism* (Boston: South End Press, 1988).
5. See also the preface. On the persistence of the elite consensus, including the media, through the period of the Iran-contra hearings and beyond, see Chomsky, *Culture of Terrorism.*
6. Laurence R. Simon and James C. Stephens, Jr., *El Salvador Land Reform 1980–1981,* Impact Audit (Boston: Oxfam America, February 1981), p. 51, citing Ambassador Robert White and land-reform adviser Roy Prosterman on "the Pol Pot left"; Raymond Bonner, *Weakness and Deceit* (New York: Times Books, 1984), p. 88, citing Ambassador White, and p. 207, citing Archbishop Rivera y Damas, who succeeded the assassinated Archbishop Romero. Jeane Kirkpatrick, "U.S. Security and Latin America," *Commentary* (January 1981).
7. *Washington Post,* May 21, 1987. The "genocide" to which Buckley refers is "of the Miskito Indians," of whom perhaps several dozen were killed by the Sandinistas in the context of attacks by U.S. mercenary forces, at a time when the U.S.-backed Guatemalan military were in the process of slaughtering tens of thousands of Indians, but not committing "genocide" by Buckley's lights.
8. Although, as we noted, with little constraint on passing along useful fabrications and rumors, even relaying tales long conceded to be fabrications.
9. W. Lance Bennett, *News: The Politics of Illusion,* 2d ed. (New York: Longman, 1988), pp. 178–79.
10. Ben Bagdikian, *The Media Monopoly* (Boston: Beacon Press, 1980), p. x.
11. Edgar Chamorro, who was selected by the CIA as press spokesman for the contras, describes Stephen Kinzer of the *New York Times* as "like an errand

boy, building up those stories that fit in with Reagan's agenda—one day it's the church, the next day the Miskitos, then the private sector. In the last two weeks I've seen at least eight articles by Kinzer which say exactly what the White House wants. Kinzer always raises questions about Sandinista intentions, whether they're truly democratic, and so on. When you analyze his articles you see he's just responding to what the White House is saying" (Interview, *Extra!* [the newsletter of FAIR, Fairness & Accuracy in Reporting], October–November 1987). FAIR is a left-liberal counterpart to the right-wing organization Accuracy in Media, therefore underfunded and regularly excluded from debate, as distinct from AIM. Its letters to editors often are refused publication, even when their accuracy is privately conceded; see the same issue for some remarkable examples.

12. For classic accounts, see Warren Breed, "Social Control in the Newsrooms: A Functional Analysis," *Social Forces* (May 1955), pp. 326–35; Gaye Tuchman, "Objectivity as Strategic Ritual," *American Journal of Sociology* (January 1972), pp. 660–70. For a useful application, see Jim Sibbison, "Environmental Reporters: Prisoners of Gullibility," *Washington Monthly* (March 1984), pp. 27–35.

13. See Chomsky, in *Z* magazine (March 1988), for discussion of these tendencies.

14. For evidence on these matters, see the specific examples discussed above and, for a broader picture, Chomsky, *Culture of Terrorism,* and sources cited.

15. The Cable Franchise and Telecommunications Act of 1984 allows cities to require public-access channels, but it permits cable operators to direct these channels to other uses if they are not well utilized. Thus nonuse may provide the basis for an elimination of public access.

16. On the differences between commercial and public television during the Vietnam War years, see Eric Barnouw, *The Sponsor* (New York: Oxford University Press, 1978), pp. 62–65.

17. See the programs spelled out for Great Britain in James Curran, Jake Ecclestone, Giles Oakley, and Alan Richardson, eds., *Bending Reality: The State of the Media* (London: Pluto Press, 1986).

Appendix 1

1. On Penniman's background, and for a study of his methods as an observer, see "Penniman on South Vietnamese Elections: The Observer-Expert as Promoter-Salesman," in Edward S. Herman and Frank Brodhead, *Demonstration Elections: U.S.-Staged Elections in the Dominican Republic, Vietnam, and El Salvador* (Boston: South End Press, 1984), appendix 2.

2. In a letter of December 20, 1984, to one of his constituents who had complained of his gullibility as an observer, Brier asserted that his obligation was to report "observed election fraud, coercion of the voters, or denials of the right to vote. . . ." On fundamental conditions, Brier wrote: "I made and make no statements concerning pre-election day freedom of speech, although the election I just witnessed in Guatemala would lead me to believe it existed

because of the 14 to 16 different political parties and based on press accounts, we have been led to believe it does not exist in Nicaragua as they prepare for elections." Actually, the occasional press accounts in the United States about state-organized murder in Guatemala might have alerted Brier to the possibility of some constraints on freedom there, but he apparently asked no questions and did no reading up on the subject. His inference from numerous parties to freedom of speech is a *non sequitur*—an authoritarian and terror-ridden state can easily allow, and may even encourage, a proliferation of candidates within a prescribed political spectrum. Brier cites press accounts on constraints on freedom of speech in Nicaragua as if this is a relevant subject, but he failed to pursue the matter with regard to Guatemala. He also makes the patriotic assumption that press accounts in the United States about conditions in client and disfavored states are objective. Brier wears blinders in U.S.-sponsored elections that he is prepared to set aside in talking about the integrity of an election in an enemy state. This dichotomization is openly employed by the State Department, and was followed by Hedrick Smith, of the *Times,* and the media more generally, as we have seen.

Brier distinguished himself as a member of the official delegation to the Philippines election of February 1986 won by Ferdinand Marcos by attacking the media's focus on negatives like "violence, vote-buying and fraud," with the result that "they missed entirely the fact that 20 million people conscientiously went to the polls without intimidation and wrote down their choice for President" (Robert Pear, quoting Jack Brier, "U.S. Observers Disagree on Extent of Philippines Fraud," *New York Times,* Feb. 12, 1986). Brier was so accustomed to focusing on the superficial in his apologies for client-state elections that he failed to grasp the fact that the administration's line was in the process of shifting—which caused him some embarrassment a few days later, when the freedom-loving Marcos was escorted out of the country.

3. He did not mention or attempt to evaluate actual institutions in Guatemala, such as the civil-defense patrols, nor did he or any other member of the observer team even mention the pacification program and killings of peasants, which had been the subject of innumerable reports. We suspect that Edwards's "research" consisted of advice by the U.S. embassy, in addition to the fact that he did not see any peasants killed in his presence.

4. In the text above, we point out that the terror in Guatemala began with the U.S. intervention in 1954, and that its subsequent growth was correlated with enlarged U.S. counterinsurgency and police aid and training. See also Edward S. Herman, *The Real Terror Network* (Boston: South End Press, 1982), pp. 175–76.

Appendix 2

1. Immediately after the shooting of the pope in 1981, Tagliabue, then a *Times* correspondent in West Germany, wrote some enlightening articles on Agca's Turkish Fascist connections. All of this material was ignored by Tagliabue after he became the *Times*'s correspondent at the Rome trial in 1985. His first

story on the trial, significantly, was coauthored with Claire Sterling, and his coverage of the trial remained faithful to her model.

2. *The Plot to Kill the Pope* (New York: Scribner's, 1985), p. 196.

3. For example, Martella's lack of control over Agca's visitors and reading materials badly compromised the case, as did the distressing number of leaks that came out of his supposedly secret investigation. See Edward S. Herman and Frank Brodhead, *The Rise and Fall of the Bulgarian Connection* (New York: Sheridan Square Publications, 1986), pp. 118–20.

4. Ibid., pp. 102ff.

5. Ibid., pp. 14–15, for further discussion of the alleged Soviet motive.

6. Ibid., chapter 5.

7. Ibid., pp. 139–41, for an analysis of Sterling's signaling theory.

Appendix 3

1. *Pentagon Papers,* Senator Gravel edition (Boston: Beacon Press, 1972), IV, 548–49; see p. 225, above. As to what Schakne actually said, we cannot be sure, since Braestrup presents only a few scattered phrases embedded in his own highly unreliable paraphrases, unsubstantiated by any text.

2. Gareth Porter, "Who Lost Vietnam?" *Inquiry,* February 20, 1978; see references of chapter 5, note 119; also Noam Chomsky and Edward S. Herman, *Political Economy of Human Rights* (Boston: South End Press, 1979), I, 5.2.3. Lengel, *Big Story,* I, 269; see p. 209, above.

3. As revealed, no doubt, by his book *Viet Cong* (Cambridge, Mass.: MIT Press, 1969), where he contrasts our side, which sympathizes with "the usual revolutionary stirrings . . . around the world," with the backers of revolutionary guerrilla warfare, which "opposes the aspirations of people while apparently furthering them," and expresses his contempt for the "gullible, misled people" who were "turning the countryside into a bedlam, toppling one Saigon government after another, confounding the Americans," etc. The fact that Pike was an employee of the U.S. government and an "admirer" and avid defender of its policies does not suggest to Braestrup that he might be something other than "independent-minded"; only Porter's alleged political preference is relevant to "Freedom House objectivity."

4. *Big Story,* I, xxviii; the same is true of Don Oberdorfer's *Tet!* (New York: Doubleday, 1971) and Stanley Karnow's *Vietnam: A History* (New York: Viking, 1983), among others.

5. Seymour Hersh. *My Lai Four* (New York: Random House, 1970), pp. 139–40.

6. Recall that "whatever losses the DRV/VC forces did suffer in the initial assaults were largely offset by the unimpeded recruiting that they conducted in the rural areas in the weeks that followed" (Wallace J. Thies, *When Governments Collide: Coercion and Diplomacy in the Vietnam Conflict, 1964–1968* [Berkeley: University of California Press, 1980], p. 201); see p. 215, above, and General Wheeler's comments, cited above, p. 225.

7. See the reviews cited in chapter 5, note 1, for many further examples.

8. Elsewhere (*Big Story,* I, 159), the same quote is attributed to Frank McGee.
9. Douglas Kinnard, *The War Managers* (Hanover, N.H.: University Press of New England, 1977), pp. 75, 47. In fact, the "body count" was unknown, since much of the air and artillery barrage was directed against targets where casualties could never be counted or even guessed at, as Kinnard and many other sources confirm. Westmoreland's subsequent writings show that reporters would have been quite justified to treat his reports with skepticism. See George M. Kahin, *Intervention: How America Became Involved in Vietnam* (New York: Knopf, 1986), p. 536, on his falsification of the record concerning the suppression of the Buddhist movement in Danang and Hué in 1966.
10. For evidence from the *Pentagon Papers,* see Noam Chomsky, *For Reasons of State* (New York: Pantheon, 1973), pp. 86ff.

Index

www.vintage-books.co.uk